Population and The Population Explosion

A Bibliography for 1970

Population and The Population Explosion

A Bibliography for 1970

by

Stephen H. Goode

The Whitston Publishing Company
Incorporated

Troy, New York

1973

Copyright 1973
Stephen H. Goode

Library of Congress Catalog Card Number: 72-87106

ISBN 0-87875-032-0

Printed in the United States of America

PREFACE

This is the first annual bibliography pertaining to population and the population explosion. It is a near-complete world bibliography covering the book and periodical literature for 1970; annual supplements will appear serially in the fall of successive years. The bibliography is divided into two sections: a title section arranged alphabetically; and a subject section arranged alphabetically by subject and alphabetically by title within subjects. Titles and subjects are provided so that researchers who do not trust subject assignments, which are always arbitrary and unique to the compiler, can conduct their own to-some-extent original literature search. Otherwise, entries are broken down into almost 100 subject heads.

The following bibliographies, abstracting services, and serials indexes, among others, have been searched in compiling this bibliography: ART INDEX; BIBLIOGRAPHIC INDEX; BOOKS IN PRINT; BRITISH HUMANITIES INDEX; BUSINESS PERIODICALS INDEX; CANADIAN PERIODICAL INDEX; CUMULATIVE BOOK INDEX; CURRENT INDEX TO JOURNALS IN EDUCATION; HOSPITAL LITERATURE INDEX; INDEX TO CATHOLIC PERIODICALS AND LITERATURE; INDEX TO LEGAL PERIODICALS; INDEX MEDICUS; INDEX TO PERIODICAL ARTICLES RELATED TO LAW; LIBRARY OF CONGRESS CATALOG: BOOKS: SUBJECTS; INTERNATIONAL NURSING INDEX; THE PHILOSOPHERS INDEX; PUBLIC AFFAIRS INFORMATION SERVICE; READERS GUIDE TO PERIODICAL LITERATURE; REVIEW FOR RELIGIOUS; and SOCIAL SCIENCES AND HUMANITIES INDEX.

In using the subject section of this bibliography, the following qualifications may be of some importance. "Birth Rate," "Population Control," "Population Growth," "Birth Control," and "Overpopulation" from time to time are not mutually exclusive subject heads, but most of the time there is a real difference; States of the United States are not entered separately but under "Population: United States;" specific drugs used, for example, in effecting contraception are not listed separately; although parenteral contraception and oral contraception are treated separately, and though oral contraceptives and mechanical (IUD) contraceptives are separate categories, complications and side effects of all contraceptives are treated as one subject head; national states are usually separate, but not in the case of Africa, the Caribbean, Central America, and South America; everything pertaining to, for example, Poland, in respect to population, demographics, statistics, economics, etc., will be found under "Population: Poland," with the exception of contraception, which proved to be too large a subject entity; although abortion as a subject head is included here, there is almost no overlap between this bibliography in that subject category and the serial, ABORTION BIBLIOGRAPHY, compiled by Mary K. Floyd (Whitston, 1970 to date); that is, abortion entries appearing here are principally concerned with that subject as a population regulator; "Sterilization" refers both to male and female sterilization; and finally, for extrauterine pregnancy and for pregnancy associated with mechanical forms of contraception, see "Contraception: Complication and Side-Effects." The author index cites page numbers only in the title section, not those in the subject section; and SOCIOLOGICAL ABSTRACTS citations are identified by number, preceded simply by "SA."

Corrections and additions applying to this bibliography, together with any suggestions enhancing its use, would be warmly welcomed and credited.

Stephen H. Goode

LIST OF ABBREVIATIONS AND PERIODICALS

Abbreviation	Title
ABA J	American Bar Association Journal (Chicago)
ACOG Nurses Bull	ACOG Nurses Bulletin (Chicago)
AIA J	American Institute of Architects Journal (New York)
Acad Mgt J	Academy of Management Journal (Eugene, Ore.)
Acta Biol Med Ger	Acta Biologica et Medica Germanica (Berlin)
Acta Biotheor	Acta Biotheoretica (Leiden)
Acta Cytol	Acta Cytologica (Baltimore)
Acta Endocrinol	Acta Endocrinologica (Copenhagen)
Acta Neurol Scand	Acta Neurologica Scandinavica (Copenhagen)
Acta Obstet Ginecol Hisp Lusit	Acta Obstetrica y Ginecologica Hispano-Lusitana (Barcelona)
Acta Obstet Gynaec Jap	Acta Obstetrica et Gynaecologica Japonica (Tokyo)
Acta Paedopsychiatr	Acta Paedopsychiatrica (Basel)
Administrative Science Q	Administrative Science Quarterly (Ithaca)
Adv Age	Advertising Age (Chicago)
Africa R	Africa Report (Washington)
Akush Ginekol	Akusherstvo I Ginekologiia (Moscow)
Ala Bus	Alabama Business (University)
Ala J Med Sci	Alabama Journal of Medical Sciences (Birmingham)
Alaska Med	Alaska Medicine (Anchorage)
Am Anthrop	American Anthropologist (Washington)
Am Federationist	American Federationist (Washington)
Am Biol Teach	American Biology Teacher (Washington)
Am Druggist	American Druggist (New York)
Am Economist	American Economist (New York)

Am Econ R	American Economic Review (Evanston)
Am Heritage	American Heritage (New York)
Am J Clin Hypn	American Journal of Clinical Hypnosis (Minneapolis)
Am J Med	American Journal of Medicine (New York)
Am J Orthopsychiatry	American Journal of Orthopsychiatry (New York)
Am J Phys	American Journal of Physics (New York)
Am J Psychother	American Journal of Psychotherapy (Jamaica, N.Y.)
Am J Sociol	American Journal of Sociology (Chicago)
Am Scientist	American Scientist (New Haven)
Am Sociol R	American Sociological Review (Washington)
Am Stat Assn J	American Statistical Association Journal (Washington)
Am Water Works Assn J	American Water Works Association Journal (New York)
Amer J Clin Nutr	American Journal of Clinical Nutrition (Bethesda)
Amer J Dis Child	American Journal of Diseases of Children (Chicago)
Amer J Hum Genet	American Journal of Human Genetics (Chicago)
Amer J Nurs	American Journal of Nursing (New York)
Amer J Obstet Gynec	American Journal of Obstetrics and Gynecology (St. Louis)
Amer J Ophthal	American Journal of Ophthalmology (Chicago)
Amer J Phys Anthrop	American Journal of Physical Anthropology (Philadelphia)
Amer J Psychiat	American Journal of Psychiatry (Hanover, N.H.)
Amer J Public Health	American Journal of Public Health and the Nation's Health (New York)
Amer J Surg	American Journal of Surgery (New York)
Amer J Trop Med or Am J Trop Med Hyg	American Journal of Tropical Medicine and Hygiene (Lawrence, Kansas)
Amer Surg	American Surgeon (Philadelphia)
America	America (San Francisco)
American Association of Colleges for Teacher	American Association of Colleges for Teacher Education Year-

Education Yearbook	book (Washington)
American Vocational Journal	American Vocational Journal (Washington)
Ann Intern Med	Annals of Internal Medicine (Philadelphia)
Ann Rev Pharmacol	Annual Review of Pharmacology (Palo Alto)
Ann Surg	Annals of Surgery (Philadelphia)
Ann Urol	Annales d'Urologie (Paris)
Annal Endocrinol	Annales d'Endocrinologie (Paris)
Annals of the American Academy of Political & Social Science	Annals of the American Academy of Political & Social Science (Philadelphia)
Annee Biol	Annee Biologique (Paris)
Anphi Pap	The Anphi Papers (Quezon City, Philippines)
Applied Econ	Applied Economics (Oxford, England)
Arch Environ Health	Archives of Environmental Health (Chicago)
Arch Forum	Architectural Forum (New York)
Arch Intern Med	Archives of Internal Medicine (Chicago)
Arch Klin Exp Derm	Archiv fur Klinische und Experimentelle Dermatologie (Berlin)
Arch Mal Coeur	Archives Des Maladies du Coeur et Des Vaisseaux (Paris)
Arch Path	Archives of Pathology (Chicago)
Arch Rec	Architectural Record (New York)
Arctic	Arctic (Montreal)
Ariz R	Arizona Review (Tucson)
Arizona Med	Arizona Medicine (Scottsdale)
Ark Bus & Econ R	Arkansas Business and Economic Review (Fayetteville)
Art Educ	Art Education (Washington)
Artha Vijnana	Artha Vijnana (Poona, India)
Arzneim Forsch	Arzneimittel-Forschung (Aulendorf)
Asian Forum	Asian Forum (Washington)
Ass Mgt	Association Management (Washington)
Assn Am Geog Ann	Association of American Geographers. Annals (Washington)
Atlan Com Q	Atlantic Community Quarterly (Washington)
Atlas	Atlas (Washington)
Audubon	Audubon Magazines (New York)
Aust New Zeal J Surg	Australia and New Zealand Journal of Surgery (Glebe)
Australian and New	Australia and New Zealand Jour-

Zealand J of Sociology	nal of Sociology (Canberra)
Barrons	Barron's (New York)
Behavioral Science	Behavioral Science (Ann Arbor)
Biochem J	Biochemical Journal (London)
Biometrics	Biometrics (Raleigh)
Bioscience	Bioscience (Washington)
Bordeaux Med	Bordeaux Medical (Bordeaux)
Brain Res	Brain Research (Amsterdam)
Bratisl Lek Listy	Bratislavske Lekarske Listy (Bratislava)
Br J Haematol	British Journal of Haematology (Oxford)
Br Med Bull	British Medical Bulletin (London)
Brit J Prev Soc Med	British Journal of Preventive and Social Medicine (London)
Brit J Psychiat	British Journal of Psychiatry (London)
Brit J of Sociology	British Journal of Sociology (London)
Brit J Urol	British Journal of Urology (Edinburgh)
Brit J Vener Dis	British Journal of Venereal Diseases (London)
Brit Med J	British Medical Journal (London)
British Geographers Transactions	British Geographers Transactions
Broadcasting	Broadcasting (Washington)
Brux Med	Bruxelles-Medical (Bruxelles)
Bsns Horizons	Business Horizons (Bloomington (Indiana)
Bsns Mgt	Business Management (Greenwich, Conn.)
Bsns Mgt	Business Management (London)
Bsns W	Business Week (New York)
Bul Atom Sci	Bulletin of the Atomic Scientists (Chicago)
Bull Bus Research	Bulletin of Business Research (Columbus, Ohio)
Bull Am Coll Nurse Midwife	Bulletin of the American College of Nurse-Midwives (Thorofare, N.J.)
Bull Fed Gynec Obstet Franc or Bull Fed Soc Gynecol Obstet Lang Fr	Bulletin de la Federation des Societes de Gynecologie et d' Obstetrique de Langue Francaise (Paris)
Bull Infirm Cath Canada	Bulletin des Infirmieres Catholiques du Canada (Quebec)
Bull NTRDA	Bulletin of the National Tuberculosis and Respiratory Disease

Bull NY Acad Med	Association (New York) The New York Academy of Medicine Bulletin (Buffalo, N.Y.)
Bull Soc Sci Med Grand Duche Luxemb	Societe des Sciences Medicales du Grand-Duche Luxembourg Bulletin (Luxembourg)
Bull Who	Who Bulletin (Geneva)
Bus & Econ Dimensions	Business and Economic Dimensions (Gainesville, Fla.)
C R Acad Sci	Comptes Rendus Herdomadaires des Seances de l'Academie des Sciences; D:Sciences Naturelles (Paris)
C R Soc Biol	Comptes Rendus des Seances de la Societe de Biologie et de Ses Filiales (Paris)
Calif L Rev	California Law Review (Berkeley)
Calif Med	California Medicine (San Francisco)
Can Aud	Canadian Audubon (Toronto)
Can Geogr J	Canadian Geographical Journal (Ottawa)
Can Hosp	Canadian Hospital (Toronto)
Can J Agric Econ	Canadian Journal of Agricultural Economics (Ottawa)
Can J Econ	Canadian Journal of Economics (Toronto)
Canad Med Ass J	Canadian Medical Association Journal (Toronto)
Canad Psychiat Ass J	Canadian Psychiatric Association Journal (Ottawa)
Cas Lek Cesk	Casopis Lekaru Ceskych (Prague)
Cent Afr J Med	Central African Journal of Medicine (Salisbury)
Ceres	Ceres (Rome, Italy)
Cesk Gynek	Ceskoslovenska Gynekologie (Prague)
Cesk Psychiat	Ceskoslovenska Psychiatrie (Prague)
Chatelaine	Chatelaine (Toronto)
Chem & Eng N	Chemical and Engineering News (Washington)
Chem & Ind	Chemistry and Industry (London)
Chem W	Chemical Week (New York)
Children	Children (Washington)
China Q	China Quarterly (London)
Chr Cent	Christian Century (Chicago)
Chr Today	Christianity Today (Washington)
Christ Nurse	Christian Nurse (Nagpur, India)
Circulation	Circulation (New York)

City	City (Washington)
Civil Eng	Civil Engineering (New York)
Clin Chim Acta	Clinica Chimica Acta (Amsterdam)
Clin Obstet Gynecol	Clinical Obstetrics and Gynecology (New York)
Clin Pediatr	Clinica Pediatrica (Bologne)
Clin Pharmacol Ther	Clinical Pharmacology and Therapeutics (St. Louis)
Clin Ter	Clinica Terapeutica (Rome)
Coeur Med Intern	Coeur et Medecine Interne (Paris)
Colum L R	Columbia Law Review (New York)
Comm & Fin Chr	Commercial and Financial Chronicle (New York)
Comm Today	Commonwealth Today (London)
Commonweal	Commonweal (New York)
Comp Stud Soc & Hist	Comparative Studies in Society and History (New York)
Comp Stud Soc & Hist	Comparative Studies in Society and History (London)
Conference Bd or Conf Bd Rec	Conference Board Record (New York)
Cong Q W Rept	Congressional Quarterly Service: Weekly Report (Washington)
Consumer Rep	Consumer Reports (Mount Vernon, N.Y.)
Contemp Educ	Contemporary Education (Terre Haute)
Cornell Internat Law J	Cornell International Law Journal (Ithaca)
Cur Anthrop	Current Anthropology (Chicago)
Curr Psychiatr Ther	Current Psychiatric Therapies (New York)
Curr Ther Res	Current Therapeutic Research (New York)
Current Dig Soviet R	Current Digest of the Soviet Press (Columbus)
Current Hist	Current History (Philadelphia)
Daily Telegraph	Daily Telegraph Magazine (London)
Delaware Med J	Delaware Medical Journal (Wilmington)
Demography	Demography (Washington)
Demosta	Demosta (Prague)
Denver L J Special	Denver Law Journal (Denver)
Dept State Bul	Department of State Bulletin (Washington)

Dept State News Letter	Department of State News Letter (Washington)
Deutsch Med Wschr	Deutsch Medizinische Wochenschrift (Stuttgart)
Develop Med Child Neurol	Developmental Medicine and Child Neurology (London)
Development Studies	Developmental Studies
Discussion	Discussion
Dokl Akad Nauk SSSR	Doklady Akademii Nauk S.S.S.R. (Washington)
Drug & Cosmetic Ind	Drug and Cosmetic Industry (New York)
Dtsch Gesundheitsw	Deutsche Gesundheitswesen (Berlin)
Duodecim	Duodecim (Helsinki)
East Afr Med J	East African Medical Journal (Nairobi)
East African Geog R	East African Geographical Review (Kampala, Uganda)
Econ Activity	Economic Activity (Nedlands, W. Australia)
Econ Affairs	Economic Affairs (Calcutta)
Econ & Social R	Economic and Social Review (Dublin)
Econ Development & Cultural Change	Economic Development and Cultural Change (Chicago)
Econ Geog	Economic Geography (Worcester, Mass.)
Econ Hist R	Economic History Review (Herts, England)
Econ J	Economic Journal (Cambridge, England)
Econ Leaflets	Economic Leaflets (Gainesville, Fla.)
Econ R	Economic Review (Kyoto)
Econ R	Economic Review (Belgrade)
Economist	Economist (London)
Editorial Research Reports	Editorial Research Reports (Washington)
Educ	Education (Indianapolis)
Egypte Contemporaine	Egypte Contemporaine (Cairo)
Encounter	Encounter (London)
Endocrinology	Endocrinology (Philadelphia)
Endokrinologie	Endokrinologie (Leipzig)
Ethnology	Ethnology (Pittsburgh)
Exchange	Exchange (New York)
Exec	Executive (Don Mills, Ont., Canada)
Experientia	Experientia (Basel)
Family Hlth	Family Health (New York)

Family L Q	Family Law Quarterly (Chicago)
Family Planning Perspectives	Family Planning Perspectives (New York)
Far Eastern Econ R	Far Eastern Economic Review (Hong Kong)
Fed Proc	Federation Proceedings: Federation of American Societies for Experimental Biology (Bethesda)
Federal Reserve Chicago	Federal Reserve Chicago. Business Conditions (Chicago)
Feldsher Akush	Fel'dsher i Akusherka (Moscow)
Fertil Steril	Fertility and Sterility (New York)
Field & S	Field and Stream (New York)
Filosofskiye Nauki	Filosopskie Nauki (Moscow)
Fin Post	Financial Post (Toronto)
Fin World	Financial World (New York)
Fla Econ Indicators	Florida Economic Indicators (Talahassee)
Fla Planning & Development	Florida Planning and Development (Boca Raton)
Folia Med Neerl	Folia Medica Neerlandica (Haarlem)
Folia Primat	Folia Primatologica (Basel)
Fortschr Neurol Psychiat	Fortschritte der Neurologie, Psychiatrie und ihre Grenzgebiete (Stuttgart)
Fortune	Fortune (Chicago)
Free China R	Free China Review (Taipei)
Free Labour World	Free Labour World (Brussels)
Freeman	Freeman (Irvington-on-Hudson, N.Y.)
Friends' Q	Friends' Quarterly (Ashford, England)
Futurist	Futurist (Washington)
Geburtsh Frauenheilk	Geburtshilfe Frauenheilkunde (Stuttgart)
Gen Comp Endocrinol	General and Comparative Endocrinology (New York)
Geog R	Geographical Review (New York)
Geographical Mag	Geographical Magazine (London)
Gerontologist	Gerontologist (St. Louis)
Ginec Obstet Mex	Ginecologia y Obstetricia de Mexico (Mexico City)
Ginek Pol	Gineklogia Polska (Lodz)
Good H	Good Housekeeping (New York)
Greater London Research Q Bull	Greater London Research Quarterly Bulletin (London)
Guardian	Guardian (New York)
Gynecol Invest	Gynecologic Investigation

	(Basel)
Gynecol Prat	Gynecologie Pratique (Paris)
Harefuah	Harefuah (Tel Aviv)
Hawaii Med J	Hawaii Medical Journal (Honolulu)
Health	Health (Chicago)
Health Visit	Health Visitor (London)
Historian	Historian (Allentown, Pa.)
Homme et la Societe	Homme et la Societe (Paris)
Hosp Manage	Hospital Management (Chicago)
Hosp Topics	Hospital Topics (Chicago)
Hospital	Hospital (Rio de Janiero)
Hum Biol	Human Biology (Detroit)
Human Organ	Human Organization (Lexington, Ky.)
Human Rights	Human Rights Journal (Paris)
Humanist	Humanist (London)
Humanist	Humanist (Amherst, N.Y.)
IEEE Spectrum	IEEE Spectrum (New York)
Illinois Med J	Illinois Medical Journal (Chicago)
Impact Sci Soc	Impact of Science on Society (New York)
Imprint	Imprint (New York)
Independ Sch Bull	Independent School Bulletin (Boston)
Indian Bus R	Indian Business Review (New Delhi)
Indian J Exp Biol	Indian Journal of Experimental Biology (New Delhi)
Indian J Med Res	Indian Journal of Medical Research (New Delhi)
Indian J Pediat	Indian Journal of Pediatrics (Calcutta)
Indian J Public Health	Indian Journal of Public Health (Calcutta)
Indian J Social Work	Indian Journal of Social Work (Bombay)
Indian J Sociol	Indian Journal of Sociology (New Delhi)
Ind & Labor Rel R	Industrial and Labor Relations Review (Ithaca)
Industry of Free China	Industry of Free China (Taipei)
Infirm Canad	Infirmiere Canadienne (Ottawa)
Inst British Geographers Transactions	Institute of British Geographers Transactions (London)
Int J Comp Sociol	International Journal of Comparative Sociology (Leiden)
Int J Fertil	International Journal of Fertility (Springfield, Mass.)

Int J Radiat Biol	International Journal of Radiation Biology and Related Studies in Physics, Chemistry and Medicine (London)
Int Labour R	International Labour Review (Geneva)
Int Surg	International Surgery (Chicago)
Inter-Am Econ Affairs	Inter-American Economic Affairs (Washington)
Internat Development	International Development Review (Washington)
Interplay	Interplay (New York)
Interpreter Releases	Interpreter Releases (New York)
Invest Urol	Investigative Urology (Baltimore)
Italy Docs & Notes	Italy Documents and Notes (Rome)
JAMA	Journal of the American Medical Association (Chicago)
J Abnorm Psychol	Journal of Abnormal Psychology (Washington)
J Admin Overseas	Journal of Administration Overseas (London)
J Am Acad Child Psychiatry	Journal of the American Academy of Child Psychiatry (New York)
J Am Folklore	Journal of American Folklore (Austin)
J Am Hist	Journal of American History (Salt Lake City)
J Am Vet Med Assoc	Journal of the American Veterinary Medical Association (Chicago)
J Amer Pharm Ass	Journal of the American Pharmaceutical Association (Washington)
J Biosoc Sci	Journal of Biosocial Science (London)
J Chromatogr	Journal of Chromatography (Amsterdam)
J Chronic Dis	Journal of Chronic Diseases (St. Louis)
J Clin Endocr	Journal of Clinical Endocrinology and Metabolism (Philadelphia)
J Comp Physiol Psychol	Journal of Comparative and Physiological Psychology (Washington)
J Comp Sociol	Journal of Comparative Sociology
J Consult Clin Psychol	Journal of Consulting and Clin-

J of Development Studies	ical Psychology (Washington) Journal of Developmental Studies (London)
J Econ Entom	Journal of Economic Entomology (College Park, Md.)
J Econ Hist	Journal of Economic History (New York)
J Egypt Med Assoc	Journal of the Egyptian Medical Association (Cairo)
J Endocr	Journal of Endocrinology (London)
J Family L	Journal of Family Law (Louisville, Ky.)
J Florida Med Ass	Journal of the Florida Medical Association (Jacksonville)
J Formosan Med Assoc	Journal of the Formosan Medical Association (Taipei)
J Geography	Journal of Geography (River Forest, Ill.)
J Geront	Journal of Gerontology (St. Louis)
J Health Soc Behav	Journal of Health and Social Behavior (Washington)
J Hist Ideas	Journal of the History of Ideas (Philedelphia)
J Hist Med	Journal of the History of Medicine and Allied Sciences (New Haven)
J Hum Resource	Journal of Human Resource (Madison, Wisc.)
J Hyg Epidemiol Microbiol Immunol	Journal of Hygiene, Epidemiology, and Immonology (Prague)
J Indian Med Ass	Journal of the Indian Medical Association (Calcutta)
J Inter-Am Stud	Journal of Inter-American Studies (Coral Gables)
J Kansas Med Soc	Journal of the Kansas Medical Society (Topeka)
J Law Reform	Journal of Law Reform (Ann Arbor)
J Louisiana Med Soc	Journal of the Louisiana State Medical Society (New Orleans)
J Mammal	Journal of Mammamology (Lawrence, Kans.)
J Marriage & Fam	Journal of Marriage and the Family (Minneapolis)
J Med Ass Georgia	Journal of the Medical Association of Georgia (Atlanta)
J Med Assoc State Ala	Journal of the Medical Association of the State of Alabama

J Med Assoc Thai	Journal of the Medical Association of Thailand (Bangkok)
J Med Chem	Journal of Medicinal Chemistry (Washington)
J Mod Afric Stud	Journal of Modern African Studies (New York)
J Nat Med Ass	Journal of the National Medical Association (New York)
J Nerv Ment Dis	Journal of Nervous and Mental Disease (Baltimore)
J Neurosurg	Journal of Neurosurgery (Chicago)
J Nurs	Journal of Nursing (Taipei)
J Obstet Gynaecol Br Commonw	Journal of Obstetrics and Gynaecology of the British Commonwealth (London)
J Occup Med	Journal of Occupational Medicine (Chicago)
J Peace Research	Journal of Peace Research (Boston)
J Postgrad Med	Journal of Postgraduate Medicine (Bombay)
J Psychol	Journal of Psychology (Provicetown, Mass.)
J R Coll Gen Pract	Journal of the Royal College of General Practitioners (Dartmouth, England)
J Rehab	Journal of Rehabilitation (Washington)
J Reprod Fertil	Journal of Reproduction and Fertility (Oxford)
J Theor Biol	Journal of Theoretical Biology (London)
J Urol	Journal of Urology (Baltimore)
J Water Pollut Contr	Journal of Water Pollution Control (London)
Jap J Midwife	Japanese Journal for Midwives (Tokyo)
Jap J Public Health Nurse	Japanese Journal of Public Health Nurse (Tokyo)
Japan Q	Japan Quarterly (Tokyo)
Jew Soc Stud	Jewish Social Studies (New York)
Jewish Frontier	Jewish Frontier (New York)
Johns Hopkins Med J	Johns Hopkins Medical Journal (Baltimore)
Kango	Kango (Tokyo)
Kango Kyoshitsu	Kango Kyoshitsu (Tokyo)
Katilolehti	Katilolehti (Helsinki)
Korea Nurse	Korea Nurse (Seoul)

Ladies Home J	Ladies Home Journal (New York)
Lakartidningen	Lakartidningen (Stockholm)
Lancet	Lancet (London)
Land Econ	Land Economics (Madison, Wis.)
Landscape Arch	Landscape Architecture (Louisville)
Life	Life (New York)
Life Sci	Life Sciences (Oxford)
Lille Med Suppl	Lille Medical (Lille)
Listener	Listener (London)
Local Historian	Local Historian (London)
Local Population Studies Mag	Local Population Studies Magazine
Long Range Planning	Long Range Planning (Elmsford, N.Y.)
Look	Look (New York)
Lyon Med	Lyon Medical (Lyon)
Mln Bull	Minnesota League of Nursing (Minneapolis)
Mc Calls	Mc Calls (New York)
Mag Macl	Magazine Maclean (Montreal)
Manchester School of Economic & Social Studies	Manchester School of Economic and Social Studies (Manchester, England)
Med Ann D C	Medical Annals of the District of Columbia (Washington)
Med Clin N Amer	Medical Clinics of North America (Philadelphia)
Med J Aust	Medical Journal of Australia (Sydney)
Med Klin	Medizinische Klinik (Munich)
Med Times	Medical Times (Manhasset)
Med Trial Techn Quart	Medical Trial Technique Quarterly (Chicago)
Med Welt	Medizinische Welt (Stuttgart)
Merrill-Palmer Q	Merrill-Palmer Quarterly of Behavior and Development (Detroit)
Metropolitan Life Stat Bul	Metropolitan Life Insurance Company. Statistical Bulletin (New York)
Middle East J	Middle East Journal (Washington)
Midwife Health Visit	Midwife and Health Visitor (London)
Midwives Chron	Midwives Chronicle (London)
Milbank Memorial Fund Q	Milbank Memorial Fund Quarterly (New York)
Milit Med	Military Medicine (Washington)
Minerva Ginecol	Minerva Ginecologica (Torino)
Minerva Med	Minerva Medica (Torino)
Minerva Pediatr	Minerva Pediatrica (Torino)

Minn Med	Minnesota Medicine (St. Paul)
Minn Munic	Minnesota Municipalities (Minneapolis)
Mlle	Madamoiselle (New York)
Mo Labor R	Monthly Labor Review (Washington)
Month	Month (London)
Mt Sinai J Med NY	Mount Sinai Journal of Medicine (New York)
Munchen Med Wschr	Muenchener Medizinische Wochenschrift (Munich)
N Carolina Med J	North Carolina Medical Journal (Winston-Salem)
N Mex Bus	New Mexico Business (Albuquerque)
N Y Times Mag	New York Times Magazine (New York)
Nat Council Social Studies Yrbk	National Council for the Social Studies. Yearbook (Washington)
Nat Parks	National Parks Magazine (Washington)
Nat Wildlife	National Wildlife (Washington)
Natur Hist	Natural History (New York)
Nature (London)	Nature (London)
Nebraska Nurse	Nebraska Nurse (Omaha)
Nederl T Geneesk	Nederlands Tijdschrift voor Geneeskunde (Amsterdam)
Nederl T Verlosk	Nederlandsch Tijdschrift voor Verloskunde en Gymaecologie (Haarlem)
Nervenarst	Nervenarst (Berlin)
Neurology	Neurology (Minneapolis)
New Eng J Med	New England Journal of Medicine (Boston)
New Engl Q	New England Quarterly (Brunswick, Me.)
New Jersey Economic Review	New Jersey Economic Review (Trenton)
New Outlook	New Outlook (London)
New Outlook	New Outlook (Tel Aviv)
New Republic	New Republic (Washington)
New Society	New Society (London)
New South	New South (Atlanta)
New Statesman	New Statesman (London)
New Times	New Times (Moscow)
New York J Med	New York State Journal of Medicine (New York)
New Zeal Med J	New Zealand Medical Journal (Wellington)
Newsette	Newsette (Makati-Rizal, Philippines)

Newsweek	Newsweek (New York)
Nigerian Nurse	Nigerian Nurse (Lagos)
Nord Med	Nordisk Medicin (Stockholm)
Northwest Med	Northwest Medicine (Seattle)
Nova	Nova (El Paso)
Nova	Nova (London)
Nova Scotia Med Bull	Nova Scotia Medical Bulletin (Halifax)
Nurs J India	Nursing Journal of India (New Delhi)
Nurs Mirror	Nursing Mirror and Midwives Journal (London)
Nurs Outlook	Nursing Outlook (New York)
Nurs Times	Nursing Times (London)
Observer	Observer (London)
Obstet Gynec	Obstetrics and Gynecology (New York)
Occup Health	Occupational Health (Auckland)
Occup Health Nurs	Occupational Health Nursing (Thorofare, N.J.)
Oeff Gesundheitswesen	Oeffentliche Gesundheitswesen (Stuttgart)
Ohio Nurses Rev	Ohio Nurses Review (Columbus)
Ohio State Med J	Ohio State Medical Journal (Columbus)
Oil Paint & Drug Rep	Oil, Paint and Drug Reporter (New York)
Op Res	Operations Research (Baltimore)
Orv Hetil	Orvoosi Hetilap (Budapest)
Oxford Economics Papers	Oxford Economic Papers (London)
P Rico Enferm	Puerto Rico y su Enferma (Rio Piedras)
Pacific Affairs	Pacific Affairs (Vancouver)
Panorama	Panorama (Denver)
Parents Mag	Parents Magazine and Better Family Living (New York)
Penn Med	Pennsylvania Medicine (Harrisburg)
Percept Motor Skills	Perceptual and Motor Skills (Missoula, Mont.)
Personnel Adm	Personnel Administration (Washington)
Personnel and Guidance Journal	Personnel and Guidance Journal (Washington)
Perspect Biol Med	Perspectives in Biology and Medicine (Chicago)
Pharmazie	Pharmazie (Berlin)
Phi Delta Kappan	Phi Delta Kappan (Bloomington, Ind.)
Philipp J Nurs	Philippine Journal of Nursing

Pol Q	Political Quarterly (London)
Pol Tyg Lek	Polski Tygodnik Lekarski (Warsaw)
Population	Population (Paris)
Population Bull	Population Bulletin (Washington)
Population Index	Population Index (Princeton)
Population Studies	Population Studies (London)
Postgrad Med	Postgraduate Medicine (Minneapolis)
Practitioner	Practitioner (London)
Presse Med	Presse Medicale (Paris)
Problems Econ	Problems of Economics (White Plains, N.Y.)
Proc R Soc Med	Proceedings of the Royal Society of Medicine (London)
Proc Soc Exp Biol	Proceedings of the Society for Experimental Biology and Medicine (New York)
Progressive	Progressive (Madison, Wis.)
Psychol Rep	Psychological Reports (Missoula, Mont.)
Psychopharmacologia	Psychopharmacologia (Berlin)
Psychosom Med	Psychosomatic Medicine (New York)
Pub Works	Public Works (Ridgewood, N.J.)
Public Affairs	Public Affairs (Dublin)
Public Health	Public Health (London)
Public Health Rep	Public Health Reports (Washington)
Public Interest	Public Interest (New York)
Q R Econ & Bus	Quarterly Review of Economics and Business (Urbana, Ill.)
R Econ & Stat	Review of Economics and Statistics (Cambridge, Mass.)
RANF Rev	RANF Review (Queensland)
R I Med J	Rhode Island Medical Journal (Providence)
Ramp Mag	Ramparts (Berkeley, Cal.)
Rass Int Clin Ter	Rassegna Internazionale di Clinica e Terapia (Napoli)
Read Digest	Readers Digest (Pleasantville, N.Y.)
Real Estate Analyst	Real Estate Analyst (St. Louis)
Redbook	Redbook Magazine (New York)
Regan Rep Nurs Law	Regan Report on Nursing Law (New York)
Relig in Life	Religion in Life (Nashville, Tenn.)

(Manila) appears before Political Quarterly entry.

Rev Chil Obstet Ginecol	Revista Chilena de Obstetricia y Ginecologia
Rev Colomb Obstet Ginecol	Revista Colombiana de Obstetricia y Ginacologia (Bogota)
Rev Fr Odontostomatol	Revue Francaise d'Odontostomatologie (Paris)
Rev Fr Psychanal	Revue Francaise de Psychanalyse (Paris)
Rev Franc Endocr Clin	Revue Francaise d'Endocrinologie Clinique Nutrition et Metabolisme (Paris)
Rev Franc Gynec Obstet	Revue Francaise de Gynecologie et d'Obstetrique (Paris)
Rev Infirm Assist Soc	Revue de l'Infirmiere et de l'Assistante Sociale (Paris)
Rev Med Lieg	Revue Medicale de Liege (Liege)
Rev Obstet Ginecol Venez	Revista Obstetricia y Ginecologia de Venezuela (Caracas)
Rev Odontostomatol Midi Fr	Revue d'Odonto-Stomatologie du Midi de la France (Bordeaux)
Rev Paul Med	Revista Paulista de Medicina (Sao Paulo)
Rev Saude Publica	Revista de Saude Publica (Sao Paulo)
Revue de l'Institut de Sociologie	Revue de l'Institute de Sociologie
Rhodesian J Econ	Rhodesian Journal of Economics (Salisbury)
Ripon Forum	Ripon Forum (Cambridge, Mass.)
Riv Sper Freniat	Rivista Sperimentale di Freniatria (Emilia)
Rivista Espanola de la Opinion Publica	Rivista Espanola de la Opinion Publica
Rocky Mountain Social Science J	Rocky Mountain Social Science Journal (Fort Collins, Colo.)
Round Tab	Round Table (London)
Royal Bank Can Mo Letter	Royal Bank of Canada. Monthly Letter (Montreal)
Rural Sociology	Rural Sociology (Madison, Wis.)
S A Nurs J	South Africa Nursing Journal (Pretoria)
Sales Mgt	Sales Management (New York)
Sanfujin Jissai	Sanfujinka no Jissai (Tokyo)
Sat R	Saturday Review (New York)
Saturday Night	Saturday Night (Toronto)
Savings & Loan News	Savings and Loan News (Chicago)
Scand J Clin Lab Invest	Scandinavian Journal of Clinical and Laboratory Investigation (Copenhagen)
Sch Sci & Math	School Science and Mathematics

	(Bloomington, Ind.)
Schol Teach Jr/Sr High	Scholastic Teacher (New York)
Schweiz Med Wochenschr	Schweizerische Medizinische Wochenschrift (Basel)
Schweizerische Zeitschrift fur Volkswirtschaft und Statistik	Schweizerische Zeitschrift fur Volkswirtschaft und Statistik (Bern)
Sci Am	Scientific American (New York)
Sci Digest	Science Digest (New York)
Sci Ed	Science Education (New York)
Sci N	Science News (Washington)
Science	Science (Washington)
Science Teacher	Science Teacher (London)
Science Teacher	Science Teacher (Washington)
Scott Med J	Scottish Medical Journal (Glasgow)
Scottish Genealogist	Scottish Genealogist
Sem Hop Paris	Semaine des Hopitaux de Paris (Paris)
Seventeen	Seventeen (New York)
Shujutsu	Shujutsu (Tokyo)
Singapore Med J	Singapore Medical Journal (Singapore)
So Econ J	Southern Economic Journal (Chapel Hill)
Soc of Archivists J	Society of Archivists Journal (London)
Soc Casework	Social Casework (New York)
Soc Prob	Social Problems (South Bend)
Soc Sci Med	Social Science and Medicine (Oxford)
Social & Econ Studies	Social and Economic Studies (Mona, Jamaica)
Social Biology	Social Biology (Chicago)
Social Ed	Social Education (Washington)
Social Trends	Social Trends (London)
Social Work	Social Work (New York)
Sociol & Soc Res	Sociology and Social Research (Los Angeles)
Sociol Q	Sociological Quarterly (Columbia, Mo.)
Sociological Symposium	Sociological Symposium (Bowling Green, Ky.)
South African J Econ	South African Journal of Economics (Johannesburg)
South Asian R	South Asian Review
Southern Med J	Southern Medical Journal (Birmingham)
Sovet Zdravookhr	Sovetskoe Zdravookhranenie (Moscow)

Sovetskaya Etnografiya	Sovetskaya Etnografiya (Moscow)
Soviet Ed	Soviet Education (White Plains, N.Y.)
Soviet R	Soviet Review (White Plains, N.Y.)
Spectator	Spectator (Philadelphia)
Spectator	Spectator (London)
Sr Schol	Senior Scholastic (New York)
Statis Observer	Statistical Observer (Ottawa)
Statis Reporter	Statistical Reporter (Washington)
Statis Reporter	Statistical Reporter (Manila)
Statist Bull Metrop Life Insur Co	Statistical Bulletin Metropolitan Life Insurance Company (New York)
Steroids	Steroids (San Francisco)
Stud Gen	Studium Generale (Berlin)
Studies in Family Planning	Studies in Family Planning (New York)
Successo	Successo (Milan)
Suffolk U L Rev	Suffolk University Law Review (Boston)
Surg Gynec Obstet	Surgical Gynecology and Obstetrics (Chicago)
Sweden Now	Sweden Now (Stockholm)
Sykepleien	Sykepleien (Oslo)
T Norsk Laegeforen	Tidsskrift for den Norske Laegeforening (Oslo)
Todays Educ	Todays Education (Washington)
Tenn Survey Bus	Tennessee Survey of Business (Knoxville)
Tex Bus R	Texas Business Review (Austin)
Tex Med	Texas Medicine (Austin)
Ther Gegenw	Therapie der Gegenwart (Berlin)
Ther Hung	Therapia Hungarica (Budapest)
Therapeutique	Therapeutique (Paris)
Tidsskrift for Samfunnsforskning	Tidsskrift for Samfunnsforskning (Oslo)
Tijdschrift voor Economische en Sociale Geografie	Tijdschrift voor Economische en Sociale Geografie (Rotterdam)
Time	Time (Chicago)
Todays Health	Todays Health Magazine (Chicago)
Town & Country Planning	Town and Country Planning (London)
Town Planning Inst J	Town Planning Institute Journal (London)
Toxic Appl Pharmacol	Toxicology and Applied Pharmacology (New York)
Trans-Action	Trans-Action - Social Science

	and Modern Society (New Brunswick, N.J.)
Trans N Y Acad Sci	New York Academy of Science. Transactions (New York)
Trans Roy Soc Trop Med Hyg	Transactions of the Royal Society of Tropical Medicine and Hygiene (London)
Trial	Trial (Cambridge, Mass.)
Trop Geogr Med	Tropical and Geographical Medicine (Haarlem)
UNESCO Courier	UNESCO Courier (New York)
U S News	U S News and World Report (Washington)
Ugeskr Laeger	Ugeskrift for Laeger (Copenhagen)
Ulster Commentary	Ulster Commentary (Belfast)
United Asia	United Asia (Bombay)
Urban Land	Urban Land (Washington)
Vict Stud	Victorian Studies (Bloomington, Ind.)
Vill L Rev	Villanova Law Review (Villanova)
Vista	Vista (New York)
Vista	Vista (Marian, Ind.)
Vital Health Statist	Vital and Health Statistics: National Center for Health Statistics (Washington)
Vital Speeches	Vital Speeches (Southold, N.Y.)
Vogue	Vogue (New York)
Vox Sang	Vox Sanguinis (Philadelphia)
WHO Technn Rep Ser	World Health Organization Technical Report Series (Geneva)
W Virginia Med J	West Virginia Medical Journal (Charleston)
Wall St J	Wall Street Journal (New York)
War-Peace Rept	War-Peace Report (New York)
Wiad Lek	Wiadomosci Lekarskie (Warsaw)
Wien Med Wochenschr	Wiener Medizinische Wochenschrift (Vienna)
Wis L R	Wisconsin Law Review (Lincoln, Nebr.)
Wis Med J	Wisconsin Medical Journal (Madison)
Wm & Mary Q	William and Mary Quarterly (Williamsburg)
World Affairs	World Affairs (Toronto)
World Affairs	World Affairs (Washington)
World Affairs	World Affairs (Wellington)
World Justice	World Justice (Louvain, Belgium)
Yorkshire Bulletin	Yorkshire Bulletin of Economic

Z Aerztl Fortbild	Zeitschfift fur Aerztliche Fortbildung (Jena)
Z Geburtshilfe Gynaekol	Zeitschrift fur Geburtshilfe und Gynaekologie (Stuttgart)
Z Klin Chem	Zeitschrift fuer Klinische Chemie und Klinische Biochemie (Berlin)
Zdrav Prac	Zdravotnicka Pracovnice (Prague)
Zdravookhr Ross Fed	Zdravookhraneniye Rossiiskoi Federatzii (Moscow)
Zentralbl Gynaekol	Zentralblatt fur Gynaekologie (Leipzig)

SUBJECT HEADINGS USED IN THIS BIBLIOGRAPHY

AMA
Abortion
Accidents & Injuries & Population
Adolescence, Youth, & Population
Aging
Agriculture, Food Supply, & Population
Anthropometry
Architecture & Population
Artificial Insemination
Baird, William R.
Birth Control & Fertility Control
Birth Rank
Birth Rate
Business & Industry & Population
Censuses
College Students & Overpopulation
Conferences, Congresses & the Like
Contraceptives: Complications & Side-Effects
Contraceptives: General
Contraceptives: IUD
Contraceptives: Male
Contraceptives: Oral
Contraceptives: Parenteral
Contraceptives: Therapeutic Use
Crowding
Developing Nations
Economics & Population
Education & Population
Environment, Ecology & Population
Family Planning
Family Structure & Relations
Fertility Control
Genetics & Population
Health, Public Health, and Medicine and Population
Isolation, Alienation, & Confinement
Labor & Population
Laws & Legislation
Life Insurance Industry & Population
Mentally Retarded
Migrant Labor
Migrations

Minority Groups & Population
Mortality & Mortality Statistics
Nursing & Population
Overpopulation: General
Politics & Population
Population: Africa
Population: Australia
Population: Belgium
Population: Bulgaria
Population: Cambodia
Population: Canada
Population: Caribbean
Population: Central America
Population: China
Population: Czechoslovakia
Population: Europe
Population: Finland
Population: France
Population: Germany
Population: Great Britain
Population: Hong Kong
Population: India
Population: Iran
Population: Ireland
Population: Israel
Population: Italy
Population: Japan
Population: Java
Population: Jordan
Population: Latin America
Population: Malaysia
Population: Norway
Population: Pakistan
Population: Poland
Population: Soloman Islands
Population: Spain
Population: Sweden
Population: Thailand
Population: Tibet
Population: Turkey
Population: United Arab Republic
Population: United States
Population: USSR
Population: Yugoslavia
Population Growth
Population Control
Population Forecasting & Theory
Population: History
Population Theory & Research
Poverty & Population
Religion & Ethics & Population
Rural Population
Sanger, Margaret
Sex, Sex Research, & Customs
Sterilization
Underdeveloped Countries
Urban Growth & Urbanization
Women & Population

TABLE OF CONTENTS

Preface..i
List of Abbreviations.................................iii
Subject Headings Used in This Bibliography........xxiii
Books..1
Periodical Literature:
    Title Index..27
    Subject Index....................................169
Author Index..346

BOOKS, MONOGRAPHS AND PAMPHLETS

A

Agarwala, S. N. A DEMOGRAPHIC STUDY OF SIX URBANISING VILLAGES. (Institute of Economic Growth Occasional Papers, no. 8). New York: Asia Publishing House, 1970.

American Enterprise Institute for Public Policy Research. THE NEW FAMILY PLANNING PROGRAM. Washington, D. C.: The Institute, 1970.

Anderson, Lewis S. TURKEY. New York: Population Council, 1970.

Arriga, Eduardo E. MORTALITY DECLINE AND ITS DEMOGRAPHIC EFFECTS IN LATIN AMERICA. (Population Monograph Series, no. 6). Berkeley, California: Institute of International Studies, 1970.

Australia. Immigration Advisory Council. IMMIGRATION AND THE BALANCE OF THE SEXES IN AUSTRALIA: REPORT TO THE MINISTER OF STATE FOR IMMIGRATION. (Parliamentary Papers no. 37). Canberra: Commonwealth Government Printing Office, 1970.

B

Borkchin, Murray. HOW MANY PEOPLE: THE MYTH IN THE POPULATION MOVEMENT. New York: Simon and Schuster, 1970.

Borrie, W. D. THE GROWTH AND CONTROL OF WORLD POPULATION. (Advancement of Science Series). London: Weidenfield and Nicholson, 1970.

Bottomley, Arthur, and Sir George Sinclair. CONTROL OF COMMONWEALTH IMMIGRATION: AN ANALYSIS AND SUMMARY OF THE EVIDENCE TAKEN BY THE SELECT COMMITTEE ON RACE RELATIONS AND IMMIGRATION, 1969-1970. London: Runnymede Trust, 1970.

British Consumers Association. CONTRACEPTIVES, 3rd ed. New York: International Publications Service, 1970.

Brody, Eugene B., ed. BEHAVIOR IN NEW ENVIRONMENTS; ADAPTATION OF MIGRANT POPULATIONS. Beverly Hills, California: Sage, 1970.

Brooks, Thomas R. LABOR AND MIGRATION: AN ANNOTATED BIBLIOGRAPHY. Brooklyn, New York: Brooklyn College Center for Migration Studies, 1970.

Brown, George H. 1985. (PRB Selection no. 34). Washington, D. C.: Population Reference Bureau, 1970.

C

Canada. Department of Manpower and Immigration. Program Development Service. THE MIGRATION OF CANADIAN-BORN BETWEEN CANADA AND UNITED STATES OF AMERICA, 1955-1968. Ottawa: Queen's Printer, 1970.

Canada. Dominion Bureau of Statistics. Census Division. THE IMPACT OF IMMIGRATION ON CANADA'S POPULATION, by Warren E. Kalbach. Ottawa: Queen's Printer, 1970.

Canada. Dominion Bureau of Statistics. INTERNAL MIGRATION IN CANADA: DEMOGRAPHIC ANALYSES, by M. V. George. Ottawa: Queen's Printer, 1970.

Canadian Welfare Council. MORE ABOUT TRANSIENT YOUTH; REPORT OF A NATIONAL CONSULTATION ON TRANSIENT YOUTH, convened by the Canadian welfare council as a followup to the Transient youth inquiry. March 30-April 2, 1970. Ste. Adele, Quebec, The Council, 1970.

Cargas, Harry J., ed. SEVENTEEN PEOPLE PER SQUARE FOOT. St. Louis: B. Herder Book Company, 1970.

Cartwright, Ann. PARENTS AND FAMILY PLANNING SERVICES. Chicago: Aldine-Atherton, 1970.

Coles, Robert, UPROOTED CHILDREN: THE EARLY LIVES OF MIGRANT FARM WORKERS. (Horace Mann Lecture Series). Pittsburgh: University of Pittsburgh Press, 1970.

Concepción, Mercedes B. THE PHILIPPINES. (Country Profiles). New York: Population Council, 1970.

Conference Board. OUR CHANGING POPULATION. (Road Maps of Industry, no. 1653). New York: The Board, 1970.

---PROFILE OF THE POPULATION: BY AREA. (Road maps of Industry, no. 1654). New York: The Board, 1970.

Conference of the Europe and Near East Region - 6th - Budapest - 1969. SOCIAL DEMOGRAPHY AND MEDICAL RESPONSIBILITY: PROCEEDINGS. New York: International Publications Service, 1970.

Cox, P. R. DEMOGRAPHY, 4th ed. (Institute of Actuaries Series). Cambridge: Cambridge University Press, 1970.

Crow, James F. and Moto Kimurs. INTRODUCTION TO POPULATION GENETICS THEORY. New York: Harper and Row, 1970.

Cyprus. Ministry of Finance. Department of Statistics and Research. DEMOGRAPHIC REPORT FOR THE YEAR 1969. (ST.R 3/5-400-7/70). Nicosia: Printing Office, 1970.

D

David, Henry P. FAMILY PLANNING AND ABORTION IN THE SOCIALIST COUNTRIES OF CENTRAL AND EASTERN EUROPE. Bridgeport, Connecticut: Key Books Service, 1970.

Demko, George J., et al, eds. POPULATION GEOGRAPHY: A READER. New York: McGraw Hill, 1970.

Du Bois, Victor D. POPULATION REVIEW 1970: IVORY COAST. (Field Staff Reports: West Africa Series, Vol. 13, no. 1). Hanover, New Hampshire: American Universities Field Staff, 1970.

Dupree, Louis. POPULATION DYNAMICS IN AFGHANISTAN. (Field Staff Reports: South Asia Series, Vol. 14, no. 7). Hanover, New Hampshire: American Universities Field Staff, 1970.

E

Ehrlich, Paul R. & Anne H. Ehrlich. POPULATION RESOURCES, ENVIRONMENT ISSUES IN HUMAN ECOLOGY. San Francisco: W. H. Freeman and Co., Publishers, 1970.

F

Fessler, Loren. POPULATION REVIEW 1970: HONG KONG. (Field Staff Reports: East Asia Series, Vol. 17, no. 8). Hanover, New Hampshire: American Universities Field Staff, 1970.

Fessler, Loren. TAIWAN AS A MODEL FOR FAMILY PLANNING: BRIEF HISTORY AND RECENT DEVELOPMENTS. (Field Staff Reports: East Asia Series, Vol. 17, no. 7). Hanover, New Hampshire: American Universities Field Staff, 1970.

Ford, Thomas R. & Gordon F. Dejong. SOCIAL DEMOGRAPHY. Englewood Cliffs, New Jersey: Prentice-Hall, 1970.

Fuller, Varden. RURAL WORKER ADJUSTMENT TO URBAN LIFE: AN ASSESSMENT OF THE RESEARCH. (Policy Papers in Human Resources and Industrial Relations, no. 15). Ann Arbor: Publications Office, Institute of Labor and Industrial Relations, University of Michigan-Wayne State University, PO Box B-1, Ann Arbor, 1970.

G

Gaisie, S. K. and S. B. Jones. GHANA. (Country Profiles). New York: Population Council, 1970.

Gallagher, Charles F. THE UNITED NATIONS SYSTEM AND POPULATION PROBLEMS. (Field Staff Reports: West Europe Series, Vol. 5, no. 5). Hanover, New Hampshire: American Universities Field Staff, 1970.

Garcia, Ts. THE SOVIET CENSUS, 1970: A BACKGROUND PAPER. (Radio liberty research paper no. 34). New York: Radio Liberty Committee, 1970.

Geary, R. C., and J. G. Hughes. INTERNAL MIGRATION IN IRELAND: WITH APPENDIX. COUNTY MIGRATION: ALTERNATIVE APPROACH, by C. J. Gillman. (Paper no. 54). Dublin, Ireland: Economic and Social Research Institute, 1970.

Gillette, Paul. PILL AND OTHER BIRTH CONTROL METHODS. New York: Bantam Books, 1970.

Goldsmith, Alfredo, et al. CHILE. (Country Profiles). New York: Population Council, 1970.

Great Britain. General Register Office. THE REGISTRAR GENERAL'S STATISTICAL REVIEW OF ENGLAND AND WALES FOR THE YEAR 1968: Pt. 1: Tables, Medical. London: British Information Services, 1970.

Great Britain. Select Committee on Race Relations and Immigration. CONTROL OF COMMONWEALTH IMMIGRATION: APPENDICES TO THE MINUTES OF EVIDENCE. (House of Commons). London: British Information Services, 1970.

H

Hahn, Harlan. URBAN RURAL CONFLICT: THE POLITICS OF CHANGE. Beverly Hills, California: Sage Publications, 1970.

Han, Dae Woo. THE REPUBLIC OF KOREA. (Country Profiles). New York: Population Council, 1970.

Hance, William A. POPULATION, MIGRATION AND URBANIZATION IN AFRICA. New York, Columbia University Press, 1970.

Hanna, Willard A. POPULATION REVIEW 1970: INDONESIA. (Field Staff Reports: Southeast Asia Series, Vol. 19, no. 3). Hanover, New Hampshire: American Universities Field Staff, 1970.

Hardee, J. Gilbert and Adaline P. Satterthwaite. PAKISTAN. (Country Profiles). New York: Population Council, 1970.

Hardin, Garrett. BIRTH CONTROL. (Science and Society Series). Indianapolis: Pegasus Publishing Co., 1970.

Harman, Alvin J. FERTILITY AND ECONOMIC BEHAVIOR OF
FAMILIES IN THE PHILIPPINES. Santa Monica, California: Rand Corporation, 1970.

Hauser, Philip M. POPULATION DILEMMA, 2nd ed. (American
Assembly Series). Englewood Cliffs, New Jersey:
Prentice-Hall, 1970.

Himes, Norman E. MEDICAL HISTORY OF CONTRACEPTION. New
York: Schocken Books, 1970.

Holland, Ruth. FORGOTTEN MINORITY: AMERICA'S TENANT
FARMERS AND MIGRANT WORKERS. New York: The Macmillan
Company, 1970.

Hollingsworth, T. H. MIGRATION: A STUDY BASED ON
SCOTTISH EXPERIENCE BETWEEN 1939 AND 1964. Edinburgh:
Glasgow University Social and Economic Studies, 1970.

Hungary. Central Statistics Office. REPORT ON THE PRELIMINARY DATA OF THE POPULATION CENSUS. Budapest,
Hungary: The Office, 1970.

I

Institute for Palestine Studies. THE PALESTINIAN
REFUGEES: A COLLECTION OF UNITED NATIONS DOCUMENTS.
Ashqar Building, Clémenceau St., P. O. Box 7164,
Beirut, Lebanon: The Institute, 1970.

International Bank Reconstruction and Development. WORLD
BANK ATLAS, 1970: POPULATION, PER CAPITA PRODUCT AND
GROWTH RATES, 5th ed. Washington, D. C.: The International Bank, 1970.

International Planned Parenthood Federation. FAMILY
PLANNING IN FIVE CONTINENTS. London: The Federation,
1970.

Iskandar, N. POPULATION PROJECTIONS FOR INDONESIA FROM
1961 TO 2001. (Serial no. 1 00/LD/'70). Djakarta,
Indonesia: Lembaga Demografi, Fakultas Ekonomi,
Universitas Indonesia, Salema 4, 1970.

Israel. Central Bureau of Statistics. THE ADMINISTERED TERRITORIES: ADDITIONAL DATA FROM THE SAMPLE ENUMERATION. (Census of population, 1967, publication no. 5). Jerusalem, Israel: The Bureau, 1970.

Israel. Central Bureau of Statistics. CENSUS OF INDUSTRY AND CRAFTS 1965: GENERAL DATA FROM STAGE B. (Publication no. 7). Jerusalem, Israel: The Bureau, 1970.

Israel. Central Bureau of Statistics. IMMIGRATION TO ISRAEL, 1966-1968. (Special series no. 308). Jerusalem, Israel: The Bureau, 1970.

J

Jacobs, Jane. ECONOMY OF CITIES. New York: Random House, 1970.

Jaffe, A. J. HANDBOOK OF STATISTICAL METHODS FOR DEMOGRAPHERS. New York: Gordon & Breach Science Publishers, 1970.

Jamaica. Department of Statistics. Division of Censuses and Surveys. JAMAICA: POPULATION CENSUS 1970; PRELIMINARY REPORT. Kingston, Jamaica, 1970.

Jansen, Clifford J., ed. READINGS IN THE SOCIOLOGY OF MIGRATION. Elmsford, New York: Pergamon Press, 1970.

Japan. Office of the Prime Minister. Bureau of Statistics. POPULATION ESTIMATES BY AGE AND SEX AS OF OCTOBER 1, 1969. (Population estimates series no. 38). Tokyo: The Bureau, 95 Wakamatsu-cho, Shinjuku-ku, 1970.

Japan. Office of the Prime Minister. Bureau of Statistics. POPULATION ESTIMATES OF JAPAN. (Population estimates series no. 36). Tokyo: The Bureau, 95 Wakamatsu-cho, Shinjuku-ku, 1970.

Johnson, Stanley. LIFE WITHOUT BIRTH: A JOURNEY THROUGH THE THIRD WORLD IN SEARCH OF THE POPULATION EXPLOSION. London: William Heinemann, 1970.

Jones, K. and A. D. Smith. THE ECONOMIC IMPACT OF COMMONWEALTH IMMIGRATION. (National Institute of Economic and Social Research). Cambridge: Cambridge University Press, 1970.

K

Keeny, S. M., et al. TAIWAN. (Country Profiles). New York: Population Council, 1970.

Kelsall, R. K. POPULATION, rev. ed. (Aspects of Modern Sociology, the Social Structure of Modern Britain Series). New York: Humanities Press, 1970.

Kennedy, David M. BIRTH CONTROL IN AMERICA: THE CAREER OF MARGARET SANGER. (Yale Publications in American Studies, 18). New Haven: Yale Universities Press, 1970.

Kippley, John. COVENANT, CHRIST AND CONTRACEPTION. Staten Island: Alba House, 1970.

Koehler, John E. THE PHILIPPINE FAMILY PLANNING PROGRAM: SOME SUGGESTIONS FOR DEALING WITH UNCERTAINTIES. Santa Monica, California: Rand Corporation, 1970.

Kopec, Ada C. DISTRIBUTION OF THE BLOOD GROUPS IN THE UNITED KINGDOM. New York: Oxford University Press, 1970.

L

Lee, Yong Leng. POPULATION AND SETTLEMENT IN SARAWAK. Detroit, Michigan: Cellar Book Shop, 1970.

Lockheimer, F. Roy. JAPAN'S NEW POPULATION POLITICS: CONCERN OVER "LABOR SHORTAGE" PROVOKES A CONTROVERSY OVER POPULATION POLICY. (Field Staff Reports: East Asia Series, Vol. 17, no. 5). Hanover, New Hampshire: American Universities Field Staff, 1970.

London School of Economic and Political Science. POPULATION INVESTIGATION COMMISSION TOWARDS A POPULATION

POLICY FOR THE UNITED KINGDOM. London: London School of Economics and Political Science, 1970.

Loraine. John A. SEX AND THE POPULATION CRISIS: AN ENDOCRINOLOGIST'S VIEW OF THE 20TH CENTURY. St. Louis: C. V. Mosby, 1970.

Love, Glen A. and Rhoda M. Love, eds. ECOLOGICAL CRISIS: READINGS FOR SURVIVAL. New York: Harcourt, Brace and Jovanovich, 1970.

M

McCormack, Arthur. POPULATION PROBLEM. New York: Thomas Y. Crowell, 1970.

McGaugh, Maurice E. GEOGRAPHY OF POPULATION AND SETTLEMENT, ed. Robert Fuson. (Foundations of Geography Series). Dubuque, Iowa: William C. Brown, 1970.

McLin, Jon. POPULATION REVIEW 1970: BELGIUM. (Field Staff Reports: West Europe Series, Vol. 5, no. 10). Hanover, New Hampshire: American Universities Field Staff, 1970.

Malta. Central Office of Statistics. DEMOGRAPHIC REVIEW OF THE MALTESE ISLANDS FOR THE YEAR 1968. Valletta, Malta: Department of Information, 1970.

Manisoff, Miriam T., ed. FAMILY PLANNING TRAINING FOR SOCIAL SERVICE: A TEACHING GUIDE IN FAMILY PLANNING FOR IN-SERVICE TRAINING IN PUBLIC WELFARE DEPARTMENTS. New York: Planned parenthood-World population, 1970.

Manwell, Clyde, and C. M. Baker. MOLECULAR BIOLOGY AND THE ORIGIN OF SPECIES: HETEROSIS, PROTEIN POLYMORPHISM AND ANIMAL BREEDING, ed. R. Phillips Dales, and Arthur W. Martin. (Biology Series). Seattle: University of Washington Press, 1970.

Marzuki, Ariffin bin and J. Y. Peng. MALAYSIA. (Country Profiles). New York: Population Council, 1970.

Meek, Ronald L., ed. MARX & ENGELS ON THE POPULATION
BOMB, tr. Dorothea Meek. New York: Simon and
Schuster, 1970.

Miller, Norman N. POPULATION REVIEW 1970: KENYA.
(Field Staff Reports: East Africa Series, Vol. 9,
no. 1). Hanover, New Hampshire: American Universities Field Staff, 1970.

Mississippi. Agricultural Experimental Station. 1968
MISSISSIPPI COUNTY POPULATION ESTIMATES BY RACE AND
AGE, by Ellen S. Bryant. (Sociology and Rural Life
Series, no. 22). State College, Mississippi: Experimental Station, 1970.

Morrison, Peter A. CHRONIC MOVERS AND THE FUTURE
REDISTRIBUTION OF POPULATION: A LONGITUDINAL
ANALYSIS. Santa Monica, California: The Rand Corporation, 1970.

---MOVERS AND STAYERS: AN ANALYSIS BASED ON TWO LONGITUDINAL DATA FILES. Santa Monica, California: The
Rand Corporation, 1970.

---THE RATIONALE FOR A POLICY ON POPULATION DISTRIBUTION.
Santa Monica, California: The Rand Corporation, 1970.

---URBAN GROWTH, NEW CITIES, AND "THE POPULATION PROBLEM".
Santa Monica, California: The Rand Corporation, 1970.

Mulvihill, Donald F. & Ruth C. Mulvihill. GEOGRAPHY,
MARKETING AND URBAN GROWTH. New York: Van Nostrand
Reinhold, 1970.

N

National Seminar on Population Education. PROCEEDINGS,
ed. T. S. Mehta et al. 2nd rev. ed. New Delhi:
Department of Social Sciences and Humanities, National
Council of Educational Research and Training, Aurobindo Marg, 1970.

Nebraska. Legislative Council. Commission on Health.
REPORT. (Commission Report no. 182). State Capitol,

Lincoln, Nebraska: The Council, 1970.

New South Wales, Australia. Department of Decentralisation and Development. A PILOT STUDY OF POPULATION MOVEMENTS FROM COUNTRY CENTRES IN NEW SOUTH WALES, 1967-1969. By Patricia Doddridge and Kate Holland. Sydney: The Department.

New York (State). Division of Human Rights. POPULATION AND HOUSING IN NEW YORK STATE, 1970. New York, New York: Division of Human Rights, 1970.

---Division of Human Rights. POPULATION AND HOUSING OF BLACKS IN NEW YORK STATE, 1970: SUMMARY REPORT OF ETHNIC CHARACTERISTICS FROM U. S. CENSUS. New York, New York: Division of Human Rights, 1970.

New Zealand. Department of Statistics. NEW ZEALAND CENSUS OF POPULATION AND DWELLINGS, 1966: MAORI POPULATION AND DWELLINGS. Wellington, New Zealand: Government Printer, 1970.

North Carolina. University. Institute of Government. NORTH CAROLINA STERILIZATION LAWS. (Health Law Bulletin no. 19). Chapel Hill: The Institute, 1970.

Nortman, Dorothy. POPULATION AND FAMILY PLANNING PROGRAMS: A FACTBOOK. (Reports on population/family planning no. 2). New York: Population Council, 1970.

Norway. Central Bureau of Statistics. VITAL STATISTICS AND MIGRATION STATISTICS 1968. (Norges offisielle statistikk XII, 259). Oslo: H. Aschehoug and Company, Sehesteds Place, 3, 1970.

O

Ontario Economic Council. IMMIGRANT INTEGRATION: OUR OBLIGATIONS--POLITICAL, SOCIAL AND ECONOMIC--TO THE 1,700,000 PEOPLE WHO HAVE COME TO ONTARIO IN THE PAST QUARTER CENTURY; a report. Toronto: Ontario Government Bookstore, Bay and Grosvenor Streets, 1970.

Organization for Economic Cooperation and Development. Development Centre. INTERNATIONAL ASSISTANCE FOR POPULATION PROGRAMMES: RECIPIENT AND DONOR VIEWS. Paris: Organization for Economic Cooperation and Development, 1970.

---Development Centre. POPULATION PROGRAMMES AND ECONOMIC AND SOCIAL DEVELOPMENT. Paris: Organization for Economic Cooperation and Development, 1970.

---Development Centre. FAMILY PLANNING PROGRAMMES IN AFRICA: A PAPER PRESENTED AT AN EXPERT GROUP MEETING HELD AT THE DEVELOPMENT CENTRE, PARIS, 6TH-8TH APRIL 1970. Pierre Pradervand. Paris: Organization for Economic Cooperation and Development, 1970.

P

Patch, Richard W. ATTITUDES TOWARD SEX, REPRODUCTION AND CONTRACEPTION IN BOLIVIA AND PERU. (Field Staff Reports: West Coast South America Series, Vol. 17, no. 11). Hanover, New Hampshire: American Universities Field Staff, 1970.

---THE LA PAZ (BOLIVIA) CENSUS OF 1970: WITH COMMENTS ON OTHER PROBLEMS OF COUNTING PEOPLE IN A DEVELOPING COUNTRY. (Field Staff Reports: West Coast South America Series, Vol. 17, no. 12). Hanover, New Hampshire: American Universities Field Staff, 1970.

---POPULATION REVIEW 1970: BOLIVIA. (Field Staff Reports: West Coast Latin America Series, Vol. 18, no. 1). Hanover, New Hampshire: American Universities Field Staff, 1970.

Pendleton, Don. NINETEEN EIGHTY-NINE: POPULATION DOOMSDAY. New York: Pinnacle Books, 1970.

PEOPLE AND PLANNING IN PAPUA AND NEW GUINEA. (New Guinea Research Bulletin no. 34). Canberra: Australian National University Press, 1970.

Poole, Peter A. THE VIETNAMESE IN THAILAND: A HISTORICAL PERSPECTIVE. Ithaca, New York: Cornell University Press, 1970.

Population Council. GOVERNMENTAL POLICY STATEMENTS ON POPULATION: AN INVENTORY. (Reports on population/family planning). New York: Population Council, 1970.

---MANUAL FOR SURVEYS OF FERTILITY AND FAMILY PLANNING: KNOWLEDGE, ATTITUDES AND PRACTICE. Bridgeport, Connecticut: Key Books Service, 1970.

POPULATION EXPLOSION: HOW SOCIALISTS VIEW IT. By Joseph Hansen. New York: Pathfinder Press, 1970.

Population Reference Bureau. Information Service. WORLD POPULATION DATA SHEET, 1970: POPULATION INFORMATION FOR 142 COUNTRIES. Washington, D. C.: Population Reference Bureau, 1970.

Presser, Harriet B. VOLUNTARY STERILIZATION: A WORLD VIEW. (Reports on population/family planning no. 5). New York: Population Council, 1970.

Preston, Samuel H. OLDER MALE MORTALITY AND CIGARETTE SMOKING: A DEMOGRAPHIC ANALYSIS. (Population monograph series, no. 7). Berkeley, California: Publications Office, Institute of International Studies, University of California, 1970.

R

Ravenholt, Albert. POPULATION REVIEW 1970: THE PHILIPPINES. (Field Staff Reports: Southeast Asia Series, Vol. 19, no. 1). Hanover, New Hampshire: American Universities Field Staff, 1970.

Robinson, Warren C. POPULATION GROWTH AND ECONOMIC WELFARE. (Reports on population/family planning, no. 6). New York: Population Council, 1970.

Rodwin, Lloyd. NATIONS AND CITIES: A COMPARISON OF STRATEGIES FOR URBAN GROWTH. Boston: Houghton Mifflin, 1970.

Rusinow, Dennison I. POPULATION REVIEW 1970: YUGOSLAVIA. (Field Staff Reports: Southeast Europe Series, Vol. 17, no. 1). Hanover, New Hampshire: American Universities Field Staff, 1970.

S

Salzano, Francisco M. and Newton Freire-Maia. PROBLEMS IN HUMAN BIOLOGY: A STUDY OF BRAZILIAN POPULATIONS. Detroit: Wayne State University Press, 1970.

Sanders, Thomas G. FAMILY PLANNING IN COLOMBIA. (Field Staff Reports: West Coast South America Series, Vol. 17, no. 3). Hanover, New Hampshire: American Universities Field Staff, 1970.

---FAMILY PLANNING IN PERU. (Field Staff Reports: West Coast South America Series, Vol. 17, no. 6). Hanover, New Hampshire: American Universities Field Staff, 1970.

---OPPOSITION TO FAMILY PLANNING IN LATIN AMERICA: THE NON-MARXIST LEFT. (Field Staff Reports: West Coast South America Series, Vol. 17, no. 5). Hanover, New Hampshire: American Universities Field Staff, 1970.

---POPULATION REVIEW 1970: BRAZIL. (Field Staff Reports: East Coast South America Series, Vol. 14, no. 6). Hanover, New Hampshire: American Universities Field Staff, 1970.

---THE RELATIONSHIP BETWEEN POPULATION PLANNING AND BELIEF SYSTEMS: THE CATHOLIC CHURCH IN LATIN AMERICA. (Field Staff Reports: West Coast South America Series, Vol. 17, no. 7). Hanover, New Hampshire: American Universities Field Staff, 1970.

Santa Clara County, California. Planning Department. CENSUS TRACT STREET INDEX--1970 edition: COUNTY OF SANTA CLARA, CALIFORNIA. San Jose, California: The Department, 70 West Hedding Street, 1970.

Schultz, T. Paul. FERTILITY PATTERNS AND THEIR DETERMINANTS IN THE ARAB MIDDLE EAST. Santa Monica, California: The Rand Corporation, 1970.

---RURAL-URBAN MIGRATION IN COLOMBIA. Santa Monica, California: The Rand Corporation, 1970.

Schultz, Paul T. and Julie DaVanzo. ANALYSIS OF DEMOGRAPHIC CHANGE IN EAST PAKISTAN: A STUDY OF

RETROSPECTIVE SURVEY DATA; a report prepared for Agency for International Development. (R-564-AID). Santa Monica, California: The Rand Corporation, 1970.

Shannon, William H. LIVELY DEBATE: RESPONSE TO HUMANAE VITAE. New York: Sheed and Ward, 1970.

Singapore. Registrar-general of births and deaths. REPORT ON THE REGISTRATION OF BIRTHS AND DEATHS AND MARRIAGES. (Cmnd. 36 of 1970). Singapore: Government Publications Bureau, Fullerton Building, 1970.

SITUACION DEMMOGRAFICA: ESTADO Y MOVIMIENTO DE LA POBLACION. (America En Cifras Ser.) Washington, D. C.: Pan American Union, 1970.

SITUACION DEMMOGRAFICA: NO. 1 AGRICULTURA, GANADERIA, SILVICULTURA, CAZA Y PESCA. (America En Cifras Ser.) Washington, D. C.: Pan American Union, 1970.

SITUACION DEMMOGRAFICA: NO. 2 INDUSTRIA. (America En Cifras Ser.) Washington, D. C.: Pan American Union, 1970.

SITUACION DEMMOGRAFICA: NO. 3 COMERCIO, TRANSPORTES, COMUNICACIONES Y TURISMO. (America En Cifras) Washington, D. C.: Pan American Union, 1970.

Smith, T. Lynn and Paul E. Zopf, Jr. DEMOGRAPHY: PRINCIPLES AND METHODS. Philadelphia: F. A. Davis, 1970.

Sollins, Alfred D. and Raymond L. Belsky. COMMERCIAL PRODUCTION AND DISTRIBUTION OF CONTRACEPTIVES. (Reports on population/family planning no. 4). New York: Population Council, 1970.

Southeast Michigan Council of Governments. Planning Division. POPULATION AND OCCUPIED DWELLING UNITS IN THE DETROIT REGION, JULY 1, 1969. (Planning data series C, report no. 16). Detroit, Michigan: The Division, 1970.

Stacey, Tom. IMMIGRATION AND ENOCH POWELL. London: Tom Stacey, 1970.

Stephen, David. IMMIGRATION AND RACE RELATIONS. (Fabian Research Series 291). London: Fabian Society, 1970.

Stone, P. A. URBAN DEVELOPMENT IN BRITAIN: STANDARDS, COSTS AND RESOURCES, 1964-2004: VOLUME I: POPULATION TRENDS AND HOUSING. (National Institute of Economic and Social Research. Economics and Social Studies 26). Cambridge: Cambridge University Press, 1970.

Stuart, Martha and William T. Liu. CHANGING WOMAN: THE IMPACT OF FAMILY PLANNING. Boston: Little, Brown and Company, 1970.

T

Tangri, Shanti S. and H. Peter Gray, eds. ECONOMIC DEVELOPMENT AND POPULATION GROWTH: A CONFLICT. (Studies in Economics Series). Lexington, Massachusetts: D. C. Heath, 1970.

Taylor, L. R., ed. THE OPTIMUM POPULATION FOR BRITAIN. (Institute of Biology. Symposia no. 19). New York: Academic Press, 1970.

Tennessee. Agricultural Experimental Station. INCOME AND MOBILITY OF TENNESSEE FARM AND NON-FARM WORKERS, 1960-1965, by Charles B. Sappington and Larry L. Bauer. Knoxville, Tennessee: The Experimental Station, 1970.

Thomson, K. W. and A. D. Trlin, ed. IMMIGRANTS IN NEW ZEALAND. New Zealand: Massey University, 1970.

Tobin, Gary Allan. THE ST. LOUIS SCHOOL CRISIS: POPULATION SHIFTS AND VOTING PATTERNS. Bridgeton, Missouri: Gary Tobin, 10965 Warwickhall, 1970.

Trobisch, Walter. PLEASE HELP ME, PLEASE LOVE ME: A CHRISTIAN VIEW OF CONTRACEPTION. (Here Is My Problem Series). Dourier's Grove, Illinois: Inter-Varsity Press, 1970.

Tunnadine, L. P. CONTRACEPTION AND SEXUAL LIFE: A THERAPEUTIC APPROACH. Ed. Michael Balint. (Mind and Medicine Monographs). Philadelphia: J. B. Lippincott, 1970.

U

United Nations. Department of Economic and Social Affairs. MANUALS ON METHODS OF ESTIMATING POPULATION: MANUAL 6, METHODS OF MEASURING INTERNAL MIGRATION. (Population Studies no. 47). New York: The Department, 1970.

---Economic and Social Council. OUTFLOW OF TRAINED PERSONNEL FROM DEVELOPING TO DEVELOPED COUNTRIES; report of the Secretary-General, June 9, 1970. New York: The Council, 1970.

---Economic and Social Council. Statistical Commission. DEMOGRAPHIC AND HOUSING STATISTICS: PRINCIPLES AND RECOMMENDATIONS FOR A VITAL STATISTICS SYSTEM; report of the Secretary-General. June 26, 1970. New York, 1970.

---Economic and Social Council. Statistical Commission. DRAFT RECOMMENDATIONS FOR THE 1973 WORLD PROGRAMME OF INDUSTRIAL STATISTICS: PART 1, GENERAL STATISTICAL OBJECTIVES; report of the Secretary General. June 12, 1970. New York, 1970.

---Economic and Social Council. Statistical Commission. AN INTEGRATED SYSTEM OF DEMOGRAPHIC, MANPOWER AND SOCIAL STATISTICS AND ITS LINKS WITH THE SYSTEM OF NATIONAL ECONOMIC ACCOUNTS. May 28, 1970. New York, 1970.

---Economic Commission for Africa. REPORT OF THE EXPORT GROUP ON POPULATION, ADDIS ABABA, 8-10 June, 1970. New York, 1970.

United Nations. Economic Commission for Africa. REPORT OF THE SEMINAR ON APPLICATION OF DEMOGRAPHIC DATA AND ANALYSIS TO DEVELOPMENT PLANNING, ADDIS ABABA, 2-9 June, 1969. New York, 1970.

---Economic Commission for Africa. REPORT OF SEMINAR ON ORGANISATION AND CONDUCT OF CENSUSES OF POPULATION AND HOUSING, ADDIS ABABA, 17-28 June, 1968: vol. 1, Seminar Report. New York, 1970.

---Economic Commission for Asia and the Far East. DIRECTORY OF KEY PERSONNEL AND PERIODICALS IN THE FIELD OF POPULATION IN THE ECAFE REGION. New York, 1970.

---Economic Commission for Latin America. REPORT OF THE WORKING GROUP ON INDUSTRIAL STATISTICS. Santiago, Chile, 3-14 August, 1970. New York, 1970.

---Executive Committee of the High Commissioner's Programme. NOTE ON EDUCATION FOR REFUGEES. September 14, 1970. New York, 1970.

---General Assembly. REPORT ON THE RESETTLEMENT OF REFUGEES. September 8, 1970. New York, 1970.

---Population Commission. REPORT OF THE AD HOC COMMITTEE OF EXPERTS ON PROGRAMMES IN DEMOGRAPHIC ASPECTS OF ECONOMIC DEVELOPMENT; on its meeting held at United Nations headquarters from June 29 to July 3, 1970. New York, 1970.

---Secretariat. AN EVALUATION OF THE FAMILY PLANNING PROGRAMME OF THE GOVERNMENT OF INDIA. November 24, 1969. New York, 1970.

---Statistics Office. DEMOGRAPHIC YEARBOOK, 1969: SPECIAL TOPIC: NATALITY STATISTICS. (21st issue). New York, 1970.

---Statistics Office. POPULATION AND VITAL STATISTICS REPORT. Data available as of October 1, 1970. New York, 1970.

United Nations. Statistics Office. REPORT OF THE SEMINAR ON CIVIL REGISTRATION AND VITAL STATISTICS FOR ASIA AND THE FAR EAST, COPENHAGEN, DENMARK. July 22 to August 10, 1968, sponsored by the Economic Commission for Asia and the Far East in cooperation with the government of Denmark, the Statistical Office of the United Nations, the United Nations office of technical cooperation. New York, 1970.

United States. Agency for International Development. Bureau for technical assistance. Office of Population. POPULATION PROGRAM ASSISTANCE: AID TO DEVELOPING NATIONS BY THE UNITED STATES, OTHER NATIONS AND INTERNATIONAL AND PRIVATE AGENCIES. Washington, D.C., 1970.

---Bureau of the Census. CENSUS USE STUDY: REPORT NO. 1. GENERAL DESCRIPTION. Washington, D. C., 1970.

---Bureau of the Census. CENSUS USE STUDY: REPORT NO. 5. DATA INTERESTS OF LOCAL AGENCIES. Washington, D.C., 1970.

---Bureau of the Census. CENSUS USE STUDY: REPORT NO. 10. DATA USES IN SCHOOL ADMINISTRATION. Takuya Maruyama and Joyce Phipps. Washington, D. C., 1970.

---Bureau of the Census. CENSUS USE STUDY: REPORT NO. 11. AREA TRAVEL SURVEY. Washington, D. C.: Superintendent of Documents, 1970.

---Bureau of the Census. ESTIMATES OF THE POPULATION OF HAWAII COUNTIES JULY 1, 1967 AND 1968. February 18, 1970. Washington, D. C.: Superintendent of Documents, 1970.

---Bureau of the Census. FERTILITY OF THE POPULATION: JANUARY 1969. July 6, 1970. Washington, D. C.: Superintendent of Documents, 1970.

---Bureau of the Census. HOUSEHOLD AND FAMILY CHARACTERISTICS, MARCH 1969. May 8, 1970. Washington, D. C.: 1970.

United States. Bureau of the Census. 1970 CENSUS USERS'
GUIDE. Washington, D. C.: Superintendent of Documents,
1970.

---Bureau of the Census. SELECTED CHARACTERISTICS OF
PERSONS AND FAMILIES MARCH 1970: INCOME, POVERTY,
EDUCATION, MOBILITY, FAMILY AND HOUSEHOLD COMPOSITION.
July 13, 1970. Washington, D. C.: Superintendent of
Documents, 1970.

---Bureau of the Census. Population Division. ESTIMATES
OF THE POPULATION OF THE UNITED STATES, BY AGE, RACE
AND SEX: JULY 1, 1967 TO JULY 1, 1969. March 19,
1970. Washington, D. C.: Superintendent of Documents, 1970.

---Bureau of the Census. Population Division. MARRIAGE,
FERTILITY AND CHILDSPACING JUNE 1965. Wilson H. Grabill and Maria Davidson. August 6, 1969. Washington,
D. C.: Superintendent of Documents, 1970.

---Bureau of the Census. Population Division. MOBILITY
OF THE POPULATION OF THE UNITED STATES, MARCH 1969
TO MARCH 1970. Larry H. Long and Karen M. Mills.
January 15, 1971. Washington, D. C.: Superintendent
of Documents, 1970.

---Bureau of the Census. Population Division. POPULATION OF PANAMA: ESTIMATES AND PROJECTIONS: 1961-
2001. Carolyn D. Yandle and Jeffrey W. Stone.
Washington, D. C.: Superintendent of Documents, 1970.

---Bureau of the Census. Population Division. PREVIOUS
AND PROSPECTIVE FERTILITY: 1967 (based on data from
the 1967 Survey of Economic Opportunity). January 26,
1971. Washington, D. C.: Superintendent of Documents, 1970.

---Bureau of the Census. Population Division. PROJECTIONS OF THE POPULATION OF THE UNITED STATES, BY AGE
AND SEX (INTERIM REVISIONS): 1970 TO 2020. August 6,
1970. Washington, D. C.: Superintendent of Documents,
1970.

United States. Bureau of the Census. Population Division. TRENDS IN SOCIAL AND ECONOMIC CONDITIONS IN METROPOLITAN AND NON-METROPOLITAN AREAS. September 3, 1970. (Current population reports series P-23, Special studies no. 23). Washington, D. C.: Superintendent of Documents, 1970.

---Bureau of the Census. Population Division. USE OF SOCIAL SECURITY'S CONTINUOUS WORK HISTORY SAMPLE FOR POPULATION ESTIMATION. Meyer Zetter and Elisabeth S. Nagy. April 10, 1970. (Current population reports series P-23, Special studies no.31). Washington,D.C.: Superintendent of Documents, 1970.

---Congressional Joint Economic Committee. Sub-committee on economic statistics. REVIEW OF FEDERAL STATISTICAL PROGRAMS: HEARINGS, APRIL 30-MAY 15, 1969. Washington, D. C.: Superintendent of Documents, 1970.

---Department of Commerce. Office of Public Affairs. UNCLE SAM COUNTS: THE STORY OF CENSUS. (Do you know your economic ABC's?) Washington, D. C.: Superintendent of Documents, 1970.

---Department of Health, Education and Welfare. Office of the Assistant Secretary (Planning and Evaluation). FAMILY PLANNING SERVICE PROGRAMS: AN OPERATIONAL ANALYSIS. Washington, D. C.: Superintendent of Documents, 1970.

---House Committee on Foreign Affairs. Sub-committee on Inter-American affairs. SELECTIVE MIGRATION PROGRAM FOR LATIN AMERICA: OPERATED BY THE INTERGOVERNMENTAL COMMITTEE FOR EUROPEAN MIGRATION (ICEM): HEARING, JULY 7, 1970.

---House Committee on Interstate and Foreign Commerce. Sub-committee on Public Health and Welfare. FAMILY PLANNING SERVICES: HEARING, AUGUST 3-7, 1970 ON H.R. 15159. Washington, D. C.: Superintendent of Documents, 1970.

---House Committee on the Judiciary. Sub-committee no. 1. AMENDMENTS TO THE IMMIGRATION LAWS (1965): HEARINGS.

DECEMBER 10, 1969, ON THE EFFECT OF THE ACT OF OCTOBER 3, 1965, ON IMMIGRATION FROM IRELAND AND NORTHERN EUROPE. Washington, D. C.: Superintendent of Documents, 1970.

---House Committee on the Judiciary. Sub-Committee no. 1. IMMIGRATION: HEARINGS, JULY 16-AUGUST 6, 1970, ON H.R. 9112, H.R. 15092, H.R. 17370, TO AMEND THE IMMIGRATION AND NATIONALITY ACT, AND FOR OTHER PURPOSES. Washington, D. C.: Superintendent of Documents, 1970.

---House Committee on Post Office and Civil Service. CONFIDENTIALITY OF CENSUS INFORMATION: REPORT, JULY 30, 1969. Washington, D. C.: Superintendent of Documents, 1970.

---House Committee on Post Office and Civil Service. Sub-committee on Census and Statistics. ACCURACY OF 1970 CENSUS ENUMERATION AND RELATED MATTERS: HEARINGS SEPTEMBER 15-30, 1970. Washington, D C.: Superintendent of Documents, 1970.

---House Committee on Post Office and Civil Service. Sub-Committee on Census and Statistics. 1970 CENSUS AND LEGISLATION RELATED THERETO: HEARINGS: PARTS 1-3, APRIL 1-JUNE 17, 1969. Washington, D. C.: Superintendent of Documents, 1970.

---National Center for Health Statistics. FACTS OF LIFE AND DEATH. Washington, D. C.: Superintendent of Documents, 1970.

---National Center for Health Statistics. Division of Vital Statistics. MORTALITY FROM SELECTED CAUSES BY MARITAL STATUS, UNITED STATES: PART A, FOR WHITE WOMEN AND MEN. A. Joan Klebba. Washington, D.C.: Superintendent of Documents, 1970.

---National Center for Health Statistics. Division of Vital Statistics. MORTALITY FROM SELECTED CAUSES BY MARITAL STATUS, UNITED STATES: PART B, FOR WOMEN AND MEN OF OTHER RACES. A. Joan Klebba. Washington, D. C.: Superintendent of Documents, 1970.

United States. National Center for Health Statistics. Division of Vital Statistics. NATALITY STATISTICS ANALYSIS: UNITED STATES, 1965-1967. Robert L. Heuser and others. Washington, D. C.: Superintendent of Documents, 1970.

---National Center for Health Statistics. Office for Health Statistics Analysis. ANNOTATED BIBLIOGRAPHY ON VITAL AND HEALTH STATISTICS. Washington, D. C.: Superintendent of Documents, 1970.

---National Center for Health Statistics. Office of Health Statistics Analysis. NEEDS FOR NATIONAL STUDIES OF POPULATION DYNAMICS: A REPORT OF THE UNITED STATES NATIONAL COMMITTEE ON VITAL AND HEALTH STATISTICS: AN ASSESSMENT OF THE TYPES OF STUDIES NEEDED IN THE FIELD OF POPULATION DYNAMICS, THE SPECIFIC TYPES OF DATA NEEDED TO YIELD SUCH STUDIES, AND THE STEPS REQUIRED TO MEET THESE NEEDS MOST EFFECTIVELY. Washington, D. C.: Superintendent of Documents, 1970.

---National Center for Health Statistics. Office of Health Statistics Analysis. REPORT OF THE TWENTIETH ANNIVERSARY CONFERENCE OF THE UNITED STATES NATIONAL COMMITTEE ON VITAL AND HEALTH STATISTICS. Washington, D. C.; Superintendent of Documents, 1970.

---National Institute of Mental Health. INTERNATIONAL FAMILY PLANNING, 1966-1968: A BIBLIOGRAPHY. David L. Kasdon. Washington, D. C.: Superintendent of Documents, 1970.

---Office of Economic Opportunity. FAMILY PLANNING PROGRAM. Provisional inventory of family planning clinics in the United States. December, 1970. OEO Pamphlet 6130-9.

---Senate. Committee on the Judiciary. Sub-committee on constitutional rights. PRIVACY, THE CENSUS AND FEDERAL QUESTIONNAIRES: HEARING APRIL 24-JULY 1, 1969 to secure personal privacy and to protect the constitutional right of individuals to ignore unwarranted requests for personal information. Washington, D.C.: Superintendent of Documents, 1970.

United States. Senate. Committee on the Judiciary.
Sub-committee to investigate the administration of
the internal security act and other internal security
laws. COMMUNIST THREAT TO THE UNITED STATES THROUGH
THE CARIBBEAN: HEARINGS: PART 21, JUNE 30, 1970.
Washington, D. C.: Superintendent of Documents, 1970.

---Senate. Committee on the Judiciary. Sub-committee
to investigate problems connected with refugees and
escapees. REFUGEE AND CIVILIAN WAR CASUALTY PROBLEMS
IN LAOS AND CAMBODIA: HEARING, MAY 7, 1970. Washington, D. C.: Superintendent of Documents, 1970.

---Senate. Committee on labor and public welfare.
Sub-committee on health. FAMILY PLANNING AND POPULATION RESEARCH, 1970: HEARINGS, DECEMBER 8, 1969-
FEBRUARY 19, 1970, ON S. 2108 TO PROMOTE PUBLIC
HEALTH AND WELFARE BY EXPANDING, IMPROVING AND BETTER
COORDINATING THE FAMILY PLANNING SERVICES AND POPULATION RESEARCH ACTIVITIES OF THE FEDERAL GOVERNMENT;
and for other purposes. Washington, D. C.: Superintendent of Documents, 1970.

---Senate. Select Committee on Small Business. Sub-
Committee on monopoly. COMPETITIVE PROBLEMS IN THE
DRUG INDUSTRY: HEARINGS: PART 15, JANUARY 14-23,
1970, on present status of competition in the pharmaceutical industry: Oral contraceptives (volume one).
Washington, D. C.: Superintendent of Documents, 1970.

---Senate. Select Committee on Small Business. Sub-
Committee on monopoly. COMPETITIVE PROBLEMS IN THE
DRUG INDUSTRY: HEARINGS: PART 16, FEBRUARY 24-MARCH
4, 1970, on present status of competition in the
pharmaceutical industry: Oral contraceptives (volume
two). Washington, D. C.: Superintendent of Documents,
1970.

---Senate. Select Committee on Small Business. Sub-
committee on monopoly. COMPETITIVE PROBLEMS IN THE
DRUG INDUSTRY: HEARINGS: PART 17, ON PRESENT STATUS
OF COMPETITION IN THE PHARMACEUTICAL INDUSTRY: ORAL
CONTRACEPTIVES (volume three). Washington, D. C.:
Superintendent of Documents, 1970.

V

Vaughan, Paul. THE PILL ON TRIAL. New York: Coward-McCann and Geoghegan, 1970.

Viva La Raza - A COMMUNIST VIEW ON CHICANO LIBERATION. New York: New Outlook Publishers, 1970.

W

Walsh, Brendan M. RELIGION AND DEMOGRAPHIC BEHAVIOUR IN IRELAND; with appendix. Migration between Northern Ireland and the Republic of Ireland, by R. C. Geary and J. H. Hughes. Dublin, Ireland: Economic and Social Research Institute, 1970.

Watson, William R. and Shirley J. Huzarski. ESTIMATES OF THE 1969 POPULATION OF NEW MEXICO COUNTIES. Business information series no. 48). (Bureau of Business Research, University of New Mexico, Albuquerque, New Mexico, 1970.

Weiner, Sandra. SMALL HANDS, BIG HANDS: SEVEN STORIES OF MEXICAN-AMERICAN MIGRANT WORKERS AND THEIR FAMILIES. New York: Pantheon Books, 1970.

Wertheimer, Richard F., II. THE MONETARY REWARDS OF MIGRATION WITHIN THE UNITED STATES. (UI 31-113-26). Washington, D. C.: Urban Institute, 1970.

WHO SHALL LIVE: MAN'S CONTROL OVER BIRTH AND DEATH. New York: Hill and Wang, 1970.

Widjojo, Nitisastro. POPULATION TRENDS IN INDONESIA. Ithaca, New York: Cornell University, 1970.

Wiens, Herold J, Han. CHINESE EXPANSION IN SOUTH CHINA. (Foreign Area Studies No. 3). Hamden, Connecticut: The Shoe String Press, 1970.

WORLD LIST OF FAMILY PLANNING AGENCIES. New York: International Publications Service, 1970.

X

Xenos, Christos. MAURITIUS. (Country Profiles). New York: Population Council, 1970.

Z

Zelinsky, Wilbur, et al. GEOGRAPHY AND A CROWDING WORLD. New York: Oxford University Press, 1970.

PERIODICAL LITERATURE BY TITLE

A

"ACOG to administer hospital family planning." ACOG NURSES BULL. 4:2, Summer, 1970.

"AMA dislikes giving OC users information." AM DRUGGIST. 162:39, October 5, 1970.

"AMA writes OC consumer booklet." AM DRUGGIST. 162:20, August 24, 1970.

"Abdominal pregnancy associated with an intrauterine contraceptive device," by L. H. Tisdall, et al. AMER J OBSTET GYNEC. 106:937-939, March 15, 1970.

"Abnormal endometrial aspects caused by prolonged use of a synthetic estro-progestinic combination," by U. Lecca, et al. MINERVA GINECOL. 22:439-440, April 30, 1970.

"Abortion and the birth rate in the USSR," by G. Hyde. J BIOSOC SCI. 2:283-292, July, 1970.

"Abortion and sterilization. Status of the law in mid-1970," by N. Hershey. AMER J NURS. 70:1926-1927, September, 1970.

"Abortion: holy innocents?" CHR TODAY. 14:39, May 8, 1970.

"Abortion is the world's most common (and worst) population regulator," by G. Machanik. SA NURS J. 36:32-33, passim. April, 1970.

"Abortive town expansion plan: Ipswich." TOWN PLAN INST J. 56:121, March, 1970.

"About planned parenthood," by M. Zelenková. ZDRAV PRAC. 20:536-540, October, 1970.

"Acadian migrations," by R. G. Leblanc. CAN GEOG J. 81:10-19, July, 1970.

"Accidental injuries: incidence and duration of disability by cause." METROPOLITAN LIFE STAT BUL. 51:10-12, June, 1970.

"Accustoming of caged animals to the cage effect. Hypothalamo-hypophyseal repercussions," by R. Roudier, et al. C R SOC BIOL. (Paris). 164:68-71, 1970.

"Action mechanism of oral contraceptives," by M. Tausk. NED TIJDSCHR VERLOSKD GYNAECOL. 70:520-527, December, 1970.

"Action of a contraceptive ovulene on mouse mammary carcinogenesis," by E. Coezy, et al. REV EUROP ETUD CLIN BIOL. 15:205-209, February, 1970.

"Action of trioxyethylrutin in women under estro-progestative treatment," by J. Laforet, et al. LYON MED. 223:327-329, February 1, 1970.

"The active mechanism of oral contraceptives," by M. Tausk. NEDERL T GENEESK. 114:1417-1418, August 22, 1970.

"Activity of certain enzymes in endometrial samples in cases of long-lasting maintenance of intrauterine contraceptive devices," by J. Jonek, et al. GINEKOL POL. 41:1195-1201, November, 1970.

"The activity record: a measure of social isolation-involvement," by A. D. Sachson, et al. PSYCHOL REP. 26:413-414, April, 1970.

"Adam Smith on population," by J. J. Spengler. POPULATION STUDIES. 24:377-388, November, 1970.

"Administration of Wagina resettlement scheme," by G. Cochrane. HUMAN ORGAN 29:123-132, Summer, 1970.

"Adrenosem therapy for bleeding coincident with the use of intrauterine contraceptive devices: a double blind study," by H. W. Horne, Jr., et al. FERTIL STERIL. 21:230-233, March, 1970.

"Advances in the control of fertility," by M. Vojta. CESK GYNEK. 35:288-289, 1970.

"Advantages and problems associated with the intrauterine device," by J. D. Loudon. MIDWIFE HEALTH VISIT. 6:97-99, passim. March, 1970.

"Adverse effects of contraceptives. I. Introduction," by J. Martinez-Manautou. GAC MED MEX. 100:821-823, August, 1970.

"Adverse effects of contraceptives. II. Adverse effects of contraceptive steroids on the liver," by B. Sepúlveda. GAC MED MEX. 100:823-831, August, 1970.

"Adverse effects of contraceptives. III. Effects on blood coagulation. The problem of thrombosis," by J. Pizzuto. GAC MED MEX. 100:831-849, August, 1970.

"Adverse effects of contraceptives. IV. The problem of potential carcinogenic effects of contraceptive steroids," by R. Hertz. GAC MED MEX. 100:849-859, August, 1970.

"Adverse reactions to oral contraceptives. Report of a case of cholestasis," by V. G. Henry. ROCKY MT MED J. 67:24-27, December, 1970.

"Affluence and effluence: U. S.," by N. Cousins. SAT R. 53:53, May 2, 1970.

"Africa's population problems," by A. E. Okorafor. AFRICA R. 15:22-23, June, 1970.

"Age distributions," by M. S. Bartlett. BIOMETRICS. 26:377-385, September, 1970.

"Age, education and occupation differentials in interregional migration; some evidence for Canada," by M. McInnis. DEMOGRAPHY. 8:195-204, May 1, 1970.

"Age-incidence of death from smoking," by S. H. Preston. AM STAT ASSN J. 65:1125-1130, September, 1970.

"Aged people among urban population," by Bohdan Kaufman. DEMOSTA. 3:5-26 no. 1/2. 1970.

"Aggressive behavior in the rat: effects of isolation, and olfactory bulb lesions," by H. Bernstein, et al. BRAIN RES. 20:75-84, May 20, 1970.

"Aging and life space in Poland and the United States," by E. J. Shanas. HEALTH SOC BEHAV. 11:183-190, September, 1970.

"Agricultural development in the humid tropics of Central America," by J. R. Taylor. INTER-AM ECON AFFAIRS. 24:41-49, Summer, 1970.

"Alarmed at birth rate figures," by S. Payne. TIMES ED SUP. 2860:5, March 13, 1970.

"Albumin metabolism in female rabbits treated with an oral oestrogen-progestogen contraceptive," by J. Dich, et al. SCAND J CLIN LAB INVEST. 26:31-34, August, 1970.

"Alienation: another dimension of underachievement," by M. M. Propper, et al. J PSYCHOL. 75:13-18, May, 1970.

"Alienation correlates of Catholic fertility," by A. G. Neal, et al. AM J SOCIOL. 76:460-473, November, 1970.

"Alienation: an essential process of the psychology of adolescence," by S. Berman. J AM ACAD CHILD PSYCHIATRY. 9:233-250, April, 1970.

"Alienation of present-day adolescents," by L. J. Wise. J AM ACAD CHILD PSYCHIATRY. 9:264-277, April, 1970.

"Alienation of youth as reflected in the Hippie movement," by F. S. Williams. J AM ACAD CHILD PSYCHIATRY. 9:251-263, April, 1970.

"Alkaline phosphatase concentration in cervical mucus," by D. C. Smith, et al. FERTIL STERIL. 21:549-554, July, 1970.

"All about food," by Stanley Johnson. VISTA. 5:24-29+. March/April, 1970.

"The alpha-fetoprotein test in pregnant women, women on oral contraceptives, newborn babies, and pyridoxine-deprived baboons," by H. Foy, et al. LANCET. 760:1336-1337, June 20, 1970.

"Alterations in brain sensitivity and barbiturate metabolism unrelated to aggression in socially deprived mice," by I. Baumel, et al. PSYCHOPHARMACOLOGIA. 18:320-324, 1970.

"Alterations in the levels of some serum proteins and serum enzymes during treatment with an oral contraceptive," by H. K. Hanel, et al. UGESKR LAEG. 132: 738-741, April 16, 1970.

"Alternatives for oral contraceptives," by A. A. Haspels. NED TIJDSCHR VERLOSKD GYNAECOL. 70:584-599, December, 1970.

"Amber light for the pill: Nelson subcommittee hearings." NEWSWEEK. 75:48-49, February 2, 1970.

"American longevity in 1968." METROPOLITAN LIFE STAT BUL. 51:9-11, AUGUST, 1970.

"American population growth in 1969." METROPOLITAN LIFE STAT BUL. 51:2-4, March, 1970.

"Analyses of census data for Greater London." GREATER LONDON RESEARCH Q. BULL. NO. 11. 46-61, June, 1970.

"Analysis of a family planning program in Guatemala," by Donald W. MacCorquodale. PUBLIC HEALTH REPORTS 85: 570-574, July, 1970.

"Analysis of migration to Israel," by F. S. Sherrow and P. Ritterband. JEW SOC STUD. 32:214-223, July, 1970.

"An analysis of 3 years' experience with intrauterine devices among women in the western area of the city of Santiago, July 1, 1964 to June 30, 1967," by B. Viel, et al. AMER J OBSTET GYNEC. 106:765-775, March, 1970.

"Anatomical and functional changes induced by oral contraception," by Y. Lefebvre. CANAD. MED. ASS J 102:621-624, March 28, 1970.

"And lest we forget: some figures to illustrate the magnitude of the problems we are facing; increasing world population and economic development." FREE LABOUR WORLD. 7-9, January, 1970.

"And the poor get babies," by Ruth Link. SWEDEN NOW.
   4:80-85+, November, 1970.

"Annals map supplement No. 13: population origin groups
   in rural Texas," by T. G. Jordan. ASSN AM GEOG ANN.
   60:404-405, June, 1970.

"Anthropometry in action. V. Age assessment by indigenous
   calendar and recalled birth intervals in village anthropometric studies," by D. A. McKay. J TROP PEDIAT.
   16:24-27, March, 1970.

"Antifertility agents," by C. W. Emmens. ANN REV PHARMACOL.
   10:237-254, 1970.

"Antifertility agents. IV. 2,3-diphenylbenzo-and 5,6-
   polymethylenebenzofurans, 1,2-diphenylnaphthofurans,
   and some related compounds," by H. P. Chawla, et al.
   J MED CHEM. 13:54-59, January, 1970.

"Antifertility drugs. Introductory remarks," by V. A.
   Drill. FED PROC. 29:1209-1210, May-June, 1970.

"Antifertility drugs. Symposium discussion," by C. R.
   Garcia. FED PROC. 29:1240-1242, May-June, 1970.

"Antifertility effects of low dose progestin," by H. W.
   Rudel. FED PROC. 29:1228-1231, May-June, 1970.

"Antispermatogenic agents," by H. Jackson. BRIT MED
   BULL. 26:79-86, January, 1970.

"Antithrombin 3 concentration in the blood," by M.
   Fagerhol, et al. NORD MED. 84:1473, November 12,
   1970.

"Antiuterotrophic activity of benzo- & naphthofurans:
   new oral antifertility agents," by B. S. Setty, et
   al. INDIAN J EXP BIOL. 8:139, April, 1970.

"Anxiety arousing effects of inappropriate crowding,"
   by J. C. Baxter, et al. J CONSULT CLIN PSYCHOL.
   35:174-178, October, 1970.

"An approach to the identification of high risk individuals in the general population," by C. E. Davis,
   et al. J FLA MED ASSOC. 57:28-30, November, 1970.

"Architectural business: economy-ecology-and zero population growth," by J. E. Carlson. ARCH REC. 148:59-60, August, 1970.

"Are there too many of us?" by P. R. Ehrlich. MCCALLS. 97:46-47+, July, 1970.

"Arkansas' population growth during the 1960's: a preliminary report," by Forrest H. Pollard and Kenneth D. Jones. ARK BUS & ECON R. 3:20-25, August, 1970.

"Artificial insemination; the dangers of a poorly kept secret," by W. Wadlington. NORTHWESTERN UNIV LAW R. 64:777-807, January-February, 1970.

"Artificial pregnancy interruption and birth rate," by K. Vacha. CESK GYNEK. 35:329-330, July, 1970.

"Ascertainment of men of Japanese ancestry in Hawaii through World War II Selective Service registration," by R. M. Worth, et al. J CHRONIC DIS. 23:389-397, November, 1970.

"Aspects of the intercommunity population balance in Northern Ireland," by P. A. Compton and F. W. Boal. ECON & SOCIAL R. 1:455-476, July, 1970.

"Assessing the demographic effect of a family planning programme," by W. Brass. PROC R SOC MED. 63:1105-1107, November, 1970.

"Association between religio-ethnic identification and fertility among contemporary Protestants and Jews," by B. Lazerwitz. SOCIOL Q. 11:307-320, Summer, 1970.

"The assumed employment generating capacity of European immigration in Rhodesia," by D. G. Clarke. RHODESIAN J ECON. 4:33-42, June, 1970.

"Attaining a stationary U. S. population: three views: Zero population growth: what is it? by Frank W. Notestein; Multiple pathe to population control by Garrett Hardin; Crisis thinking-rhetoric vs. action." by Jeannie I. Rosoff. FAMILY PLANNING PERSPECTIVES. 2:20-28, June, 1970.

"Attitudes of married college students on overpopulation and family planning," by P. D. Darney. PUBLIC HEALTH

REP. 85:412-418, May, 1970.

"Attitudes toward family planning among peri-urban Africans in Uganda," by R. E. Brown. TROP GEOGR MED. 22:87-100, March, 1970.

"Atypical cytology with contraceptive hormone medication. A preliminary report," by T. S. Kline, et al. AMER J CLIN PATH. 53:215-222, February, 1970.

"The autifertility effect of Butea frondosa petals (alcoholic extract and its crystalline fraction)," by K. Kapila, et al. J INDIAN MED ASS. 55:60-61, July, 1970.

B

"Baboon menstrual cycles affected by social environment," by T. E. Rowell. J REPROD FERTIL. 21:133-141, February, 1970.

"Baby shortage." ECONOMIST. 235:43-44, May 2, 1970.

"A bacteriological study in women with early post-partum intrauterine contraceptive device insertion," by G.R. Umabai, et al. INDIAN J MED RES. 58:258-267, February, 1970.

"Bacteriological study on the users of intrauterine contraceptive devices," by A. Ishihama, et al. ACTA OBSTET GYNAEC. 17:77-80, April, 1970.

"Bacteriology of fallopian tube in relation to puerperal sterilization," by M. A. Mustafa, et al. J OBSTET GYNAEC BRIT COMM. 77:171-173, February, 1970.

"Bajau sex and reproduction," by H. A. Nimmo. ETHNOLOGY. 9:251-262, July, 1970.

"The behavior of the immunoglobulin level during administration of oral contraceptives," by T. Pulay, et al. ORV HETIL. 111:1931-1933, August 16, 1970.

"Behavioral approaches to family and couple therapy," by R. Liberman. AMER J ORTHOPSYCHIAT. 40:106-118, January, 1970.

"Berkeley's demographic challenge: adjusting to population change," by Gerald Fox. PUBLIC AFFAIRS REPT. 11:1-5, October, 1970.

"Beyond the exponentials; the role of geography in the great transition," by W. Zelinsky. ECON GEOG. 46: 498-535, July, 1970.

"Big as it is, Canada doesn't need more people," by D.A. Chant. MACL MAG. 83:13, August, 1970.

"Big city syndrome," by D. Behrman. UNESCO COURIER. 23:20+, August, 1970.

"A big family isn't fun any more," by Gillian Tindall. GUARDIAN, April 1, 1970.

"Big shifts in political power: impact of 1970 census." U S NEWS. 69:26-28, September 21, 1970.

"The bigger the better." BULL NTRDA. 56:14+, July-August, 1970.

"Bill Shaw's gate to the promised land," by A. Edmonds. MACL MAG. 83:30, January, 1970.

"Biologic mode of action of the Lippes loop in intrauterine contraception," by N. Sagiroglu, et al. AMER J OBSTET GYNEC. 106:506-515, February 15, 1970.

"Birth control," by R. S. Kirk, et al. SCIENCE. 170: 1256, passim, December 18, 1970.

"Birth control. Moral theological, medico-gynecologic and penal aspects," by H. D. Hiersche, et al. GEBURTSH FRAUENHEILK. 30:289-301, April, 1970.

"Birth control. Problem of the gynecologist from the medical, moral and religious point of view," by S. Fossati. MINERVA GINECOL. 22:664-668, July 15, 1970.

"Birth control after 1984," by C. Djerassi. SCIENCE. 169:941-951, September 4, 1970.

"Birth control and Jewish Law," by D. M. Feldman. REVIEW CHR CENT. 87:632-633, May 20, 1970.

"Birth control and sex ratio," by R. Cruz-Coke. LANCET. 2:426, August 22, 1970.

"Birth control; a better method." CHEM & ENG N. 48:12, September 28, 1970.

"Birth control by the FDA," by G. G. Liddle. JAMA. 212:159, April 6, 1970.

"Birth control success story no. 1," by A. Gordon. READ DIGEST. 96:80-84, January, 1970.

"Birth control--the views of women," by J. A. Hurst. MED J AUST. 2:835-838, October 31, 1970.

"Birth control wars," by J. Deedy. COMMONWEAL. 92:2+, March 13, 1970.

"Birth pills' marketing freedom is just about coming to an end; curbs, lower dosages in offing." OIL PAINT & DRUG REP. 197:3+, January 19, 1970.

"Birth rank bias due to changes in birth rate," by J. S. Price, et al. BRIT J PREV SOC MED. 24:62, February, 1970.

"Birth rank in schizophrenia: with a consideration of the bias due to changes in birth-rate," by E. H. Hare, et al. BRIT J PSYCHIAT. 116:409-420, April, 1970.

"Birth rate and work load," by E. Nurge. AM ANTHROP. 72:1434-1439, December 9, 1970.

"Blood clotting, plasma kinins and fibrinolysis," by H. Gjonnaess, et al. THROMB DIATH HAEMORRH. 24:308-310, October 31, 1970.

"Blood glucose levels and glucose tolerance in women with subclinical diabetes receiving an oral contraceptive," by J. A. Goldman, et al. AMER J OBSTET GYNEC. 107:325-327, May 15, 1970.

"Blood-testis barrier--the key to male contraception in the future?" by M. Kormano. DUODECIM. 86:672-679, 1970.

"Botswana, another developing country," by L. Buhring. SYKEPLEIEN. 57:456-457, July 1, 1970.

"Brain cholinesterase in grouped and singly adrenal-demedullated rats," by T. D. McKinney. AMER J PHYSIOL.

219:331-334, August, 1970.

"The brain drain: a case study," by Joseph Chataparampil. ASIAN FORUM. 2:236-244, October-December, 1970.

"The brain drain: reality and paradox," by Roger Du Pasquier. PANORAMA. 2-8, July-August, 1970.

"Brain weight and acetylcholinesterase activity in differentially-grouped cottontail rabbits," by T. D. McKinney, et al. J MAMMAL. 51:389-391, May, 1970.

"Brave new world: can the law bring order within traditional concepts of due process?" SUFFOLK U L REV. 4:894, Spring, 1970.

"Breast cancer during oral contraceptive therapy," by R. E. Fechner. CANCER. 26:1204-1211, December, 1970.

"British experience of the pill," by C. R. Kay. J ROY COLL GEN PRACT. 19:251-257, May, 1970.

"The Bureau of business research as a summary-tape processing center." by Larry D. Adcock. N MEX BUS. 23:6-9, July. 1970.

C

"The CBI industrial trends survey," by David J. Reid. APPLIED ECON. 1:183-203, May, 1970.

"CFM and the Pill," by J. Deedy. COMMONWEAL. 91:442, January 23, 1970.

"Calhoun's horrible mousery; effects of overcrowding on mice," by S. Alsop. NEWSWEEK. 76:96, August 17, 1970.

"Call for an institute on demography: scientific council on problems of demography," by L. Degtyar. CURRENT DIGEST SOVIET PR. 22:15-16, July 14, 1970.

"Can the measurement of antithrombin-3 point out women who run the risk of thrombosis with the use of P-pills?" by M. K. Fagerhol, et al. T NORSK LAEGEFOREN. 90: 1559-1560, August 15, 1970.

"Canadian censuses and parish registers in the 1665-1668 period; a critical examination," by H. Charbonneau, et al. POPULATION. 25,1:97-124, January-February, 1970. SA # F0127.

"Canadian county-sponsored family planning. 3. A second survey," by J. E. Tyson, et al. OBSTET GYNEC. 35: 377-380, March, 1970.

"Canadian government view on immigrant services." INTERPRETER RELEASES. 47:220-223, September 14, 1970.

"Canadian immigration," by V. Del Buono. WORLD AFFAIRS. 35:23-24, April, 1970.

"Cancer and the pill," by T. W. Anderson. BR MED J. 3:773, September 26, 1970.

"Cancer and the pill," by P. Strickland. BRIT MED J. 3:165-166, July 18, 1970.

"Carbohydrate metabolism and oral contraceptives," by W. D. Reitsma. NED TIJDSCHR VERLOSKD GYNAECOL. 70:562-567, December, 1970.

"Carbohydrate metabolism and oral contraceptives," by W. D. Reitsma. NEDERL T GENEESK. 114:1427-1428, August 22, 1970.

"The carpal tunnel syndrome-a new complication ascribed to the pill," by M. S. Sabour, et al. AMER J OBSTET GYNEC. 107:1265-1267, August 15, 1970.

"The case for voluntary sterilization," by W. C. Rattan. WIS MED J. 69:20-21, August, 1970.

"A case of acute myelogenic leukemia seemingly induced by intrauterine contraceptive devices," by A. Ishihama, et al. YOKOHAMA MED BULL. 20:83-86, June, 1970.

"A case of thromboembolic complication following use of oral contraceptives," by A. Kaindl, et al. WIEN MED WOCHENSCHR. 120:323-325, May 2, 1970.

"A case of thrombophlebitis in a woman on oral contraceptive," by M. K. Rajakumar. MED J MALAYA. 25:68-69, September, 1970.

"Case reports. Hyperlipaemic pancreatitis and the pill,"
by S. Bank, et al. POSTGRAD MED J. 46:576-578,
September, 1970.

"Catastrophic death toll lower in first half of 1970."
METROPOLITAN LIFE STAT BUL. 51:8, August, 1970.

"Causes of fertility decline in eastern Europe and the
Soviet Union: the influence of demographic factors,"
by Jerzy Berent. POPULATION STUDIES. 24:35-58, March,
1970 and 247-292, July, 1970.

"Census and apportionment: states' gains and losses in
House seats as projected from preliminary 1970 data."
CONG Q W REPT. 28:2193-2196, September 4, 1970.

"Census data by computer-for you," by J. C. Baker.
STORES. 52:74+, November, 1970.

"Census data: tailored to suit you." NATIONS BSNS.
58:52, August, 1970.

"The census is over, but--." U. S. NEWS. 68:50, April
13. 1970.

"Census is winner as direct mail operation." ADV AGE.
41:3+, September 7, 1970.

"Census of industrial production, 1968: principal results
in 1968 and some comparisons with earlier years."
STATIS BUL. 45:283-305, December, 1970.

"Census of 1970--an important source of information on
problems of social hygiene in public health," by M.
S. Bednyi, et al. ZDRAVOOKHR ROSS FED. 14:8-15,
January, 1970.

"Census ranking of cities is misleading." IND W.
167:23-24, October 5, 1970.

"Census '70: people on the move." FIRST NATIONAL CITY
BANK. p.114-117, October, 1970.

"Census taker and you: what to expect: the great American head count, the decennial census, is at hand."
U S NEWS. 68:32, March 23, 1970.

"Census taking, 1970," by William Gerber. EDITORIAL
RESEARCH REPORTS, p. 205-218, March 18, 1970.

"The center for population research," by J. F. O'Donnell.
J AM VET MED ASSOC. 157:1786-1794, December 1, 1970.

"Cerebrovascular accidents during oral contraception,"
by R. Fogelholm, et al. ACTA NEUROL SCAND. 46:Suppl.
43:252+, 1970.

"Cerebrovascular accidents in young women. Etiological
analysis. Pathogenetic role of oral contraceptive
drugs," by M. Mumenthaler, et al. Z NEUROL. 198:
46-64, 1970.

"Cerebrovascular disease and oral contraceptives."
J MED ASS GEORGIA. 59:125-126, March, 1970.

"Cerebrovascular diseases associated with the use of oral
contraceptives. A review of the English-language
literature," by A. T. Masi, et al. ANN INTERN MED.
72:111-121, January, 1970.

"Certain cultural and familial factors contributing to
adolescent alienation," by J. D. Noshpitz. J AM
ACAD CHILD PSYCHIATRY. 9:216-223, April, 1970.

"Cervical cytology and sequential birth control pills,"
by C. M. Dougherty. OBSTET GYNECOL. 36:741-744,
November, 1970.

"Cervico-vaginal cytology in women fitted with intrauterine devices (197 cases)," by M. Ancla, et al.
REV FR GYNECOL OBSTET. 65:585-590, October, 1970.

"Cesarean hysterectomy," by G. T. Schneider, et al.
SURG GYNEC OBSTET. 130:501-504, March, 1970.

"The challenge of family planning," by H. Hill. NURS
MIRROR. 131:27-32, August 21, 1970.

"Changes in antithrombin 3 and plasminogen induced by
oral contraceptives," by R. A. Peterson, et al.
AMER J CLIN PATH. 53:468-473, April, 1970.

"Changes in carbohydrate metabolism during the administration of progestational hormones," by P. Vela.

REV CHIL OBSTET GINECOL. 35:40-49, 1970.

"Changes in the cytology of the pars distalis of pituitary of green frog, Rana esculenta, under laboratory confinement," by R. K. Rastogi, et al. GEN COMP ENDOCRINOL. 15:488-491, December, 1970.

"Changes in fertility in Japan by region: 1920-1965," by Yoshihiro Tsubouchi. DEMOGRAPHY. 7:121-134, May, 1970.

"Changes in psychological symptoms in women taking oral contraceptives," by B. Herzberg, et al. BRIT J PSYCHIAT. 116:161-163, February, 1970.

"Changes in the trend of crude birth rate and crude death rate of Cairo and the U. A. R. during the past ten years (1958-1968)," by S. Abdou, et al. J EGYPT MED ASSOC. 53:433-441, 1970.

"Changing distribution of negroes within metropolitan areas: the emergence of black suburbs," by R. Farley. AM J SOCIOLOGY. 75:512-529, January, 1970.

"The changing environment: some implications for health," by A.J. Diekema. OCCUP HEALTH NURS (NY). 18:20-22, July, 1970.

"Changing pattern of immigration. METROPOLITAN LIFE STATIS BUL. p. 7-9, November, 1970.

"Changing patterns of family growth: the value of linked vital records as a source of data," by Howard B. Newcombe and Martha E. Smith. POPULATION STUDIES. 24:193-203, July, 1970.

"Changing sex norms in America and Scandinavia," by H. T. Christensen and C. F. Gregg. J MARRIAGE & FAM. 32:616-627, November, 1970.

"Changing urban spatial patterns; central places," by A. Getis. NAT COUNCIL SOCIAL STUDIES WRBK. 40: 101-120, 1970.

"Characteriological deterrants to economic progress in people of Appalachia," by C.E. Goshen. SOUTHERN MED J. 63:1053-1061, September, 1970.

"Charting the future; graphs," by J. Kettle. EXEC. 12:38, October, 1970.

"Chemical composition of the deposity formed on the Lippes loop after prolonged use," by A. D. Engineer, et al. AMER J OBSTET GYNEC. 106:315-316, January 15, 1970.

"Chemical composition of I.U.C.D.'s," by P. R. Myerscough. LANCET. 2:1316-1317, December 19, 1970.

"Child plan organization endorses pill." AM DRUGGIST. 161:57, May 18, 1970.

"Childlessness, intentional and unintentional," by E. J. Pohlman. J NERV MENT DIS. 151:2-12, July, 1970.

"China's birth control action programme, 1956-1964," by Pi-Chao Chen. POPULATION STUDIES. 24:141-158, July, 1970.

"Chinese provincial population data," by Robert Michael Field. CHINA Q. 195-202, October-December, 1970.

"Chlormadinone acetate in microdosis as a contraceptive," by J. Botero, et al. REV OBSTET GINECOL VENEZ. 21: 503-508, September-October, 1970.

"Chlormadinone contraceptive withdrawn," by L. Poller. BRIT MED J. 1:303-304, January 31, 1970.

"Choices of parenthood." SCIENCE. 170:257-262, October 16, 1970.

"Chromosomal abnormalities in the human population: estimation of rates based on New Haven newborn study," by H. A. Lubs and F. H. Ruddle. SCIENCE. 169:495-497, July 31, 1970.

"Chromosome studies in selected spontaneous abortions. 1. Conception after oral contraceptives," by D. H. Carr. CANAD MED ASS J. 103:343-348, August 15, 1970.

"Chronic steroid overloadings and contraception. Importance of conjunctive changes in the corporeal human uterine mucosa," by R. Moricard. BULL ACAD

NATL MED. 154:588-599, June 30, 1970.

"Chronic urticaria caused by allergy to the "pill" controlled and analysed by T.T.L.," by J. J. Meyer de Schmid, et al. BULL SOC FRANC DERM SYPH. 77:158-159, 1970.

"Circulatory effects of estrogen," by S. Kushner. OHIO STATE MED J. 66:1016-1021, October, 1970.

"Claustroxenscopophobia as a model of obessional syndrome formation," by O. N. Kznetsov. ZH NEVROPATOL PSIKHIATR. 70:551-556, 1970.

"The climax of population growth--past and future perspective," by K. Davis. CALIF MED. 113:33-39, November, 1970.

"The clinical and microscopic study of the inhibition of spermatic fertilizing power by 799 R. Trial of contraception in 114 cases," by A. Notter, et al. BULL FED GYNEC OBSTET FRANC. 22:58-60, January-March, 1970.

"Clinical aspects of the administration of gestagen preparations (Volidan, Cyclofarlutal, Ovulen, Ciba AC-101 and Steridil)," by Z. Sternadel. GINEK POL. 41:771-776, July, 1970.

"Clinical aspects of Ovulen application as a contraceptive and in gynecological disorders," by M. Bulska, et al. GINEK POL. 41:877-882, 1970.

"Clinical, biochemical, and experimental studies on lactation. V. Clinical effects of steroids on the initiation of lactation," by I. Kamal, et al. AM J OBSTET GYNECOL. 108:655-658, October 15, 1970.

"Clinical changes and histological aspect of the endometrium, during and after the end of treatment in 5 patients amenorrheic from hormonal contraception," by H. Voegeli, et al. BULL FED SOC GYNECOL OBSTET LANG FR. 22:286-287, June-August, 1970.

"Clinical evaluation of Madinon-s, an oral contraceptive," by R.Borenstein, et al. HAREFUAH. 79:8-11, July 1, 1970.

"A clinical evaluation of a monthly injection for conception control," by W. S. Keifer, et al. AMER J OBSTET GYNEC. 107:400-410, June 1, 1970.

"Clinical studies in United Arabic Republic with SH 850 (Eugynon), a low dose oral contraceptive, with special reference to its effect on lactation," by A. H. Shaaban, et al. MED WELT. 40:1730-1734, October 3, 1970.

"Clinical study of a once-a-month oral contraceptive: quinestrol-quingestanol," by E. Guiloff, et al. FERTIL STERIL. 21:110-118, February, 1970.

"Clinical study of an oral contraceptive, in a single monthly dose: quinestrol quingestanol," by D. Rubio, et al. GINEC OBSTET MEX. 27:123-133, February, 1970.

"A clinical study with continuous low doses of megestrol acetate for fertility control. Oil solution versus tablet formulation," by S. Avendano, et al. AMER J OBSTET GYNEC. 106:122-127, January 1, 1970.

"Clinical trial of medroxyprogesterone acetate during postpartum," by L. Beco. REV MED LIEGE. 25:226-230, April 1, 1970.

"Clinical trials of a low-dose inhibitor of ovulation," by C. Poiret, et al. LILLE MED SUPPL. 4:737-739, May, 1970.

"Clinical use of steroids hormones in the control of fertility," by E. Mears. CLIN TER. 52:499-507, March 31, 1970.

"Coexistence of pregnancy with Lippes' loop," by A. Lipinski, et al. WIAD LEK. 23:1603-1605, September 15, 1970.

"College policy on abortion and sterilization." ACOG NURSES BULL. 4:2, Fall, 1970.

"Colonial New England demography: a sampling approach," by R. Higgs and H. L. Stettler, 3rd. WM & MARY Q. 27:282-294, April, 1970.

"Color film spots tell the story," by I. Neiger. PUB REL J. 26:8-9, August, 1970.

"Colour and colonization," by H. Tinker. ROUND TAB. 60:405-416, November, 1970.

"Colpocytology in users of oral contraceptives. Findings in the Praia do Pinto Ambulatory clinic and in the Central Hospital of the IASEG (Department of Pathological Anatomy)," by A. F. Moura, et al. REV BRAS MED. 27:341-344, July, 1970.

"Combined oral contraceptives. A statement by the committee on safety of drugs." BRIT MED J. 2:231-232, April 25, 1970.

"Comment on "high school yearbooks: a nonreactive measure of social isolation in graduates who later became schizophrenic," by J. C. Schwarz. J ABNORM PSYCHOL. 75:317-318, June, 1970.

"A commentary on oral contraceptive therapy and contact lens wear," by J. B. Goldberg. J AMER OPTOM ASS. 41:237:241, March, 1970.

"Comments on the current status of contraception," by J. Ledr. CESK GYNEK. 35:40-41, February, 1970.

"Comments on the current status of our peroral contraception," by R. Sterba, et al. CESK GYNEK. 35:189-190, April, 1970.

"The committee and the pill," by P. Diggory. LANCET. 1:86, January 10, 1970.

"Commonsense advice on contraceptives," by L. M. Hellman. FAMILY HLTH. :37+, January, 1970.

"Community homogeneity and exclusion of the mentally ill: rejection versus consensus about deviance," by A. S. Linsky. J HEALTH SOC BEHAV. 11:304-311, December, 1970.

"Companion therapy for hospitalized psychotics," by A. M. Ludwig, et al. CURR PSYCHIATR THER. 10:182-190, 1970.

"Comparative clinical studies with oral contraceptives," by R.H. Richter. MED WELT. 40:1715-1726, October 3, 1970.

"A comparative study of blood fibrinolytic activity in normal women, pregnant women and women on oral contraceptives," by I. S. Menon, et al. J OBSTET GYNAEC BRIT COMM. 77:752-756, August, 1970.

"Comparative study of the influence of pregnancy and oral contraceptives on the gingivae," by G. M. El-Ashiry, et al. ORAL SURG. 30:472-475, October, 1970.

"Comparison of the metabolic effects of chlormadinone acetate and conventional contraceptive steroids in man," by P. J. Beck. CLIN ENDOCR. 30:785-791, June, 1970.

"Comparison of the migration process to an urban barrio and to a rural community: two case studies," by W. L. Flinn and D. G. Cartano. INTER-AM ECON AFFAIRS. 24:37-48, Autumn, 1970.

"Comparison: population densities, land values and socioeconomic class in four Latin American cities," by P. W. Amato. LAND ECON. 46:447-455, November, 1970.

"The complete family planning service at King's College Hospital, by P. Newton. NURS TIMES. 66:1399-1400, October 29, 1970.

"Complexities of morality," by S. Perlman. ANN INTERN MED. 72:761-762, May, 1970.

"Complications of the contraceptive pill." WISCONSIN MED J. 69:84-91, February, 1970.

"Conception control and embryonic development," by B. J. Poland. AMER J OBSTET GYNEC. 106:365-368, February 1, 1970.

"Conception control in doctors' families," by R. Levin, et al. PRACTITIONER. 204:694-699, May, 1970.

"Confusion on the pill: Nelson Hearings," by M. Mintz. NEW REPUB. 162:10-11, January 31, 1970.

"Congress on optimum population and environment. 1st, Chicago." CHEM & ENG N. 48:34-35, June 22, 1970.

"Constitutional problems of population control," by
Bettye S. Elkins. J LAW REFORM. 4:63-68, Fall,
1970.

"Containing the explosion." NATURE. 227:110, July
11, 1970.

"Context and consex: a cautionary tale," by R. M.
Hauser. AM J SOCIOL. 75:645-664+. January,
1970.

"Continuance of contraception post partum by patients
of Cook County Hospital," by P. B. Tamblyn, et al.
PUBLIC HEALTH REP. 85:220-224, March, 1970.

"Continuance of family planning in a health department
clinic," by J. J. Speidel, et al. AM J OBSTET
GYNECOL. 108:1134-1140, December 1, 1970.

"Continued or discontinued use of contraceptives," by
G. J. Kloosterman. NEDERL T GENEESK. 114:1429-
1432, August 22, 1970.

"Continued or intermittent use of contraceptives," by
G. J. Kloosterman. NED TIJDSCHR VERLOSKD GYNAECOL.
70:576-583, December, 1970.

"Continuous microdoses of chloramadinone during lactation," by C. González. GINECOL OBSTET MEX. 28:563-566, November, 1970.

"Contraception," by H. Winn. CLIN OBSTET GYNECOL.
13:701-712, September, 1970.

"Contraception and abortion: American catholic responses,"
by D. Callhan. ANNALS OF THE AMERICAN ACADEMY OF
POLITICAL & SOCIAL SCIENCE. 387:109-117, January,
1970. SA #E7669.

"Contraception before and during marriage," by V. Bartak, et al. CAS LEK CESK. 109:599-604, June 9,
1970.

"Contraception by an injectable long-acting oestrogen-progestogen agent. II. Evaluation of cycles, menstrual
flows and side effects," by R. Plesner. ACTA ENDOCRINOL. 65:683-697, December, 1970.

"Contraception by intra-uterine device," by M. Lancet, et al. HAREFUAH. 78:223-226, March 1, 1970.

"Contraception by means of a silastic vaginal ring impregnated with medroxyprogesterone acetate," by D. R. Mishell, Jr., et al. AMER J OBSTET GYNEC. 107:100-107, May 1, 1970.

"Contraception: the chemical control of fertility," by D. Lednicer. Review by V. Petrow. CHEM & IND. 1105-1106, August 22, 1970.

"Contraception: the fourth stage of labour," by P. A. Last. NURS MIRROR. 130:25-29, April 3, 1970.

"Contraception in general practice. A research project from general practice. II. Presentation of cases with special attention to the contraceptive pattern," by P. Backer, et al. UGESKR LAEG. 132:227-231, January 29, 1970.

"Contraception sine comstockery," by S. H. Sturgis. NEW ENG J MED. 283:595-596, September 10, 1970.

"Contraception using the intrauterine device Super-DANA in combination with the rhythm method," by M. Vojta, et al. CESK GYNEK. 35:32-35, February, 1970.

"Contraception with chlormadinone acetate in woman with previous contraceptive jaundice," by R. P. Thompson, et al. BRIT MED J. 1:152-153, January 17, 1970.

"Contraception with a novel sequential preparation (Ovanon)," by D. Tenhaeff. MUNCHEN MED WSCHR. 112:851-857, May 1, 1970.

"Contraceptive effect of varying dosages of progestogen in silastic vaginal rings," by D. R. Mishell, Jr., et al. FERTIL STERIL. 21:99-103, February, 1970.

"Contraceptive hormones," by B. N. Branch. J INDIAN MED ASSOC. 55:359-362, November 16, 1970.

"Contraceptive methods prior to hospital discharge: the first city-wide program," by E. F. Daily. AMER J PUBLIC HEALTH. 60:965-967, June, 1970.

"Contraceptive pill and thyroid nodule," by M. T.

Diamond, et al. NEW YORK J MED. 70:295-297, January 15, 1970.

"The contraceptive pill, side effects and personality: report of a controlled double blind trial," by D. Grounds, et al. BRIT J PSYCHIAT. 116:169-172, February, 1970.

"Contraceptive technology: advances needed in fundamental research," by L. J. Carter. SCIENCE. 168: 805-809, May 15, 1970.

"Contraceptives," by P. A. Corfman, et al. SCIENCE. 167:1315-1316, March 6, 1970.

"Contraceptives and dysplasia: higher rate for pill choosers," by E. Stern, et al. SCIENCE. 169:497-498, July 31, 1970.

"Contraceptives and hypertension." JAMA. 214:136-137, October 5, 1970.

"Contraceptives and serum proteins," by M. H. Briggs, et al. BRIT MED J. 3:521, August 29, 1970.

"Contraceptives, brain serotonin, and liver tryptophan pyrrolase," by G. Nistico, et al. LANCET. 2:213, July 25, 1970.

"Contraceptives; once-a-month pill." CHEM & ENG N. 48:22, May 11, 1970.

"Control of fertility," by M. L. Peterson. NEW ENG J MED. 282:1432-1433, June 18, 1970.

"Control of human fertility." BRIT MED J. 1:449-450, February 21, 1970.

"Control of population: excerpt from The social contract," by R. Ardrey. LIFE. 68:48-52+, February 20, 1970.

"Control of population: excerpt from The social contract," by R. Ardrey. READ DIGEST. 96:116-120, June, 1970.

"A controlled trial of oral contraceptives in haemophilia," by P. Beck, et al. BR J HAEMATOL. 19:667-673, December, 1970.

"Controlling human fertility." CANAD MED ASS J. 102: 871-872, April 25, 1970.

"Controversy over the pill," by B. Surface. GOOD H. 170:64-65+, January, 1970.

"The convention of the Organisation of African unity governing the specific aspects of refugee problems in Africa," by Paul Weis. HUMAN RIGHTS J. 3:449-464, September, 1970.

"Cooperation of general practitioner in birth control. Legal questions about prescription of the "pill"," by W. Becker. THER GEGENW. 109:428 passim. March, 1970.

"COPE-ing with the environment," by A. Mull. IMPRINT. 17:7, September-October, 1970.

"Coping with executive mobility," by W. A. Dressel. BSNS HORIZONS. 13:53-58, August, 1970.

"Correlates of marital dissolution in a prospective fertility study: a research note," by L. C. Coombs and Z. Zumeta. SOC PROB. 18:92-102, Summer, 1970.

"Correlation of folate metabolism and socioeconomic status in pregnancy and in patients taking oral contraceptives," by S. B. Kahn, et al. AM J OBSTET GYNECOL. 108:931-935, November 15, 1970.

"Counting heads in Africa: the experience of Zambia, 1963 and 1969," by Patrick O. Ohadike. J ADMIN OVERSEAS. 9:247-254, October, 1970.

"Court-Ordered Contraception; a reasonable alternative to institutionalization for juvenile unwed mothers?" WIS L R. 1970:899, 1970.

"Crackdown; FDA withdraws." C-Quens and Provest. NEWSWEEK. 76:100, November 2, 1970.

"Creation of new knowledge and our way of life," by D. J. Zinn. SCH SCI & MATH. 70:18-25, January, 1970.

"Critical aspects of the future of the human species," by D. Dubarle. STUD GEN. 23:998-1009, 1970.

"Critical examination of request for sterilization of
mentally defective persons," by K. Grunewald.
LAKARTIDNINGEN. 67:5091-5095, October 28, 1970.

"Cross-sectional investigation of carbohydrate metabolism
in women taking a sequential or combination type
oral contraceptive: measurements of blood glucose,
plasma insulin and plasma growth hormone during an
oral glucose tolerance test," by W. N. Spellacy, et
al. SOUTHERN MED J. 63:152-155, February, 1970.

"Crossing of mortality curves." METROPOLITAN LIFE
STAT BUL. 51:10-11, November, 1970.

"Cryofibrinogenaemia in patients on oral contraceptives,"
by S. E. Ritzmann. LANCET. 1:522, March 7, 1970.

"Cryofibrinogenaemia in women using oral contraceptives,"
by I. R. Fisch. LANCET. 1:775, April 11, 1970.

"Cryofibrinogenaemia in women using oral contraceptives,"
by J. Pindyck, et al. LANCET. 1:51-53, January 10,
1970.

"Cuban population estimates, 1953-1970," by L. Nelson.
J INTER-AM STUD. 12:392-400, July, 1970.

"Cultural determinants of population stability in the
Havasupai Indians," by A. L. Alvarado. AMER J PHYS
ANTHROP. 33:9-14, July, 1970.

"The culture of poverty in relation to disease in Latin
America," by L. S. Miranda. P RICO ENFERM. 45:14-
15, March, 1970.

"Current aspects of fertility control," by V. Petrow.
CHEM BRIT. 6:167-171, April 4, 1970.

"Current method of birth control, with special reference
to oral contraceptives," by S. Suziki. JAP J MIDWIFE.
24:35-40, December, 1970.

"Current morality report; standard ordinary policyholders,
Metropolitan Life insurance company first half 1970."
METROPOLITAN LIFE STAT BUL. 51:11, October, 1970.

"Current status of fertility restraint in males," by
R. Petry, et al. DEUTSCH MED WSCHR. 95:855-858,
April 10, 1970.

"Current status of oral contraceptives," by R. E. Cleary, et al. MED CLIN N AMER. 54:163-171, January, 1970.

"Current status of population research in schools of public health," by I. W. Gabrielson, et al. AMER J PUBLIC HEALTH. 60:913-918, May, 1970.

"The current status of treatment with hormonal contraceptives," by E. Robecchi. MINERVA MED. 61:2394-2404, May 30, 1970.

"Current trends in sexual sterilization in women," by Z. Lapinski, et al. GINEK POL. 41:219-225, February, 1970.

"Curriculum should include fertility regulation," by H. E. Mizer. NURS OUTLOOK. 18:42-43, November, 1970.

"Cutaneous eruptions and in vitro lymphocyte hypersensitivity. Associated with oral contraceptives and mestranol " by H. Savel, et al. ARCH DERM. 101:187-190, February, 1970.

"Cutaneous side effects of oral contraceptives," by J. E. Jelinek. ARCH DERM. 101:181-186, February, 1970.

"Cybernetic concepts in population dynamics," by H. Wilbert. ACTA BIOTHEOR. 19:54-81, 1970.

"Cyclic and step-up administration of ethynodiol diacetate as an oral contraceptive," by K. R. Heber. MED J AUST. 2:21-24, July 4, 1970.

"Cytogenetic studies on women using oral contraceptives and their progeny," by H. G. McQuarrie, et al. AM J OBSTET GYNECOL. 108:659-665, October 15, 1970.

"Cytologic studies after insertion of intrauterine contraceptive devices," by A. Ishihama, et al. ACTA CYTOL. 14:35-41, January, 1970.

"Cytological findings and oral contraceptives," by A. L. Schmidt. NED TIJDSCHR VERLOSKD GYNAECOL. 70:539-545, December, 1970.

"The cytology of intrauterine contraceptive devices," by N. Sagiroglu, et al. ACTA CYTOL. 14:58-64, February, 1970.

D

"Dawn of the morning-after pill?" AM DRUGGIST. 161: 35-36, February 23, 1970.

"Deaths among users of oral and nonoral contraceptives," by A. Fuertes-de la Haba, et al. OBSTET GYNECOL. 36:597-602, October, 1970.

"Deceptive birth rates," by P. R. Ehrlich and J. P. Holdren. SAT R. 53:58, October 3, 1970.

"The decline in mortality in British Guiana, 1911-1960," by Jay R. Mandle. DEMOGRAPHY. 7:301-315, August, 1970.

"The decline of the size of the domestic group in England. A comment on J. W. Nixon's note," by Peter Laslett. POPULATION STUDIES. 24:449-454, November, 1970.

"Defective infants in a feral monkey group," by G. Berkson. FOLIA PRIMAT. 12:284-289, 1970.

"Demographic adaptations to urban conditions," by G.M. Korostelev, et al. SOV ZDRAVOOKHR. 29:35-36, 1970.

"Demographic boom--doom or dud." RI MED J. 53:688-690, December, 1970.

"Demographic comments on family planning," by H. Arnold. OEFF GESUNDHEITSWESEN. 32:68-70, February, 1970.

"Demographic effectiveness of sterilization programme in India," by O. P. Vig. ARTHA VIINANA. 12:398-405, September, 1970.

"The demographic effects of birth control and legal abortion," by H. Sjovall. LAKARTIDNINGEN. 67: 5261-5272, November 4, 1970.

"Demographic factors and borough occupancy rates," by Jane Peretz and Hywel Davies. GREATER LONDON RESEARCH Q. BULL. NO. 10. 22, March, 1970.

"Demographic history of the West: Manistee county, Michigan, 1860," by G. Blackburn and S. L. Ricards, Jr.

J AM HIST. 57:600-618, December, 1970.

"Demographic problem: female employment and the birth-rate." SOVIET R. 11:76-81, Spring, 1970.

"Demographic study of an Eskimo village on the north slope of Alaska: with summaries in French and Russian," by F. A. Milan. ARCTIC. 23:82-99, June, 1970.

"A demographic study on the relationships of nuptiality, child mortality, and attitude toward fertility to actual fertility in Hsueh-Chia township in Taiwan. I. Relationship of marriage cohort and marriage age to actual fertility," by H. Y. Wu. J FORMOSAN MED ASSOC. 69:243-255, May 28, 1970.

"Demographic transition: threat to developing nations," by George A. Schnell. J GEOGRAPHY. 69:164-171, March, 1970.

"Demography and human ecology; some apparent trends," ANNALS OF THE AMERICAN ACADEMY OF POLITICAL & SOCIAL SCIENCE. 390:120-128, July, 1970. SA #F0139.

"Demography and thermodynamics," by E. Fein. AM J PHYS. 38:1373-1379, December, 1970.

"Demography in the nineteenth century," by Roger Smith. LOCAL HISTORIAN. 9:27-35, February, 1970.

"Demography of primitive populations," by N. McArthur. SCIENCE. 167:1097-1102, February 20, 1970.

"Denver school dramatizes population pollution," by B. J. Meadows. AM BIOL TEACH. 32:281-283, May, 1970.

"Depo-medroxyprogesterone acetate as a contraceptive." by R. J. Seymour, et al. OBSTET GYNECOL. 36:589-596, October, 1970.

"Depopulation of the central Andes in the 16th Century," by C. T. Smith. CUR ANTHROP. 11:453-464, October-December, 1970.

"Depot-gestagen for contraception," by A. A. Haspels. NEDERL T GENEESK. 114:61-63, January 10, 1970.

"Depression and oral contraception." BR MED J. 4:127-128, October 17, 1970.

"Depression and oral contraception," by E. C. Grant. BR MED J. 4:367, November 7, 1970.

"Depression and oral contraception," by J. T. Hart. BR MED J. 4:367, November 7, 1970.

"Depressive symptoms and oral contraceptives," by B. N. Herzberg, et al. BR MED J. 4:142-145, October 17, 1970.

"Deprivation: an essay in definition with special consideration of the Australian Aboriginal, by R. Nurcombe. MED J AUST. 2:87-92, July 11, 1970.

"Dermatologic side effects of ovulation inhibitors," by H. Tronnier. ARCH KLIN EXP DERM. 237:197-200, 1970.

"The detection of incidence of congenital malformations in the community," by J. A. Weatherall. PROC R SOC MED. 63:1251-1252, December, 1970.

"The determinants of emigration to South Africa, 1950-1967," by Gene L. Chapin, et al. SOUTH AFRICAN J ECON. 38:374-381, December, 1970.

"The determinants of fertility: a theoretical forecasting model," by M. Fish, et al. BEHAV SCI. 15:381-328, July, 1970.

"Determinants of premarital sexual permissiveness: a secondary analysis," by C. P. Middendorp, et al. J MARRIAGE & FAM. 32:369-380, August, 1970.

"Determining the labor force status of men missed in the census: special labor force report describes pilot use of a new technique for securing labor force data in urban poverty areas," by Deborah P. Klein. MO LABOR R. 93:26-32, March, 1970.

"A deterministic model for handling the birth, death, and migration processes of spatially distributed populations," by M. B. Usher, et al. BIOMETRICS. 26:1-12, March, 1970.

"Development and trends in maternal-child welfare towards
the idea of family welfare," by Manciaux. REV INFIRM
ASSIST SOC. 20:542-545, June, 1970.

"The development of tool using in wild-born and restriction-reared chimpanzees," by E. W. Menzel, Jr., et al.
FOLIA PRIMAT. 12:273-283, 1970.

"Developments in steroidal hormonal contraception," by
A. Klopper. BRIT MED BULL. 26:39-44, January, 1970.

"Develops his-or-her birth curb." AM DRUGGIST. 161:35,
June 29, 1970.

"Did the pill get a fair shake from Nelson?" CHEM W.
106:21, January 28, 1970.

"Differential fertility and socioeconomic status of
Shirazi women: a pilot study," by A. A. Paydarfar
and M. Sarram. J MARRIAGE & FAM. 32:692-699,
November, 1970.

"Differential susceptibility to a viral agent in mice
housed alone or in groups," by S. B. Friedman, et al.
PSYCHOSOM MED. 32:285-299, May-June, 1970.

"Diffusion model for selected demographic variables:
an application to Soviet data," by G. J. Demko and
E. Casetti. ASSN AM GEOG ANN. 60:533-539, September,
1970.

"Disease patterns and vaccine-response studies in isolated Micronesian populations," by P. Brown, et al.
AMER J TROP MED. 19:170-175, January, 1970.

"Disengagement and morale," by M. Tallmer, et al.
GERONTOLOGIST. 10:317-320, Winter, 1970.

"The dispossessed: in a remarkable instance of
generosity India has opened some half dozen settlements for Tibetans within her borders." VISTA.
6:16-21, November-December, 1970.

"Distributional effects in demand analysis; observations
and predictive tests," by D. J. Laughhunn. AM STAT
ASSN J. 65:576-585, June, 1970.

"D-norgestrel combined with ethinyl oestradiol as an oral contraceptive," by W. G. McBride. CURR THER RES. 12:177-185, April, 1970.

"Does sterilization cause psychic faulty development?" by H. Kind, et al. NERVENARZT. 41:287-289, June, 1970.

"Drive to stop population growth: Zero population growth plan." U S NEWS. 68:36-38, March 2, 1970.

"Dropping of pills not serious loss to Kallir, Corbett," by N. Giges. ADV AGE. 41:16, November 2, 1970.

"Drug environment interactions: acute hypoxia and chronic isolation," by J.J. DeFeo, et al. FED PROC. 29:1985-1990, November-December, 1970.

"Drug photosensitivity. I. Light and photo sensitivities observed during oral contraceptive therapy. A review," by I. W. Mathison, et al. OBSTET GYNEC SURVEY. 25:389-401, April, 1970.

"Dual challenge of health and hunger: a global crisis; reprint," by G. A. Borgstrom. BUL ATOM SCI. 26:42-46, October, 1970.

"Dural sinus and cerebral venous thrombosis. Incidence in young women receiving oral contraceptives," by D. S. Buchanan, et al. ARCH NEUROL. 22:440-444, May, 1970.

"Dynamics of sexual behavior of college students," by G. R. Kaats & K. E. Davis. J MARRIAGE & FAM. 32:390-399, August, 1970.

E

"Early effect of humanae vitae?" by R. Cruz-Coke. LANCET. 2:525, September 5, 1970.

"Ecological consequences of island colonization by southwest Pacific birds. II. The effect of species diversity on total population density," by J. M. Diamond. PROC NATL ACAD SCI USA. 67:1715-1721, December, 1970.

"Ecological destruction is a condition of American life; interview, ed. by P. Collier," by P. Ehrlich. MLLE. 70:188-189+, April, 1970.

"Ecology: the new religion?" by R. L. Schueler. AMERICA. 122:292-295. March 21. 1970.

"Economic growth: new doubts about an old ideal." TIME. 95:72-74, March 2, 1970.

"Economic value of preventing births: reply to Simon," by S. Enke. POPULATION STUDIES. 24:455-456, November, 1970.

"The economy doesn't need more people," by John G. Welles. WALL ST J. 175:22, April 22, 1970.

"Economy, ecology, and zero population growth; conditions affecting construction industry," by J. E. Carlson. ARCH REC. 148:59-60, August, 1970.

"Ectopic Lippes' intrauterine devices; Hysterography," by E. Villablanca. REV CHIL OBSTET GINECOL. 35:59-66, 1970.

"Educating teachers and children in law: an approach to reduced alienation in inner-city schools," by A. Elson, et al. AM J ORTHOPSYCHIATRY. 40:870-878, October, 1970.

"Education and religion as factors influencing attitudes toward population growth in the United States," by Larry D. Barnett. SOCIAL BIOLOGY. 17:26-36, March, 1970.

"Educational status and differential fertility in India," by I. Z. Husain. SOCIAL BIOLOGY. 17:132-139, June, 1970.

"Edward Foote's Medical Common Sense: an early American comment on birth control," by V. J. Cirillo. J HIST MED. 25:341-345, July, 1970.

"The effect of age, sex, parity, haemoglobin level, and oral contraceptive preparations on the normal leucocyte count," by J. M. Cruickshank, et al. BRIT J HAEMAT. 18:541-550, May, 1970.

"Effect of anovulatory drugs on the human urinary tract and urinary tract infections," by J. N. Corriere, Jr., et al. OBSTET GYNEC. 35:211-216, February, 1970.

"Effect of combined oestrogen-progestogen oral contraceptives, oestrogen, and progestogen on antiplasmin and antithrombin activity," by P. W. Howie, et al. LANCET. 2:1329-1332, December 26, 1970.

"Effect of combined oestrogen-progestogen oral contraceptives on serum-levels of alpha 2-macroglobulin, transferrin, albumin, and IgG," by C. H. Horne, et al. LANCET. 1:49-50, January 10, 1970.

"Effect of contraceptive pills on the distribution of sexual activity in the menstrual cycle," by J. R. Udry, et al. NATURE. 227:502-503, August 1, 1970.

"Effect of the duration of social isolation on instrumental learning acquisition in mice," by A. Ungerer. C R ACAD SCI. 271:350-352, July 20, 1970.

"The effect of Enovid on the binding of thyroxine to plasma proteins in vitro," by H. A. Moses, et al. J NATL MED ASSOC. 62:331-333, September, 1970.

"The effect of the great blackout of 1965 on births in New York City," by J. Richard Udry. DEMOGRAPHY. 7:325-327, August, 1970.

"Effect of induced abortion on birth rate; a simulation model," by S. Mukherji, et al. INDIAN J PUBLIC HEALTH. 14:49-58, January, 1970.

"Effect of infecundin in combination with ethimizol on the reproductive capacity of white rats," by A. N. Poskalenko, et al. AKUSH GINEKOL. 46:46-49, March, 1970.

"Effect of intrauterine contraceptive suture on the response of rat uterus to prolonged estrogen treatment," by B. Malaviya, et al. INDIAN J EXP BIOL. 8:19-21, January, 1970.

"The effect of intrauterine copper and other metals on implantation in rats and hamsters," by C. C. Chang, et al. FERTIL STERIL. 21:274-278, March, 1970.

"The effect of an intrauterine thread on tissue changes in the endometrium of the pseudopregnant rat," by J. C. Wood. J PHYSIOL. 207:545-555, May, 1970.

"Effect of melengestrol acetate on the bleeding & clotting times of blood in Indian water buffalo," by G. N. Memon, et al. INDIAN J EXP BIOL. 8:220-222, July, 1970.

"Effect of the new hormonal contraceptive mixtures on the intrauterine environment," by K. Rezabek, et al. CAS LEK CESK. 109:1100-1102, November, 1970.

"Effect of 19-norsteroids on the motility of human fallopian tubes," by A. Jakobovits, et al. INT J FERTIL. 15:36-39, January-March, 1970.

"Effect of nonsteroidal compounds on fertility," by G. W. Duncan, et al. FED PROC. 29:1232-1239, May-June, 1970.

"The effect of oestrogens and progestogens on serum protein levels," by C. H. Horne, et al. J CLIN PATH. 23:378, May, 1970.

"Effect of an oral contraceptive agent on blood pressure response to renin," by B. H. Douglas, et al. PROC SOC EXP BIOL MED. 133:1142-1144, April, 1970.

"Effect of an oral contraceptive on spontaneous running activity of female rats," by M. J. Fregly, et al. CANAD J PHYSIOL PHARMACOL. 48:107-114, February, 1970.

"The effect of oral contraceptive steroids on bile secretion and bilirubin Tm in rats," by T. A. Heikel, et al. BRIT J PHARMACOL. 38:593-601, May, 1970.

"Effect of the oral-contraceptive steroids on the ultrastructure of human cervical mucus--a preliminary communication," by A. Singer, et al. J REPROD FERTIL. 23:249-255, November, 1970.

"The effect of oral contraceptives on the histology of carcinoma of the breast," by H. G. Penman. J PATH. 101:66-68, May, 1970.

"Effect of oral contraceptives on leukocyte count in hemophiliacs," by O. Kiran, et al. CLIN PEDIATR. 9:656-657, November, 1970.

"Effect of oral contraceptives on lipoprotein lipase activity and platelet stickiness," by J. H. Adams, et al. LANCET. 2:333-335, August 15, 1970.

"Effect of oral contraceptives on the oral and vaginal mucosa," by G. Klinger, et al. DTSCH STOMATOL. 20:664-669, September, 1970.

"Effect of oral contraceptives on serum folic acid content," by O. M. Castren, et al. J OBSTET GYNAEC BRIT COMM. 77:548-550, June, 1970.

"Effect of oral contraceptives on serum protein concentrations," by H. W. Mendenhall. AMER J OBSTET GYNEC. 106:750-753, March, 1970.

"Effect of out-migration on regional employment," by J. Vanderkamp. CAN J ECON. 3:541-549, November, 1970.

"Effect of some contraceptive steroids on pituitary growth hormone content in female rats," by F. T. Liu, et al. PROC SOC EXP BIOL MED. 133:1354-1357, April, 1970.

"Effect of some steroid contraceptives on serum inorganic constituents of lactating goats," by M. M. Abdel Kader, et al. J EGYPT MED ASSOC. 53:170-178, 1970.

"Effect of tubal obstruction, salpingectomy, or intrauterine devices on estrous cycle lengths and mating behavior of the ewe," by H. H. Conley, et al. J FERTIL. 15:115-119, April-June, 1970.

"Effect of two days' monotonous confinement on conditioned eyelid frequency and topography," by P. Gendreau, et al. PERCEPT MOTOR SKILLS. 31:291-293, August, 1970.

"Effect on unemployment rates of weekly enumeration of the current population survey," by Marie D. Wann. STATIS REPORTER. 93-98, December, 1970.

"Effect of unilateral hysterectomy and separation or ligation of uterine horns on luteolytic action of intrauterine device in sheep," by O. J. Ginther. AM J VET RES. 31:2127-2130, December, 1970.

"The effect of vasectomy upon the incidence and morbidity

of post-prostatectomy epididymitis," by A. D Beck.
AUST NEW ZEAL J SURG. 39:286-289, February, 1970.

"Effect of Washington hearings on contraceptive use,"
by E. B. Connell. DELAWARE MED J. 42:212 passim,
August, 1970.

"Effectiveness and adverse effects of the IUD (contraceptive loop) manufactured in Hungary," by Z. Szereday,
et al. ORV HETIL. 111:2303-2305, September 27, 1970.

"Effectiveness and risks of birth-control methods," by
D. M. Potts, et al. BRIT MED BULL. 26:26-32,
January, 1970.

"Effectiveness of protective confinement therapy of
alcoholics," by H. Skopkova. CESK PSYCHIAT. 66:165-172, June, 1970.

"Effects of certain contraceptive pills on uterine myomas,"
by B. C. West, Jr. N CAROLINA MED J. 31:14-16,
January, 1970.

"Effects of combined and low-dose gestagen oral contraceptives on plasma lipids; including individual
phospholipids," by U. Larsson-Cohn, et al. ACTA
ENDOCR. 63:717-735, April, 1970.

"Effects of different systemic contraceptives on blood
fibrinolysis," by P. Brakman, et al. AMER J OBSTET
GYNEC. 106:187-192, January 15, 1970.

"The effects of dwelling density on mental disorders in
Filipino men," by A. J. Marsella, et al. J HEALTH
SOC BEHAV. 11:288-294, December, 1970.

"Effects of early experience and differential housing on
susceptibility to gastric erosions in lesion-susceptible rats," by R. Ader. PSYCHOSOM MED. 32:569-580,
November-December, 1970.

"Effects of the intrauterine contraceptive device on
endometrial enzyme and carbohydrate histochemistry,"
by L. L. Hester, Jr., et al. AMER J OBSTET GYNEC.
106:1144-1154, April 15, 1970.

"Effects of an intra-uterine contraceptive device on
mitosis in the rat uterus on different days of pregnancy," by R. R. Chaudhury, et al. J REPROD FERTIL.

22:33-40, June, 1970.

"The effects of intrauterine devices on preimplantation changes in the mouse uterus," by L. Martin, et al. J ENDOCRINOL. 46:19-20, February, 1970.

"The effects of an intra-uterine device on uterine cell division and epithelial morphology during early pregnancy in the mouse," by L. Martin, et al. J ENDOCRINOL. 48:347-354, November, 1970.

"Effects of obesity, glucocorticoid, and oral contraceptive therapy on plasma glucose and blood pyruvate levels," by J. W. Doar, et al. BRIT MED J. 1:149-152, January 17, 1970.

"Effects of oral contraceptives on carbohydrate metabolism," by A. Vermeulen, et al. DIABETOLOGIA. 6:519-523, October, 1970.

"Effects of oral contraceptives on the fetus," by F. Neumann, et al. LANCET. 2:1258-1259, December 12, 1970.

"Effects of oral contraceptives on urinary bacterial growth rate," by M. Silk, et al. INVEST UROL. 8:239-241, September, 1970.

"Effects of rearing experiences on development in rhesus monkey," by G. Sackett. ELECTROENCEPH CLIN NEUROPHYSIOL. 28:422, April, 1970.

"The effects of small doses of megestrol acetate on the cervical mucus," by P. E. Lebech, et al. INT J FERTIL. 15:65-76, April-June, 1970.

"Effects of a surface active contraceptive agent (nonylphenoxypolyethoxyethanol) on the vagina; a new functional approach to assessing the actions on the vagina of spermicides," by F. Edwards, et al. J PHYSIOL. 208:35-36, May, 1970.

"Effects upon the palmar sweat index of hormonal changes related to the menstrual cycle," by P. S. Yoder. NURS RES. 19:165-168, March-April, 1970.

"The egg that never was," by E. Wachtel, et al. ACTA CYTOL. 14:1-2, January, 1970.

"Eight assumptions concerning rural-urban migration
in Colombia: a three-shanty-towns test," by W. L.
Flinn and J. W. Converse. LAND ECON. 46:456-466,
November, 1970.

"Elective vasectomy by American urologists in 1967,"
by J. E. Davis, et al. FERTIL STERIL. 21:615-621,
August, 1970.

"Electrical activity of the human uterus in the presence
of intrauterine contraceptive device," by D. M. Serr,
et al. OBSTET GYNEC. 35:217-220, February, 1970.

"Electroencephalographic recording during progestation
treatment," by A. H. Ansari, et al. FERTIL STERIL.
21:873-882, December, 1970.

"Electron microscopic changes in the rat liver after
administration of the oral contraceptive lynestrenol,"
by I. Bartok, et al. ACTA HEPATOSPLEN. 17:1-10,
January-February, 1970.

"Eleven myths of family planning," by Ashish Bose.
SOUTH ASIAN R. 3:323-330, July, 1970.

"Emigrants to Canada few but independent." FIN POST.
64, July 2-August 22, 1970.

"Emigration of Finns to Sweden: drain or benefit for
Finland," by Vilho A. Koiranen. ECON R. 2:47-52,
1970.

"Emotional aspects of contraception," by M. E. Lane.
BULL AMER COLL NURSE MIDWIFE. 15:16-25, February,
1970.

"Employment injuries in Canada in 1969." LABOUR GAZ.
70:484-485, 533-543, July, 1970.

"The encyclical "Humanae Vitae" and birth rate," by D.
Hoogendoorn. NEDERL T GENEESK. 114:1294-1297,
August 1, 1970.

"The end of rapid increase in the use of oral anovulants? some problems in the interpretation of time
series of oral use among married women," by John D.
Allingham, et al. DEMOGRAPHY. 7:31-41, February,
1970.

"Ending the trek to the towns," by A. Trotter. TOWN & COUNTRY PLANNING. 38:540-543, December, 1970.

"Endocrine properties and mechanism of action of oral contraceptives," by F. J. Saunders. FED PROC. 29: 1211-1219, May-June, 1970.

"Endometrial carbonic anhydrase after diethylstilbestrol as a postcoital antifertility agent," by J. A. Board. OBSTET GYNEC. 36:347-349, September, 1970.

"Endometrial changes in women receiving oral contraceptives," by J. Song, et al. AMER J OBSTET GYNEC. 107:717-728, July 1, 1970.

"Endometrial findings after insertion of stainless steel spring IUD," by W. B. Ober, et al. OBSTET GYNEC. 36:62-68, July, 1970.

"Endometrial leukocytes in patients using intrauterine contraceptive devices," by A. Sedlis, et al. AM J OBSTET GYNECOL. 108:1209-1212, December 15, 1970.

"Endometrial regeneration in patients discontinuing oral contraceptives," by M. Maqueo, et al. FERTIL STERIL. 21:224-229, March, 1970.

"Endometrium pattern after intrauterine device (Lippes loop) insertion," by M. Bulska, et al. POL TYG LEK. 25:565-566, April 20, 1970.

"English population in the early sixteenth century," by Julian Cornwall. ECONOMIC HISTORY R. 23:32-44, April, 1970.

"Enough to move FDA; relation of estrogen to blood-clotting." SCI N. 97:430-431, May 2, 1970.

"The Environmental Crisis: Through A Glass Darkly," by W. G. Rosen. BIOSCIENCE. 20,22:1209-1211,1216, November, 1970.

"Environmental hucksterism." NATURE. 227:118, July 11, 1970.

"Environmental quality: its significance in our society," by W. R. Barclay. JAMA. 213:1890-1892, September 14, 1970.

"Establishing family planning services in Kenya," by
N. R. Fendall, et al. PUBLIC HEALTH REP. 85:131-
139, February, 1970.

"Estimated net migration for Tennessee counties, 1960-
1970," by Richard A. Engels. TENN SURVEY BUS.
6:3-4+, September, 1970.

"Estimating the effective size of human populations,"
by J. W. MacCluer, et al. AMER J HUM GENET. 22:176-
183, March, 1970.

"The estimation of potential fertility for family planning evaluation: a critical discussion," by D.
Wolfers. PROC R SOC MED. 63:1107-1110, November,
1970.

"Estrogen content of oral contraceptives and thromboembolitic processes," by C. J. Rubsaam. NEDERL
T GENEESK. 114:1101-1103, June 27, 1970.

"Estrogen therapy and glucose tolerance test," by G.
Di Paola, et al. AMER J OBSTET GYNEC. 107:124-132,
May 1, 1970.

"The ethics of biomedical interventions," by D. J. Ingle.
PERSPECT BIOL MED. 13:364-387, Spring, 1970.

"The ethics of population control in the twentieth
century," by R. Craig. CENT AFR J MED. 16:109-
114, May, 1970.

"Ethinylated steroids," by D. Onken, et al. PHARMAZIE.
25:3-9, January 1, 1970.

"European political emigrations: a lost subject," by
R. C. Williams. COMP STUD SOC & HIST. 12:140-148,
April, 1970.

"Evaluating the training of nurses to do family planning
work in India," by J. B. Weisbuch, et al. PUBLIC
HEALTH REP. 85:707-715, August, 1970.

"Evaluation of cesarean section hysterectomy as a sterilization procedure," by P. Brenner, et al. AM J OBSTET
GYNECOL. 108:335-339, October 1, 1970.

"An evaluation of demographic data pertaining to the non-white population of South Africa: the population of Asian origin; the coloured population; the Bantu population," by J. L. Sadie. SOUTH AFRICAN J ECON. 38:1-34, March; 171-191, June, 1970.

"Evaluation of fertility control of periodic abstinence," by W. M. Moore. PRACTITIONER. 205:38-43, July, 1970.

"Evaluation of an injectable progestin-estrogen as a contraceptive," by A. Scommegna, et al. AMER J OBSTET GYNEC. 107:1147-1155, August 15, 1970.

"An evaluation of the intrauterine contraceptive device," by H. C. Chia. SINGAPORE MED J. 11:46-51, March, 1970.

"Evaluation of Lippes loop in planned parenthood. Present status," by S. A. Kaufman, et al. NEW YORK J MED. 70:2103-2107, August 15, 1970.

"Evaluation of a program for preventing adolescent pregnancy," by L. Gordis, et al. NEW ENG J MED. 282:1078-1081, May 7, 1970.

"Evaluation of rare adverse effects of systemic contraceptives," by R. Doll, et al. BRIT MED BULL. 26:33-38, January, 1970.

"Evaluation of the results of intrauterine contraception. 2 year analysis of the Rostock studies by means of the life table method of Tietze and Potter," by H. G. Neumann. GEBURTSHILFE FRAUENHEILKD. 30:537-547, June, 1970.

"Evaluation of 300 cases of intrauterine devices," by G. Marty. BULL FED GYNEC OBSTET FRANC. 22:111-112, January-March, 1970.

"Evaluation of a variation in the simultaneous method of oral contraceptions," by A. Alvarado Duran, et al. GINECOL OBSTET MEX. 27:597-604, May, 1970.

"Every child a wanted child," by P. M. Wilkinson. NURS TIMES. 66:1308-1309, October 8, 1970.

"Everybody's guilty. The ecological dilemma," by G. Hardin. CALIF MED. 113:40-47, November, 1970.

"Evolution of endogenous infant mortality in France in the second half of the 19th century." POPULATION. 25, 1:49-58, January-February, 1970. SA #F0135.

"Evolutionary Response to Human Infectious Diseases," by G. J. Armelagos. BIOSCIENCE. 20,5:271-275, March, 1970.

"Ex-F.A.O. head charges contradiction in Pope's policies on birth control." CHR CENT. 87:135, February 4, 1970.

"Existing stocks may be used up." AM DRUGGIST. 162:37, November 16, 1970.

"Experience in education of couples about birth control in under-developed countries," by R. Traissac. BULL FED SOC GYNECOL OBSTET LANG FR. 22:187-190, April-May, 1970.

"The experience of living in cities," by S. Milgram. SCIENCE. 167:1461-1468, March 13, 1970.

"Experience with DANA Super Fix contraception," by J. Sracek. CESK GYNEK. 35:277-279, 1970.

"Experience with double-coil intrauterine contraceptive device," by B. J. Vaughn, et al. POSTGRAD MED. 47:170-183, February, 1970.

"Experience with IUD; first insertions," by J. H. Gerende, et al. PENN MED. 73:56-60, March, 1970.

"Experience with intrauterine pessaries," by M. Schulz. Z AERZTL FORTBILD. 64:1138-1141, November 15, 1970.

"Experience with oral contraceptives in the immediate puerperium: effect on breast engorgement and menstrual flow," by J. A. Bowman, Jr. FERTIL STERIL. 21:39-42, January, 1970.

"Experience with Ovosiston for contraception," by H. Geschke. DEUTSCH GESUNDH. 25:201-206, February 5, 1970.

"Experiences in rural family planning," by Philipp Flavier. J NURS. 39:6+, January-March, 1970.

"Experiences with IUD complications," by S. C. Green,
et al. TEX MED. 66:60-63, November, 1970.

"Experiences with Ovosiston in a new dosage form," by
C. Zwahr. DTSCH GESUNDHEITSW. 25:635-639, April 8,
1970.

"Experiments with the contraceptive effectiveness of
the intrauterine DANA-Super devices," by M. Semczuk,
et al. POL TYG LEK. 25:1710-1711, November 9, 1970.

"The expression of induced sterility in Glossina austeni,"
by C. F. Curtis. TRANS ROY SOC TROP MED HYG. 64:186,
1970.

"Extended birth control: abortion on request," by John
G. Howells. CAN'S MENTAL HEALTH. 18:3-8, September-
October, 1970.

"Extended family structure and fertility: some conceptual
and methodological issues," by T. K. Burch and M.
Gendell. J MARRIAGE & FAM. 32:227-236, May, 1970.

"Extending family planning services," by H. A. Hutcheson,
et al. AMER J NURS. 70:1516-1518, July, 1970.

"Extra-uterine pregnancy with intra-uterine prevention,"
by T. Bakke. TIDSSKR NOR LAEGEFOREN. 90:1878-1879,
October 15, 1970.

"Extra-uterine pregnancy under oral contraceptive," by
G. Zographos, et al. BULL FED SOC GYNECOL OBSTET
LANG FR. 22:295-296, June-August, 1970.

"Extramarital sexual intercourse: a methodological
note," by R. E. Johnson. J MARRIAGE & FAM. 32:279-
282, May, 1970.

"Eye disorders and contraceptive agents," by G. Payeur,
et al. BULL SOC OPHTALMOL FR. 70:699-703, May-June,
1970.

F

"FDA chief says Rxmen have role in educating users about the pill," by D. Wickware. AM DRUGGIST. 161:17-19, February 9, 1970.

"FDA: efficiency drive stumbles over the issue of drug efficiency; effects of Demulen," by T. P. Southwick. SCIENCE. 169:1188-1189, September 18, 1970.

"FDA goes to the consumer." SCI N. 97:266, March 14, 1970.

"FDA is facing court action for access to pill information as a result of secrecy policy." OIL PAINT & DRUG REP. 198:7, July 6, 1970.

"FDA offers milder version OC insert." AM DRUGGIST. 161:16, April 20, 1970.

"FDA set to weigh stricter standards for the birth pills." OIL PAINT & DRUG REP. 197:5+, January 12, 1970.

"FDA will look again into the pill's dangers." OIL PAINT & DRUG REP. 197:7+, January 26, 1970.

"FDA writes another warning." SCI N. 97:599, June 20, 1970.

"Faces from the past; M. Sanger," by R. M. Ketchum. AM HERITAGE. 21:52-53, June, 1970.

"Factors associated with involvement of low-income women in a public family planning program," by E. Siegel, et al. AM J PUBL HLTH. 60:1382+, August, 1970.

"The failure of the copper IUD to inhibit fertilization in the rabbit," by J. P. Polidoro, et al. J REPROD FERTIL. 23:151-154, October, 1970.

"Failure of a pure progestogen contraceptive to affect serum levels of iron, transferrin, protein-bound iodine, and transaminase," by L. W. Powell, et al. BRIT MED J. 1:194-195, July 25, 1970.

"Failure of the rhythm method." GOOD H. 170:10+, February, 1970.

"Failure of tubal sterilization accompanying cesarean section," by M. E. Husbands, Jr., et al. AMER J OBSTET GYNEC. 107:966-967, July 15, 1970.

"Failures of contraception on the lower dose ethinyl estradiol sequential therapy: a clinical trial," by J. Miyamoto. AM J OBSTET GYNECOL. 108:990-991, November 15, 1970.

"The family. Is it basic?" by Jean West. FRIENDS' Q. 16:480-484, January, 1970.

"Family breakdown and social networks," by Trevor Noble. BRIT J OF SOCIOLOGY. 21:135-150, June, 1970.

"Family, fertility, and sex ratios in the British Caribbean," by Anthony Marino. POPULATION STUDIES. 24:159-172, July, 1970.

"Family history." METROPOLITAN LIFE STAT BUL. 51:4-7, May, 1970.

"Family life education in a family planning clinic," by S. Okrent. BULL AM COLL NURSE MIDWIFE. 15:78-84, August, 1970.

"Family patterns of migrant and nonmigrant retirees," by G. L. Bultena and D. G. Marshall. J MARRIAGE & FAM. 32:89-93, February, 1970.

"Family planning," by A. O. Sokoya. NIGERIAN NURSE. 2:61+, January, 1970.

"Family planning," by R. L. Standard. MED ANN DC. 39:280-281, May, 1970.

"Family planning. The pace of bumbledom." NATURE. 226:96, April 11, 1970.

"Family planning and conjugal roles in New York City poverty areas," by S. Polgar, et al. SOC SCI MED. 4:135-139, July, 1970.

"Family planning and fertility in Tunisia," by Robert J. Lapham. DEMOGRAPHY. 7:241-253, May, 1970.

"Family planning and the poor," by W. M. Hern. NEW REPUB. 163:17-19, November 14, 1970.

"Family planning and population control in developing countries," by Harry M. Raulet. DEMOGRAPHY. 7:211-234, May, 1970.

"Family planning and population problems. Concepts of 4 different eras," by M. Muramatsu. JAP J MIDWIFE. 24:27-30, December, 1970.

"Family planning: a basic human right," by J. D. Tydings. MLN BULL. 18:7-10, January, 1970.

"Family-planning bonds." CHATELAINE. 43:10, February, 1970.

"Family planning coordinator in a city hospital," by E. Smith. AMER J NURS. 70:2363-2365, November, 1970.

"Family planning counselling," by E. F. Daily. BRIT MED J. 3:345-346, August 8, 1970.

"Family planning from the viewpoint of the gynecologist," by R. Elert. OEFF GESUNDHEITSWESEN. 32:25-32, January, 1970.

"Family planning--a health priority." J MED ASSOC STATE ALA. 40:414-415, December 1970.

"Family planning in China," by Han Suyin. JAPAN Q. 17:433-442, October-December, 1970.

"Family planning in the developing world," by W. G. Povey. OBSTET GYNECOL. 36:948-952, December, 1970.

"Family planning in England," by E. Funke. OEFF GESUNDHEITSWESEN. 32:412-419, August, 1970.

"Family planning in New York City: recommendations for action: prepared by Planned parenthood of New York City. FAMILY PLANNING PERSPECTIVES. 2:25-31, October, 1970.

"Family planning in a rural area using intrauterine devices," by Carlos R. Ramirez. REV CHIL OBSTET GINECOL. 35:11-13, 1970.

"Family planning in rural areas: Colorado: enlisting private physicians," by Sheri S. Tepper. FAMILY PLANNING PERSPECTIVES. 2:30-34, June, 1970.

"Family planning in Taiwan, 1949-1970," by Shihchu Hsu. INDUSTRY OF FREE CHINA. 34:2-20, December, 1970.

"Family planning in Taiwan, Republic of China: progress and prospects," by L. P. Chow. POPULATION STUDIES. 24:339-352, November, 1970.

"Family planning in the war on poverty," by G. D. London. FERTIL STERIL. 21:189-192, March, 1970.

"Family planning--much more than the "pill"," by S. J. Elsea. NEBRASKA NURSE. 3:12-15, May, 1970.

"Family planning or population control?" by J. Reston. READ DIGEST. 97:163-164, December, 1970.

"Family planning problems," by J. Priddle. OCCUP HEALTH. 22:145-149, May, 1970.

"Family planning program evaluation by use of a sample survey. The Emory University Family Planning Program, Atlanta, Georgia," by C. W. Tyler, Jr., et al. AMER J PUBLIC HEALTH. 60:1264-1270, July, 1970.

"Family planning project," by J. Sigamoney. CHRIST NURSE, 232:16-17, October, 1970.

"Family planning prospects in less-developed countries, and a cost-benefit analysis of various alternatives," by J. L. Simon. ECON J. 80:58-71, March, 1970.

"Family planning: respectability at last." NATURE. 226:992-993, June 13, 1970.

"Family planning seminars for health visitors," by D. Barnard. HEALTH VISIT. 43:81-83, March, 1970.

"A family planning services data system, Atlanta,

Georgia," by Jack C. Smith and James B. Goldsby. FAMILY PLANNING PERSPECTIVES. 2:41-46, June, 1970.

"Family planning services within hospitals," by S. J. Steele. LANCET. 1:514-515, March 7, 1970.

"Family planning: A suggested supplementary course to health care in the home." PHILIPP J NURS. 39:12+, January-March, 1970.

"Family size and sex-role stereotypes," by F. E. Clarkson, et al. SCIENCE. 167:390-392, January 23, 1970.

"Family therapy; an adjunct to hemodialysis and transplantation," by P. Kossoris. AMER J NURS. 70:1730-1733, August, 1970.

"Fatal embolism and progestational hormones. Apropos of a case," by L. Bardonnet. LYON MED. 223:809-810, April 12, 1970.

"Fatal pulmonary embolism during oral contraception," by J. C. Giertsen, et al. TIDSSKR NOR LAEGEFOREN. 90:2252-2253, December 15, 1970.

"Fate of personal adjustment in the process of modernization," by A. Inkeles and D. H. Smith. INT J COMP SOCIOL. 11:81-114, June, 1970.

"Fear of the pill aids an industry; mass-media advertising." BSNS W. p. 89, March 21, 1970.

"Federal Action for Population Policy-What More Can We Do Now?" by R. W. Lamson. BIOSCIENCE. 20,15:854-857, August, 1970.

"Federal Association of Physicians: "No pills" for girls under 16 years of age." MUNCH MED WOCHENSCHR. 42:43, October 16, 1970.

"Federal family planning programs: choice or coercion?" by Julia B. Rauch. SOCIAL WORK. 15:68-75, October, 1970.

"Fees for family planning services," by K. L. Oldershaw. BRIT MED J. 1:502, February 21, 1970.

"Female fertility in the Kingdom of Jordan; a statistical analysis," by W. A. Ettema. TIJDSCHRIFT VOOR ECONOMISCHE EN SOCIALE GEOGRAFIE. 61:195-206, July-August, 1970.

"Female sterilisation by tubal electrocoagulation under laparoscopic control," by W. A. Liston, et al. LANCET. 1:382-383, February 21, 1970.

"Femigen forte and mite preparations in contraception and gynecological disorders," by Z. Sternadel, et al. GINEKOL POL. 41:1227-1236, November, 1970.

"Fertile period after vasectomy," by J. B. Deisher. SCIENCE. 169:816-817, August 28, 1970.

"Fertility after removal of the intrauterine ring," by G. Waintraub. FERTIL STERIL. 21:555-564, July, 1970.

"Fertility and family planning in Africa," by T. E. Dow, Jr. J MOD AFRIC STUD. 8:445-457, October, 1970.

"Fertility control: health and educational factors for the 1970's. Contraception or abortion?" by J. H. Hughes. J BIOSOC SCI. 2:161:166, April, 1970.

"Fertility control: health and educational factors for the 1970's. Family planning in the next 10 years," by E. Brooks. J BIOSOC SCI. 2:171-180, April, 1970.

"Fertility control: health and educational factors for the 1970's. The future of oral contraception," by G. A. Christie. J BIOSOC SCI. 2:191-197, April, 1970.

"Fertility control: health and educational factors for the 1970's. The role of the local authority," by D. Barnard. J BIOSOC SCI. 2:181-189, April, 1970.

"Fertility control: health and educational factors for the 1970's. Trends in contraception," by A. C. Turnbull. J BIOSOC SCI. 2:157-160, April, 1970.

"Fertility control--when?" JAMA. 214:1878, December 7, 1970.

"Fertility control with drugs," by E. T. Tyler. POSTGRAD MED. 47:82-86, January, 1970.

"Fertility of American women since 1920," by W. Sanderson. J ECON HIST. 30:271-272, 285-287, March, 1970.

"The fertility of migrants to and within North America," by Larry H. Long. MILBANK MEMORIAL FUND Q. 48:297-315, July, 1970.

"Fertility patterns among religious groups in Canada," by Larry H. Long. DEMOGRAPHY. 7:135-149, May, 1970.

"Fibrin proteolysis in the monkey uterine cavity: variations with and without IUD," by S. T. Shaw, Jr., et al. NATURE. 228:1097-1099, December 12, 1970.

"Fibrinolytic activity and oral contraception," by I. S. Menon, et al. BR MED J. 4:621, December 5, 1970.

"Fibroadenomas in patients receiving oral contraceptives: a clinical and pathologic study," by R. E. Fechner. AM J CLIN PATHOL. 53:857-864, June, 1970.

"Fibrocystic disease in women receiving oral contraceptive hormones," by R. E. Fechner. CANCER. 25: 1332-1339, June, 1970.

"Final 1970 census figures for New Mexico." N MEX BUS. 23:12, October, 1970.

"Final population figures will help US to move forward in the 70s." COMM TODAY. 1:22, November 30, 1970.

"Final warning? revised pamphlet with birth-control pills." NEWSWEEK. 75:76, June 22, 1970.

"1st clinical experiences on the use of oral contraceptive Ovosiston in diabetics," by E. Godel, et al. DTSCH GESUNDHEITSW. 25:627-631, April 8, 1970.

"1st experiences with Ovosiston in new dosage--a comparative study of oral contraception with 'old' and 'new' Ovosiston." "Experiences with Ovosiston in contraception. II. "Viewpoint concerning works of Chr. Zwahr and H. Geschke," by D. Kuhne. DTSCH GESUNDHEITSW. 25:2245-2247, November 19, 1970.

"1st experiences with Ovosiston in a new dosage--a comparative study of oral contraception with 'old' and 'new' Ovosiston." "Experiences with Ovosiston in contraception. II. "Reply to the viewpoint of D. Kuhne," by C. Zwahr. DTSCH GESUNDHEITSW. 25:2247-2250, November 19, 1970.

"The first National congress on optimum population and environment." POPULATION BUL. 26:2-18, November, 1970.

"5-hydroxytryptamine content of rat uterus with intrauterine device in one horn," by O. P. Gulati, et al. INDIAN J EXP BIOL. 8:142-143, April, 1970.

"Five Scientists View the Impacts of Technology," by C. H. Waddington. IMPACT SCI SOC. 20,2:137-150, April-June, 1970.

"Flesh in the afternoon," by J. Weightman. ENCOUNTER. 34:30-32, June, 1970.

"Flocculation tests in women taking oral contraceptives," by M. J. Halpern. LANCET. 1:1065, May 16, 1970.

"Flocculation tests, oral contraceptives, and malaria," by J. F. Currin. LANCET. 1:103, July 11, 1970.

"Flood insurance for the data deluge." SALES MGT. 104:76+, May 1, 1970.

"Folate deficiency and oral contraceptives," by R. R. Streiff. JAMA. 214:105-108, October 5, 1970.

"46, XY female: anti-androgenic effect of oral contraceptive?" by L. I. Gardner, et al. LANCET. 2:667-668, September 26, 1970.

"Free abortion," by L. Valvanne. KATILOLEHTI. 75:91, March, 1970.

"Freedom in family planning. The abortion law and women's liberation," by H. Muramatsu. JAP J MIDWIFE. 24:10-19, December, 1970.

"Frequency of expulsion of intrauterine pessaries depending upon the type and time of introduction," by S. I. Sleptsova. AKUSH GINEKOL. 46:52-55, March, 1970.

"Frightening talk," by J. Kettle. EXEC. 12:20-21,
December, 1970.

"From gentleman to player." NATURE. 226:579, May 16,
1970.

"Frustrated America: symptoms, causes, and cures,"
by H. K. Smith. HUMANIST. 30:14-16, January-February,
1970.

"Function of neighborhood in ecological stratification,"
by G. K. Hesslink. SOCIOL & SOC RES. 54:441-459,
July, 1970.

"Furor over the '70 census: did the recent head count
of Americans produce a monumental goof? some city
and state officials are convinced it did; there is
much at stake-financially and politically; a cross-
country survey show what the grumbling is all about."
U S NEWS. 69:28-32, July 27, 1970.

"Further doubts about oral contraceptives." BRIT MED
J. 1:252, January 31, 1970.

"Further experience wtth intrauterine contraceptive
devices," by W. Mills. LANCET. 2:921-923, October,
1970.

G

"Game of human shuttlecock," by C. Adam. NEW STATESM.
79:280-281, February 27, 1970.

"Genealogy and demography," by D. J. Steel. GENEALOGISTS'
MAG. 16:203-211, March, 1970.

"General congress of the international union for scientific population study." POPULATION. 25,1:9-48,
January-February, 1970. SA #F0142

"General review of side effects of oral contraceptives,"
by J. Janssens. NED TIJDSCHR VERLOSKD GYNAECOL.
70:528-539, December, 1970.

"General view of the oral prevention of pregnancy," by
D. M. Potts. KATILOLEHTI. 75:414-418, October, 1970.

"General theory of population, by A. Sauvy. A review," by E. Hammond. TOWN & COUNTRY PLAN. 38:415, September, 1970.

"Generation life tables." METROPOLITAN LIFE STAT BUL. 51:8-11, September, 1970.

"Generational succession as a source of foreign policy attitudes: a cohort analysis of American opinion, 1946-1966," by Neal E. Cutler. J PEACE RESEARCH. 1:33-47, 1970.

"Genetic patterns," by G. E. Moore. SCIENCE. 169:328, July 24, 1970.

"Genetics of the HL-A system. A population and family study," by A. Svejgaard, et al. VOX SANG. 18:97-133, February, 1970.

"Genital candidasis and oral contraceptives," by J. J. Rohatiner, et al. J OBSTET GYNAECOL BR COMMONW. 77:1013-1015, November, 1970.

"Geographic distribution of need for family planning and subsidized services in the United States; conference paper," by Raymond C. Lerner. AM J PUBLIC HEALTH. 60:1945-1955, October, 1970.

"Geography of internal migration movements in Belgium," by R. Andre. REVUE DE L'INSTITUT DE SOCIOLOGIE. 2:383-402, 1970. SA #E9001

"Glucose, insulin and growth hormone studies in long-term users of oral contraceptives," by W.N. Spellacy, et al. AMER J OBSTET GYNEC. 106:173-182, January 15, 1970.

"Glucose metabolism during the menstrual cycle. Glucose tolerance during the one cycle and under the effect of ovulatory suppressants," by J. A. Goldman, et al. OBSTET GYNEC. 35:207-210, February, 1970.

"Glucose tolerance in gestational diabetic women during and after treatment with a combination-type oral contraceptive," by A. J. Szabo, et al. NEW ENG J MED. 282:646-650, March 19, 1970.

"Goals and some methods in psychotherapy: hypnosis and

isolation," by I. Wickram. AM J CLIN HYPN. 13:95-100, October, 1970.

"Government seeks ways to limit population growth (background, population and resources, government activities, contraceptive research)." CONG Q W REPT. 28:1554-1558, June 12, 1970.

"Gravidic cholestatic icterus, icterus due to estro-progestogen substances and incomplete anicteric sarcoidosic cholestasis," by H. Merillon, et al. ANN MED INTERN. 121:711-716, August-September, 1970.

"Gravidity inspite of "coitus ante portas"," by G. Ladanji. MUNCHEN MED WSCHR. 112:3, August 14, 1970.

"The great death happening," by B. J. Nerone. IMPRINT. 17:11, January, 1970.

"Great head count." TIME. 95:33, March 23, 1970.

"Growth in the east." NATURE. 227:430-431, August 1, 1970.

"The growth of population to the turn of the century," by Jean Thompson. SOCIAL TRENDS. 1:21-32, 1970.

"Growth versus the quality of life," by J. A. Wagar. SCIENCE. 168:1179-1184, June 5, 1970.

"Guidelines governing the use of synthetic progestational hormones as contraceptives," by J. Okla. GINEK POL. 41:573-576, May, 1970.

"Gynecologic indications for oral contraceptives," by A. M. Cohen. NED TIJDSCHR VERLOSKD GYNAECOL. 70:569-576, December, 1970.

H

"Haemodynamic changes in women taking oral contraceptives," by W. A. Walters, et al. J OBSTET GYNAECOL BR COMMONW. 77:1007-1012, November, 1970.

"Haemophilus endometritis in woman fitted with Lippes loop," by R. Hurley. BRIT MED J. 1:566, February 28, 1970.

"Half-cock at the sex fair," by T. Baistow. NEW STATESM. 79:436, March 27, 1970.

"Hallelujah the pill?" by R. B. Dixon. TRANS-ACTION. 8:44-49+, November, 1970.

"Handier & dandier data for marketers (interview with Census bureau's G. Brown)." SALES MGT. 105:21-22+, December 15, 1970.

"Have a baby for Brezhnev," by Victor Zorza. GUARDIAN. p. 9, January 7, 1970.

"Hazardous avocations." METROPOLITAN LIFE STAT BUL. 51:2-4, June, 1970.

"Hazards of oral contraceptive therapy," by R. K. Chandra. INDIAN J PEDIAT. 37:44-45, January, 1970.

"Headache and treatment with oral contraceptives," by U. Larsson-Cohn, et al. ACTA NEUROL SCAND. 46:267-278, 1970.

"Heading for dramatic increase of younger adults, and in income," by G. H. Brown. COMM & FIN CHR. 212:1474-1475+, November 19, 1970.

"Healing our sick environment," by M. Michaelson. TODAY'S HEALTH. 48:21+, April, 1970.

"Health and disease from the sociological viewpoint," by K. D. Stumpfe. THER GEGENW. 109:153-170, February, 1970.

"Health aspects of family planning, report of a WHO Scientific Group." WHO TECHN REP SER. 442:1-50, 1970.

"Health hazards associated with urbanization and overpopulation," by B. Walker, Jr. J NAT MED ASS. 62:259-264, July, 1970.

"Health, population growth, and development in Taiwan," by Te-Hsiung Sun. INDUSTRY OF FREE CHINA. 33:17-30, June, 1970.

"Health protection and irreversible contraception (sterilization) in women," by J. Rothe. DTSCH GESUNDHEITSW. 25:555-560, March 25, 1970.

"Health standards of a populated locality." FELDSHER AKUSH. 35:35-38, September, 1970.

"Health visitors and family planning," by A. Cartwright. BRIT J PREV SOC MED. 24:64, February, 1970.

"Health visitors' attitudes towards family planning," by P. Woodward. HEALTH VISIT. 43:360-361, November, 1970.

"Hearings cause pill sales to flatten out." AM DRUGGIST. 161:18, March 23, 1970.

"Hereditary haemorrhagic telangiectasia: aggravation by oral contraceptives?" by P. T. Rowley, et al. LANCET. 1:474-475, February 28, 1970.

"Hereditary haemorrhagic telangiectasia and oral contraceptives," by E. K. Blackburn. LANCET. 1:616, March 21, 1970.

"Hereditary haemorrhagic telangiectasia and oral contraceptives," by P. W. Harris. LANCET. 1:615-616, March 21, 1970.

"Hereditary haemorrhagic telangiectasia and oral contraceptives," by D. F. Harrison. LANCET. 1:721, April 4, 1970.

"Here's where to get information and advice." CHATELAINE. 43:50, August, 1970.

"Hidden effects of overpopulation," by P. R. Ehrlich and J. P. Holdren. SAT R. 53:52, August 1, 1970.

"Histologic study of the uterine cervix during oral contraception with ethynodiol diacetate and mestranol," by E. Carbia, et al. OBSTET GYNEC. 35:381-388, March, 1970.

"Histological changes in the ovum following failure of intrauterine contraception," by F. Havranek, et al. CESK GYNEK. 35:377-378, July, 1970.

"Histopathological pictures of the endometrium a few years after a Lippes loop insertion," by A. Cekanski, et al. GINEK POL. 41:171-177, February, 1970.

"The historical calendar as a method of estimating age;

the experience of the Moroccan multi-purpose sample survey of 1961-63," by Christopher Scott and Georges Sabagh. POPULATION STUDIES. 24:93-109, March, 1970.

"Home ownership, life cycle stage, and residential mobility," by Alden Speare, Jr. DEMOGRAPHY. 7:449-458, November, 1970.

"Home begins with, but ends without, the "H"," by L. J. Polskin. MED TIMES. 98:109-112, March, 1970.

"Hong Kong's fertility decline, 1961-1968," by Ronald Freedman, et al. POPULATION INDEX. 36:3-18, January-March, 1970.

"Hormonal contraception," by E. Imparato. RASS INT CLIN TER. 50:86-96, January 31, 1970.

"Hormonal contraception," by R. Vokaer, et al. BULL SOC SCI MED GRAND DUCHE LUXEMB. 107:263-272, October, 1970.

"Hormonal contraception. Clinical experience, gained up to now and present-day problems," by J. Teter. POL TYG LEK. 25:1641-1643, November 2, 1970.

"Hospital-based nurses in family planning," by A. N. K. Dan. NURS J INDIA. 61:264, August, 1970.

"Hospitals may assume role of information centres." CAN HOSP. 47:25, October, 1970.

"Housing--surplus or shortage?" by J. Macey. TOWN AND COUNTRY PLAN. 38:202-206, April, 1970.

"How Catholics are making up their minds on birth control," by J. E. Allen. CHR CENT. 37:915-918, July 29, 1970.

"How Green is the Green Revolution?" by W. C. Paddock. BIOSCIENCE. 20,16:897-902, August, 1970.

"How many is a crowd?" NEW STATESMAN. p. 429-430, March 27, 1970.

"How many people?" LANCET. 2:553-554, September 12, 1970.

"How many people is enough?" by Gerald Leach. OBSERVER.

p. 8   January 4, 1970.

"How preventable are unwanted pregnancies?" by W. H. James. LANCET. 2:1257-1258, December 12, 1970.

"How they kept Canada almost lily white: the previous untold story of the Canadian immigration officials who stopped American blacks from coming to Canada," by Trevor W. Sessing. SATURDAY NIGHT. 85:30-32, September, 1970.

"How 334 gynecologists view the pill," by N. D'Amelio. MED TIMES. 98:206-212, October, 1970.

"How to insure effective implementation of family planning activities in critical population areas," by J. P. Pasaporte. NEWSETTE. 10:4-9, January-March, 1970.

"How to snatch survival from the jaws of pollution and overpopulation," by Anthony D'Amato. RIPON FORUM. 6:16-19, January, 1970.

"The Hull family survey. I. The survey couples, 1966," by J. Peel. J BIOSOC SCI. 2:45-70, January, 1970.

"Human fertility control by transvaginal application of quinacrine on the fallopian tube," by J. A. Zipper, et al. FERTIL STERIL. 21:581-589, August, 1970.

"Human food production as a process in the biosere," by L. R. Brown. SCI AMER. 223:161-170, September, 1970.

"Human genetic aspects of family planning," by W. Lenz. OEFF GESUNDHEITSWESEN. 32:61-67, February, 1970.

"Human population problems," by T. C. Emmel and M. M. Sligh. SCI ED. 54:363-372, October, 1970.

"Human survival (menace to human survival caused by over-population)," by Royal Bank. CAN MO LETTER. 51:1-4, August, 1970.

"Humberside; employment, unemployment and migration, the evolution of industrial structure, 1951-1966," by J. Craig, et al. YORKSHIRE BULLETIN. 22:123-142, November, 1970.

"Hypertension in young females receiving anovulatory steroids," by A. M. Lansing. ANN SURG. 171:731-734, May, 1970.

"Hysterotomy and insertion of an intrauterine device for endometrial sclerosis: importance of long term followup," by J. A. Wider, et al. FERTIL STERIL. 21:240-243, March, 1970.

I

"Ideal means of fertility control?" by A. Gillespie, et al. LANCET. 1:717, April 4, 1970.

"Ideal means of fertility control?" by J. J. Speidel, et al. LANCET. 1:565, March 14, 1970.

"Identification of migrants and their descendants in the United States," by W. Haenszel. J CHRONIC DIS. 23:383-387, November, 1970.

"An ideological reading of the essay on the principle of population," by A. Mattelart. L'HOMME ET LA SOCIETE. 15:183-219, January-March, 1970. SA #E7686.

"If population stops growing: impact on U. S." U S NEWS. 69:80-82, September 28, 1970.

"If you want publicity, pan the pill; editorial," by D. Anderson. CHATELAINE. 43:3, April, 1970.

"Immediate postpartum oral contraception," by R. D. Gambrell, Jr. OBSTET GYNEC. 36:101-106, July, 197 .

"Immigrants and municipal voting turnout: implications for the changing ethnic impact on urban politics," by D. N. Gordon. AM SOCIOL R. 35:665-681, August, 1970.

"Immigration from the U.S.A." WORLD AFFAIRS. 35:10, February, 1970.

"Immigration service statistics on immigrants with occupational preferences and other immigrants admitted by occupation." INTERPRETER RELEASES. 47:208-213, August 24, 1970.

"Immigration statistics for 1969." INTERPRETER RELEASES. 47:131-145, June 19, 1970.

"Immigration tap still turned on with skilled young people in lead," by C. Baxter. FIN POST. 64:5, August 22, 1970.

"Immigration under review." INST PUBLIC AFFAIRS R. 24:75-79, July-September, 1970.

"Immigration yields," by G. Keeleric, et al. SCIENCE. 169:817, August 28, 1970.

"Immunosuppression and simultaneous contraception," by W. Creutzfeldt. DEUTSCH MED WSCHR. 95:1581, July 24, 1970.

"The impact of family planning propaganda of the younger generation," by A. Abraham. NURS J INDIA. 61:110 passim, April, 1970.

"The impact of high altitudes on human populations," by E. J. Clegg, et al. HUM BIOL. 42:486-518, September, 1970.

"The implementation of Leninist national policy among the people of the USSR far north," by I. S. Gurvich. SOVETSKAYA ETNOGRAFIYA. 45,1:15-34, January-February, 1970. SA #F0131.

"Implications of the changing environment to occupational health," by F. D. Yoder. OCCUP HEALTH NURS. 18:23-25, July, 1970.

"Implications of the 1970 census for health and medicine," by O. K. Sagen. ANN INTERN MED. 72:134-136, January, 1970.

"The importance of data on the age and sex structure of the population," by A. Vostrikova. PROBLEMS ECON. 12:27-39, March, 1970.

"The importance of the pediatrician in family planning," by C. C. De Silva. CLIN PEDIAT. 9:69-71, February, 1970.

"Improving mechanical birth control methods; intrauterine devices," by B. J. Cullition. SCI N. 98:121-123, August 8, 1970.

"Improving population estimates with the use of dummy variables," by Donald E. Pursell. DEMOGRAPHY. 7: 87-91, February, 1970.

"Improving the quality of life," by C. E. Flowers, Jr. ALA J MED SCI. 7:297-299, July, 1970.

"In-migration and growth of non-metropolitan urban places," by James J. Zuiches. RURAL SOCIOL. 35:410-420, September, 1970.

"In my opinion; we must stop multiplying!" by R. Gordon. SEVENTEEN. 29:234, May, 1970.

"In warmer markets, hottest growth." BROADCASTING. 79:40, September 14, 1970.

"Inaugural address: 7th National Conference of the Indian Academy of Pediatrics," by S. K. Shah. INDIAN PEDIATR. 7:1-3, January, 1970.

"Incidence of pregnancy with the IUD in private practice in New Orleans," by L. L. Doyle, et al. LOUISIANA MED SOC. 122:45-47, February, 1970.

"Incorporation of (3H) uridine into the ribonucleic acid of rat uterus during pseudopregnancy and in the presence of I.C.I. 46474. (trans-1-(p-beta-dimethylaminoethoxyphenyl)-1,2-diphenylbut-1-ene)," by J. E. O'Grady, et al. BIOCHEM J. 119:609-613, October, 1970.

"Increased antipyrine half-life in women taking oral contraceptives," by K. O'Malley, et al. SCOTT MED J. 15:454-456, December, 1970.

"India: a bleak demographic future." POPULATION BUL. 26:2-12, November, 1970.

"Indiana's metropolitan population," by Morton J. Marcus. INDIANA BUS R. 45:13-26, September-October, 1970.

"Indications for sterilization of the mentally disturbed have to be reevaluated," by K. Grunewald. LAKARTID-

NINGEN. 67:5096-5102, October 28, 1970.

"Indications for surgical sterilization," by J. R. Bopp, et al. OBSTET GYNEC. 35:760-764, May, 1970.

"Induction of hepatic delta-amino-levulinic acid synthetase by oral contraceptive steroids," by A. B. Rifkind, et al. J CLIN ENDOCR. 30:330-335, March, 1970.

"Industrial decentralization policy in Victoria and its effect on the distribution of population and industry," by A. Kan. ECON ACTIVITY. 13:47-53, January, 1970.

"Industrial pressure and the population problem--the FDA and the pill," by I. C. Winter. JAMA. 212:1067-1068, May 11, 1970.

"Infant mortality; an urgent national problem," by F. Falkner. CHILDREN. 17:83-87, May-June, 1970.

"Infibulation, population control, and the medical profession," by G. S. Schwarz. BULL NY ACAD MED. 46:964-996, November, 1970.

"Influence of administrative reform on the immigration and naturalization service," by Justin J. Green. ADMINISTRATIVE SCIENCE Q. 15:353-359, September, 1970.

"Influence of being caged together on mammary carcinogenesis due to 7,12-dimethylbenzanthracene in female rats," by J. C. Guillon, et al. C R ACAD SCI. 270:1066-1068, February 16, 1970.

"The influence of biphasic hormonal contraceptives on hair growth," by H. Zaun, et al. ARCH KLIN EXP DERMATOL. 238:197-206, 1970.

"Influence of cyclic Ovosiston therapy on plasma lipid fractions of free cholesterol, total cholesterol and phospholipid," by W. Carol, et al. ENDOKRINOLOGIE. 57:108-114, 1970.

"Influence of an IUD on the leucocytic content of the uterus and on the duration of pseudopregnancy in mice," by A. J. Bartke. J REPROD FERTIL. 23:243-247, November, 1970.

"The influence of a mono- and biphasic oral contraceptives on colpitis of diverse etiology," by L. Mettler, et al. Z GEBURTSHILFE GYNAEKOL. 173:168-180, 1970.

"The influence of oral contraceptive and progestational drugs upon the mechanical activity of the non-pregnant human uterus in vivo," by T. K. Eskes, et al. NEDERL T VERLOSK. 70:47-56, February, 1970.

"The influence of an oral contraceptive on glucose, F.F.A., triglyceride and insulin levels after glucose loading," by P. Terpstra, et al. FOLIA MED NEERL. 13:44-50, 1970.

"Influence of ovulation inhibitors on body height growth," by G. K. Doering. DEUTSCH MED WSCHR. 95:241, January 30, 1970.

"The influence of several ovulation inhibiting hormone preparations on scalp hair growth," by H. Zaun. DEUTSCH MED WSCHR. 95:1433-1436, July 3, 1970.

"The influence of sex, age, synthetic oestrogens, progestogens and oral contraceptives on the excretion of urinary tryptophan metabolites," by G. E. Moursi, et al. BULL WHO. 43:651-661, 1970.

"The influence of two different doses of HMG in counteracting the inhibitory effect of an oral contraceptive observed at laparotomy," by P. Pujol-Amat, et al. J REPROD FERTIL. 22:188-189, June, 1970.

"Inhabitants of Northmavine, Shetland 18th and 19th Century," by J. C. Mowat. SCOTTISH GENEALOGIST. 17,3:91-104, 1970.

"Inhibition of sperm capacitation in vitro by contraceptive steroids," by R. B. Gwatkin, et al. NATURE. 227:182-183, July 11, 1970.

"An injectable contraceptive with prolonged action," by P. Simon. REV FR ODONTOSTOMATOL. 46:1029-1032, December, 1970.

"Injectable long-acting progestogens for contraception," by B. S. Karstadt. AFR MED J. 44:480-481, April 18, 1970.

"Insertion and supervision of an intrauterine device,"

by J. H. Ravina. PRESSE MED. 78:31-32, January 3,
1970.

"Insertion of IUD following artificial abortion," by
J. Koukal, et al. CESK GYNEKOL. 35:465-467,
October, 1970.

"Integrated incentives for fertility control," by L.
W. Kangas. SCIENCE. 169,3952:1278-1283, September
25, 1970. "Discussion," 170:1256+, December 18, 1970.

"An integrated social and demographic statistical system," by Kjeld Bjerke. STATISTISK TIDSKRIFT. 8:173-197, November 3, 1970.

"Interference with human life; some jurisprudential reflections," by W. Friedman. COLUM L R. 70:1058,
June, 1970.

"Interference with reproduction in water buffalo by
intra-uterine devices," by K. Janakiraman, et al.
J REPROD FERTIL. 22:499-507, August, 1970.

"Internal-external locus of control and the practice
of birth control," by A. P. MacDonald, Jr. PSYCHOL
REP. 27:206, August, 1970.

"An international comparison of excessive adult mortality,"
by Samuel H. Preston. POPULATION STUDIES. 24:5-20,
March, 1970.

"International conference on family planning, Budapest,
September 15-17, 1969," by M. Zelenkova. CESK GYNEK.
35:47-49, February, 1970.

"International migration of professionals," by Judith
A. Fortney. POPULATION STUDIES. 24:217-232, July,
1970.

"International symposium on work and urbanization in
modernizing societies. City and country in the
third world: issues in the modernization of Latin
America," by Arthur J. Field. xi+303 p., 1970.

"International variations in the motor vehicle hazard."
METROPOLITAN LIFE STAT BUL. 51:2-4, September, 1970.

"Interprovincial migration and economic adjustment,"
by T. J. Courchene. CAN J ECON. 3:550-576, November,
1970.

"Interval tubal sterilization via laparoscopy," by M. R. Cohen, et al. AM J OBSTET GYNECOL. 108: 458-461, October 1, 1970.

"Intracranial venous thrombosis as complication of oral contraception," by E. A. Atkinson, et al. LANCET. 1:914-918, May 2, 1970.

"Intracranial venous thrombosis complicating oral contraception," by C. Sissons, et al. LANCET. 2:419, August 22, 1970.

"Intra-urban dualism in developing economics," by D. L. McKee and W. H. Leahy. LAND ECON. 46:486-489, November, 1970.

"Intrauterine administration of progesterone by a slow releasing device," by A. Scommegna, et al. FERTIL STERIL. 21:201-210, March, 1970.

"Intra-uterine contraception," by D. F. Hawkins. PRACTITIONER. 205:20-29, July, 1970.

"Intrauterine contraception and the Armed Forces," by R. Israel. MILIT MED. 135:490-494, June, 1970.

"Intrauterine contraception in Indians of the American Southwest," by C. C. Bollinger, et al. AMER J OBSTET GYNEC. 106:669-675, March, 1970.

"The intrauterine contraceptive device and uterine perforation," by H. C. Hodes. J KANSAS MED SOC. 71: 318-323, August, 1970.

"Intra-uterine contraceptive device with ectopic gestation. A case report," by A. N. Rijhwani, et al. J POSTGRAD MED. 16:42-43, January, 1970.

"Intra-uterine device and embryonic survival in the rat," by K. F. DeBoer, et al. J REPROD FERTIL. 21:343-346, March, 1970.

"Intrauterine device and pituitary follicle-stimulating hormone and luteinizing hormone in the rat," by A. P. Labhsetwar. FERTIL STERIL. 21:177-181, February, 1970.

"Intrauterine devices and cervico-vaginal cytology," by M. Ancla, et al. PRESSE MED. 78:1541-1542,

July 25, 1970.

"Intrauterine spiral and extrauterine pregnancy," by J. R. Giraud. MUNCHEN MED WSCHR. 112:2, September 25, 1970.

"Introducing the world population crises to secondary social studies classes: an inquiry-oriented instructional strategy," by R. C. Anderson. SOCIAL ED. 34:27-35, January, 1970.

"Introduction of mass psychology of animals to pharmacology. I. Influence of the 3d party on the legal questions about prescription of the 'pill'," by W. Becker. THER GEGENW. 109:428 passim, March, 1970.

"Iranian censuses 1956 and 1966: a comparative analysis," by Ferydoon Firoozi. MIDDLE EAST J. 24:220-228, Spring, 1970.

"Irish fertility ratios before the famine," by G. S. L. Tucker. ECON HIST R. 23:267-284, August, 1970.

"Iron and oral contraceptives." BRIT MED J. 1:320, February 7, 1970.

"Is dispersal the answer to urban overgrowth?" by Jerome P. Pickard. URBAN LAND. 29:3-10, January, 1970.

"Is overpopulation really the problem? achieving a better American way of life is not primarily a question of numbers," by Herman P. Miller. CONFERENCE BD REC. 7:19-22, May, 1970.

"Is the "pill" a cause of vaginal candidiasis? Culture study," by B. Lapan. NEW YORK J MED. 70:949-951, April 15, 1970.

"Is the pill safe?" SR SCHOL. 96:15, March 16, 1970.

"Is pregnancy interruption necessary following failure of the intrauterine device (IUD)," by M. Kohoutek, et al. CESK GYNEK. 35:341-342, July, 1970.

"Is sterilization the answer?" by M. Nag, et al. SCIENCE. 168:62, April 3, 1970.

"Isolated and migratory population groups: health

problems and epidemiologic studies. I. Introduction"
by C. D. Gajdusek. AMER J TROP MED. 19:127-129,
January, 1970.

"Isolation, a challenge of disability," by H. H. Hanson.
J REHAB. 36:2, May-June, 1970.

"Israel's drive for manpower," by Vivian Craddock Williams.
DAILY TELEGRAPH. p. 11, October 29, 1970.

"Italian communities abroad: migration to European
and non-European nations." ITALY DOCS & NOTES.
19:7-17, January-February, 1970.

"It's an ill pill." ECONOMIST. 234:40, January 24, 1970.

J

"Japan: a crowded nation wants to boost its birthrate,"
by P. M. Boffey. SCIENCE. 167:960-962, February
13, 1970.

K

"Key points of our method of transvaginal tubal sterilization," by I. Kai. SANFUJIN JISSAI. 19:408-411,
April, 1970.

"Knowledge and attitude of nursing students toward
population control and family planning," by M. I.
Kim, et al. KOREAN NURSE. 9:41-53, June 25, 1970.

"Knowledge of and employment of contraception by young
mothers," by A. Braestrup. UGESKR LAEG. 132:232-
240, January 29, 1970.

"Kymographic studies of the Fallopian tubes after insertion of intrauterine contraceptive devices using
the Lippes loop and the nylon ring," by A. M. Makhlouf,
et al. AMER J OBSTET GYNEC. 106:759-764, March,
1970.

L

"L. A. County still tops in population-census. BROAD-CASTING. 79:33, September 21, 1970.

"Labor mobility and regional payment adjustments," by C. W. Hultman. LAND ECON. 46:467-473, November, 1970.

"Laboratory studies on radiation-induced dominant lethality in sperms in population control of the mosquito Culex pipiens fatigans Wied," by T. Koshy, et al. INT J RADIAT BIOL. 18:521-530, 1970.

"Lactation and genital involution effects of a new low-dose oral contraceptive on breast-feeding mothers and their infants," by G. H. Miller, et al. OBSTET GYNEC. 35:44-50, January, 1970.

"Lactation and lactational amenorrhoea with post-partum IUCD insertions," by V. Hingorani, et al. J REPROD FERTIL. 23:513-515, December, 1970.

"Land speculation, promotion and failure: the Northern Pacific railroad, 1870-1873," by J. L. Harnsberger. J WEST. 9:33-45, January, 1970.

"Large families: for MDs only?" JAMA. 213:454, July 20, 1970.

"Lateness of contraception among recipients of subsidized family planning service," by C. F. Bennett. AM J PUBLIC HEALTH. 60:2110-2117, November, 1970.

"Latin America's unemployment problem," by I. Beller. MO LABOR R. 93:8, November, 1970.

"The law concerning voluntary sterilization as it affects doctors," by M. Mackay, et al. J UROL. 103:482-484, April, 1970.

"Law, policy, and behavior: educational exchange policy and student migration," by P. Ritterband. AM J SOCIOL. 76:71-82, July, 1970.

"Laws to limit family size," by L. Lader. PARENTS MAG. 45:58-61, October, 1970.

"A leaf from the Koran," by Auberon Waugh. TIMES. p. 6, March 14, 1970.

"Legal effects of 1970 census on Minnesota municipalities," by Jon Lunde. MINN MUNIC. 55:73-75, March, 1970.

"Legal responsibility for unsuccessful sterilization," by E. Havt. HOSP MANAGE. 109:13 passim. February, 1970.

"Legality of sterilization." BRIT MED J. 1:704-705, March 21, 1970.

"Leibenstein on the benefits and costs of birth control programmes," by S. Enke. POPULATION STUDIES. 24:115-116, March, 1970.

"Lessons from a "primitive" people," by J. V. Neel. SCIENCE. 170:815-822, November 20, 1970.

"Licensing: for cars and babies," by B. M. Russett. BUL ATOM SCI. 26:15-19, November, 1970.

"Life without birth," by Stanley Johnson. OBSERVER. Colour suppt. p. 27+, June 28, 1970.

"Ligature of the salpinx," by H. Adachi. SHUJUTSU. 24:576-581, May, 1970.

"Lilly, Upjohn praised: swallowed a bitter pill." OIL PAINT & DRUG REP. 198:7+, November 2, 1970.

"Limits to the use of energy," by A. M. Weinberg and R. P. Hammond. AM SCIENTIST. 58:412-418, July, 1970. "Discussion," 58:618-620, November, 1970.

"Limousin: regional crisis and change," by Hugh D. Clout. TIJDSCHRIFT VOOR ECONOMISCHE EN SOCIALE GEOGRAFIE. 61:288-299, September-October, 1970.

"The Lippes loop in general practice," by N. H. Fursdon, et al. NZ MED J. 72:239-243, October, 1970.

"The literature of ethical problems in medicine," by J. R. Elkinton, Jr. ANN INTERN MED. 73:662-666, October, 1970.

"Liver function in patients using depot anti-ovulation

agents," by Arguelles J. Rodriguez. GINEC OBSTET MEX. 27:107-113, January, 1970.

"Lochia and menstrual patterns in women with postpartum IUCD insertions," by V. Hingorani, et al. AM J OBSTET GYNECOL. 108:989-990, November 15, 1970.

"The loneliness of old age," by M. L. Conti. NURS OUTLOOK. 18:28-30, August, 1970.

"Long cycles, late ovulation, and calendar rhythm," by R. G. Potter, Jr., et al. INT J FERTIL. 12: 127-140, January-March, 1970.

"Long-term application of steroids enclosed in dimethylpolysiloxane (silastic): in vitro and in vivo experiments," by R. Schuhmann, et al. ACTA BIOL MED GER. 24:897-910, 1970.

"Long-term effect of an intrauterine contraceptive device on genital organs of rhesus monkeys. A 4 and one-half year study," by A. B. Kar, et al. AMER J OBSTET GYNEC. 106:457-462, February 1, 1970.

"Long term effect of medroxyprogesterone acetate in human ovarian morphophysiology and sperm transport," J. Zanartu, et al. FERTIL STERIL. 21:525-533, July, 1970.

"The long-term effects of steroid contraceptives," by R. Doll. J BIOSOC SCI. 2:367-389, October, 1970.

"Long-term isolation in rats reduces morphine response," by D. M. Katz, et al. NATURE. 228:469-471, October 31, 1970.

"Long-term toxicologic and tumorigenesis studies on an oral contraceptive agent in albino rats," by J. L. Schardein, et al. TOXIC APPL PHARMACOL. 16:10-23, January, 1970.

"Longevity of members of Congress." METROPOLITAN LIFE STAT BUL. 51:2-5, December, 1970.

"A Look at Indiana's Pupil Population in the Decade Ahead," by J. C. Hill. CONTEMP EDUC. 41,6:280-284, May, 1970.

"A look at preliminary 1970 census data," by Diane H. Rush. BUS & ECON DIMENSIONS. 6:16-17, October, 1970.

"Looking back upon our guidance in conception control," by Y. Ashimura. KANGO. 22:91-94, December, 1970.

"Les Loop; medicolegal aspects," by J. E. Deming. MED TRIAL TECHN QUART. 16:1-8, June, 1970.

"Louisiana's quiet revolution in family planning," by A. Gordon. TODAY'S HLTH. 48:38+, January, 1970.

"Low-oestrogen oral contraceptives," by S. M. Wood, et al. BR MED J. 4:54, October 3, 1970.

"Lymphoid follicles of the endometrium in women wearing an intrauterine device," by A. Ishihama, et al. AMER J OBSTET GYNEC. 107:535-537, June 15, 1970.

M

"MDs blast pill's safety during Nelson hearings." AM DRUGGIST. 161:22, January 26, 1970.

"Magnitude of rate-of-growth effects on aggregate savings," by M. J. Farrell. ECON J. 80:873-894, December, 1970.

"Major federal resources for family planning programs and services: a summary." FAMILY PLANNING PERSPECTIVES. 2:40-41, March, 1970.

"Major vascular complications during treatment with oral contraceptives and retrospective discovery of idiopathic hyperlipemia. 9 cases," by J. L. de Gennes, et al. PRESSE MED. 78:541-546, March 7, 1970.

"Majzlin intrauterine contraceptive spring. Report of a clinical study," by A. J. Sobrero, et al. OBSTET GYNECOL. 36:911-918, December, 1970.

"Make love, not babies; childlessness; views of the Nathaniel Freedlands," by M. Kasindorf. NEWSWEEK. 75:111, June 15, 1970.

"Making plans." LANCET. 2:807-808, October 17, 1970.

"Malabsorption of folate polyglutamates associated with oral contraceptive therapy," by T. F. Necheles, et al. NEW ENG J MED. 282:858-859, April 9, 1970.

"Malaria control and population growth," by Peter Newman. J OF DEVELOPMENT STUDIES. 6:133-158, January 6, 1970.

"Malaria eradication and the fall of mortality, a note," by H. Frederiksen. POPULATION STUDIES. 24:111-113, March, 1970.

"Male antifertility compounds: U-5897 as a rat chemosterilant," by R. J. Ericsson. J REPROD FERTIL. 22:213-222, July, 1970.

"Male contraceptive: a better pill?" by L. Witt. TODAY'S HEALTH. 48:16-19+, June, 1970.

"Male Preserves," by A. Brien. NEW STATESMAN. 80:335, September 18, 1970.

"Male sex-role and response to a community problem," by F. L. Strodtbeck, et al. SOCIOL Q. 11:291-306, Summer, 1970.

"Male sterilisation; an ultimate in family planning," by A. D. Gunn. NURS TIMES. 66:627, May 14, 1970.

"A male sterilization clinic," by P. Jackson, et al. BR MED J. 4:295-297, October 31, 1970.

"Malthus can turn in his grave." NATURE. 225:1-2 January 3, 1970.

"Malthus versus Marx: China's population is growing more slowly than that of the US; to achieve this, its leaders have ignored Marx, exploited every method; but they still have to find jobs for today's youth," by Charles Snyder. FAR EASTERN ECON R. 69:28+, December 26, 1970.

"Man and His Environment," by A. J. Coale. SCIENCE. 170,3954:132-136, October, 1970.

"Man as an Endangered Species," by M. K. Udall. AMERICAN ASSOCIATION OF COLLEGES FOR TEACHER EDUCATION YEARBOOK. 69-77, 1970.

"Man in the north," by V. Ianovskii. SOVIET R. 10:24-34, Winter, 1969-1970.

"Man is the endangered species; interview," by P. R. Ehrlich. NAT WILDLIFE. 8:38-39, April, 1970.

"Manpower developments," by R. J. Brown. PERSONNEL ADM. 33:2+, May, 1970.

"Man's decline as a species," by A. H. Drummond. SCI DIGEST. 68:26-31, July, 1970.

"Man's place in the ecological pattern," by John C. Robertson. GEOGRAPHICAL MAG. 42:254-265, January, 1970.

"Marital moratorium and fertility control in China," by H. Yuan Tien. POPULATION STUDIES. 24:311-323, November, 1970.

"Marriage and malevolence: the uses of sexual opposition in a Hindu pantheon," by L. A. Babb. ETHNOLOGY. 9:137-148, April, 1970.

"Marriage rates and population pressure: Ireland, 1871 and 1911," by Brendan M. Walsh. ECONOMIC HISTORY R. 23:148-162, April, 1970.

"A mass social-hygienic investigation of a very old population in various areas of the Soviet Union: program, procedure, results," by N. N. Sachuk. J GERONT. 25:256-261, July, 1970.

"Mate choice and domestic life in the nineteenth-century marriage manual," by M. Gordon and M. C. Bernstein. J MARRIAGE AND FAM. 32:665-674, November, 1970.

"Maternal effects on behavior and white blood cells of isolated female mice," by A. S. Weltman, et al. LIFE SCI. 9:291-300, March 1, 1970.

"Maternal nutrition and family planning," by J. G. Chopra, et al. AM J CLIN NUTR. 23:1043-1058, August, 1970.

"Measures of longevity of American Indians," by Charles A. Hill, Jr. PUBLIC HEALTH REPTS. 85:233-239, March, 1970.

"Measuring rural-urban drift in developing countries; a suggested method," by L. Roussel. INT LABOUR R. 101:229-246, March, 1970.

"Mechanical methods of contraception," by E. Stewart. PRACTITIONER. 205:13-19, July, 1970.

"Mechanism of action of intrauterine contraceptives in women," by H. J. Davis, et al. OBSTET GYNEC. 36:350-358, September, 1970.

"Mechanism of the contraceptive effect of intrauterine devices," by V. I. Sakharov, et al. AKUSH GINEKOL. 46:56-57, March, 1970.

"Mechanisms of action of intra-uterine contraceptive devices in women and other mammals," by P. Eckstein. BRIT MED BULL. 26:52-59, January, 1970.

"Medical aspects of oral contraceptives," by N. J. Elgee. ANN INTERN MED. 72:409-418, March, 1970.

"Medical correlates of termination of use of intrauterine contraceptive devices in Taichung," by J. Y. Peng, et al. INT J FERTIL. 15:102-126, April-June, 1970.

"Medical Grand Rounds from the University of Alabama Medical Center," SOUTH MED J. 63:1297-1303, November, 1970.

"'Medicalized' sex," by S. Goldsmith. NEW ENG J MED. 283:709, September 24, 1970.

"'Medicalized' sex," by L. Gordis. NEW ENG J MED. 283:709-710, September 24, 1970.

"'Medicalized' sex," by A. Pinzello. NEW ENG J MED. 283:709, September 24, 1970.

"Medicine's survival in the seventies," by W. M. Krigsten. J IOWA MED SOC. 60:443-446, July, 1970.

"The Mediterranean mother," by A. S. Falconer. J ROY NAV MED SERV. 56:18-25, Spring, 1970.

"Megalobiastic anemia precipitated by the use of oral contraceptive. A case report," by R. P. Holmes. N CAROLINA MED J. 31:17-18, January, 1970.

"Mendeleev; demographics in addition to chemistry." CHEM & ENG NEWS. 48:43, September 28, 1970.

"Menstrual dysfunction following use of oral contraceptives," by H. D. Homesley, et al. OBSTET GYNEC. 35:734-739, May, 1970.

"The mental and sexual aspects of contraceptives," by J. P. Hes. HAREFUAH. 78:299-300, March 15, 1970.

"Mental health and family planning," by H. P. David. J NERV MENT DIS. 151:1, July, 1970.

"Metabolic effects of oral contraceptives." BRIT MED J. 3:121, July 18, 1970.

"Metabolic effects of oral contraceptives," by E. C. Grant. BRIT MED J. 3:402-403, August 15, 1970.

"Metabolism of protestogen administered in oral contraceptives," by V. Brockner, et al. MED J AUST. 1:1229-1230, June 13, 1970.

"Method of analysis of a table of 'origin-destination' migrations," by Yves Tugault. POPULATION. 25,1: 59-68, January-February, 1970. (SA #F0140)

"A method of tubal ligation," by S. J. Barr. AMER J OBSTET GYNEC. 107:324-325, May 15, 1970.

"Methodological issues in health statistics." MILBANK MEMORIAL FUND Q. 48:1-87, October, 1970.

"Metropolitan area projections through 1975." SALES MGT. 105:57-107, November 10, 1970.

"Mexico ambivalent on birth control," by F. U. Ross. CHR CENT. 87:1428-1429, November 25, 1970.

"Micro-dosage of a new progestogen (quingestanol) used as a contraceptive," by J. J. Medina del Campo, et al. GINEC OBSTET MEX. 27:471-475, April, 1970.

"Microbiological study of secretion in the vagina, cervical canal and uterine cavity in women with IUD," by M. Nishijima, et al. SANFUJIN JISSAI. 19:40-43, January, 1970.

"Microdose intrauterine progestagen associated with intrauterine contraceptive devices," by H. W. Horne, Jr., et al. INT J FERTIL. 15:210-213, October-December, 1970.

"Migraine and oral contraceptives," by L. Moreau, et al. THERAPEUTIQUE. 46:279-281, March, 1970.

"Migrant labour and agricultural output in Ghana," by Ralph E. Beals and Carmen F. Menezes. OXFORD ECONOMIC PAPERS. 22:109-127, March, 1970.

"Migrant labour and economic development," by Marvin P. Miracle and Sara S. Berry. OXFORD ECONOMIC PAPERS. 22:86-108, March, 1970.

"Migration and economic opportunities in West Virginia; a statistical analysis," by G. L. Rutman. RURAL SOCIOLOGY. 35,2:206-217, June, 1970. (SA #F0138)

"Migration and industrial development: the southern Italian experience," by A. Rodgers. ECON GEOG. 46:111-135, April, 1970.

"Migration and modernization," by Fred W. Reed. INDIAN J SOCIOL. 1:104-129, September, 1970.

"Migration as investment; empirical tests of the human investment approach to geographical mobility," by S. Bowles. R ECON & STAT. 52:356-362, November, 1970.

"Migration, employment and race in the deep South," by J. J. Persky and J. F. Kain. SO ECON J. 36:268-276, January, 1970.

"Migration flows in intraurban space: place utility considerations," by L. A. Brown and D. B. Longbrake. ASSN AM GEOG ANN. 60:368-384, June, 1970.

"Migration, functional distance, and the urban hierarchy," by L. A. Brown, et al. ECON GEOG. 46:472-485, July, 1970.

"Migration in an urban population," by A. E. Bennett. BRIT J PREV SOC MED. 24:63-64, February, 1970.

"Migration of native-born Ohioans: 1850-1960," by Lowell E. Gallaway and Richard K. Vedder. BUL BUS RESEARCH. 45:4-5, June, 1970.

"Migration to and from Scotland since 1961," by Huw R. Jones. INST BRITISH GEOGRAPHERS TRANSACTIONS. pp. 145-158, March, 1970.

"Migration, unemployment and development; a two-sector analysis," by J. R. Harris, et al. AM ECON R. 60: 126-142, March, 1970.

"Migration within the U. S. 1800-1960: some new estimates," by S. Lebergott. J ECON HIST. 30:839-847, December, 1970.

"Minipill in limbo." SCI N. 97:93, January 24, 1970.

"Minority-group status and fertility: an extension of Goldscheider and Uhlenberg," by D. F. Sly. AM J SOCIOL. 76:443-459, November, 1970.

"Miss Stephanie Mills vs. motherhood," by A. Wolff. LOOK. 34:58-59, April 21, 1970.

"Mobility among business faculty," by L. J. Shuster. ACAD MGT J. 13:325-335, September, 1970.

"Mode of action of intra-uterine devices," by J. H. Ravina. PRESSE MED. 78:1063-1064, May 9, 1970.

"Model for the dispersion of the migrant labor force and some results for the United States, 1880-1920," by T. J. Orsagh, et al. R ECON & STAT. 52:306-312, August, 1970.

"Model for Zero Population Growth," by S. M. Dickson. BIOSCIENCE. 20,23:1245-1246, December, 1970.

"Modern contra conception and veneral diseases." LAKART IDNINGEN. 67:Suppl.III:16, October 12, 1970.

"Monilial vulvovaginitis following 'the Pill'," by G. Perl. MT SINAI J MED NY. 37:699-701, November-December, 1970.

"Monitoring of adverse reactions to drugs in the United Kingdom," by W. H. Inman. PROC R SOC MED. 63: 1302-1304, December, 1970.

"More about the pill: UCLA findings." NEWSWEEK. 76:78+, October 12, 1970.

"More babies needed, not fewer; interview ed. by L. Kent," by J. Jacobs. VOGUE. 156:86-87, August 15, 1970.

"More fuel for the pill controversy; use of beagles in testing," by B. J. Culliton. SCI N. 98:402, November 21, 1970.

"More on pitfalls," by Harvey Leibenstein. POPULATION STUDIES. 24:117-119, March, 1970.

"More or less people; thoughts on feeding the hungry," by W. H. Davis. NEW REPUB. 162:19-21, June 20, 1970.

"More working wives, fewer children," by H. Woods Bowman. FEDERAL RESERVE CHICAGO. pp. 7-12, August, 1970.

"Morocco: family planning knowledge, attitudes, and practice in the rural areas; Morocco: family planning and an attitude survey in the urban areas." STUDIES IN FAMILY PLANNING. 58:1-10, October, 1970.

"Morphologic changes in the uterus associated with steroid contraceptives and intrauterine contraceptive devices," by W. B. Ober. ACTA CYTOL. 14:156, March, 1970.

"Morphological effects of intrauterine contraceptive devices," by R. M. Wynn. ILLINOIS MED J. 137:333-337, April, 1970.

"Morphological findings on the endometrium, decia and chorlon following long-term use of intrauterine anticonceptive devices," by M. Stopekova, et al. BRATISL LEK LISTY. 53:146-152, February, 1970.

"Morphology of ovaries and oral contraceptives," by W. P. Plate. NEDERL T GENEESK. 114:1422-1424, August 22, 1970.

"Mortality from coronary occlusion in young women with reference to oral contraceptives as a possible etiological factor," by A. Fischer, et al. UGESKR LAEGER. 132:2480-2482, December 24, 1970.

"Mortality from diabetes mellitus at ages 45-64." METROPOLITAN LIFE STAT BUL. 51:2-4, July, 1970.

"Mothers of disabled children-the value of weekly group meetings," by R. Linder. DEVELOP MED CHILD NEUROL. 12:202-206, April, 1970.

"The motivation for reproduction and the new population dimensions of Ghana," by D. A. Ampofo. E AFR MED J. 47:217-222, April, 1970.

"Mouth manifestations and oral contraceptives," by M. E. Chevallier. REV ODONTOSTOMATOL MIDI FR. 28:96-103, 1970.

"Mr. Maudling's chance." ECONOMIST. 236:19-20, August 22, 1970.

"Much useful data coming from census." ED & PUB. 103:18, November 7, 1970.

"Multiply thy kind and perish," by C. E. Gillham. FIELD & S. 75:8+, July, 1970.

"A multivariate regression analysis of differences in fertility in United States counties," by David M. Heer and John W. Boynton. SOCIAL BIOLOGY. 17:180-194, September, 1970.

"Mumps in a general population. A sero-epidemiologic study," by L. P. Levitt, et al. AMER J DIS CHILD. 120:134-138, August, 1970.

"Myometrial activity and the IUCD. 3. Effect of contraceptive pills," by G. Beyer, et al. AMER J OBSTET GYNEC. 106:87-92, January 1, 1970.

N

"Natality statistics analysis. United States, 1965-1967," by R. L. Heuser, et al. VITAL HEALTH STATIST. 19:1-38, May, 1970.

"National family-planning programs: where we stand," by B. Berelson. SCIENCE. 169:931, September 4, 1970.

"The National Goals Research Staff report," by P. H. Abelson. SCIENCE. 169:537, August 7, 1970.

"National population programs and policy: social and legal implications-a symposium: introduction," by D. A. Giannella; "Federal population policy: a decade of change," by C. S. Schultz; "National population problems and standardization of family size," by H. Y. Tien; "Population programs and policy," by S. M. Wishik; "Population policies of state governments in the United States: some preliminary observations," by E. D. Driver; "Constitutional aspects of a national population policy," by C. C. Means, Jr.; panel discussion. VILL L REV. 15:785, Summer, 1970.

"National surveillance network for occupational health," by V. E. Rose, et al. J OCCUP MED. 12:193-197, June, 1970.

"National survey of U. K. births. Obstetrics in the United Kingdom," by R. Chamberlain, et al. MIDWIVES CHRON. 83:78-83, March, 1970.

"Natural selection in ecologically and genetically defined populations," by C. Istock. BEHAVIORAL SCIENCE. 15,1:101-115, January, 1970. (SA #E9021)

"Naturalistic rationale for women's reform: Lester Frank Ward on the evolution of sexual relations," by C. H. Scott. HISTORIAN. 33:54-67, November, 1970.

"The nature and effects of Latin America's non-western trend in fertility," by E. E. Arriaga. DEMOGRAPHY. 7:483-501, November, 1970.

"Nature and site of action of 3-chloro-1, 2-propanediol--an oral antifertility agent for the male," by B. S. Setty, et al. INDIAN J EXP BIOL. 8:49-50, January, 1970.

"Necrotecture: the underground population explosion and its impact on cemetery design," by R. Slusarenko. LANDSCAPE ARCH. 60:297-300, July, 1970.

"Need for a global population policy-now," by V. P. Nanda. DENVER L J SPECIAL. 17, 1970.

"Needed: a population policy for Arizona," by M. H. Goodwin, Jr., et al. ARIZONA MED. 27:18-22, June, 1970.

"Negro migration and unemployment," by D. E. Kaun. J HUMAN RESOURCES. 5:191-207, Spring, 1970.

"Net delay of next conception by contraception: a highly simplified case," by R. G. Potter, A. K. Jain and B. McCann. POPULATION STUDIES. 24:173-192, July, 1970.

"Neuro-ophthalmological complications in the wake of
   oral contraceptives," by J. Jablonski. POL TYG LEK.
   25:1555-1557, October 12, 1970.

"Neurologic complications after oral contraceptives,"
   by M. Orzechowska, et al. WIAD LEK. 23:2199-2201,
   December 15, 1970.

"Never mind the Pill---." NURS MIRROR. 131:31-33,
   October 2, 1970.

"The "new" Americans--who is coming to U. S. now."
   U S NEWS. 69:70-71, October 5, 1970.

"New baby boom on the way?" METROPOLITAN LIFE STAT
   BUL. 51:2-3, May, 1970.

"New biology and the prenatal child," by D. W. Brodie.
   J FAMILY L. 9:391, 1970.

"A new deterministic model for the interaction between
   predator and prey," by C. Pearce. BIOMETRICS. 26:
   387-392, September, 1970.

"New doubts about the pill." LIFE. 68:28-29, February
   27, 1970.

"New draft of OC insert is awaited." AM DRUGGIST.
   161:20, April 6, 1970.

"New environment of the south," by G. Clay. ARCH FORUM.
   133:42-45, December, 1970.

"New facts on construction: the 1967 census of construction industries," by G. H. Brown. CONSTR R.
   16:4-8, October, 1970.

"New feminism: potent force in birth-control policy,"
   by L. J. Carter. SCIENCE. 167:1234-1236, February
   27, 1970.

"A new intrauterine contraceptive device. An open ring,"
   by S. Rozin, et al. OBSTET GYNEC. 36:304-305, August,
   1970.

"New Jersey Economic Review, number 4, 1970, is a special
   issue entitled, "1970 preliminary census counts."
   NEW JERSEY ECONOMIC REVIEW. No. 4, 1970.

"New look at the great landlords of eighteenth-century

New York," by S. B. Kim. WM & MARY Q. 3,27:581-614, October, 1970.

"New oral contraceptive methods," by A. Suzuki. JAP J PUBLIC HEALTH NURSE. 26:58-59, November, 1970.

"A new oral contraceptive with a 7 plus 15 sequential formulation," by I. Brosens, et al. ARZNEIMITTEL-FORSCHUNG. 20:236-237, February, 1970.

"New report on oral contraceptives of the Advisory committee to the Food and Drug Administration. A comment on the new report," by J. W. Goldzieher. AMER J OBSTET GYNEC. 107:1106-1109, August 1, 1970.

"New report on oral contraceptives of the Advisory Committee to the Food and Drug Administration. Reply to Dr. Goldzieher's comment on the new report," by L. M. Hellman. AMER J OBSTET GYNEC. 107:1109-1110, August 1, 1970.

"New tasks for the '70s: we are awakening to the realization that all mankind depends on the same scarce and relatively shrinking resource pool," by Richard N. Gardner. VISTA. 5:39+, May-June, 1970.

"A 'new town' planned for the urban and rural poor: the University of Louisville develops a controversial strategy to change the flow of migration," by Simpson Lawson. CITY. 4:35-38, June-July, 1970.

"A new type of oral contraceptive," by W. McBride. MED J AUST. 1:212-215, January 31, 1970.

"New use recommendations for birth control pills." GOOD H. 171:153, August, 1970.

"Next decade shows promise but raises many serious urban questions." AIA J. 53:8, January, 1970.

"Nice baby." JAMA. 214:1108, November 9, 1970.

"Nimble with the pill." NATURE. 225:4-5, January 3, 1970.

"19 Canada dailies reject Schmid ads for prophylactics." ADV AGE. 41:68, April 6, 1970.

"1984 the era of young marrieds." NATURE. 228:206, October 17, 1970.

"1984 plus one," by G. H. Brown. CONF BD REC. 7:20-24, December, 1970.

"1970 census: changes and innovations," by G. McGimsey. AM INST PLAN J. 36:198-203, May, 1970.

"The 1970 census: a statistical gold mine: the 1970 census will contain many of the facts and figures that associations need to define and achieve their goals in the 70's." ASSN MGT. 22:52-55, February, 1970.

"1970 Census: Tool for Vocational Planning wealth," by J. C. Baker. AMERICAN VOCATIONAL JOURNAL. 45, 8:83-84,86,88-89, November, 1970.

"The 1970 census: controversy and change," by C. A. Keyko. PUBLIC AFFAIRS COMMENT. 16:1-6, March, 1970.

"No greater challenge: the US urban problem," by T. L. Ashley. DISCUSSION. 53:86, February, 1970.

"No more unwanted children." UNESCO COURIER. 23:24-27+, February, 1970.

"No Teacher Surplus," by M. M. Chambers. PHI DELTA KAPPAN. 52,2:118-119, October, 1970.

"No universal birth control agent seen." AM DRUGGIST. 161:53, June 1, 1970.

"Noli me tangere," by R. Seidenberg. PSYCHOANAL REV. 57:196-202, 1970.

"Nonmonetary commodity incentives in family planning programs: a preliminary trial," by Gordon W. Perkin. STUDIES IN FAMILY PLANNING. pp. 12-15, September, 1970.

"Nonsense explosion," by B. Wattenberg. NEW REPUB. 162:18-23, April 4, 1970; "Discussion," 162:24-26+, May 2; 44-46, May 9; 29-31, May 16, 1970.

"Nonwage benefits of vocational training: employability and mobility," by R. L. Bowlby and W. R. Schriver. IND & LABOR REL R. 23:500-509, July 9, 1970.

"Northampton-centre of megalopolis? Northampton master plan," by J. B. McLoughlin. TOWN AND COUNTRY PLAN.

38:197-199, April, 1970.

"Note on asocial populations dispersing in two dimensions," by E. Bradford, et al. J THEOR BIOL. 29: 27-33, October, 1970.

"Note on intercensal estimates of the Australian population, classified by country of birth, 1961-1966," by P. F. Gourley. ECON REC. 46:419-423, September, 1970.

"Notes on current drugs: oral contraceptives and thromboemboembolic disease," by C. B. Cox. MED J AUST. 2:202-203, July 25, 1970.

"Number, types and duration of human lives," by R. H. Williams. NORTHWEST MED. 69:493-496, July, 1970.

"Nurse, make it well," by E. H. Naugle. NO. 18:41, November, 1970.

"Nurse's role in family planning at a municipal hospital," by N. Herzig. HOSP TOP. 48:101 passim, February, 1970.

O

"O A U convention governing the specific aspects of refugee problems in Africa." HUMAN RIGHTS J. 3:170-181, March, 1970.

"OBG: Nurse's role in family planning at a municipal hospital," by N. Herzig. HOSP TOPICS. 48:101+, February, 1970.

"O-C makers told to give MDs consumer booklets." AM DRUGGIST. 161:24, June 29, 1970.

"Observation upon patients following vasectomy in Nepal," by B. P. Sharma. SOUTHERN MED J. 63:771-772, July, 1970.

"Observations concerning the increase of mankind, peopling of countries, etc.," by B. Franklin. PERSPECT BIOL MED. 13:469-475, Summer, 1970.

"Observations on the instruction of family planning for outpatients of the Aiiku Hospital," by M. Horiguchi, et al. JAP J MIDWIFE. 24:50-53, March, 1970.

"Observations on 1970 census data," by William R. Watson. N MEX BUS. 23:17-25, November-December, 1970.

"Obstacles to sterilization in one community," by Susan C. Scrimshaw and Bernard Pasquariella. FAMILY PLANNING PERSPECTIVES. 2:40-42, October, 1970.

"The obstetrician and society," by D. Baird. AMER J PUBLIC HEALTH. 60:628-640, April, 1970.

"Oestrogen content of oral contraceptives and thromboembolism," by E. G. McQueen. NEW ZEAL MED J. 71:317, May, 1970.

"Oestrogens and thromboembolism." BRIT MED J. 2:189-190, April 25, 1970.

"Oestrogens in the pill." LANCET. 1:929-930, May 2, 1970.

"Off the pill?" by J. Coburn. RAMP MAG. 8:46-49, June, 1970.

"On a case of thrombosis of the middle cerebral artery during progestogen therapy," by G. G. Cavalca, et al. RIV SPER FRENIAT. 94:83-94, February 28, 1970.

"On measuring geographic mobility," by L. H. Long. AM STAT ASSN J. 65:1195-1203, September, 1970.

"On population and environment: address, June 8, 1970," by P. M. Hauser. VITAL SPEECHES. 36:696-701, September 1, 1970.

"On population matters and family planning programs." DEPT STATE NEWS LETTER. pp. 12-13, September, 1970.

"On the preliminary results of the 1970 all-union population census: report of the U.S.S.R. Central statistical administration. CURRENT DIG SOVIET PR. 22:22-26, May 19, 1970.

"On the relation between economic status and family size preferences when status differentials in contraceptive instrumentalities are eliminated," by N. Krishnan Namboodiri. POPULATION STUDIES. 24:233-239, July, 1970.

"On some psychiatric complications of oral contraception," by M. Bourgeois, et al. BORDEAUX MED. 3:1273-1292, May, 1970.

"Once a bad'n?" by E. Williams. LANCET. 1:299-300, February 7, 1970.

"Once-a-month oral contraceptive: quinestrol and quingestanol," by B. R. Lotvin, et al. OBSTET GYNEC. 35:933-936, June, 1970.

"One hundred years of population change. Growth rate of the 100 largest metropolitan areas." REAL ESTATE ANALYST. 39:455-466, November 17, 1970.

"One in 20 who prefers it abroad." ECONOMIST. 236:239, September 5, 1970.

"One man's answer to overpopulation; vasectomy." LIFE. 68:42-47, March 6, 1970.

"One myth less." NATURE. 227:874-875, August 29, 1970.

"Operative laparoscopy: removal of intra-abdominal IUD with biopsy tongs," by M. B. Taylor, et al. OBSTET GYNEC. 35:981, June, 1970.

"Opinion: the case for compulsory birth control," by E. Chasteen. MLLE. 70:142+, January, 1970.

"Opposition to birth control law wanes," by Norman C. Miller. WALL ST J. 176:8, August 14, 1970.

"Optimizing the distribution of housing in large-scale developments," by Alan Walter Steiss and John W. Dickey. TOWN PLANNING INST J. 56:95-99, March, 1970.

"Optimum population and environment: a Georgian microcosm," by Eugene P. Odum. CURRENT HIST. 58: 355-359+, June, 1970.

"Optimum World Population," by H. R. Hulett. BIOSCIENCE. 20,3:160-161, February, 1970.

"Oral contraception," by H. Hill. PRACTITIONER. 205:5-12, July, 1970.

"Oral contraception. An application in family planning programme in Calcutta city," by A. S. Gupta. J INDIAN MED ASS. 54:187-194, March 1, 1970.

"Oral contraception among special clinic patients. With particular reference to the diagnosis of gonorrhoea," by A. B. Hewitt. BRIT J VENER DIS. 46:106-107, April, 1970.

"The oral contraception controversy." CANAD MED ASS J. 102:1407 passim, June 20, 1970.

"Oral contraceptive steroids: effects on various nutrient balances and body composition in adult female rats," by K. Manoharan, et al. PROC SOC EXP BIOL MED. 133:774-779, March, 1970.

"Oral contraceptives. Current status of therapy." JAMA. 241:2316-2321, December 28, 1970.

"Oral contraceptives and acute surgery," by A. Pedersen Berget. UGESKR LAEG. 132:1628-1629, August 27, 1970.

"Oral contraceptives and amino acid utilization," by I. L. Craft, et al. AM J OBSTET GYNECOL. 108:1120-1125, December 1, 1970.

"Oral contraceptives and blood lipids." POSTGRAD MED. 47:256, May, 1970.

"Oral contraceptives and blood pressure," by M. P. Chidell. PRACTITIONER. 205:58-64, July, 1970.

"Oral contraceptives and copper metabolism," by M. Briggs, et al. NATURE. 225:81, January 3, 1970.

"Oral contraceptives and depression," by J. Braham. BRIT MED J. 1:237, January 24, 1970.

"Oral contraceptives and female mortality trends," by T. W. Anderson. CANAD MED ASS J. 102:1156-1160, May 30, 1970.

"Oral contraceptives and gastrointestinal disorders," by R. L. Hurwitz, et al. ANN SURG. 172:892-896, November, 1970.

"Oral contraceptives and gestational diabetes." BRIT MED J. 1:190, January 24, 1970.

"Oral contraceptives and glucose tolerance," by P. D. Hansten. ANN INTERN MED. 73:492, September, 1970.

"Oral contraceptives and hypertension." BRIT MED J. 1:378, May 16, 1970.

"Oral contraceptives and hypertension," by D. F. Horrobin, et al. BRIT MED J. 1:285, August 1, 1970.

"Oral contraceptives and hypertension," by A. M. Macintosh. BRIT MED J. 3:346-347, August 8, 1970.

"Oral contraceptives and hypertension: the effect of guanethidine," by T. M. Clezy. MED J AUST. 1:638-640, March 28, 1970.

"Oral contraception and hypertension-once more," by O. Stenbaek. T NORSK LAEGEFOREN. 90:790-791, April 15, 1970.

"Oral contraceptives and hypertensive disease: a cybernetic overview," by J.H. Laragh. CIRCULATION. 42:983-985, December, 1970.

"Oral contraceptives and the incidence of thrombosis," by A. F. Abrahamsen. T NORSK LAEGEFOREN. 90:403-408, February 15, 1970.

"Oral contraceptives and low antithrombin-3 activity," by P. Wolf. LANCET. 1:144, January 17, 1970.

"Oral contraceptives and low antithrombin-3 concentration," by M. K. Fagerhol, et al. LANCET. 1:1175, May 30, 1970.

"Oral contraceptives and low antithrombin-3 activity," by E. von Kaulla, et al. LANCET. 1:36, January 3, 1970.

"Oral contraceptives and myocardial infarction," by M. F. Oliver. BRIT MED J. 2:210-213, April 25, 1970.

"Oral contraceptives and neurologic complications," by H. H. Janzik, et al. MED WELT. 10:395-399, March 7, 1970.

"Oral contraceptives and premenstrual depression," by B. Herzberg, et al. LANCET. 1:775, April 11, 1970.

"Oral contraceptives and serum lipids," by G. M. Barton, et al. J OBSTET GYNAEC BRIT COMM. 77:551-554, June, 1970.

"Oral contraceptives and serum-proteins," by M. Elstein. LANCET. 1:367, February 14, 1970.

"Oral contraceptives and thromboembolism." NEW ZEAL MED J. 71:305, May, 1970.

"Oral contraceptives and thrombosis. Introduction," by H. Stormorken. NORD MED. 84:1472-1473, November 12, 1970.

"Oral contraceptives and thrombosis. Pathological-anatomical viewpoint," by L. Jorgensen. NORD MED. 84:1473, November 12, 1970.

"Oral contraceptives and thrombosis. Some coagulation and fibrinolysis changes," by H. Gjonnaess. NORD MED. 84:1473, November 12, 1970.

"Oral contraceptives and vascular anomalies," by L. Goldman. LANCET. 1:108-109, July 11, 1970.

"Oral contraceptives; background, motivation, education, application," by A. Sikkel. NED TIJDSCHR VERLOSKD GYNAECOL. 70:599-604, December, 1970.

"Oral contraceptives, depression, and aminoacid metabolism," by A. R. Green, et al. LANCET. 1:1288, June 13, 1970.

"Oral contraceptives, depression, and aminoacid metabolism," by D. P. Rose, et al. LANCET. 1:1117-1118, May 23, 1970.

"Oral contraceptives: depressions and frigidity," by V. Huffer, et al. J NERV MENT DIS. 151:35-41, July, 1970.

"Oral contraceptives, hypertension, and toxemia," by S. M. Carmichael, et al. OBSTET GYNEC. 35:371-376, March, 1970.

"Oral contraceptives-prescribe or proscribe?" by P. E. Sartwell. AMER J PUBLIC HEALTH. 60:1187-1189, July, 1970.

"Oral contraceptives: a review of certain metabolic effects and an examination of the question of safety," by J. W. Goldzieher. FED PROC. 29:1220-1227, May-June, 1970.

"Oral contraceptives: turmoil and aftermath," by C. A. Paulsen. JAMA. 212:873, May 4, 1970.

"Oral contraceptives warning notice is planned for
every package by FDA." OIL PAINT & DRUG REP.
197:3+, March 9, 1970.

"Oral contraceptives: Which pill for which patient?"
PT CARE. 4:135+, June 15, 1970.

"Oral ovulation inhibitors in the treatment of skin
diseases," by J. Vankos. THER HUNG. 18:33-39, 1970.

"An orally active long-acting estrogen (AY-20,121),"
by U. K. Banik, et al. STEROIDS. 16:289-296,
September, 1970.

"Ortho 1557-0. A new oral contraceptive," by W. J.
Ledger. INT J FERTIL. 15:88-92, April-June, 1970.

"Orthopedics and oral administration of contraceptives,"
by W. S. Kaden. JAMA. 213:301, July 13, 1970.

"Other side of the pill." NEWSWEEK. 75:45-46, March
9, 1970.

"Our affluent economy will be bursting at seams by '85:
Brown." ADV AGE. 41:1+, October 12, 1970.

"Our experience with the IUD (contraceptive loop) inserted immediately after interruption of pregnancy,"
by Z. Szereday, et al. ORV HETIL. 111:2299-2300,
September 27, 1970.

"Outpatient tubal sterilization," by C. R. Wheeless.
OBSTET GYNEC. 36:208-211, August, 1970.

"Ovarian pregnancy and the intrauterine device," by
H. Lehfeldt, et al. AM J OBSTET GYNECOL. 108:
1005-1009, December 1, 1970.

"Ovarian pregnancy with in situ IUCD: report of 2
cases," by A. Pane, et al. AM J OBSTET GYNECOL.
108:672-673, October 15, 1970.

"Ovarian suppressants in dogs: pilot study of an approach to rabies control," by C. Yasmuth, et al.
LANCET. 760:1312-1315, June 20, 1970.

"Ovary morphology and oral contraceptives," by W. P.
Plate. NED TIJDSCHR VERLOSKD GYNAECOL. 70:545-
550, December, 1970.

"Overpopulated America," by W. H. Davis. NEW REPUB. 162:28-30, January 31, 1970.

"Overpopulation and the American Catholic conscience," by Peter J. Riga. WORLD JUSTICE. 12:199-215, December, 1970.

"Overpopulation: crisis today, disaster tomorrow." PARENTS MAG. 45:30, January, 1970.

"The oversuppression syndrome," by S. C. MacLeod, et al. AMER J OBSTET GYNEC. 106:359-364, February 1, 1970.

"The oversuppression syndrome," by W. N. Spellacy, et al. AMER J OBSTET GYNEC. 107:1270-1271, August 15, 1970.

"Ovostat, a low dose oral contraceptive," by G. Linthorst, et al. BRUX MED. 50:433-437, June, 1970.

"Ovulation after the pill," by H. P. Dunn. BRIT MED J. 1:237, January 24, 1970.

"Ovulation inhibition with a long-acting injectable contraceptive. IV. Return of reproductive function after discontinuation," by M. A. Yussman, et al. AM J OBSTET GYNECOL. 108:901-907, November 15, 1970.

"Ovulation inhibitor and pancreopathy, by H. Bauer-Hack. MED WELT. 40:1739-1745, October 3, 1970.

"Oxytocin levels in female rats with bilateral intrauterine devices," by K. S. Raghavan, et al. J ENDOCR. 47:255-256, June, 1970.

P

"Packaging accuracy with good tabletting speeds," by J. Colligas. DRUG & COSMETIC IND. 106:96-97+, February, 1970.

"Palace and pollution," by A. C. Mason, et al. NATURE. 228:693, November 14, 1970.

"Panel discussion on problems in population screening for cervical cancer. ACTA CYTOL. 14:161-163, March, 1970.

"Parathion, embryonic development, sterilization and estrogen effects in birds. Comparison with the effects of aldrin," by Y. Lutz-Ostertag, et al. ANNEE BIOL. 9:501-507, July-October, 1970.

"Parent population," by F. Linden. CONF BD REC. 7:24-26, March, 1970.

"Parenthood: right or privilege?" by G. Hardin. SCIENCE. 169:427, July 31, 1970; "Discussion," 170:257-259+, October 16, 1970.

"Parents under strain: families with a mentally handicapped child," by Susie Gilderdale. NEW SOCIETY. pp. 777-778, May 7, 1970.

"The Parliament requested overhaul in sterilization law." LAKARTIDNINGEN. 67:5732, December 2, 1970.

"Participation of low-income urban women in a public health birth control program," by Z. L. Janus, et al. PUBLIC HEALTH REP. 85:859-867, October, 1970.

"Pasquia land settlement project in Manitoba," by L. Harrington. CAN GEOG J. 80:92-97, March, 1970.

"Patterns of migration in relation to local community structure, a study in Karasjok," by R. Mook, et al. TIDSSKRIFT FOR SAMFUNNSFORSKNING. 11,1:13-31, 1970. (SA #F0134)

"Paul R. Ehrlich: A biologist's remarks on the "population explosion"," by M. Sloan. ILLINOIS MED J. 138:246-247, September, 1970.

"Paying Mum and motivation." PERSONNEL MANAGEMENT. 2:30-32, January, 1970.

"People, an affluent society, and pollution," by W. R. Barclay. BULL NTRDA. 56:14+, October, 1970.

"People and politics," by J. Kettle. EXEC. 12:35-36, October, 1970.

"People & pollution: the challenge to planning," by Colin Hutchinson. LONG RANGE PLANNING. 2:2-7, March, 1970.

"People and spending power, state by state," by F. Linden. CONF BD REC. 7:44-47, December, 1970.

"People of York: 1538-1812," by U. M. Cowgill. SCI AM. 222:104-10+, January, 1970.

"People pollution," by P. R. Ehrlich. AUDUBON. 72: 4-9, May, 1970.

"People pollution; excerpt from The doomsday book," by G. R. Taylor. LADIES HOME J. 87:74+, October, 1970.

"People problem," by P. R. Ehrlich and J. P. Holdren. SAT R. 53:42-43, July 4, 1970.

"Per-celloscopic tubal sterilization by isthmic electrocoagulation," by R. Palliez, et al. BULL FED SOC GYNECOL OBSTET LANG FR. 22:449-51, September-October, 1970.

"Perceptual differences between married and single college women for the concepts of self, ideal woman, and man's ideal woman," by A. F. Rappaport, et al. J MARRIAGE & FAM. 32:441-442, August, 1970.

"The "perfect contraceptive" population," by L. Bumpass, et al. SCIENCE. 169:1177-1182, September 18, 1970.

"Perforation of bicornuate uterus by intrauterine contraceptive device," by S. D. Gupta. J OBSTET GYNAECOL BR COMMONW. 77:1140-1141, December, 1970.

"Perforation of the uterus by an intrauterine contraceptive device (1 case)," by M. Dumont, et al. REV FRANC GYNEC OBSTET. 65:115-117, March, 1970.

"Perils of the pill; Senate hearings." NEWSWEEK. 75:21, January 26, 1970.

"Perinatal mortality in Hawkshead, Lancashire 1581-1710," by R. S. Schofield. LOCAL POPULATION STUDIES MAG. 4:11-16, Spring, 1970.

"Permanent contraception using K 18 IUD," by R. Jinno. SANFUJIN JISSAL. 19:51-53, January, 1970.

"Peroral contraception (1): drugs," by J. Dolby, et al. LAKARTIDNINGEN. 67:Suppl III:33+, October 12, 1970.

"Peroral contraception (2): pharmacodynamics and

"clinical experiences," by G. Rybo. LAKARTIDNINGEN.
67:Suppl III:38+, October 12, 1970.

"Peroral contraception (3): clinical viewpoint," by
M. Bygdeman, et al. LAKARTIDNINGEN. 67:Suppl III:
45+, October 12, 1970.

"Peroral contraception (4): pregnancies," by M.
Rutenskold. LAKARTIDNINGEN. 67:Suppl III:51+,
October 12, 1970.

"Peroral contraception (5): continuing low dosage
treatment," by U. Larsson-Cohn. LAKARTIDNINGEN.
67:Suppl III:56+, October 12, 1970.

"Peroral contraception (6): adverse effects," by B.
Westerholm. LAKARTIDNINGEN. 67:Suppl III:63+,
October 12, 1970.

"Peroral contraception (7): metabolic changes," by
U. Larsson-Cohn. LAKARTIDNINGEN. 67:Suppl III:71+,
October 12, 1970.

"Peroral contraception (8): changes in laboratory test
results," by S. Lindstedt, et al. LAKARTIDNINGEN.
67:Suppl III:76+, October 12, 1970.

"Peroral contraception (9): use of oral contraceptives
in Sweden in 1969," by U. Larsson-Cohn, et al.
LAKARTIDNINGEN. 67:Suppl III:85+, October 12, 1970.

"Pharmacologic approach to contraception," by H. D.
Johnson. J AMER PHARM ASS. 10:261-263, May, 1970.

"The photosynthetic apparatus of Euglena gracilis. I.
Adaptation to population density change," by B. A.
Melandri. ARCH BIOCHEM. 138:598-605, June, 1970.

"Physicians and methods of birth planning," by P. J.
Donaldson. RI MED J. 53:419-423 passim, August,
1970.

"Physiologic responses to conception control methods
in domestic animals," by H. W. Hawk. J AM VET MED
ASSOC. 157:1795-1799, December 1, 1970.

"Pigeon control by chemosterilization; population model
from laboratory results," by J. Sturtevant. SCIENCE.
170:322-324, October 16, 1970.

"The Pill," by G. L. Swyer. NURS MIRROR. 130:19-21, June 19, 1970.

"The Pill," by G. L. Swyer. NURS MIRROR. 130:34-36, June 26, 1970.

"The "pill". Why not?" by M. Curwen. J R COLL GEN PRACT. 19:365-366, June, 1970.

"The pill, amenorrhea and ovarian cysts. Conservative surgical treatment. Pregnancy," by A. Paoli, et al. BULL FED GYNEC OBSTET FRANC. 22:90-92, January-March, 1970.

"The pill and the breast," by H. P. Leis, Jr. NY STATE J MED. 70:2911-2918, December 1, 1970.

"The pill and hypertension," by R. P. Russell, et al. JOHNS HOPKINS MED J. 127:287-293, November, 1970.

"The Pill and the Pathologist." NZ MED J. 72:45-47, July, 1970. "Demulen: hastily approved drug," by D. C. Goldberg. SCIENCE. 170:491, October 30, 1970.

"The pill and the public's right to know," by M. Mintz. PROGRESSIVE. 34:25-27, May, 1970.

"The pill and thrombosis," by G. J. Ottolander. NED TIJDSCHR VERLOSKD GYNAECOL. 70:556-562, December, 1970.

"Pill and your skin." VOGUE. 155:216+, May, 1970.

"Pill caution." TIME. 95:46, April 20, 1970.

"The pill controversy," by J. W. Records. SOUTHERN MED J. 63:608-610, May, 1970.

"Pill: do its benefits outweigh its hazards?" CONSUMER REP. 35:314-319, May, 1970.

"Pill: fewer takers." OIL PAINT & DRUG REP. 197:7, March 9, 1970.

"Pill for pigeons." CHEM & ENG N. 48:14-15, February 23, 1970.

"Pill goes to Washington." BSNS W. pp. 31-32, January 10, 1970.

"Pill: how much warning is enough?" CONSUMER REP. 35:329, June, 1970.

"Pill in court." CHEM W. 107:17, September 30, 1970.

"Pill in perspective," by E. B. Connell. READ DIGEST. 97:118-122, October, 1970.

"Pill is hard to follow." BSNS W. p. 80, January 31, 1970.

"Pill: is it safe?" U S NEWS. 68:10, January 26, 1970.

"Pill is safe; ed. by R. H. Berg," by E. T. Tyler. LOOK. 34:65-66, June 30, 1970.

"The pill; loyalty in spite of everything," by P. Vaughan. HEALTH. 7:6-7, Autumn, 1970.

"The pill on campus: many university clinics yield to co-ed pressure for contraceptives; single girls may obtain them at Michigan, Cornell, Yale; some schools fear furor; adapting to changing mores," by Henry Elliot Weinstein. WALL ST J. 175:1+, January 19, 1970.

"Pill on trial." TIME. 95:60+, January 26, 1970.

"The pill parallels the placenta. A method of teaching oral contraception," by W. B. Beasley. J INDIAN MED ASS. 54:20-22, January 1, 1970.

"The pill: past, present and future," by E. J. Servy, et al. GYNECOL PRAT. 21:285-298, 1970.

"Pill-pessimism overdone?" FIN WORLD. 133:10+, February 25, 1970.

"Pill poll," by E. Damude. CHATELAINE. 43:18, March, 1970.

"The "pill", promiscuity, and venereal disease," by L. Cohen. BRIT J VENER DIS. 46:108-110, April, 1970.

"The pill-safe? Clinical evaluation of oral contraceptives," by S. T. Thierstein. J KANS MED SOC. 71:465-470, December, 1970.

"Pill scare on Washington scene is blamed for worldwide panic as Stetler reviews PMA year." OIL PAINT & DRUG REP. 197:22+, April 20, 1970.

"Pill talk at a whisper." OIL PAINT & DRUG REP. 197:5, March 30, 1970.

"Pill trial." TIME. 95:32+, March 9, 1970.

"Pills and thrombosis (platelets, estrogens and magnesium)," by J. Durlach. REV FRANC ENDOCR CLIN. 11:45-54, January-February, 1970.

"Pilot study of patient time spent and cost analysis in a demonstration family planning and gynecology clinic, July-September, 1970, Taipei, Taiwan," by S. Fong. J NURS. 17:16-21, October, 1970.

"La pilule fait peur," by M. J. Dulac. MAG MACL. 10:40-42, May, 1970.

"Plain talk about the pill." NEWSWEEK. 75:93, March 16, 1970.

"Plan for a Palestinian state," by Averroes. NEW OUTLOOK. 13:19-26, May, 1970.

"Planning and implementing a large-scale family planning program in Georgia," by R. W. O'Connor, et al. AMER J PUBLIC HEALTH. 60:78-86, January, 1970.

"Planning better families: education and voluntary control measures have brought Taiwan's population explosion under control even in rural areas where big families are the rule," by Yulin Hsueh. FREE CHINA R. 20:20-22, March, 1970.

"Planning population," by T. Bendixson. TOWN AND COUNTRY PLAN. 38:124, February, 1970.

"Plans for the 1970 census of population and housing," by David L. Kaplan. DEMOGRAPHY. 7:1-18, February, 1970.

"Plans for the 1971 census of Canada." STATIS OBSERVER. 3:3-5, July, 1970.

"Plasma-proteins and oral contraceptives." LANCET. 1:72-73, January 10, 1970.

"Platelet adhesiveness in women using oral contraceptives," by N. Oishi, et al. HAWAII MED J. 29:365-367, May-June, 1970.

"Plea for reconciliation; break between the Archbishop of Washington and his priests." AMERICA. 122:446, April 25, 1970. Reply with rejoinder: by J. C. Ford. 122:571, May 30, 1970.

"A policy for urban growth: Where shall they live?" by James L. Sundquist; "Where shall the money come from?" by Charles M. Haar and Peter A. Lewis. PUBLIC INTEREST. pp. 88-112, Winter, 1970.

"Poliomyelitis surveillance in England and Wales, 1965-1968," by D. L. Miller, et al. PUBLIC HEALTH. 84:265-285, September, 1970.

"Political affiliation and attitudes toward population limitation," by Larry D. Barnett. SOCIAL BIOLOGY. 17:124-131, June, 1970.

"Poll on the pill." NEWSWEEK. 75:52-53, February 9, 1970.

"Pollution: whence and whither," by W. H. Davis. ARCH ENVIRON HEALTH. 21:3-4, July, 1970.

"Polyethylene intrauterine contraceptive device. Endometrial changes following long-term use," by W. B. Ober, et al. JAMA. 212:765-769, May 4, 1970.

"Popollution-are we all guilty? The higher and higher wisdom," by J. Lederberg. CALIF MED. 113:61-62, December, 1970.

"Population alert-a case of control." BSNS MGT. 39:24-29, December, 1970.

"Population and accessibility: an analysis of Turkish railroads," by J. Kolars and H. J. Malin. GEOG R. 60:229-246, April, 1970.

"Population and the dignity of man," by R. L. Shinn. CHR CENT. 87:442-448, April 15, 1970.

"Population and economic change: the emergence of the rice industry in Guyana, 1895-1915," by J. R. Mandle. J ECON HIST. 30:785-801, December, 1970.

"Population and the law: a symposium. Where does individual freedom conflict with a citizen's duty to society and the future of the environment? New role for government?" by R. O. Egeberg; "Incentives for the two-child family," by B. Packwood; "Alternative to the ant-hill society," by M. H. Stans. TRIAL. 6:10, August-September, 1970.

"Population and people," by W. H. Wisely. CIVIL ENG. 40:27, December, 1970.

"Population and the social, political and environmental crisis," by R. B. Ragland. J FLORIDA MED ASS. 57:24-30, October, 1970.

"Population, birth control and West Virginia," by D. T. Allen, et al. W VIRGINIA MED J. 66:167-170, May, 1970.

"Population change and employment policy in India," by S. V. Khandewale. ECON AFFAIRS. 15:229-236, May, 1970.

"Population change and mobility: a case study of an Arkansas state economic area," by D. G. Bennett. LAND ECON. 46:206-208, May, 1970.

"Population change, enclosure, and the early Tudor economy," by I. Blanchard. ECON HIST R. 23:427-445, December, 1970.

"Population change in the Springfield-Chicopee-Holyoke commuter region," by Louis Seig. ROCKY MOUNTAIN SOCIAL SCIENCE J. 7:77-87, April, 1970.

"Population changes in leading metropolitan areas." METROPOLITAN LIFE STAT BUL. 51:5-7, February, 1970.

"Population control in India," by John P. Lewis; comment by Robert Muscat. POPULATION BUL. 26:12-31, November, 1970.

"Population control: the legal approach to a biological imperative." CALIF L REV. 58:1414, November, 1970.

"Population control-a necessity for survival," by S. Pustek. COLO NURSE. 70:18-19 passim, December, 1970.

"Population control, sterilization, and ignorance; results of Cornell university survey," by T. Eisner, et al. SCIENCE. 167:337, January 23, 1970; "Discussion," 168:62, April 3, 1970.

"Population crisis and extremism," by R. B. Kelman. SCIENCE. 168:777, May 15, 1970.

"Population crisis and extremism," by H. H. Suter. SCIENCE. 168:777, May 15, 1970.

"Population density vs. per capita solid waste production," by G. P. Westerhoff and R. M. Gruninger. PUB WORKS. 101:86-87, February, 1970.

"Population development and recent population projection," by Milan Kucera. DEMOSTA. 3:177-183, 1970.

"Population; EQ Index." NAT WILDLIFE. 8:38-39, October, 1970.

"Population; EQ Index." SCHOL TEACH JR/SR HIGH. pp. 14-15, October 5, 1970.

"Population education: a challenge of the seventies." POPULATION BUL. 26:1-40, 1970.

"Population estimates for Texas counties, April 1, 1969," by Benjamin S. Bradshaw. TEX BUS R. 44:77-83, March, 1970.

"Population explosion," by W. G. Heim. AM BIOL TEACH. 32:244, April, 1970.

"Population explosion," by W. P. Mauldin. AM WATER WORKS ASSN J. 62:735-739, December, 1970.

"The population explosion," by W. Veerhusen. MLN BULL. 18:3-5, July, 1970.

"Population explosion falls flat." NATURE. 227:994-995, September 5, 1970.

"Population explosion--impact on business: huge markets will open in the 1970s as the growing numbers of young adults form households; but there will be problems, too, as U. S. becomes more and more crowded." U. S. NEWS. 68:32-34, January 12, 1970.

"Population explosion--a universal threat," by G. Lapointe. INFIRM CANAD. 12:25-28, October, 1970.

"Population growth," by H. C. Wallich. NEWSWEEK. 75:70, June 29; 76:60, August 10, 1970.

"Population growth and economic development," by David R. Kamerschen. SCHWEIZERISCHE ZEITSCHRIFT FUR VOLKSWIRTSCHAFT UND STATISTIK. 106:79-89, March, 1970.

"Population growth and international law," by Alfred C. Kellogg. CORNELL INTERNAT LAW J. 3:93-103, Winter, 1970.

"Population growth and the multi-type Galton-Watson process," by E. Seneta. NATURE. 225:766, February 21, 1970.

"Population growth in Java in the 19th century. A new interpretation," by Bram Peper. POPULATION STUDIES. 24:71-84, March, 1970.

"Population heads for a zero growth rate." BSNS W. pp. 102-104, October 24, 1970.

"Population implications for forecasting highway demand," by Robert W. Paterson. TRAFFIC Q. 24:121-136, January, 1970.

"Population increase and Public Health," by M. I. Kim. KOREAN NURSE. 9:19-24, August 25, 1970.

"Population increase and social norms," by B. M. Chung. KOREAN NURSE. 9:25-26, August 25, 1970.

"Population migration and its evaluation in Lenin's works," by V. V. Pokshishevskii. SOVIET ED. 12:86-100, January, 1970.

"Population migration and the utilization of labor resources," by V. Perevedentsev. CURRENT DIG SOVIET PR. 23:1-6, February 9, 1971. Translated from Voprosy Ekonomiki, September, 1970.

"Population movement in seventeenth century England," by Peter Spufford. LOCAL POPULATION STUDIES MAG. 4:41-50, Spring, 1970.

"The population of Cambodia 1945-1980," by George S. Siampos. MILBANK MEMORIAL FUND Q. 48:317-360, July, 1970.

"Population of London boroughs by sex, age, and marital

status," by Martin Daly. GREATER LONDON RESEARCH Q BULL. 11:28-45, June, 1970.

"The population of tropical Africa in the 1980s," from AFRICA IN THE SEVENTIES AND EIGHTIES. p 247-303, 1970.

"Population overgrowth, the fertile curse," by P. R. Ehrlich. FIELD & S. 75:58+, June, 1970.

"Population package; Family planning services and Population research act of 1970." TIME. 96:36, December 21, 1970.

"Population patterns of the sixties," by Ronald E. Beller. BUS & ECON DIMENSIONS. 6:18-20, January, 1970.

"Population patterns of the sixties," by Ronald E. Beller. FLA ECON INDICATORS. 2:1-2+, January, 1970.

"The population phenomenon: its implications and the growing crisis," by P. M. Hauser. ARIZ R. 19:1-5, June-July, 1970.

"Population policy," by J. Burkinshaw. LANCET. 2:608, September 19, 1970.

"Population policy," by P. W. Gifford. LANCET. 2:463, August 29, 1970.

"Population policy: the crucial factor," by B. Dasgupta. SOUTH ASIAN R. 3:331-346, July, 1970.

"A population policy for Britain," by M. Lancet, et al. HAREFUAH. 78:223-226, March 1, 1970.

"Population pollution," by R. T. Osborne. J PSYCHOL. 76:187-192, November, 1970.

"Population pressure and crop rotational changes among the Tiv of Nigeria," by D. E. Vermeer. ASSN AM GEOG ANN. 60:299-314, June, 1970.

"Population pressure and the social evolution of agriculturalists," by M. J. Harner. SW J ANTHROP. 26:67-86, Spring, 1970.

"Population problem: in search of a solution," by J. J. Spengler. SCIENCE. 167:1438-1439, March 13, 1970.

"Population problems," by J. M. Yang. KOREAN NURSE. 9:12-18, August 25, 1970.

"Population projections [comparing distribution of ages of mortgagors with the various age groups in the United States population, 1950-1990]." REAL ESTATE ANALYST. 39:417-433, October 26, 1970.

"The population question in Northeast Brazil: its economic and ideological dimensions," by Herman E. Daly. ECON DEVELOPMENT & CULTURAL CHANGE. 18: 536-574, July, 1970.

"Population residing in the United States, 1790 to 1970." METROPOLITAN LIFE STAT BUL. 51:2, January, 1970.

"Population rocket," by B. Schlesinger. CHATELAINE. 43:10, September 12, 1970.

"Population strategy," by A. W. Smith. NAT PARKS. 44:2, February, 1970.

"Population survey for detection of frank and latent diabetes in one part of Cuttack, Orissa," by B. B. Tripathy, et al. J INDIAN MED ASS. 54:55-61, January 16, 1970.

"Population: time to put the brake on," by Gerald Leach. OBSERVER. 29:11, November, 1970.

"Population trends in an Indian village," by C. E. Taylor. SCI AMER. 223:106-112 passim, July, 1970.

"Population; where have all the babies gone?" ECONOMIST. 234:22+, February 21, 1970.

"Portrait of a decade," by D. H. Wrong. N Y TIMES MAG. pp. 22-23+, August 2, 1970.

"A possible mechanism for hypertension induced by oral contraceptives. Diminished feedback suppression of renin release," by T. Saruta, et al. ARCH INTERN MED. 126:621-626, October, 1970.

"Postcoital contraception," by C. W. Emmens. BRIT MED BULL. 26:45-51, January, 1970.

"Postcoital contraception," by J. M. Morris. ANN INTERN MED. 73:656, October, 1970.

"Postnatal family planning at St. Mary's Hospital and Westminster Welfare Centre, London," by A. W. Giles. MIDWIVES CHRON. 83:346-347, October, 1970.

"Postoperative thromboembolism and the use of oral contraceptives," by M. P. Vessey, et al. BRIT MED J. 3:123-126, July 18, 1970.

"Powell, the minorities, and the 1970 election," by Nicholas Deakin and Jenny Bourne. POL Q. 41:399-415, October-December, 1970.

"Power-politics and population," by P. M. Sharma. UNITED ASIA. 22:28-34, January-February, 1970.

"A pox on the Pill." JAMA. 213:1481, August 31, 1970.

"The predicament of mankind," by Aurelio Peccei. SUCCESSO. 12:149-156, June, 1970.

"Predicting ovulation-a reply," by C. S. Marwick, et al. SCIENCE. 169:717, August 21, 1970.

"Prediction in family planning. Factors associated with involvement of low-income women in a public family planning program," by E. Siegel, et al. AMER J PUBLIC HEALTH. 60:1382-1394, August, 1970.

"Prediction in family planning. Prediction of the adoption and continued use of contraception," by D. McCalister, et al. AMER J PUBLIC HEALTH. 60:1372-1381, August, 1970.

"Predominance of male authors in social work publications," by A. Rosenblatt, et al. SOC CASEWORK. 51:421-430, July, 1970.

"Pregnancy and chlormadinone acetate," by G. R. Daniel. BRIT MED J. 1:174-175, January 17, 1970.

"Pregnancy and delivery with an intrauterine contraceptive device in situ. An analysis of 44 cases," by P. Damsgaard-Sorensen, et al. UGESKR LAEG. 132:736-738, April 16, 1970.

"Premarital pregnancy and status before and after marriage," by L. C. Coombs et al. AM J SOCIOL. 75:800-820, March, 1970.

"Premarital sex as deviant behavior: an application of current approaches to deviance," by I. L. Reiss. AM SOCIOL R. 35:78-87, February, 1970.

"Premarital sexual experience among coeds, 1958 and 1968," by R. R. Bell and J. B. Chaskes. J MARRIAGE & FAM. 32:81-84, February, 1970.

"Pre-pregnancy care-a logical extension of prenatal care," by R. F. Friesen. CAN MED ASSOC J. 103: 495-497, September 12, 1970.

"President Nixon is wrong," by J. Kettle. MON TIMES. 138:22-23, April, 1970.

"Presidential address: 7th National Conference of the Indian Academy of Pediatrics," by J. N. Pohowalla. INDIAN PEDIATR. 7:4-7, January, 1970.

"Prevention of pregnancy in the rabbit by subcutaneous implantation of silastic tube containing oestrogen," by M. C. Chang, et al. NATURE. 226:1262-1263, June 27, 1970.

"Preview of the 1970 census. STATIST BULL METROP LIFE INSUR CO. 51:2-4, January, 1970.

"Primary drug resistance: a continuing study of drug resistance in tuberculosis in a veteran population within the United States. VII. September 1965 to September 1969," by G. L. Hobby, et al. AMER REV RESP DIS. 102:347-355, September, 1970.

"Primary sex-ratio and size of family," by M. H. Shokeir. LANCET. 1:245, January 31, 1970.

"Primate populations and biomedical research," by C. H. Southwick, et al. SCIENCE. 170:1051-1054, December 4, 1970.

"Principle of population as political theory; Godwin's Of population and the Malthusian controversy," by F. Rosen. J HIST IDEAS. 31:33-48, January, 1970.

"The problem of birth control. Need for deeper research on numerous aspects of the problem," by A. Barraciu. MINERVA MED. 61:Suppl 59-60+, July-August, 1970.

"The problem of cot deaths." ULSTER COMMENTARY. 293:4-5, September, 1970.

"Problem of the people bomb." SR SCHOL. 97:19-20, September 28, 1970.

"The problem of speech disorders and their psychosocial aspects," by L. Rubinato, et al. MINERVA PEDIATR. 22:2271-2272, November 17, 1970.

"Problems concerning oral contraception," by A. Salvati, et al. MINERVA MED. 61:Suppl.43:10-12, May, 1970.

"Problems in industry," by S. J. Vaughan. OCCUP HLTH. 22:151+, May, 1970.

"Problems of economic demography," by B. Urlanis. PROBLEMS ECON. 13:69-89, January, 1971; translated from VOPROSY EKONOMIKI, no. 5, 1970.

"Problems of expanding populations," by D. Wolfers. NATURE. 225:593-597, February 14, 1970.

"Problems of health and development," by A. A. Angara. BULL INFIRM CATH CANADA. 37:133-144, May-August, 1970.

"Problems of population pressure in tropical Africa," by Robert W. Steel. INST BRITISH GEOGRAPHERS TRANSACTIONS. pp. 1-13, March, 1970.

"Problems of rural-urban migration: some suggestions for investigation," by D. Warriner. INT LAB R. 101:441-451, May, 1970.

"Process of cultural stripping and reintegration: the rural migrant in the city," by M. Leeds; with reply by L. E. Gary and rejoinder. J AM FOLKLORE. 83:259-270, April, 1970.

"Procreation and the future of mankind. Implications of artificial insemination," by H. Muramatsu. KANGO KYOSHITSU. 14:28-31, August, 1970.

"Product pushers vs. the people," by C. F. Wurster. FIELD & S. 75:60+, June, 1970.

"Profile of our children." STATIST BULL METROP LIFE INSUR CO. 51:10-11, July, 1970.

"Profiles of American youth, ages 14-24, 1950-1969,

with projections to 1980." METROPOLITAN LIFE STATIS BUL. 51:4-7, November, 1970.

"Profit from 1970 census data: more refined data available on computer tapes can bring users greater rewards," by A. R. Eckler. HARVARD BUS R. 48: 4-6+, July-August, 1970.

"Prognosis for the development of new chemical birth-control agents," by C. Djerassi. SCIENCE. 166: 468-473, October 24, 1969; Discussion, P. A. Corfman. 167:1315; Reply. 1315-1316, March 6, 1970.

"Program for a farm population data base; the 1971 census," by R. P. Shaw; "A master sampling plan for Canadian agriculture," by J. E. Graham. CAN J AGRIC ECON. 18:60-73, July, 1970.

"Program of the Data access and use laboratory, U. S. Bureau of the Census," by Benjamin Gura. STATIS REPORTER. pp. 1-7, July, 1970.

"A program of indigent obstetric care and planned parenthood in a rural North Carolina county," by J. E. Clement. AMER J OBSTET GYNEC. 108:63-67, September 1, 1970.

"Progress in contraception," by M. Vojta. CESK GYNEK. 35:129-130, March, 1970.

"Progressive inhibition of uterine sensitivity in rats fitted with intra-uterine sutures," by J. C. Wood, et al. J REPROD FERTIL. 22:339-343, July, 1970.

"Projected effects of family planning on the incidence of perinatal mortality in a lower-class nonwhite population," by D. V. McCalister, et al. AMER J OBSTET GYNEC. 106:573-580, February 15, 1970.

"Projections of the growth of the coloured immigrant population of England and Wales," by C. J. Thomas. J BIOSOC SCI. 2:265-281, July, 1970.

"Proliferation of the species." NATUR HIST. 79:50-51, January, 1970.

"Prolonged amenorrhea following oral contraception," by B. A. Hayes, Jr. N CAROLINA MED J. 31:352-354, September, 1970.

"Promiscuity and contraception in a sample of patients
attending a clinic for venereal diseases," by A.
Linken, et al. BRIT J VENER DIS. 46:243-246,
June, 1970.

"Prophylactic tubal sterilization," by C. Colmeiro-
Laforet. ACTA OBSTET GINECOL HISP LUSIT. 18:263-
278, November, 1970.

"A proposed new vital event numeration unitary system
for developed countries," by F. E. Linder. MILBANK
MEM FUND Q. 48:Suppl 77-87, October, 1970.

"Proposed package insert for the pill," by D. Wickware.
AM DRUGGIST. 161:12-14+, March 23, 1970.

"Proposition d'un indice de jeunesse: methode et application a Montreal; avec commentaire "A propos
d'indices simplifies de la structure par age", par
Hubert Charbonneau," by M. Pruvot. R DE GEOG DE
MONTREAL. 24,1:96-99; 4:457-459, 1970.

"Pros and cons of oral contraceptives," by D. Deer.
J KANSAS MED SOC. 71:43-49, February, 1970.

"Proselytizers for prophylactics; Population services,
inc. promotes condoms." TIME. 96:97+, December 7,
1970.

"The prospects for zero population growth," by Richard
A. Engels. TENN SURVEY BUS. 5:3-6+, August, 1970.

"Pseudopregnancy Treatment of periodic psychiatric
illness: a pilot study," by I D. Glick, et al.
PSYCHIATR Q. Suppl 44:403-407, 1970.

"Psychiatric care: Patients isolated from society
during treatment time," by L. Gustafsson. LAKARTID-
NINGEN. 67:704-708, February 11, 1970.

"Psychoendocrine study of oral contraceptive agents,"
by F. J. Kane, et al. AMER J PSYCHIAT. 127:443-
450, October, 1970.

"Psychologic aspects of the basal body temperature
method of regulating births," by J. Marshall, et al.
FERTIL STERIL. 21:14-19, January, 1970.

"Psychological aspects of oral contraceptives," by F.
J. Huygens. NEDERL T GENEESK. 114:1436, August 22,
1970.

"Psychological aspects of oral contraceptives," by F. J. Huygens. NED TIJDSCHR VERLOSKD GYNAECOL. 70:610-617, December, 1970.

"Psychological aspects of the use of anovulatory agents," by Y. Rouleau, et al. CANAD PSYCHIAT ASS J. 15:295-300, June, 1970.

"Psychological disturbance and oral contraceptives." LANCET. 1:1378, June 27, 1970.

"Psychological sources of resistance to family planning," by A. B. Keller, et al. MERRILL-PALMER Q. 16:286-302, July, 1970.

"Psychomotor assessment and rehabilitation of socioculturally deprived children," by H. Feldmann. ACTA PAEDOPSYCHIATR. 37:268-293, December, 1970.

"Psychopathology of the pill." CANAD MED ASS J. 102:217, January 31, 1970.

"Psychophysiologic changes accompanying oral contraceptive use," by D. B. Marcotte, et al. BRIT J PSYCHIAT. 116:165-167, February, 1970.

"Psychosocial studies in family planning behavior in Central and Eastern Europe. A preliminary report of a developing program," by H. P. David. J PSYCHIATR NURS. 8:28-33, September-October, 1970.

"Psychosomatic effects of ovulation inhibitors," by H. J. Prill. GEBURTSH FRAUENHEILK. 30:212-224, March, 1970.

"Putting the 1970 census of population to use," by Charlotte R. Menke. ECON LEAFLETS. 29:1-4, January, 1970.

"Pyridoxine and oral contraceptives," by A. L. Luhby, et al. LANCET. 2:1083, November 21, 1970.

"Pyridoxine and the pill," by M. J. Baumblatt, et al. LANCET. 1:832-833, April 18, 1970.

Q

"Qualitative and quantitative problems in generation," by R. H. Williams. NORTHWEST MED. 69:92-93, February, 1970.

"Qualitative and quantitative problems in generation," by R. H. Williams. NORTHWEST MED. 69:497-501, July, 1970.

"Quality of life; a proposed program for global action by the UN; address, April 21, 1970," by R. N. Gardner. VITAL SPEECHES. 36:466-470, May 15, 1970.

"A question of numbers," by Alma Birk. TIMES. p. 5, July 27, 1970.

R

"R.C.O.G. statement on oral contraceptives," by T. N. Jeffcoate. BRIT MED J. 1:293, May 2, 1970.

"Rabbit uterine contractile activity in the presence of an intrauterine device," by D. K. Michael, et al. AMER J OBSTET GYNEC. 107:188-193, May 15, 1970.

"The race toward misery," by David T. Rogers, Jr. ALA BUS. 41:1-3+, October 15, 1970.

"Radical changes in migration." REAL ESTATE ANALYST. 39:35-37, January 28, 1970.

"Rapid disruption of sperm transport mechanisms by intra-uterine devices in the ewe," by H. W. Hawk. J REPROD FERTIL. 23:139-142, October, 1970.

"Rate of plasma protein normalization after parturition and withdrawal of oral contraceptives," by C. B. Laurell, et al. SCAND J CLIN LAB INVEST. 26:345-348, December, 1970.

"Raynaud-like clinical picture during the treatment with an oral contraceptive," by H. Ebert. DTSCH GESUNDHEITSW. 25:1642-1643, August 27, 1970.

"Reactions of human endometrium to the intrauterine

device. I. Correlation of the endometrial histology with the bacterial environment of the uterus following short-term insertion of the IUD," by D. L. Moyer, et al. AMER J OBSTET GYNEC. 106:799-809, March 15, 1970.

"The reader asks to be told: on migration of the population," by V. Boldyrev. CURRENT DIG SOVIET PR. 22:18-19, September 22, 1970. Translated and condensed from PRAVDA. August 22, 1970.

"Recalling a pill; chlormadinone." TIME. 95:39, February 9, 1970.

"Recent advances in surgical methods of control of fertility and infertility," by P. C. Steptoe. BRIT MED BULL. 26:60-64, January, 1970.

"Recent mortality from cerebral vascular diseases." METROPOLITAN LIFE STAT BUL. 51:5-7, September, 1970.

"Recent mortality trends for emphysema and other chronic respiratory diseases." METROPOLITAN LIFE STAT BUL. 51:2-6, August, 1970.

"Recent progress on systemic contraceptives," by S. Matsumoto. ACTA OBSTET GYNAEC JAP. 17:211-219, July, 1970.

"Recent results of the sterilization of women by the Madlener's method," by J. Higier, et al. WIAD LEK. 23:637-640, April 15, 1970.

"Recent trends in infant and maternal health in Minnesota," by A. B. Rosenfield, et al. MINN MED. 53:807-816, July, 1970.

"Recent trends in pharmacologic contraception," by L. Gregoire. REV MED LIEGE. 25:224-225, April 1, 1970.

"Recurrent polyneuropathy with pregnancy and oral contraceptives," by R. Calderon-Gonzalez, et al. NEW ENG J MED. 282:1307-1308, June 4, 1970.

"Red man's plight: urban Indians, driven to cities by poverty, find harsh existence," by Barbara Isenberg. WALL ST J. 175:1+, March 9, 1970.

"Reduced population growth as related to the urbanization process: Medellin, Colombia," by C. L. Marshall, et al. CLIN PEDIATR. 9:736-741, December, 1970.

"Reducing the environmental impact of population growth," by S. F. Singer. SCIENCE. 169:1233, September 18, 1970.

"Reduction of plasma tyrosine by oral contraceptives and oestrogens: a possible consequence of tyrosine aminotransferase induction," by D. P. Rose, et al. CLIN CHIM ACTA. 29:49-53, July, 1970.

"Re-examination of some recent criticisms of transition theory," by K. C. W. Kammeyer. SOCIOL Q. 11:500-510, Fall, 1970.

"Regional aspects of the 1969 Uganda census," by Stephen R. Taber. EAST AFRICAN GEOG R. pp. 78-80, April, 1970.

"Regional population geography of the northeastern United States," by M. P. Donahue. GEOG R. 60:566-568, October, 1970.

"Regionalization of population densities in Kansas," by R. T. Aangeenbrug and F. C. Caspall. TIJDSCHRIFT VOOR ECONOMISCHE EN SOCIALE GEOGRAFIE. 61:85-90, March-April, 1970.

"Regression of cerebral lesions after cessation of oral contraceptives," by H. R. McFarland. SOUTHERN MED J. 63:145-151, February, 1970.

"Regulation of birth rate in Bulgaria as a social experiment," by D. Sepetliev, et al. AKUSH GINEKOL. 9:115-123, 1970.

"A rejoinder to Miss Spencer's comments on pre-marital pregnancies and ex-nuptial births in Australia, 1911-1966," by K. G. Basavarajappa. AUSTRALIAN AND NEW ZEALAND J OF SOCIOLOGY. 6,1:79-84, 1970. (SA #E9003)

"Relation between estrogen content and the risk of thromboembolism in peroral contraception." UGESKR LAEG. 132:846, April 30, 1970.

"The relation of migration to regional unemployment,"

by Bruce D. Phillips. AM ECONOMIST. 14:26-42, Fall, 1970.

"The relationship between endometrial mast cell count and bleeding in women following insertion of an intrauterine device," by U. Mehra, et al. AMER J OBSTET GYNEC. 107:852-856, July 15, 1970.

"Relationship of family planning to pediatrics and child health," by H. M. Wallace, et al. CLIN PEDIATR. 9:699-701, December, 1970.

"Relationships among population, income and retail sales in SMSAs, 1952-1966," by B. C. Liu. Q R ECON & BUS. 10:25-40, Spring, 1970.

"The relative importance of selected behavioral characteristics of group members in an extreme environment," by R. E. Doll, et al. J PSYCHOL. 75:231-237, July, 1970.

"Religiosity and premarital sexual permissiveness: reexamination of Reiss's traditionalism proposition," by M. E. Heltsley and C. B. Broderick. "Discussion," 32:647-655, November, 1970.

"Religious and moral aspects of population control," by H. L. Smith. RELIG IN LIFE. 39:193-204, Summer, 1970.

"The removal method for two and three samples," by G. A. Seber, et al. BIOMETRICS. 26:393-400, September, 1970.

"Removal of barriers to family planning." WIEN MED WOCHENSCHR. 120:129, May 2, 1970.

"Removal of Lippes loop through laparoscope," by M. O. Farooqui, et al. PRACTITIONER. 205:65-66, July, 1970.

"Rep. Rogers calls for restrictions on pill advertising." ADV AGE. 41:3, April 13, 1970.

"A report from the Australian drug evaluation committee: oral contraceptives and thromboembolic disease." MED J AUST. 1:1267-1269, June 20, 1970.

"Reproduction and astrology," by M. Vojta. CESK GYNEK. 35:38-40, February, 1970.

"Reproductive revolution," by R. D. Lamm. ABA J. 56:41. January, 1970.

"Research techniques in structure planning experience from the South Hampshire plan: the design and calibration of a population projection model," by M. K. Francis and P. F. Menczer. TOWN PLAN INST J. 56:216-220, June, 1970.

"Reserving a womb: case for the small family," by E. J. Lieberman. AMER J PUBLIC HEALTH. 60:87-92, January, 1970.

"Reversal of sterilization in the female," by G. Williams. NURS J INDIA. 61:145+, May, 1970.

"Reversibility of ovarian function and general management," by L. A. Joosse. NEDERL T GENEESK. 114:1434-1436, August 22, 1970.

"Reversibility of ovarian function and general supervision," by L. A. Joosse. NED TIJDSCHR VERLOSKD GYNAECOL. 70:604-610, December, 1970.

"Reversing the brain drain: a case study from India," by M. F. Merriam. INTERNAT DEVELOPMENT R. 12:16-22, November 3, 1970.

"Review of the current status of research in steroid contraception," by M. Vojta. CESK GYNEKOL. 35:431-433, September, 1970.

"Review of the demographic levels and trends in Africa and their impact on the economic development of the region," by A. K. M. Zirky. L'EGYPTE CONTEMPORAINE. 61:351-374, October, 1970.

"Review of side effects of oral contraceptives," by J. Janssens. NEDERL T GENEESK. 114:1418-1422, August 22, 1970.

"Rhythm method doubted." SCI DIGEST. 67:73, May, 1970.

"Richter's hernia resulting from displaced intrauterine contraceptive device," by G. F. Schwartz, et al. AMER SURG. 36:502-504, August, 1970.

"The right to live," by J. Stallworthy. J ROY COLL GEN PRACT. 19:187-190, April, 1970.

"Rising population: its effect on environment," by S. J. McNaughton." CONS. 24:14-16, June, 1970.

"Role of drug-reaction monitoring in the investigation of thrombosis and "the pill"," by W. H. Inman. BR MED BULL. 26:248-256, September, 1970.

"The role of family planning in prevention of pregnancy wastage," by E. M. Gold, et al. CLIN OBSTET GYNEC. 13:145-156, March, 1970.

"Role of operations research in population planning," by W. A. Reinke. OP RES. 18:1099-1111, November, 1970.

"The role of the pharmacist in family planning," by N. N. Wagner, et al. J AMER PHARM ASS. 10:258-260, May, 1970.

"Rural slums or rural desert?" by M. Hederman. INTERPLAY. 3:23-26, June, 1970.

"Rural-urban migration: a clue to rural-urban relations in India," by C. R. Prasada Rao. INDIAN J SOCIAL WORK. 30:335-342, January, 1970.

"Russia is growing up-but not fast enough; baby shortage." ECONOMIST. 235:43-44, May 2, 1970.

"Russia takes a census-what it shows." U S NEWS. 68:50-51, May 18, 1970.

S

"SC11800 sequential paper," by M. G. Tompkins. FERTIL STERIL. 21:77-79, January, 1970.

"Safeguarding the quality of life." AMERICA. 122:548, May 23, 1970.

"Safety of oral contraception," by L. Mastroianni, Jr. FERTIL STERIL. 21:281, March, 1970.

"Safety of oral contraceptives," by J. Frankenberg. BRIT MED J. 1:285, August 1, 1970.

"Safety of the pill," by J. Infield. BRIT MED J. 1:294, May 2, 1970.

"Sagittal sinus thrombosis related to oral contraceptives. Case report," by M. C. Shende, et al. J NEUROSURG. 33:714-717, December, 1970.

"Schmid plans first national ads for prophylactic brands." ADV AGE. 41:6, March 16, 1970.

"Science, Birth Control, and the Roman Catholic Church," by J. J. Baker. BIOSCIENCE. 20,3:143-150, February, 1970.

"Scientist looks at the human zoo," by D. Morris. U S NEWS. 68:38, March 2, 1970.

"Search for a preparation to prevent venereal disease and pregnancy," by R. C. Arnold, et al. PUBLIC HEALTH REP. 85:1062, December, 1970.

"Searching of truth on abortion," by E. Hervet. GYNEC OBSTET. 69:287-295, May-July, 1970.

"Seasonal variations in the blood corticosterone level in animals kept in groups and in isolation," E. V. Naumenko, et al. DOKL AKAD NAUK SSSR. 195:750-752, 1970.

"Seasonal variations in infant mortality in Belgium," by R. Andre, et al. REVUE DE L'INSTITUT DE SOCIOLOGIE. 3:587-598, 1970. (SA #F0121)

"2nd generation IUDs are here," by H. Goldstein. AM DRUGGIST. 162:37-39, November 2, 1970.

"Second-guessing the census takers." BSNS W. p. 86, September 19, 1970.

"Second trimester foetal death associated with an intra-uterine contraceptive device," by E. Tischler, et al. MED J AUST. 1:441-442, February 28, 1970.

"Sees OC pill needing no Rx in 5 years." AM DRUGGIST. 161:39, June 1, 1970.

"A self-regulating system of human population control," by L. Thompson. TRANS NY ACAD SCI. 32:262-270, February, 1970.

"Semen examinations after vasectomy," by J. G. Temple. et al. LANCET. 2:1258, December 12, 1970.

"Sensory deprivation versus sensory variation," by M. Zuckerman, et al. J ABNORM PSYCHOL. 76:76-82, August, 1970.

"Serious sequelae of intrauterine contraceptive devices," by G. F. Schwartz, et al. JAMA. 211:959-960, February 9, 1970.

"Serum fucose levels during pregnancy and while taking oral contraceptives," by W. N. Spellacy, et al. OBSTET GYNEC. 35:39-43, January, 1970.

"The serum level of immunoreactive LH in intact and spayed androgen-sterilized rats," by A. P. Labhsetwar. J REPROD FERTIL. 23:349-352, November, 1970.

"The serum levels of nonesterified fatty acids and free amino acids under the effect of the oral contraceptive, Ovosiston," by H. D. Methfessel, et al. Z AERZTL FORTBILD. 64:880-882, September 1, 1970.

"Serum lipids during oral contraceptive exposure," by D. G. Corredor, et al. CLIN PHARMACOL THER. 11:188-193, March-April, 1970.

"Serum protein-(Xh)-changes in pregnancy and use of ovulation inhibitions in women and men," by G. Geserick, et al. ZENTRALBL GYNAEKOL. 92:1195-1200, September 12, 1970.

"Settlement patterns of Canadian emigrants to the United States, 1850-1960; with French summary," by R. K. Vedder and L. E. Gallaway. CAN J ECON. 3:476-486, August, 1970.

"'70 census: the final figures." U S NEWS. 69:31, December 14, 1970.

"The '70 census: how many Americans and where they are. How states have changed in the past decade." U S NEWS. 69:22-25, September 14, 1970.

"The '70 census: rich new data source for retailers," by C. E. Treas. MISSISSIPPI'S BUS. 28:1-5, February, 1970.

"Severe arterial hypertension, stenosis of the renal artery, a disorder of glycoregulation and the contraceptive pill," by H. Bour, et al. COEUR MED INTERN. 9:239-243, April, 1970.

"Sex education hits the British airwaves." ATLAS. 19:16, April, 1970.

"Sex education in New Orleans: the Birchers win a victory," by D. R. Mackintosh, et al. NEW SOUTH. 25:46-56, Summer, 1970.

"Sex Education: A Key to the Population Crisis," by W. G. Peter. BIOSCIENCE. 20,3:173-174, February, 1970.

"Sex-role identity and pragmatic action," by W. Bezdek and F. L. Strodtbeck. AM SOCIOL R. 35:491-502, June, 1970.

"Sexual attitudes of Thai students: an exploratory cross-cultural study," by J. Wohl and A. Dunlop. HUMAN ORGAN. 29:190-196, Fall, 1970.

"Sexual inversion among the Azande," by E. E. Evans-Pritchard. AM ANTHROP. 72:1428-1434, December, 1970.

"Sexual responsibility in our permissive society-is it just an impossible dream?" by D. Evagorou. NURS TIMES. 66:628, May 14, 1970.

"Sexual revolution; myth or reality," by R. L. Worsnop. EDITORIAL RESEARCH REPORTS. 241:58, April 1, 1970.

"Sexual sterilization for non-medical reasons." CANAD MED ASS J. 102:211, January 31, 1970.

"Sexual sterilization, legal position of a doctor," by I. Maxwell. NOVA SCOTIA MED BULL. 49:18, February, 1970.

"Sexuality, contraception and the mentally retarded," by B. Fujita, et al. POSTGRAD MED. 47:193-197, May, 1970.

"The shape of things to come," by E. H. Hutten. HUMANIST. 85:182-183, June, 1970.

"The shield intrauterine device. A superior modern

contraceptive," by H. J. Davis. AMER J OBSTET GYNEC. 106:455-456, February 1, 1970.

"A short run model of inter-regional migration," by A. B. Jack. MANCHESTER SCHOOL OF ECONOMIC AND SOCIAL STUDIES. 38:15-28, March, 1970.

"Should P-pills be prescribed for teenagers?" by P. Bergsjo. T NORSK LAEGEFOREN. 90:1711-1712, September 15, 1970.

"Should public policy give incentives to welfare mothers to limit the number of their children?" by N. Dembitz; "A dissenting viewpoint," by H. F. Pilpel. FAMILY L Q. 4:130, June, 1970.

"Should teenagers be given contraceptive pills?" by B. Dahlberg. LAKARTIDNINGEN. 67:1453-1456, March 25, 1970.

"Side effect: pill sales slump." CHEM W. 106:26, April 1. 1970.

"Side effects of contraceptive drugs," by W. E. Schreiner. SCHWEIZ MED WOCHENSCHR. 100:778-784, May 2, 1970.

"Side effects of contraceptive steroids. I," by E. J. Plotz. GEBURTSH FRAUENHEILK. 30:193-211, March, 1970.

"Side effects of contraceptive steroids. II," by E. J. Plotz. GEBURTSH FRAUENHEILK. 30:362-379, April, 1970.

"Side effects of contraceptives (review of the literature)," by I. V. Skorodumova. AKUSH GINEKOL. 46:41-46, March, 1970.

"Side effects of the oral contraceptive Ovosiston on the blood coagulation system," by W. Carol, et al. ZENTRALBL GYNAEKOL. 92:1641-1650, December 12, 1970.

"Side effects of synthetic progestagens," by L. A. De Luca. REV PAUL MED. 76:34-36, March, 1970.

"A simple technique of re-anastomosis after vasectomy," by K. C. Mehta, et al. BRIT J UROL. 42:340-343, June, 1970.

"The Singapore Family Planning Program: further
evaluation data," by D. Wolfers. AM J PUBLIC
HEALTH. 60:2354-2360, December, 1970.

"Single monthly injection for contraception," by J.
Artner, et al. GEBURTSHILFE FRAUENHEILKD. 30:
554-564, June, 1970.

"61st decree of the Council of Ministers on birth
rate and its results during the past 2 years,"
by G. Stoimenov, et al. AKUSH GINEKOL. 9:331-
336, 1970.

"Size and structure of the household in England over
three centuries; a comment," by J. W. Nixon.
POPULATION STUDIES. 24:445-447, November, 1970.

"Small-for-dates babies and the pill," by K. J.
Dennis. LANCET. 1:195, January 24, 1970,

"Small-town population change and distance from larger towns: a replication of Hassinger's study,"
by J. E. Butler and G. V. Fuguitt. RURAL SOCIOL.
35:396-409, September, 1970.

"Smaller families: a national imperative," by G. J.
Hecht. PARENTS MAG. 45:24+, July, 1970.

"Smoking, air pollution, bronchitis, and population
mobility," by R. M. Acheson, et al. LANCET.
760:1340-1341, June 20, 1970.

"Social class and premarital sexual permissiveness:
a subsequent test," by G. M. Maranell, et al.
J MARRIAGE & FAM. 32:85-88, February, 1970.

"Social deprivation, housing density, and gregariousness in rats," by B. Latane, et al. J COMP
PHYSIOL PSYCHOL. 70:221-227, February, 1970.

"The social ecology of hyper-fertility," by D. M.
Recio. ANPHI PAP. 5:16-23, April-June, 1970.

"Social isolates and urbanites in perceptual isolation," by A. As, et al. J ABNORM PSYCHOL. 76:
1-9, August, 1970.

"Social isolation, activeness and leisure reading
among the blind," by S. S. Guterman. SOC SCI

MED. 3:349-361, January, 1970.

"Social isolation and bereavement," by F. G. Wilson. LANCET. 2:1356-1357, December 26, 1970.

"Social nutrition and malnutrition," by L. Havens. ARCH INTERN MED. 126:198 passim, August, 1970.

"Social planning for the family," by R. Dore. J OF DEVELOPMENT STUDIES. 6:57-66, July, 1970.

"Social research and privileged data," by U. L. Val. REV. 4:368, Spring, 1970.

"Socio-economic status and family planning knowledge, attitudes and practices in rural East Pakistan," by J. Stoeckel. SOCIAL & ECON STUDIES. 19:213-225, June, 1970.

"Sociological problems of sexual morality," by S. I. Golod. SOVIET R. 11:127-147, Summer, 1970.

"Solitude and transference: a study on character neuroses," by M. Neyraut. REV FR PSYCHANAL. 34:81-100, January, 1970.

"Some aspects of immigration into the Glamorgan coalfield between 1881 and 1911," by P. N. Jones. HONOURABLE SOC OF CYMMRODORION TRANS. 1969 SESSION PART I. pp. 82-98, 1970.

"Some aspects of the interaction between natural and synthetic female sex hormones and the liver," by H. Adlercreutz, et al. AM J MED. 49:630-648, November, 1970.

"Some aspects of the nonagenarian's environment," by F. W. Wigzell. GERONT CLIN. 12:175-185, 1970.

"Some correlates of extramarital coitus," by R. E. Johnson. J MARRIAGE & FAM. 32:449-456, August, 1970.

"Some economic aspects of Norwegian population movements 1740-1940: an econometric study," by T. Moe. J ECON HIST. 30:267-270; 285-287, March, 1970.

"Some international implications of environmental challenges," by L. Hartley. ATLAN COM Q. 8:234-241, Summer, 1970.

"Some methodological aspects of the 1971 census in Canada," by T. G. Beynon, et al. CAN J ECON. 3:95-110, February, 1970.

"Some obstacles to family planning in India," by P. Singh. ECON AFFAIRS. 15:293-303, August, 1970.

"Some relations between social isolation and communicable diseases," by F. D. Schofield. AMER J TROP MED. 19:167-169, January, 1970.

"Some remarks on factors influencing the failure of intra-uterine devices," by A. Sadovsky, et al. HAREFUAH. 78:247-248, March 1, 1970.

"Some variations in the normal haemoglobin concentration," by J. M. Cruickshank. BRIT J HAEMAT. 18:523-529, May, 1970.

"The Soviet census." NEW TIMES. pp. 13-14. January 13, 1970.

"Spiralists: their careers and family lives," by S. Edgell. BRIT J OF SOCIOLOGY. 21:314-323, September, 1970.

"The spread of anti-natal knowledge and practice in Nigeria," by J. C. Caldwell and A. I. Igun. POPULATION STUDIES. 24:21-34, March, 1970.

"Stabilising the population," by R. Haughton. MONTH. 2:150-151, November, 1970.

"Stability of steady distributions of asocial populations dispersing in one dimension," by E. Bradford, et al. J THEOR BIOL. 29:13-26, October, 1970.

"Starvation or plenty? by C. Clark. A review." NAT R. 22:631-632, June 16, 1970.

"The state: an ecological phenomenon." JAMA. 214:905, November 2, 1970.

"Statement on the thromboembolic risk while taking

oral contraceptives," by H. Rozenbaum. THERA-
PEUTIQUE. 46:439-441, April, 1970.

"Statistical and sociological aspects after sterilization surgery," by H. E. Schneider. GEBURTSHILFE FRAUENHEILKD. 30:1064-1070, December, 1970.

"Statistical observations on IUD in the Tokyo Teishin Hospital," by I. Fuchi. SANFUJIN JISSAI. 19:44-50, January, 1970.

"Stemming the tide of rural migration," by W. Eustis. MINN MUNIC. 55:344-345+, November, 1970.

"Sterilization," by J. S. Scott. LANCET. 2:417, August 22, 1970.

"Sterilization, an alternative to contraceptive pills," by G. Berggren. LAKARTIDNINGEN. 67:348-350, January 21, 1970.

"Sterilization and family planning," by M. Elstein. PRACTITIONER. 205:30-37, July, 1970.

"Sterilization as legitimate medical task," by R. Hellmann. MED WELT. 1:41-47, January 3, 1970.

"Sterilization by ovariotexy, a reversible technic," by C. Wood, et al. GYNECOL PRAT. 21:299-305, 1970.

"Sterilization for both sexes; vasectomy and new gynecological technique called laparoscopy." TIME. 95:33, June 1, 1970.

"Sterilization in India. The pill: daily bread. Cold demographic calculation should prevail over every other sentiment," by A. Fiore. MINERVA MED SUPPL. 78:20-24, September 25, 1970.

"Sterilization of the fallopian tubes by electrocoagulation of the isthmus under celioscopy," by J. Thoyer-Rozat, et al. BULL FED GYNEC OBSTET FRANC. 22:11-13, January-March, 1970.

"Sterilization of fallopian tubes during laparoscopy," by M. Vojta. CESK GYNEKOL. 35:602-603, December, 1970.

"Sterilization of women," by L. N. Jackson. LANCET. 2:463, August 29, 1970.

"Sterilization of women," by E. A. Williams. LANCET. 2:361, August 15, 1970.

"Sterilization of women," by G. F. Williams. LANCET. 2:608, September 19, 1970.

"Sterilization of women in the light of Polish legislation," by W. Wieszczycki, et al. GINEKOL POL. 41:1153-1156, October, 1970.

"Sterilizing doses of gamma irradiation for the imported cabbageworm, Pieris rapae, and effects on longevity, mating, and fecundity," by H. M. Flint, et al. J ECON ENTOM. 63:1008-1009, June, 1970.

"Steroid contraceptives," by R. L. Vande Wiele. GYNECOL INVEST. 1:Suppl:55-68, 1970.

"Steroidal conception. Statement by the IPPF central medical committee." (International Planned Parenthood Federation). SA NURS J. 37:17-18 passim, July, 1970.

"Stimulation by ovarian hormones and intrauterine devices of vascular function in the endometrium of the ewe," by B. S. Cooper, et al. AMER J OBSTET GYNEC. 106:93-97, January 1, 1970.

"The strange society of the physician," by N. Roth. AM J PSYCHOTHER. 24:494-498, July, 1970.

"The stresses of urban living," by A. I. Adams. RANF REV. 1:7+, October, 1970.

"Stroke, sickle cell trait, and oral contraceptives," by J. G. Greenwald. ANN INTERN MED. 72:960, June, 1970.

"Strokes in women of childbearing age. A population study," by B. S. Schoenberg, et al. NEUROLOGY. 20:181-189, February, 1970.

"The structure and change of mortality in a Maya community," by J. D. Early. MILBANK MEMORIAL FUND Q. 48:179-201, April, 1970.

"Structure and dynamics of the Spanish human resources," by A. de Miguel. REVISTA ESPANOLA DE LA OPINION PUBLICA. 19:71-104, January-March, 1970. (SA # E7671)

"Studies on the site of action of oral contraceptive steroids. II. Plasma LH and FSH levels after administration of antifertility steroids and LH-releasing hormone (LH-RH)," by A. V. Schally, et al. ENDOCRINOLOGY. 86:530-541, March, 1970.

"Study of cause of natural abortion: based on the data on natural abortion in 1967 socioeconomic population survey," by T. Suganuma, et al. JAP J PUBLIC HEALTH NURSE. 26:49-51, October, 1970.

"A study of disease in migrants and their siblings: development of sibling rosters," by K. Magnus, et al. J CHRONIC DIS. 23:405-410, November, 1970.

"A study of the endometrium in intrauterine contraceptive device users," by S. Rimdusit, et al. J MED ASSOC THAI. 53:843-848, December, 1970.

"A study of glucose tolerance in women taking oral contraceptives," by Z. Domany. ORV HETIL. 111: 1511-1513, June 28, 1970.

"Study of oral contraceptives and risk determination for life insurance," by J. G. Defares. NEDERL T GENEESK. 114:647-648, April 11, 1970.

"A study of the public activity of the population in Bulgaria," by M. Radeva. FILOSOFSKIYE NAUKI. 13,1:138-145, 1970. (SA #E9032)

"Study on the cause of natural abortion-based on the 1967 socio-economic population survey," by T. Suganuma, et al. JAP J MIDWIFE. 24:50-56, October, 1970.

"Suburb hegira's extent startles census folk." ADV AGE. 41:1+, August 31, 1970.

"Suggestions on adding family planning to the curriculums of medical schools," by D.T. Rice. PUBLIC HEALTH REP. 85:889-895, October, 1970.

"Summary of the social sciences and population policy: a survey," by E. D. Driver. DEMOGRAPHY. 7:379-392, August, 1970.

"The summary report of the seminar on nursing education and family planning," by M. I. Kim. KOREAN NURSE. 9:27-34, December 25, 1970.

"Suppression of oestradiol secretion and luteinising-hormone release during oestrogen-progestagen oral contraceptive therapy," by M. Dufau, et al. LANCET. 1:271-274, February 7, 1970.

"Suprascrotal vasectomy," by S. M. Gupta. J INDIA MED ASSOC. 54:561-563, June 16, 1970.

"Surgical control of population," by W. E. Lockhart. TEX MED. 66:24-26, November, 1970.

"Surgical nursing: abortions and sterilizations." REGAN REP NURS LAW. 11:1, June, 1970.

"Surprise for 1980s: the big city, population explosion will fizzle," by E. B. Weiss. ADV AGE. 41:65-66, May 4, 1970.

"Surprises from the census." BSNS W. pp. 16-17, August 8, 1970.

"Surprises in the '70 census." U S NEWS. 69:17, August 31, 1970.

"Surprising trends found in 1970 census figures." COMM TODAY. 1:24-26, October 19, 1970.

"Surveillance of poliomyelitis in Czechoslovakia in 1966-1968," by J. Vobecky, et al. J HYG EPIDEMIOL MICROBIOL IMMUNOL. 14:404-412, 1970.

"Survey of buying power: a preview." SALES MGT. 104:28-29, May 15, 1970.

"Survey of buying power; special issue." SALES MGT. 104:A1-E41, June 10, 1970.

"Survey on induced abortion and use of contraceptives in Bogota. Method of approach," by S. Gomez, et al. REV COLOMB OBSTET GINECOL. 21:427-439, July-August, 1970.

"Survival in the seventies," by M. L. Brown. OHIO NURSES REV. 45:12-20, April, 1970.

"The survival of the chosen: three new books on the contraceptive pill," by H. Miller. LISTENER. 84:489-490, October 8, 1970.

"Sweden: a case of population policies." POPULATION BUL. 26:19-27, November, 1970.

"Symposium: oral contraceptives. Opening address," by R. F. Wering. NEDERL T GENEESK. 114:1416-1417, August 22, 1970.

"Syntex denies that its O-C price to OEO is unfair." AM DRUGGIST. 161:25, June 15, 1970.

T

"Tackling the refugee problem," by M. Louvish. JEWISH FRONTIER. 37:6-8, May, 1970; "What future for the Palestine Arabs." WAR/PEACE REPT. 10:3-11, June-July, 1970.

"Taiwan: implications of fertility at replacement levels," by R. Freedman and R. Avery. STUDIES IN FAMILY PLANNING. 59:1-4, November, 1970.

"Taiwan's population characteristics and dynamics," by S. C. Hsu. J FORMOSAN MED ASSOC. 69:455-468, September 28, 1970.

"Taking the pill is just following Nature's law," by A. Jay. NOVA. pp. 47-48, October, 1970.

"Tax-supported sterilization wins in London despite Catholic drive." CHR CENT. 87:591, May 13, 1970.

"The teaching of fertility control and population problems in the medical schools of Brazil," by J. Yunes. REV SAUDE PUBLICA. 4:79-84, June, 1970.

"Teaching population dynamics with a simulation exercise," by E. van de Walle and J. Knodel. DEMOGRAPHY. 7:433-448, November, 1970.

"The teen, the pill, the physician," by P. H. Heersema. MED INSIGHT. 2:16+, September, 1970.

"Teenagers in a family planning clinic," by J. T. Cassidy. NURS OUTLOOK. 18:30-31, November, 1970.

"The temperature method for family planning," NURS J INDIA. 61:399, December, 1970.

"The temporal relationship between bead-induced luteolysis and luteal growth during early pregnancy in the guinea-pig," by F. R. Blatchley, et al. J ENDOCRINOL. 48:1xvi+, December, 1970.

"Temporary occlusion of ductus deferens," by K. H. Moon, et al. INVEST UROL. 8:292-298, November, 1970.

"Temporary psychosis caused by isolation," by L. Palmgren. LAKARTIDNINGEN. 67:1280-1282, March 18, 1970.

"Texan Appalachia," by T. G. Jordan. ASSN AM GEOG ANN. 60:409-427, September, 1970.

"Therapeutic considerations of side effects of hormonal contraceptives on the liver," by S. F. Gomes da Costa, et al. ARZNEIM FORSCH. 20:1246-1247, September, 1970.

"Therapy of the alienated college student," by S. Halleck. CURR PSYCHIATR THER. 10:76-82, 1970.

"Thin-layer chromatographic identification of estrogens and progestogens in oral contraceptives," by M. B. Simard, et al. J CHROMATOGR. 51:517-524, September 23, 1970.

"Thin layer chromatography separation of oral contraceptives and some sex steroids," by I. Szekacs, et al. Z KLIN CHEM. 8:131-133, March, 1970.

"Third fish," by K. S. Norris. NEW REPUB. 162:16-18, May 9, 1970.

"3 interesting cases of insertion of the wing," by T. Fukuda, et al. SANFUJIN JISSAI. 19:763-766, July, 1970.

"300 million people in 30 years: where will they all live?" SAVINGS & LOAN NEWS. 91:46-49, June, 1970.

"Three million new southerners: depopulation and migration in five southeast states, 1950 to 1968," by L. A. Eyre. FLA PLANNING & DEVELOPMENT. 21: 1+, February, 1970.

"Three's a crowd," by P. J. Smith. SPECTATOR. pp. 74-75, January 17, 1970.

"Thromboembolic complications during treatment by estro-progestational drugs. Critical study of 3 cases," by L. Croccel, et al. SEM HOP PARIS. 46:101-108, January 8, 1970.

"Thromboembolic disease and the pill," by L. F. Nanni. BR MED J. 3:644, September 12, 1970.

"Thromboembolic disease and the steroidal content of oral contraceptives. A report to the Committee on Safety of Drugs," by W. H. Inman, et al. BRIT MED J. 2:203-209, April 25, 1970.

"Thromboembolism and oral contraception." MED J AUST. 1:1025, May 23, 1970.

"Thromboembolism, oral contraceptives, and cigarettes," by H. Frederiksen, et al. PUBLIC HEALTH REP. 85:197-205, March, 1970.

"Thromboembolism, oral contraceptives, and cigarettes," by A. T. Masi. ANN INTERN MED. 73:486-487, September, 1970.

"Thrombosis and the content of estrogens in oral anticonceptives," by T. J. Skobba. T NORSK LAEGEFOREN. 90:1223-1224, June 1, 1970.

"Thrombosis of a Blalock's anastomosis for Fallot's tetralogy, in the course of a contraceptive treatment (by an anovulatory steroid)," by J. C. Pony, et al. ARCH MAL COEUR. 63:277-290, February, 1970.

"Thrombosis prophylaxis and the pill," by K. K. Meyer, et al. AMER J SURG. 119:619, June, 1970.

"Thrombotic complications in a young woman during ovocyston therapy," by Z. Babinska, et al. WIAD LEK. 23:333-336, February 15, 1970.

"Thyroid-function tests in women taking norgestrel," by A. W. Goolden, et al. LANCET. 1:624, March 21, 1970.

"Tibetan refugees in a decade of exile," by G. Woodcock. PACIFIC AFFAIRS. 43:410-420, Fall, 1970.

"To teach or not to teach family planning in Kenyan primary schools," by J. B. Maathuis. EAST AFR MED J. 47:545-549, November, 1970.

"Tomorrow's robot reports today." COMM TODAY. 1:28. December 14, 1970.

"Too many children or too many pediatricians?" by P. Banister. CANAD MED ASS J. 103:157-159, July 18, 1970.

"Toward a third world theology: reaction to-- Humanae vitae. AMERICA. 122:90, January 31, 1970.

"Towards a more physiological hormonal contraception," by R. Sterba. ZENTRALBL GYNAEKOL. 92: 303-312, March 7, 1970.

"Towards a Rural Urban Balance," by D. L. Freeman. FUTURIST. 4,5:159-162, October, 1970.

"The training of nurses in family planning," by N. Loudon. NURS MIRROR. 131:28-29, July 24, 1970.

"Transferred to U. S. office? Your move may come soon," by D. Townson. FIN POST. 64:1-2, March 21, 1970.

"Transition in the concept of birth control," by T. Tada. JAP J MIDWIFE. 24:20-26, December, 1970.

"Transmission of life: certain generalizations about the demography of Europe's nations in 1939-41," by J. Lukacs. COMP STUD SOC & HIST. 12: 442-451, October, 1970.

"Transvaginal Madlener's surgery, introduction of glassfiber illumination and variation in operative method," by T. Ishii, et al. SANFUJINKA JISSAI. 19:1071-1075, October, 1970.

"Treatment of intrauterine adhesions with the use of intrauterine devices," by J. Danezis. INT J FERTIL. 15:14-23, January-March, 1970.

"Treatment with an ovulation-inhibiting hormone combination with lower progestin component. Cytologic and histologic studies," by H. Breinl, et al. MED KLIN. 65:195-199, January 30, 1970.

"Trend to sterilization." NEWSWEEK. 76:90, December 21, 1970.

"Trends in distances moved by interstate migrants," by J. D. Tarver and R. Douglas McLeod. RURAL SOCIOL. 35:523-533, December, 1970.

"Trends in human ecology and demography," by L. F. Schnore. DEMOGRAPHY, 1970. (SA # E6341)

"Trends in pregnancy and fertility in a rural area of East Pakistan," by J. Stoeckel, et al. J BIOSOC SCI. 2:329-335, October, 1970.

"Trends in US population," by F. Pollara. AM FEDERATIONIST. 77:9-13, June, 1970.

"A trial of a one dose a month oral contraceptive," by A. D. Claman. AMER J OBSTET GYNEC. 107: 461-464, June 1, 1970.

"Trouble with the IUD." NEWSWEEK. 75:73, May 25, 1970.

"True precautions; true to life, published by Atlanta's Emory University." NEWSWEEK. 76: 55, October 26, 1970.

"Truncation effect in closed and open birth interval data," by M. C. Sheps, et al. AM STAT ASSN J. 65:678-693, June, 1970.

"Tubal electrocoagulation under laparoscopic control," C. H. De Boer, et al. LANCET. 1:997, May 9, 1970.

"Tubal ligation and abortion in the State of Alabama," by C. E Flowers, Jr. J MED ASS ALABAMA. 39:

945-947, April, 1970.

"Tubal ligation in population control." BRIT MED J. 1:770-771, March 28, 1970.

"Tubal occlusion: a comparative study," by K. F. Omran, et al. INT J FERTIL. 15:226-241, October-December, 1970.

"Tubal pregnancy and oral contraceptive by continual administration," by A. Fonder, et al. BULL FED SOC GYNECOL OBSTET LANG FR. 22:329-330, June-August, 1970.

"Tubal sterilization. Morbidity on a charity hospital service," by C. R. Mabray, et al. OBSTET GYNEC. 36:204-207, August, 1970.

"Tubal sterilization in an indigent population. Report of fourteen years' experience," by D. M. Haynes, et al. AMER J OBSTET GYNEC. 106:1044-1053, April 1, 1970.

"Turkish international migrant labor," by J. Kolars. GEOG R. 60:262-264, April, 1970.

"Twice as many people in next thirty-six years." U S NEWS. 69:29-30, November 9, 1970.

"Two and a half centuries of demographic history in a Bavarian village," by J. Knodel. POPULATION STUDIES. 24:353-376, November, 1970.

"2 cases of coralloid renal lithiasis developed in young women under prolonged treatment with the contraceptive pill," by S. Reziciner. ANN UROL. 4:269-274, December, 1970.

U

"US funded study hits Enovid; FDA demurs." AM DRUGGIST. 162:33, December 14, 1970.

"The U. S. labor force: projections to 1985: special labor force report sets forth BLS projections of the growth of the labor force to more than 100 million in 1980 and 107 million in 1985," by S. C.

Travis. MO LABOR R. 93:3-12, May, 1970.

"U.S. lifts personnel transfer ban--for some," by D. Townson. FIN POST. 64:16, April 25, 1970.

"U.S. population growth and family planning: a review of the literature." FAMILY PLANNING PERSPECTIVES. 2:16-page section following p. 24, October, 1970.

"US population growth: would slower be better?" by L. A. Mayer. FORTUNE. 81:80-83+, June, 1970.

"US voting age population totals more than 124 million." COMM TODAY. 1:26, November 2, 1970.

"U.S.S.R. census returns," by V. Pokshishevsky. NEW TIMES. pp. 30-31, May 9, 1970.

"Under 18--the younger population," by F. Linden. CONF BD REC. 7:22-24, February, 1970.

"Undesirable effects of sex hormone therapy." PRESSE MED. 78:2135-2136, November 14, 1970.

"Uneasy present, uncertain future." LANCET. 2:643-644, September 26, 1970.

"Unemployment: challenge to development," by E. Thorbecke, et al. CERES. 3:24-51, November-December, 1970.

"United States population policy, origins and development; address, August 21, 1970," by P. P. Claxton, Jr. DEPT STATE BUL. 63:317-326, September 21, 1970.

"United States: utilization of a family planning program in a metropolitan area," by J. D. Beasley and R. F. Frankowski. STUDIES IN FAMILY PLANNING. 59:7-16, November, 1970.

"The unmarried father-the forgotten man," by R. Pannor. NURS OUTLOOK. 18:36-37, November, 1970.

"Uptake of 59Fe as a tool for study of the crowding effect in Blomphalaria Glabrata," by G. Gazzinelli, et al. AM J TROP MED HYG. 19:1034-1037, November, 1970.

"Urban development in Britain: standards, costs
and resources, 1964-2004; Population trends
and housing," by P. A. Stone. V. 1 reviewed
by C. Barr. RIBA J. 77:380, August, 1970.

"Urban Growth Policy," by C. W. Brubaker. ART
EDUC. 23,7:16-17, October, 1970.

"Urban influence on the fertility and employment
patterns of women living in homogeneous areas,"
by J. D. Tarver, et al. J MARRIAGE & FAM.
32:237-241, May, 1970.

"The urban setting. 3. Mental health services
and the isolated citizen," by M. Mitchell-Bateman.
RHODE ISLAND MED J. 53:263-266 passim, May,
1970.

"Urban U.S.A.--A chaotic society," by P. M. Hauser.
NO. 18:48+, March, 1970.

"Ureteral dilatation and oral contraceptives," by
S. Marshall. JAMA. 211:2157, March 30, 1970.

"Urinary oestrogens in pill-users may be artefacts."
LANCET. 2:598, September 19, 1970.

"Urinary tract dilatation and oral contraceptives,"
by P. B. Guyer, et al. BR MED J. 4:588-590,
December 5, 1970.

"Use of the Chandrasekar-Deming technique in the
Liberian fertility survey," by J. C. Rumford.
PUBLIC HEALTH REP. 85:965-974, November, 1970.

"The use of client characteristics as predictors
of utilization of family planning service," by
S. M. Wishik. AMER J PUBLIC HEALTH. 60:1394-
1397, August, 1970.

"The use of continuous progestogen contraception in
the treatment of migraine," by B. W. Somerville,
et al. MED J AUST. 1:1043-1045, May 23, 1970.

"The use of contraceptives in internal medicine,"
by K. Rak. ORV HETIL. 111:1913, August 9, 1970.

"Use of intrauterine devices," by H. G. Neumann.
DTSCH GESUNDHEITSW. 25:1957-1958, October 8, 1970.

"Use of intrauterine devices for contraception," by
G. V. Truevtseva, et al. AKUSH GINEKOL. 46:49-
52, March, 1970.

"Use of oxytocics in the control of hemorrhages after
the insertion of intrauterine devices," by M.de M.
Marques, et al. HOSPITAL. 78:177-189, July,
1970.

"Use of the "pill" on Taiwan," by F. L. Chen, et al.
INDUSTRY OF FREE CHINA. 33:18-31, April, 1970.

"Use of subcutaneous Silastic capsules for long-
term steroid contraception," by S. Tejuja. AMER
J OBSTET GYNEC. 107:954-957, July 15, 1970.

"Useful rules in the use of estro-progestative
steroids," by M. Albeaux-Fernet, et al. ANNEE
ENDOCRINOL. 22:131-140, 1970.

"Users and non-users of contraception: tests of
stationarity applied to members of a family
planning programme," by G. E. Ebanks. POPU-
LATION STUDIES. 24:85-91, March, 1970.

"Uterine activity and oral contraceptives," by T.
K. Eskes. NED TIJDSCHR VERLOSKD GYNAECOL.
70:550-556, December, 1970.

"Uterine bleeding in rhesus monkeys after intrauterine contraceptive device insertion: effect
of adrenosem salicylate and p-aminomethylbenzoic
acid," by A. B. Kar, et al. INDIAN J EXP BIOL.
8:48, January, 1970.

"Uterine perforation by Lippes loop," by P. S.
Alberts. OBSTET GYNEC. 36:164-166, July, 1970.

"Uterotrophic action of an intrauterine contraceptive device in Rhesus monkeys," by H. Chandra,
et al. INDIAN J EXP BIOL. 8:50, January, 1970.

"Uterus activity and oral contraceptives," by T. K.
Eskes. NEDERL T GENEESK. 114:1424-1426,
August 22, 1970.

"Vaginal cytology in a study of cumulative effects of an oral contraceptive: acid mucopolysaccharide and keratin as indicators for cycle stages," by E. Stern, et al. ACTA CYTOL. 14:382-385, July-August, 1970.

"Vaginal smear patterns in women taking ethynodial diacetate as an oral contraceptive," by K. R. Heber. MED J AUST. 1:379-381, February 21, 1970.

"The value of human abortuses in the surveillance of developmental anomalies. I. General overview," by J. R. Miller, et al. CAN MED ASSOC J. 103:501-502, September 12, 1970.

"The value of human abortuses in the surveillance of developmental anomalies. II. Reduction deformities of the limbs," by J. R. Miller, et al. CAN MED ASSOC J. 103:503-505, September 12, 1970.

"Variations in the renin-angiotensin-aldosterone system and in the antidiuretic hormone induced within 5 days by a contraceptive drug. Rapid action of a contraceptive drug on the hormones controlling water and salt metabolism," by J. Menard, et al. PRESSE MED. 78:415-419, February 21, 1970.

"Various problems of the population in Africa," by O. P. Shchepin. SOVET ZDRAVOOKHR. 29:57-60, 1970.

"Various viewpoints about contraceptive pills and their use," by C. A. Ehrnrooth. KATILOLEHTI. 75:419-427, October, 1970.

"Vascular lesions in women taking oral contraceptives," by N.S. Irey, et al. ARCH PATH. 89:1-8, January, 1970.

"Vasectomies increase as concern over 'pill' overpopulation grows," by E. Graham. WALL ST J. 176:1+, November 11, 1970.

"Vasectomy," by L. N. Jackson. LANCET. 1:140-141, January 17, 1970.

"Vasectomy," by D. R. Rogers. ALASKA MED. 12:60, June, 1970.

"Vasectomy and A.I.H.," by B. Herzberg. LANCET. 1:90, January 10, 1970.

"Vasectomy and A.I.H.," by H. Hill. LANCET. 1:191, January 24, 1970.

"Vasectomy and A.I.H.," by J. K. Monro. LANCET. 1:354-355, February 14, 1970.

"Vasectomy and adverse psychological reactions," by F. J. Ziegler. ANN INTERN MED. 73:853, November, 1970.

"Vasectomy of election," by H. E. Carlson. SOUTHERN MED J. 63:766-770, July, 1970.

"Vasectomy on the N.H.S." BRIT MED J. 1:312-313, May 9, 1970.

"Vasectomy: research proposal," by A. Roe. SCIENCE. 168:1523-1525, June 26, 1970.

"Victims in flight." ECONOMIST. 234:18, February 14, 1970.

"Victorian women and menstruation," by E. Showalter and E. Showalter. VICT STUD. 14:83-89, September, 1970.

"Village campaign in China to foster birth control," by R. Harris. TIMES. 23:7, January, 1970.

"Visual loss associated with oral contraceptives," by M. S. Smith, et al. AMER J OPHTHAL. 69:874-876, May, 1970.

"Vital statistics and census tract data used to evaluate family planning," by N. H. Wright. PUBLIC HEALTH REP. 85:383-389, May, 1970.

"Vital statistics publications of the registration areas of the United States," by A. S. Lunde. POPULATION INDEX. 36:125-146, April-June, 1970.

"Vitiating Humanae vitae; Catholic renewal movements leaflet," by T. Beeson. CHR CENT. 87:1032-1033, September 2, 1970.

"Voluntary confinement among lepers," by M. Bloombaum, et al. J HEALTH SOC BEHAV. 11:16-20, March, 1970.

"Voluntary sterilization," by C. P. Blacker. BRIT MED J. 1:499, February 21, 1970.

"Voluntary sterilization," by S. T. DeLee. INT SURG. 54:304-311, October, 1970.

"Voluntary sterilization," by B. Gonzales. AM J NURS. 70:2581-2583, December, 1970.

"Voluntary sterilization and reform of the criminal law," by A. Eser. MED WELT. 40:1751-1759, October 3, 1970.

"Voluntary sterilization as a family planning measure," by P. Petersen. FORTSCHR NEUROL PSYCHIAT. 38:33-52, January, 1970.

"Voluntary sterilisation in the male," by D. Urquhart-Hay. NEW ZEAL MED J. 71:230-232, April, 1970.

"Voluntary sterilization law recommended forms," by J. L. Moore, Jr., et al. J MED ASS GEORGIA. 59:374-377, September, 1970.

"Voluntary sterilization, a necessary alternative?" by P. Tierney. FAMILY LAW Q. 4:373, December, 1970.

W

"Wall Street and the pill." AM DRUGGIST. 161:23-24, March 9, 1970.

"Warnings," by P. Ehrlich. LISTENER. 84:215-216, August 13, 1970.

"Watching for the small print." ECONOMIST. 236:18, July 11, 1970.

"Water pollution--an ecological perspective," by A. F. Bartsch. J WATER POLLUT CONTR FED. 42:819-823, May, 1970.

"The weight of numbers: family planning in India,"

by F. J. Thierry. ILO (Internat Labour Office) PANORAMA. pp. 24-32, January-February, 1970.

"Welfare of expectant mothers and family planning. Statistical observations on the health guidance of expectant mothers." JAP J MIDWIFE. 24:42-46, December, 1970.

"We're standing on the edge of the earth," by P. Ehrlich. NAT WILDLIFE. 8:16-17, October, 1970.

"West Virginia's approach to a statewide family planning program," by L. C. Landman. FAMILY PLANNING PERSPECTIVES. 2:21-24, October, 1970.

"What the census saw." ECONOMIST. 237:50, November 7, 1970.

"What future for the Palestine Arabs." WAR/PEACE REPT. 10:3-11, June-July, 1970.

"What is overpopulation?" by R. J. Rushdoony. FREEMAN. 20:98-105, February, 1970.

"What kids still don't know about sex," by T. Fleming and A. Fleming." LOOK. 34:59-69+, July 28, 1970; Same abr. READ DIGEST. 97:153-156, December, 1970.

"What the 1970s will bring." SALES MGT. 105:28, July 15, 1970.

"What state governments can do," by D. Weinberg. FAMILY PLANNING PERSPECTIVES. 2:30-34, March 4, 1970.

"What you must tell the census taker: How secret is the census? interview with associate director of Census bureau Conrad Taeber." U S NEWS. 68:36-40, January 12, 1970.

"What you should know about the pill; text of AMA pamphlet." TODAYS HEALTH. 48:9-10, September, 1970.

"What zero population growth will mean to marketers," by E. B. Weiss. ADV AGE. 41:80+, June 15, 1970.

"What's happened since the pill scared everyone:

sales of the pill are still down, but as sales of other contraceptives rise markedly, makers of the pill tone down its potency," by G. Pluenneke. EXCHANGE. 31:1-5, August, 1970.

"What's off at the pictures?", by J. J. O'Connor. WALL ST J. 176:16, November 30, 1970.

"When numbers don't mean strength," by G. Tagliacarne. SUCCESSO (Internat Ed). 12:90-94, November, 1970.

"Where have all the babies gone?" ECONOMIST. 234: 22+, February 21, 1970.

"Where is 1970 US population center?" COMM TODAY. 1:25, November 16, 1970.

"Which exit for the rural poor?" by R. Cumming. INTERPLAY. 3:42-45, December, 1969-January, 1970.

"Who rules here? random reflections on the national origins of those set in authority over us," by W. M. Whitehill. NEW ENGL Q. 43:434-449, September, 1970.

"Who should take the pill? excerpt from Two children by choice," by I. Rossman. PARENTS MAG. 45:54-57+, February, 1970.

"Who's to blame?" by J. Liss. NEW SOCIETY. pp. 96-98, July 16, 1970.

"Who's worrying?" by M. Holt. NURS MIRROR. 131:23, October 16, 1970.

"Whose baby is the population problem?" by R. E. Miles. POPULATION BUL. 16:3-36, February, 1970.

"Why are plants important to snowy owls and Arctic foxes? population cycle in a cold climate." INSTR. 79:103, June, 1970.

"Why do people move?" by P. R. Ehrlich and J. P. Holdren. SAT R. 53:51, September 5, 1970.

"Why the global income gap grows wider," by C.

Ogburn, Jr. POPULATION BUL. 26:5-36, June, 1970.

"Why I'll give my daughter the pill," by P. H. Wade. REDBOOK. 135:30+, June, 1970.

"Why the population bomb is a Rockefeller baby," by S. Weissman. RAMP MAG. 8:42-47, May, 1970.

"Why there is growing concern about the safety of the pill." GOOD H. 170:129-131, January, 1970.

"Why young people leave the villages," by M. Garin and A. Druzenko. CURRENT DIG SOVIET PR. 22:4-6, September 15, 1970; translated and condensed from IZVESTIA. July 12, 1970.

"Will the exploding human population succeed in conserving nature," by P. A. Tschumi. EXPERIENTIA. 26:572-576, May 15, 1970.

"Will mankind survive?" by T. Philpot. HUMANIST. 85:111-112, April, 1970.

"Will a miracle child be born this year?" by P. S. Buck. LADIES HOME J. 87:63+, December, 1970.

"Will we say "it just happened" when the world overpopulates itself to extinction?" Louisiana family planning program," by J. Lelyveld. N Y TIMES MAG. pp. 24-25+, July 19, 1970.

"William R. Baird (Baird WR)," by J. Arlen. NEW ENG J MED. 282:755, March 26, 1970.

"Without sugar-coating; Jim Balog takes a searching look at drug research, the pill." BARRONS. 50:5+, February 23, 1970.

"Wolf children--truth or fallacy?" by V. B. Abello. CLIN PEDIAT. 9:425-429, July, 1970.

"Women's magazines vs public opinion," by D. E. Schuller, et al. OHIO STATE MED J. 66:1107-1110, November, 1970.

"A world agricultural plan," by A. H. Boerma. SCI AMER. 223:54-69 passim, August, 1970.

"World population." NATUR HIST. 79:60-62, January, 1970.

"World population." WORLD AFFAIRS. 35:11, April, 1970.

"World population growth and related technical problems," by A. L. Austin and J. W. Brewer. IEEE SPECTRUM. 7:43-54, December, 1970,

"World population trends and controls," by D. V. Glass. PROC R SOC MED. 63:Suppl:1172-1176, November, 1970.

"World wildlife fund stresses human population; a brief review of the second international conference of the world wildlife fund," by E. Ashpole. CAN AUD. 32:127, September-December, 1970.

"World's biggest data bank," by P. Hirsch. DATAMATION. 16:66-73, May, 1970.

X, Y, Z

"ZPG; new movement challenges the U. S. to stop growing." LIFE. 68:32-37, April 17, 1970.

"Zero population growth by the year 2000?" by W. H. Draper, Jr. WAR/PEACE REPT. 10:16-17, April, 1970.

SUBJECT INDEX

AMA

"AMA dislikes giving OC users info." AM DRUGGIST. 162:39, October 5, 1970.

"AMA writes OC consumer booklet." AM DRUGGIST. 162:20, August 24, 1970.

ABORTION

"Abortion and the birth rate in the USSR," by G. Hude. J BIOSOC SCI. 2:283-292, July, 1970.

"Abortion and sterilization. Status of the law in mid-1970," by N. Hershey. AMER J NURS. 70:1926-1927, September, 1970.

"Abortion: holy innocents?" CHR TODAY. 14:39, May 8, 1970.

"Abortion is the world's most common (and worst) population regulator," by G. Machanik. SA NURS J. 36:32-33, passim, April, 1970.

"Artificial pregnancy interruption and birth rate," by K. Vacha. CESK GYNEK. 35:329-330, July, 1970.

"College policy on abortion and sterilization." ACOG NURSES BULL. 4:2, Fall, 1970.

"Contraception and abortion: american catholic responses." ANNALS OF THE AMERICAN ACADEMY OF POLITICAL AND SOCIAL SCIENCE. 387:109-117, January, 1970.

"The demographic effects of birth control and legal abortion," by H. Sjovall. LAKARTIDNINGEN. 67: 5261-5272, November 4, 1970.

"Effect of induced abortion on birth rate; a simulation model," by S. Mukherji, et al. INDIAN J PUBLIC HEALTH. 14:49-58, January, 1970.

"Extended birth control: abortion on request," by John G. Howells. CAN'S MENTAL HEALTH. 18:3-8, September-October, 1970.

"Fertility control: health and educational factors for the 1970s. Contraception or abortion?" by J. H. Hughes. J BIOSOC SCI. 2:161-166, April, 1970.

ABORTION

"Free abortion," by L. Valvanne. KATILOLEHTI. 75:91, March, 1970.

"Freedom in family planning. The abortion law and women's liberation," by H. Muramatsu. JAP J MIDWIFE. 24:10-19, December, 1970.

"The right to live," by J. Stallworthy. J ROY COLL GEN PRACT. 19:187-190, April, 1970.

"Searching of truth on abortion," by E. Hervet. GYNEC OBSTET. 69:287-295, May-July, 1970.

"Study of cause of natural abortion: based on the data on natural abortion in 1967 socioeconomic population survey," by T. Suganuma, et al. JAP J PUBLIC HEALTH NURSE. 26:49-51, October, 1970.

"Study on the cause of natural abortion--based on the 1967 socio-economic population survey," by T. Suganuma, et al. JAP J MIDWIFE. 24:50-56, October, 1970.

"Surgical nursing: Abortions and sterilizations." REGAN REP NURS LAW. 11:1, June, 1970.

ACCIDENTS & INJURIES & POPULATION
SEE ALSO: LIFE INSURANCE INDUSTRY & POPULATION

"An approach to the identification of high risk individuals in the general population," by C. E. Davis, et al. J FLA MED ASSOC. 57:28-30, November, 1970.

"Catastrophic death toll lower in first half of 1970." METROPOLITAN LIFE STAT BUL. 51:8, August, 1970.

"Employment injuries in Canada in 1969." LABOUR GAZ. 70:484-485, 533-543, July, 1970.

"Accidental injuries: incidence and duration of disability by cause." METROPOLITAN LIFE STAT BUL. 51:10-12, June, 1970.

"Hazardous avocations." METROPOLITAN LIFE STAT BUL. 51:2-4, June, 1970.

"International variations in the motor vehicle hazard." METROPOLITAN LIFE STAT BUL. 51:2-4, September, 1970.

ADOLESCENCE, YOUTH, & POPULATION

"Alienation: an essential process of the psychology of adolescence," by S. Berman. J AM ACAD CHILD PSYCHIATRY. 9:233-250, April, 1970.

"Alienation of present-day adolescents," by L. J. Wise. J AM ACAD CHILD PSYCHIATRY. 9:264-277, April, 1970.

"Alienation of youth as reflected in the Hippie movement," by F. S. Williams. J AM ACAD CHILD PSYCHIATRY. 9:251-263, April, 1970.

"Certain cultural and familial factors contributing to adolescent alienation," by J. D. Noshpitz. J AM ACAD CHILD PSYCHIATRY. 9:216-233, April, 1970.

"Evaluation of a program for preventing adolescent pregnancy," by L. Gordis, et al. NEW ENG J MED. 282:1078-1081, May 7, 1970.

"Federal Association of Physicians: 'No pills' for girls under 16 years of age." MUNCH MED WOCHENSCHR. 42:3, October 16, 1970.

"Should P-pills be prescribed for teenagers?" by P. Bergsjo. T NORSK LAEGEFOREN. 90:1711-1712, September 15, 1970.

"Should teenagers be given contraceptive pills?" by B. Dahlberg. LAKARTIDNINGEN. 67:1453-1456, March 25, 1970.

"The teen, the pill, the physician," by P. H. Heersema. MED INSIGHT. 2:16+, September, 1970.

"Teenagers in a family planning clinic," by J. T. Cassidy. NURS OUTLOOK. 18:30-31, November, 1970.

"Under 18-the younger population," by F. Linden. CONF BD REC. 7:22-24, February, 1970.

"What kids still don't know about sex," by T. Fleming and A. Fleming. LOOK. 34:59-60+, July 28. 1970; same abr. READ DIGEST. 97:153-156, December, 1970.

AGING

"Aged people among urban population," by B. Kaufman. DEMOSTA. 3,1-2:5-26, 1970.

"Aging and life space in Poland and the United States,"

AGING

by E. Shanas. J HEALTH SOC BEHAV. 11:183-190, September, 1970.

"American longevity in 1968." METROPOLITAN LIFE STAT BUL. 51:9-11, August, 1970.

"Disengagement and morale," by M. Tallmer, et al. GERONTOLOGIST. 10:317-320, Winter, 1970.

"The ecological distribution of the elderly in the florida counties," by S. R. Ahsan. SOCIOLOGICAL SYMPOSIUM. 1969, 2, Spr 1-13.

"The loneliness of old age," by M. L. Conti. NURS OUTLOOK. 18:28-30, August 1970.

"Some aspects of the nonagenarian's environment," by F. W. Wigzell. GERONT CLIN (BASEL). 12:175-185, 1970.

AGRICULTURE, FOOD SUPPLY & POPULATION

"Agricultural development in the humid tropics of Central America," by J. R. Taylor. INTER-AM ECON AFFAIRS. 24:41-49, Summer, 1970.

"All about food," by Stanley Johnson. VISTA. 5:24-29+, March-April, 1970.

"Dual challenge of health and hunger: a global crisis; reprint," by G. A. Borgstrom. BUL ATOM SCI. 26:42-46, October, 1970.

"Human food production as a process in the biosere," by L. R. Brown. SCI AMER. 223:161-170, September, 1970.

"Malthus can turn in his grave." NATURE (LONDON). 225:1-2, January 3, 1970.

"A master sampling plan for Canadian agriculture," by J. E. Graham. CAN J AGRIC ECON. 18:60-73, July, 1970.

"Migrant labour and agricultural output in Ghana," by R. E. Beals, et al. OXFORD ECONOMIC PAPERS. 22: 109, March, 1970.

"More or less people; thoughts on feeding the hungry," by W. H. Davis. NEW REPUB. 162:19-21, June 20, 1970.

AGRICULTURE, FOOD SUPPLY & POPULATION

"Population pressure and crop rotational changes among the Tiv of Nigeria," by D. E. Vermeer. ASSN AM GEOG ANN. 60:299-314, June, 1970.

"Population pressure and the social evolution of agriculturalists," by M. J. Harner. SW J ANTHROP. 26:67-86, Spring, 1970.

"Program for a farm population data base: the 1971 census," by R. P. Shaw. CAN J AGRIC ECON. 18:60-73, July, 1970.

"Social nutrition and malnutrition," by L. Havens. ARCH INTERN MED. 126:198 passim, August, 1970.

"Starvation or plenty? by C. Clark. A review." NAT R. 22:631-632, June 16, 1970.

"A world agricultural plan," by A. H. Boerma. SCI AMER. 223:54-69 passim, August, 1970.

ANTHROPOMETRY

"Anthropometry in action. V. Age assessment by indigenous calendar and recalled birth intervals in village anthropometric studies," by D. A. McKay. J TROP PEDIAT. 16:24-27, March, 1970.

ARCHITECTURE & POPULATION

"Architectural business: economy-ecology-and zero population growth," by J. E. Carlson. ARCH REC. 148:59-60, August, 1970.

ARTIFICIAL INSEMINATION

"Artificial insemination; the dangers of a poorly kept secret," by W. Wadlington. NORTHWESTERN UNIV LAW R. 64:777-807, January-February, 1970.

"Procreation and the future of mankind. Implications of artificial insemination," by H. Muramatsu. KANGO KYOSHITSU. 14:28-31, August, 1970.

BAIRD, WILLIAM R.

"William R. Baird," by J. Arlen. NEW ENG J MED. 282:755, March 26, 1970.

BIRTH CONTROL & FERTILITY CONTROL

"Advances in the control of fertility," by M. Vojta. CESK GYNEK. 35:288-289, 1970.

BIRTH CONTROL & FERTILITY CONTROL

"Baboon menstrual cycles affected by social environment," by T. E. Rowell. J REPROD FERTIL. 21:133-141, February, 1970.

"Birth control," by R. S. Kirk, et al. SCIENCE. 170: 1256 passim, December 18, 1970.

"Birth control. Moral theological. medico-gynecologic and penal aspects," by H. D. Hiersche, et al. GEBURTSH FRAUENHEILK. 30:289-301, April, 1970.

"Birth control. Problem of the gynecologist from the medical, moral and religious point of view," by S. Fossati. MINERVA GINECOL. 22:664-668, July 15, 1970.

"Birth control after 1984," by C. Djerassi. SCIENCE. 169:941-951, September 4, 1970.

"Birth control and sex ratio," by R. Cruz-Coke. LANCET. 2:426, August 22, 1970.

"Birth control; a better method." CHEM & ENG N. 48:12, September 28, 1970.

"Birth control by the FDA," by G. G. Liddle. JAMA. 212:159, April 6, 1970.

"Birth control success story no. 1," by A. Gordon. READ DIGEST. 96:80-84, January, 1970.

"Birth control--the views of women," by J. A. Burst. MED J AUST. 2:835-838, October 31, 1970.

"China's birth control action programme, 1956-1964," by Pi-Chao Chen. POPULATION STUDIES. 24:141-158, July, 1970.

"Birth control--color film spots tell the story," by I. Neiger. PUB REL J. 26:8-9, August, 1970.

"Control of fertility," by M. L. Peterson. NEW ENG J MED. 282:1432-1433, June 18, 1970.

"Control of human fertility." BRIT MED J. 1:449-450, February 21, 1970.

"Controlling human fertility." CANAD MED ASS J. 102:

BIRTH CONTROL & FERTILITY CONTROL

871-872, April 25, 1970.

"Current aspects of fertility control," by V. Petrow. CHEM BRIT. 6:167-171, April 4, 1970.

"The demographic effects of birth control and legal abortion," by H. Sjovall. LAKARTIDNINGEN. 67:5261-5272, November 4, 1970.

"Ecology: the new religion?" by R. L. Schueler. AMERICA. 122:292-295, March 21, 1970.

"Edward Foote's Medical Common Sense; an early American comment on birth control," by V. J. Cirillo. J HIST MED. 25:341-345, July, 1970.

"Evaluation of fertility control of periodic abstinence," by W. M. Moore. PRACTITIONER. 205:38-43, July, 1970.

"Every child a wanted child," by P. M. Wilkinson. NURS TIMES. 66:1308-1309, October 8, 1970.

"Experience in education of couples about birth control in under developed countries," by R. Traissac. BULL FED SOC GYNECOL OBSTET LANG FR. 22:187-190, April-May, 1970.

"Faces from the past; M. Sanger," by R. M. Ketchum. AM HERITAGE. 21:52-53, June, 1970.

"Failure of the rhythm method." GOOD H. 170:10+, February, 1970.

"How preventable are unwanted pregnancies?" by W. H. James. LANCET. 2:1257-1258, December 12, 1970.

"Internal-external locus of control and the practice of birth control," by A. P. MacDonald, Jr. PSYCHOL REP. 27:206, August, 1970.

"Leibenstein on the benefits and costs of birth control programmes," by S. Enke. POPULATION STUDIES. 24:115-116, March, 1970.

"Make love, not babies; childlessness; views of the Nathaniel Freedlands," by M. Kasindorf. NEWSWEEK. 75:111, June 15, 1970.

BIRTH CONTROL & FERTILITY CONTROL

"Medicalized" sex," by S. Goldsmith. NEW ENG J MED. 283:709, September 24, 1970.

"Medicalized" sex," by L. Gordis. NEW ENG J MED. 283:709-710, September 24, 1970.

"Medicalized" sex," by A. Pinzello. NEW ENG J MED. 283:709, September 24, 1970.

"Medicine's survival in the seventies," by W. M. Krigsten. J IOWA MED SOC. 60:443-446, July, 1970.

"Miss Stephanie Mills vs. motherhood," by A. Wolff. LOOK. 34:58-59, April 21, 1970.

"More babies needed, not fewer; interview," ed. by L. Kent and J. Jacobs. VOGUE. 156:86-87, August 15, 1970.

"New feminism: potent force in birth-control policy," by L. F. Carter. SCIENCE. 167:1234-1236, February 27, 1970.

"No more unwanted children." UNESCO COURIER. 23:24-27+, February, 1970.

"No universal birth control agent seen." AM DRUGGIST. 161:53, June 1, 1970.

"Opinion: the case for compulsory birth control," by E. Chasteen. MLLE. 70:142+, January, 1970.

"Parent population," by F. Linden. CONF BD REC. 7:24-26, March, 1970.

"Parenthood: right or privilege?" by G. Hardin. SCIENCE. 169:427, July 31, 1970; DISCUSSION. 170: 257-259, October 16, 1970.

"Participation of low-income urban women in a public health birth control program," by Z. L. Janus, et al. PUBLIC HEALTH REP. 85:859-867, October, 1970.

"Predicting ovulation--a reply," by C. S. Marwick, et al. SCIENCE. 169:717, August 21, 1970.

"The problem of birth control. Need for deeper research on numerous aspects of the problem," by A. Barraciu.

BIRTH CONTROL & FERTILITY CONTROL

MINERVA MED. 61:Suppl 59-60+, July-August, 1970.

"Psychologic aspects of the basal body temperature method of regulating births," by J. Marshall, et al. FERTIL STERIL. 21:14-19, January, 1970.

"Rhythm method doubted." SCI DIGEST. 67:73, May, 1970.

"The spread of anti-natal knowledge and practice in Nigeria," by J. C. Caldwell and A. I. Igun. POPULATION STUDIES. 24:21-34, March, 1970.

"The temperature method for family planning." NURS J INDIA. 61:399, December, 1970.

"Transition in the concept of birth control," by T. Tada. JAP J MIDWIFE. 24:20-26, December, 1970.

"True precautions; True to life, by Atlanta's Emory University." NEWSWEEK. 76:55, October 26, 1970.

BIRTH RANK
"Birth rank bias due to changes in birth rate," by J. S. Price, et al. BRIT J PREV SOC MED. 24:62, February, 1970.

"Birth rank in schizophrenia; with a consideration of the bias due to changes in birth-rate," by E. H. Hare, et al. BRIT J PSYCHIAT. 116:409-420, April, 1970.

BIRTH RATE
"Abortion and the birth rate in the USSR," by G. Hyde. J BIOSOC SCI. 2:283-292, July, 1970.

"Alarmed at birth rate figures," by S. Payne. TIMES ED SUP. 2860:5, March 13, 1970.

"Artificial pregnancy interruption and birth rate," by K. Vacha. CESK GYNEK. 35:329-330, July, 1970.

"Baby shortage." ECONOMIST. 235:43-44, May 2, 1970.

"Birth rank bias due to changes in birth rate," by J. S. Price, et al. BRIT J PREV SOC MED. 24:62, February, 1970.

"Birth rank in schizophrenia: with a consideration of

BIRTH RATE

the bias due to changes in birth-rate," by E. H. Hare, et al. BRIT J PSYCHIAT. 116:409-420, April, 1970.

"Birth rate and work load," by E. Nurge. AM ANTHROP. 72:1434-1439, December 1970.

"Deceptive birth rates," by P. R. Ehrlich and J. P. Holdren. SAT R. 53:58, October 3, 1970.

"Effect of induced abortion on birth rate; a simulation model," by S. Mukherji, et al. INDIAN J PUBLIC HEALTH. 14:49-58, January, 1970.

"Proliferation of the species." NATUR HIST. 79:50-51, January, 1970.

"61st decree of the Council of Ministers on birth rate and its results during the past 2 years," by G. Stoimenov, et al. AKUSH GINEKOL. 9:331-336, 1970.

"Trends in human ecology and demography," by L. F. Schnore. DEMOGRAPHY. 1970. SA #E6341

"Trends in world population; factors accounting for progress to date; address, February 24, 1971," by B. Berelson. VITAL SPEECHES. 37:349-352, March 15, 1971.

"Truncation effect in closed and open birth interval data," by M. C. Sheps, et al. AM STAT ASSN J. 65:678-693, June, 1970.

"Twice as many people in next thirty-six years." U S NEWS. 69:29-30, November 9, 1970.

"Uneasy present, uncertain future." LANCET. 2:643-644, September 26, 1970.

"Where have all the babies gone?" ECONOMIST. 234:22+, February 21, 1970.

BUSINESS & INDUSTRY & POPULATION
SEE ALSO: CENSUSES & POPULATION
ECONOMICS & POPULATION

"Census data by computer--for you," by J. C. Baker. STORES. 52:74 plus, November, 1970.

BUSINESS & INDUSTRY & POPULATION

"Census data: tailored to suit you." NATIONS BSNS. 58:52, August, 1970.

"Census is winner as direct mail operation." ADV AGE. 41:3 plus, September 7, 1970.

"Census of industrial production, 1968; principal results in 1968 and some comparisons with earlier years." IRISH STATIS BUL. 45:283-305, December, 1970.

"Economy, ecology, and zero population growth; conditions affecting construction industry," by J. E. Carlson. ARCH REC. 148:59-60, August, 1970.

"Fear of the pill aids an industry; mass-media advertising." BSNS W. March 21, 1970, p. 89.

"Flood insurance for the data deluge." SALES MGT. 104:76+, May 1, 1970.

"Handier and dandier data for marketers." SALES MGT. 105:21-22 plus, December 15, 1970.

"Heading for dramatic increase of younger adults and in income," by G. H. Brown. COMM & FIN CHR. 212: 1474-1475 plus, November 19, 1970.

"Humberside; employment, unemployment and migration, the evolution of industrial structure, 1951-1966," by J. Craig, et al. YORKSHIRE BULLETIN. 22:123-142, November, 1970.

"In warmer markets, hottest growth." BROADCASTING. 79:40, September 14, 1970.

"Industrial decentralization policy in Victoria and its effect on the distribution of population and industry," by A. Kan. ECON ACTIVITY. 13:47-53, January, 1970.

"Industrial pressure and the population problem--the FDA and the pill," by I. C. Winter. JAMA. 212: 1067-1068, May 11, 1970.

"Migration and industrial development: the southern Italian experience," by A. Rodgers. ECON GEOG. 46:111-135, April, 1970.

BUSINESS & INDUSTRY & POPULATION

"New facts on construction: the 1967 census of construction industries," by G. H. Brown. CONSTR R. 16:4-8, October, 1970.

"The 1970 census: a statistical gold mine: the 1970 census will contain many of the facts and figures that associations need to define and achieve their goals in the 70's." ASSN MGT. 22:52-55, February, 1970.

"Paying Mum and motivation." PERSONNEL MANAGEMENT. 2:30-32, January, 1970.

"Plans for the 1970 census of population and housing," by D. L. Kaplan. DEMOGRAPHY. 7:1-18, February, 1970.

"Population implications for forecasting highway demand," by R. W. Paterson. TRAFFIC Q. 24:121-136, January, 1970.

"Population projections." REAL ESTATE ANALYST. 39:417-433, October 26, 1970.

"Population projects (comparing distribution of ages of mortgagors with the various age groups in the United States population, 1950-1990)." REAL ESTATE ANALYST. 39:417-433, October 26, 1970.

"Problems in industry," by S. J. Vaughan. OCCUP HLTH. 22:151+, May, 1970.

"Product pushers vs. the people," by C. F. Wurster. FIELD & S. 75:60 plus, June, 1970.

"Profit from 1970 census data: more refined data available on computer tapes can bring users greater rewards," by R. Eckler. HARVARD BUS R. 48:4-6 plus, July-August, 1970.

"The 1970 census: rich new data source for retailers," by C. E. Treas. MISSISSIPPI'S BUS. 28:1-5, February, 1970.

"Relationships among population, income and retail sales in SMSAs, 1952-1966," by B. C. Liu. Q R ECON & BUS. 10:25-40, Spring, 1970.

BUSINESS & INDUSTRY & POPULATION

"Wall Street and the pill." AM DRUGGIST. 161:23-24, March 9, 1970.

"What the 1970s will bring." SALES MGT. 105:28, July 15, 1970.

"What zero population growth will mean to marketers," by E. B. Weiss. ADV AGE. 41:80+, June 15, 1970.

CENSUSES
"Analyses of census data for Greater London." GREATER LONDON RESEARCH Q. BULL. 11:46-61, June, 1970.

"Big shifts in political power: impact of 1970 census." US NEWS. 69:26-28, September 21, 1970.

"The Bureau of business research as a summary-tape processing center," by L. D. Adcock. N MEX BUS. 23:6-9, July, 1970.

"The CBI industrial trends survey," by D. R. Glynn and D. J. Reid. APPLIED ECON. 1:183-203, May, 1970.

"Census and apportionment: states' gains and losses in House seats as projected from preliminary 1970 data." CONG Q W REPT. 28:2193-2196, September 4, 1970.

"Census data by computer--for you," by J. C. Baker. STORES. 52:74+, November, 1970.

"Census data: tailored to suit you." NATIONS BSNS. 58:52, August, 1970.

"Census enumerators' schedules." LOCAL POPULATION STUDIES. 3:5-6, Autumn, 1969.

"The census is over, but--1970." U S NEWS. 68:50, April 13, 1970.

"Census is winner as direct mail operation." ADV AGE. 41:3+, September 7, 1970.

"Census of industrial production, 1968 principal results in 1968 and some comparisons with earlier years." IRISH STATIS BUL. 45:283-305, December, 1970.

"Census of 1970--an important source of information on problems of social hygiene in public health," by M.

CENSUSES

S. Bednyi, et al. ZDRAVOOKHR ROSS FED. 14:8-15, January, 1970.

"Census ranking of cities is misleading." IND W. 167: 23-24, October 5, 1970.

"Census 1970: people on the move." FIRST NATIONAL CITY BANK. p. 114-117, October, 1970.

"Census taker and you: what to expect: the great American head count, the decennial census, is at hand." U S NEWS. 68:32, March 23, 1970.

"Census taking, 1970," by W. Gerber. EDITORIAL RESEARCH REPTS. p. 205-218, March 18, 1970.

"Changing patterns of family growth: the value of linked vital records as a source of data," by H. B. Newcombe, et al. POPULATION STUDIES. 24:193-203, July, 1970.

"Determining the labor force status of men missed in the census," by D. P. Klein. MO LABOR R. 93:26-32, March, 1970.

"Final 1970 census figures for New Mexico." N MEX BUS. 23:12, October, 1970.

"Final population figures will help US to move forward in the 70s." COMM TODAY. 1:22, November 30, 1970.

"Furor over the 1970 census." U S NEWS. 69:28-32, July 27, 1970.

"Handier & dandier data for marketers." SALES MGT. 105:21-22+, December 15, 1970.

"Implications of the 1970 census for health and medicine," by O. K. Sagen. ANN INTERN MED. 72:134-136, January, 1970.

"Iranian censuses 1956 and 1966: a comparative analysis," by F. Firoozi. MIDDLE EAST J. 24:220-228, Spring, 1970.

"Legal effects of 1970 census on Minnesota municipalities," by J. Lunde. MINN MUNIC. 55:73-75, March, 1970.

CENSUSES

"A look at preliminary 1970 census data," by D. H. Rush. BUS & ECON DIMENSIONS. 6:16-17, October, 1970.

"Much useful data coming from census." ED & PUB. 103:18, November 7, 1970.

"1970 preliminary census counts." NEW JERSEY ECONOMIC REVIEW. no. 4, 1970.

"1970 census: changes and innovations," by G. McGimsey. AM INST PLAN J. 36:198-203, May, 1970.

"The 1970 census: a statistical gold mine: the 1970 census will contain many of the facts and figures that associations need to define and achieve their goals in the 70's." ASSN MGT. 22:52-55, February, 1970.

"The 1970 census (United States): controversy and change," by C. A. Keyko. PUBLIC AFFAIRS COMMENT. 16:1-6, March, 1970.

"Observations on 1970 census data," by W. R. Watson. N MEX BUS. 23:17-25, November-December, 1970.

"On the preliminary results of the 1970 all-union population census: report of the USSR Central statistical administration." CURRENT DIG SOVIET PR. 23:22-26, May 19, 1970.

"Plans for the 1970 census of population and housing," by D. L. Kaplan. DEMOGRAPHY. 7:1-18, February, 1970.

"Plans for the 1971 census of Canada." STATIS OBSERVER. 3:3-5, July, 1970.

"Preview of the 1970 census." STATIS BULL METROP LIFE INSUR CO. 51:2-4, January, 1970.

"Profit from 1970 census data: more refined data available on computer tapes can bring users greater rewards," by A. R. Eckler. HARVARD BUS R. 48:4-6+, July-August, 1970.

"Program for a farm population data base: the 1971 census," by R. P. Shaw. CAN J AGRIC ECON. 18:60-73, July, 1970.

CENSUSES

"Program of the Data access and use laboratory, U. S. bureau of the census," by B. Gura. STATIS REPORTER. p. 1-7, July, 1970.

"Putting the 1970 census of population to use," by C. R. Menke. ECON LEAFLETS. 29:1-4, January, 1970.

"Regional aspects of the 1969 Uganda census," by S. R. Tabor. EAST AFRICAN GEOG R. pp. 78-80, April, 1970.

"Russia takes a census--what it shows." US NEWS. 68: 50-51, May 18, 1970.

"Second-guessing the census takers (1970)." BSNS W. p. 86, September 19, 1970.

"1970 census: the final figures." U S NEWS. 69:31, December 14, 1970.

"The 1970 census: how many Americans and where they are." U S NEWS. 69:22-25, September 14, 1970.

"The 1970 census: rich new data source for retailers," by C. E. Treas. MISSISSIPPI'S BUS. 28:1-5, February, 1970.

"Some methodological aspects of the 1971 census in Canada," by T. G. Beynon and others. CAN J ECON. 3:95-110, February, 1970.

"The Soviet census." NEW TIMES. p. 13-14, January 13, 1970.

"Suburb hegira's extent startles census folk." ADV AGE. 41:1 plus, August 31, 1970.

"Surprises from the census." BSNS W. p. 16-17, August 8, 1970.

"Surprises in the 1970 census." U S NEWS. 69:17, August 31, 1970.

"Surprising trends found in 1970 census figures." COMM TODAY. 1:24-26, October 19, 1970.

"U.S.S.R. census returns," by V. Pokshishevsky. NEW TIMES. p. 30-31, May 9, 1970.

CENSUSES

"Vital statistics and census tract data used to evaluate family planning," by N. H. Wright. PUBLIC HEALTH REP. 85:383-389, May, 1970.

"What the census saw." ECONOMIST. 237:50, November 7, 1970.

"What you must tell the census taker: How secret is the census? Interview with associate director of Census bureau (Conrad Taeber)." U S NEWS. 68:36-40, January 12, 1970.

"World's biggest data bank," by P. Hirsch. DATAMATION. 16:66-73, May, 1970.

COLLEGE STUDENTS & OVERPOPULATION

"Attitudes of married college students on overpopulation and family planning," by P. D. Darney. PUBLIC HEALTH REP. 85:412-418, May, 1970.

"College policy on abortion and sterilization." ACOG NURSES BULL. 4:2, Fall, 1970.

"Dynamics of sexual behavior of college students," by G. R. Kaats, et al. J MARRIAGE & FAM. 32:390-399, August, 1970.

"The pill on campus," by H. E. Weinstein. WALL ST J. 175:1+, January 19, 1970.

CONFERENCES, CONGRESSES & THE LIKE

"Congress on optimum population and environment." CHEM & ENG N. 48:34-35, June 22, 1970.

"The first National congress on optimum population and environment." POPULATION BUL. 26:2-18, November, 1970.

"General congress of the international union for scientific population study." POPULATION. 25,1:9-48, January-February, 1970. SA#F0142

"Inaugural address: 7th National Conference of the Indian Academy of Pediatrics," by S. K. Shah. INDIAN PEDIATR. 7:1-3, January, 1970.

CONTRACEPTIVES: COMPLICATIONS & SIDE-EFFECTS

"Abdominal pregnancy associated with an intrauterine

contraceptive device," by L. H. Tisdall, et al. AMER J OBSTET GYNEC. 106:937-939, March 15, 1970.

"Abnormal endometrial aspects caused by prolonged use of a synthetic estro-progestinic combination," by U. Lecca, et al. MINERVA GINECOL. 22:439-440, April 30, 1970.

"Action of a contraceptive (ovulene) on mouse mammary carcinogenesis," by E. Coezy, et al. REV EUROP ETUD CLIN BIOL. 15:205-209, February, 1970.

"Activity of certain enzymes in endometrial samples in cases of long-lasting maintenance of intrauterine contraceptive devices," by J. Jonek, et al. GINEKOL POL. 41:1195-1201, November, 1970.

"Adrenosem therapy for bleeding coincident with the use of intrauterine contraceptive devices: a double blind study," by H. W. Horne, Jr., et al. FERTIL STERIL. 21:230-233, March, 1970.

"Adverse effects of contraceptives. I. Introduction," by J. Martinez-Manautou. GAC MED MEX. 100:821-823, August, 1970.

"Adverse effects of contraceptives. II. Adverse effects of contraceptive steroids on the liver," by B. Sepdiveda. GAC MED MEX. 100:823-831, August, 1970.

"Adverse effects of contraceptives. III. Effects on blood coagulation. The problem of thrombosis," by J. Pizzuto. GAC MED MEX. 100:831-849, August, 1970.

"Adverse effects of contraceptives. IV. The problem of potential carcinogenic effects of contraceptive steroids," by R. Hertz. GAC MED MEX. 100:849-859, August, 1970.

"Adverse reactions to oral contraceptives. Report of a case of cholestasis," by V. G. Henry. ROCKY MT MED J. 67:24-27, December, 1970.

"Albumin metabolism in female rabbits treated with an oral oestrogen-progestogen contraceptive," by J. Dich, et al. SCAND J CLIN LAB INVEST. 26:31-34, August, 1970.

CONTRACEPTIVES: COMPLICATIONS & SIDE-EFFECTS

"Alkaline phosphatase concentration in cervical mucus," by D. C. Smith, et al. FERTIL STERIL. 21:549-554, July, 1970.

"The alpha-fetoprotein test in pregnant women, women on oral contraceptives, newborn babies, and pyridoxine-deprived baboons," by H. Foy, et al. LANCET. 760:1336-1337, June 20, 1970.

"Alterations in the levels of some serum proteins and serum enzymes during treatment with an oral contraceptive," by H. K. Hanel, et al. UGESKR LAEG. 132:738-741, April 16, 1970.

"Amber light for the pill; Nelson subcommittee hearings." NEWSWEEK. 75:48-49, February 2, 1970.

"Anatomical and functional changes induced by oral contraception," by Y. Lefebvre. CANAD MED ASS J. 102:621-624, March, 1970.

"Antithrombin 3 concentration in the blood," by M. Fagerhol, et al. NORD MED. 84:1473, November 12, 1970.

"Atypical cytology with contraceptive hormone medication. A preliminary report," by T. S. Kline, et al. AMER J CLIN PATH. 53:215-222, February, 1970.

"The behavior of the immunoglobulin level during administration of oral contraceptives," by T. Pulay, et al. ORV HETIL. 111:1931-1933, August 16, 1970.

"Blood clotting, plasma kinins and fibrinolysis," by H. Gjonnaess, et al. THROMB DIATH HAEMORRH. 24:308-310, October 31, 1970.

"Blood glucose levels and glucose tolerance in women with subclinical diabetes receiving an oral contraceptive," by J. A. Goldman, et al. AMER J OBSTET GYNEC. 107:325-327, May 15, 1970.

"Breast cancer during oral contraceptive therapy," by R. E. Fechner. CANCER. 26:1204-1211, December, 1970.

"Can the measurement of antithrombin-3 point out women who run the risk of thrombosis with the use of P-pills?" by M. K. Fagerhol, et al. T NORSK LAEGEFOREN. 90:1559-1560, August 15, 1970.

"Cancer and the pill," by T. W. Anderson. BR MED J. 3:773, September 26, 1970.

"Cancer and the pill," by P. Strickland. BRIT MED J. 3:165-166, July 18, 1970.

"Carbohydrate metabolism and oral contraceptives," by W. D. Reitsma. NED TIJDSCHR VERLOSKD GYNAECOL. 70:562-567, December, 1970.

"Carbohydrate metabolism and oral contraceptives," by W. D. Reitsma. NEDERL T GENEESK. 114:1427-1428, August 22, 1970.

"The carpal tunnel syndrome--a new complication ascribed to the "pill"," by M. S. Sabour, et al. AMER J OBSTET GYNEC. 107:1265-1267, August 15, 1970.

"A case of acute myelogenic leukemia seemingly induced by intrauterine contraceptive devices," by A. Ishihama, et al. YOKOHAMA MED BULL. 20:83-86, June, 1970.

"A case of thromboembolic complication following use of oral contraceptives," by A. Kaindl, et al. WIEN MED WOCHENSCHR. 120:323-325, May 2, 1970.

"A case of thrombophlebitis in a woman on oral contraceptive," by M. K. Rajakumar. MED J MALAYA. 25: 68-69, September, 1970.

"Case reports. Hyperlipaemic pancreatitis and the pill," by S. Bank, et al. POSTGRAD MED J. 46:576-578, September, 1970.

"Cerebrovascular accidents during oral contraception," by R. Fogelholm, et al. ACTA NEUROL SCAND. 46:Suppl, 43:252+, 1970.

"Cerebrovascular accidents in young women. Etiological analysis. Pathogenetic role of oral contraceptive drugs," by M. Mumenthaler, et al. Z NEUROL. 198: 46-64, 1970.

"Cerebrovascular disease and oral contraceptives."

J MED ASS GEORGIA. 59:125-126, March, 1970.

"Cerebrovascular diseases associated with the use of oral contraceptives. A review of the English-language literature," by A. T. Masi, et al. ANN INTERN MED. 72:111-121, January, 1970.

"Cervical cytology and sequential birth control pills," by C. M. Dougherty. OBSTET GYNECOL. 36:741-744, November, 1970.

"Cervico-vaginal cytology in women fitted with intrauterine devices (197 cases)," by M. Ancla, et al. REV FR GYNECOL OBSTET. 65:585-590, October, 1970.

"Changes in antithrombin 3 and plasminogen induced by oral contraceptives," by R. A. Peterson, et al. AMER J CLIN PATH. 53:463-473, April, 1970.

"Changes in carbohydrate metabolism during the administration of progestational hormones," by P. Vela. REV CHIL OBSTET GINECOL. 35:40-49, 1970.

"Changes in psychological symptoms in women taking oral contraceptives," by B. Herzberg, et al. BRIT J PSYCHIAT. 116:161-163, February, 1970.

"Chromosome studies in selected spontaneous abortions. I. Conception after oral contraceptives," by D. H. Carr. CANAD MED ASS J. 103:343-348, August 15, 1970.

"Chronic steroid overloadings and contraception. Importance of conjunctive changes in the corporeal human uterine mucosa," by R. Moricard. BULL ACAD NATL MED. 154:588-599, June 30, 1970.

"Chronic urticaria caused by allergy to the "pill" controlled and analysed by T.T.L.," by J. J. Meyer de Schmid, et al. BULL SOC FRANC DERM SYPH. 77:158-159, 1970.

"Circulatory effects of estrogen," by S. Kushner. OHIO STATE MED J. 66:1016-1021, October, 1970.

"Claustroxenscopophobia as a model of obessional syndrome formation," by O. N. Kzetsov. ZH NEVROPATOL PSIKHIATR. 70:551-556, 1970.

CONTRACEPTIVES: COMPLICATIONS & SIDE-EFFECTS

"Clinical, biochemical, and experimental studies on lactation. V. Clinical effects of steroids on the initiation of lactation," by I. Kamal, et al. AM J OBSTET GYNECOL. 108:655-658, October 15, 1970.

"Clinical changes and histological aspect of the endometrium, during and after the end of treatment, in 5 patients amenorrheic from hormonal contraception," by H. Voegell, et al. BULL FED SOC GYNECOL OBSTET LANG FR. 2:286-287, June-August, 1970.

"Clinical studies in United Arabic Republic with SH 850 (Eugynon), a low dose oral contraceptive, with special reference to its effect on lactation," by A. H. Shaaban, et al. MED WELT. 40:1730-1734, October 3, 1970.

"Coexistence of pregnancy with Lippes' loop," by A. Lipinski, et al. WIAD LEK. 23:1603-1605, September 15, 1970.

"Colpocytology in users of oral contraceptives. Findings in the Praia do Pinto Ambulatory clinic and in the Central Hospital of the IASEG (Department of Pathological Anatomy)," by A. F. Moura, et al. REV BRAS MED. 27:341-344, July, 1970.

"A commentary on oral contraceptive therapy and contact lens wear," by J. B. Goldberg. J AMER OPTOM ASS. 41:237-241, March, 1970.

"A comparative study of blood fibrinolytic activity in normal women, pregnant women and women on oral contraceptives," by I. S. Menon, et al. J OBSTET GYNAEC BRIT COMM. 77:752-756, August, 1970.

"Comparative study of the influence of pregnancy and oral contraceptives on the gingivae," by G. M. El-Ashiry, et al. ORAL SURG. 30:472-475, October, 1970.

"Comparison of the metabolic effects of chlormadinone acetate and conventional contraceptive steroids in man," by P. Beck. J CLIN ENDOCR. 30:785-791, June, 1970.

"Complications of the contraceptive pill." WISCONSIN MED J. 69:84-91, February, 1970.

CONTRACEPTIVES: COMPLICATIONS & SIDE-EFFECTS

"Conception control and embryonic development," by B. J. Poland. AMER J OBSTET GYNEC. 106:365-368, February 1, 1970.

"Confusion on the pill: Nelson hearings," by M. Mintz. NEW REPUB. 162:10-11, January 31, 1970.

"Contraception with chlormadinone acetate in woman with previous contraceptive jaundice," by R. P. Thompson, et al. BRIT MED J. 1:152-153, January 17, 1970.

"Contraceptive pill and thyroid nodule," by M. T. Diamond, et al. NEW YORK J MED. 70:295-297, January 15, 1970.

"The contraceptive pill, side effects and personality: report of a controlled double blind trial," by D. Grounds, et al. BRIT J PSYCHIAT. 116:169-172, February, 1970.

"Contraceptives and dysplasia: higher rate for pill choosers," by E. Stern, et al. SCIENCE. 169:497-498, July 31, 1970.

"Contraceptives and hypertension." JAMA. 214:136-137, October 5, 1970.

"Contraceptives and serum proteins," by M. H. Briggs, et al. BRIT MED J. 3:521, August 29, 1970.

"Contraceptives, brain serotonin, and liver tryptophan pyrrolase," by G. Nistico, et al. LANCET. 2:213- July 25, 1970.

"Correlation of folate metabolism and socioeconomic status in pregnancy and in patients taking oral contraceptives," by S. B. Kahn, et al. AM J OBSTET GYNECOL. 108:931-935, November 15, 1970.

"Crackdown; FDA withdraws C-Quens and Provest." NEWSWEEK. 76:100, November 2, 1970.

"Cross-sectional investigation of carbohydrate metabolism in women taking a sequential or combination type oral contraceptive: measurements of blood glucose, plasma insulin and plasma growth hormone during an oral glucose tolerance test," by W. N.

Spellacy, et al. SOUTHERN MED J. 63:152-155, February, 1970.

"Cryofibrinogenaemia in patients on oral contraceptives," by S. E. Ritzmann. LANCET. 1:522, March 7, 1970.

"Cryofibrinogenaemia in women using oral contraceptives," by I. R. Fisch. LANCET. 1:775, April 11, 1970.

"Cryofibrinogenaemia in women using oral contraceptives," by J. Pindyck, et al. LANCET. 1:51-53, January 10, 1970.

"Cutaneous eruptions and in vitro lymphocyte hypersensitivity. Associated with oral contraceptives and mestranol," by H. Savel, et al. ARCH DERM. 101: 187-190, February, 1970.

"Cutaneous side effects of oral contraceptives," by J. E. Jelinek. ARCH DERM. 101:181-186, February, 1970.

"Cytogenetic studies on women using oral contraceptives and their progeny," by H. G. McQuarrie, et al. AM J OBSTET GYNECOL. 108:659-665, October 15, 1970.

"Cytologic studies after insertion of intrauterine contraceptive devices," by A. Ishihama, et al. ACTA CYTOL. 14:35-41, January, 1970.

"Cytological findings and oral contraceptives," by A. L. Schmidt. NED TIJDSCHR VERLOSKD GYNAECOL. 70: 539-545, December, 1970.

"The cytology of intrauterine contraceptive devices," by N. Sagiroglu, et al. ACTA CYTOL. 14:58-64, February, 1970.

"Deaths among users of oral and nonoral contraceptives," A. Fuertes-de la Haba, et al. OBSTET GYNECOL. 36: 597-602, October, 1970.

"Depression and oral contraception." BR MED J. 4:127-128, October 17, 1970.

" Depression and oral contraception," by E. C. Grant. BR MED J. 4:367, November 7, 1970.

"Depression and oral contraception," by J. T. Hart. BR

CONTRACEPTIVES: COMPLICATIONS & SIDE-EFFECTS

MED J. 4:367, November 7, 1970.

"Depressive symptoms and oral contraceptives," by B. N. Herzberg, et al. BR MED J. 4:142-145, October 17, 1970.

"Dermatologic side effects of ovulation inhibitors," by H. Tronnier. ARCH KLIN EXP DERM. 237:197-200, 1970.

"The detection of incidence of congenital malformations in the community," by J. A. Weatherall. PROC R SOC MED. 63:1251-1252, December, 1970.

"Drug photosensitivity. I. Light-and photo-sensitivities observed during oral contraceptive therapy. A review," by I. W. Mathison, et al. OBSTET GYNEC SURVEY. 25:389-401, April, 1970.

"Dural sinus and cerebral venous thrombosis. Incidence in young women receiving oral contraceptives," by D. S. Buchanan, et al. ARCH NEUROL. 22:440-444, May, 1970.

"Effect of anovulatory drugs on the human urinary tract and urinary tract infections," by J. N. Corriere, Jr. et al. OBSTET GYNEC. 35:211-216, February, 1970.

"Effect of combined oestrogen-progestogen oral contraceptives, oestrogen, and progestogen on antiplasmin and antithrombin activity," by P. W. Howie, et al. LANCET. 2:1329-1332, December 26, 1970.

"Effect of contraceptive pills on the distribution of sexual activity in the menstrual cycle," by J. R. Udry, et al. NATURE (LONDON). 227:502-503, August 1, 1970.

"Effect of combined oestrogen-progestogen oral contraceptives on serum-levels of alpha 2-macroglobulin, transferrin, albumin, and IgG," by C. H. Horne, et al. LANCET. 1:49-50, January 10, 1970.

"The effect of Enovid on the binding of thyroxine to plasma proteins in vitro," by H. A. Moses, et al. J NATL MED ASSOC. 62:331-333, September, 1970.

CONTRACEPTIVES: COMPLICATIONS & SIDE-EFFECTS

"Effect of gestogens on lactation maintenance in the albino rat," by M. M. Abdel-Kader, et al. J EGYPT MED ASSOC. 52:306-312, April, 1969.

"Effect of intrauterine contraceptive suture on the response of rat uterus to prolonged estrogen treatment," by B. Malaviya, et al. INDIAN J EXP BIOL. 8:19-21, January, 1970.

"The effect of intrauterine copper and other metals on implantation in rats and hamsters," by C. C. Chang, et al. FERTIL STERIL. 21:274-278, March, 1970.

"The effect of an intrauterine thread on tissue changes in the endometrium of the pseudopregnant rat," by J. C. Wood. J PHYSIOL. 207:545-555, May, 1970.

"Effect of melengestrol acetate on the bleeding & clotting times of blood in Indian water buffalo," by G. N. Memon, et al. INDIAN J EXP BIOL. 8: 220-222, July, 1970.

"Effect of the new hormonal contraceptive mixtures on the intrauterine environment," by K. Rezabek, et al. CAS LEK CESK. 109:1100-1102, November, 1970.

"Effect of 19-norsteroids on the motility of human fallopian tubes," by A. Jakobovits, et al. INT J FERTIL. 15:36-39, January-March, 1970.

"The effect of oestrogens and progestogens on serum protein levels," by C. H. Horne, et al. J CLIN PATH. 23:378, May, 1970.

"Effect of an oral contraceptive agent on blood pressure response to renin," by B. H. Douglas, et al. PROC SOC EXP BIOL MED. 133:1142-1144, April, 1970.

"Effect of an oral contraceptive on spontaneous running activity of female rats," by M. J. Fregly, et al. CANAD J PHYSIOL PHARMACOL. 48:107-114, February, 1970.

"The effect of oral contraceptive steroids on bile secretion and bilirubin Tm in rats," by T. A. Heikel, et al. BRIT J PHARMACOL. 38:593-601,

May, 1970.

"Effect of the oral-contraceptive steroids on the ultrastructure of human cervical mucus--a preliminary communication," by A. Singer, et al. J REPROD FERTIL. 23:249-255, November, 1970.

"The effect of oral contraceptives on the histology of carcinoma of the breast," by H. G. Penman. J PATH. 101:66-68, May, 1970.

"Effect of oral contraceptives on leukocyte count in hemophiliacs," by O. Kiran, et al. CLIN PEDIATR. 9:656-657, November, 1970.

"Effect of oral contraceptives on lipoprotein lipase activity and platelet stickiness," by J. H. Adams, et al. LANCET. 2:333-335, August 15, 1970.

"Effect of oral contraceptives on the oral and vaginal mucosa," by G. Klinger, et al. DTSCH STOMATOL. 20:664-669, September, 1970.

"Effect of oral contraceptives on serum folic acid content," by O. M. Castren, et al. J OBSTET GYNAEC BRIT COMM. 77:548-550, June, 1970.

"Effect of oral contraceptives on serum protein concentrations," by H. W. Mendenhall. AMER J OBSTET GYNEC. 106:750-753, March, 1970.

"Effect of some contraceptive steroids on pituitary growth hormone content in female rats," by F. T. Liu, et al. PROC SOC EXP BIOL MED. 133:1354-1357, April, 1970.

"Effect of some steroid contraceptives on serum inorganic constituents of lactating goats," by M. M. Abdel Kader, et al. J EGYPT MED ASSOC. 53:170-178, 1970.

"Effect of tubal obstruction, salpingectomy, or intrauterine devices on estrous cycle lengths and mating behavior of the ewe," by H. H. Conley, et al. INT J FERTIL. 15:115-119, April-June, 1970.

"Effect of unilateral hysterectomy and separation or ligation of uterine horns on luteolytic action of intrauterine device in sheep," by O. J. Ginther. AM J VET RES. 31:2127-2130, December, 1970.

"Effectiveness and risks of birth-control methods," by D. M. Potts, et al. BRIT MED BULL. 26:26-32, January, 1970.

"Effects of certain contraceptive pills on uterine myomas," by B. C. West, Jr. N CAROLINA MED J. 31:14-16, January, 1970.

"Effects of combined and low-dose gestagen oral contraceptives on plasma lipids; including individual phospholipids," by U. Larsson-Cohn, et al. ACTA ENDOCR. 63:717-735, April, 1970.

"Effects of different systemic contraceptives on blood fibrinolysis," by P. Brakman, et al. AMER J OBSTET GYNEC. 106:187-192, January 15, 1970.

"Effects of the intrauterine contraceptive device on endometrial enzyme and carbohydrate histochemistry," by L. L. Hester, Jr., et al. AMER J OBSTET GYNEC. 106:1144-1154, April 15, 1970.

"Effects of an intra-uterine contraceptive device on mitosis in the rat uterus on different days of pregnancy," by R. R. Chaudhury, et al. J REPROD FERTIL. 22:33-40, June, 1970.

"The effects of intrauterine devices on preimplantation changes in the mouse uterus," by L. Martin, et al. J ENDOCRINOL. 46:19-20, February, 1970.

"The effects of an intra-uterine device on uterine cell division and epithelial morphology during early pregnancy in the mouse," by L. Martin, et al. J ENDOCRINOL. 48:347-354, November, 1970.

"Effects of obesity, glucocorticoid, and oral contraceptive therapy on plasma glucose and blood pyruvate levels," by J. W. Doar, et al. BRIT MED J. 1:149-152, January 17, 1970.

"Effects of oral contraceptives on carbohydrate metabolism," by A. Vermeulen, et al. DIABETOLOGIA. 6:519-523, October, 1970.

CONTRACEPTIVES: COMPLICATIONS & SIDE-EFFECTS

"Effects of oral contraceptives on the fetus," by F. Neumann, et al. LANCET. 2:1258-1259, December 12, 1970.

"Effects of oral contraceptives on urinary bacterial growth rate," by M. Silk, et al. INVEST UROL. 8:239-241, September, 1970.

"The effects of small doses of megestrol acetate on the cervical mucus," by P. E. Lebech, et al. INT J FERTIL. 15:65-76, April-June, 1970.

"Effects of a surface active contraceptive agent (nonylphenoxypolyethoxyethanol) on the vagina; a new functional approach to assessing the actions on the vagina of spermicides," by F. Edwards, et al. J PHYSIOL. 208:35-36, May, 1970.

"Effects upon the palmar sweat index of hormonal changes related to the menstrual cycle," by P. S. Yoder. NURS RES. 19:165-168, March-April, 1970.

"Electrical activity of the human uterus in the presence of intrauterine contraceptive device," by D. M. Serr, et al. OBSTET GYNEC. 35:217-220, February, 1970.

"Electroencephalographic recording during progestation treatment," by A. H. Ansari, et al. FERTIL STERIL. 21:873-882, December, 1970.

"Electron microscopic changes in the rat liver after administration of the oral contraceptive lynestrenol," by I. Bartok, et al. ACTA HEPATOSPLEN. 17:1-10, January-February, 1970.

"Endometrial findings after insertion of stainless steel spring IUD," by W. B. Ober, et al. OBSTET GYNEC. 36:62-68, July, 1970.

"Emotional aspects of contraception," by M. E. Lane. BULL AMER COLL NURSE MIDWIFE. 15:16-25, February, 1970.

"Endocrine properties and mechanism of action of oral contraceptives," by F. J. Saunders. FED PROC. 29:1211-1219, May-June, 1970.

"Endometrial carbonic anhydrase after diethylstilbestrol as a postcoital antifertility agent," by J. A. Board. OBSTET GYNEC. 36:347-349, September, 1970.

"Endometrial changes in women receiving oral contraceptives," by J. Song, et al. AMER J OBSTET GYNEC. 107:717-728, July 1, 1970.

"Endometrial leukocytes in patients using intrauterine contraceptive devices," by A. Sedlis, et al. AM J OBSTET GYNECOL. 108:1209-1212, December 15, 1970.

"Endometrial regeneration in patients discontinuing oral contraceptives," by M. Maqueo, et al. FERTIL STERIL. 21:224-229, March, 1970.

"Endometrium pattern after intrauterine device (Lippes loop) insertion," by M. Bulska, et al. POL TYG LEK. 25:565-566, April 20, 1970.

"Enough to move FDA; relation of estrogen to bloodclotting." SCI N. 97:430-431, May 2, 1970.

"Estrogen content of oral contraceptives and thromboembolitic processes," by C. J. Rubsaam. NEDERL T GENEESK. 114:1101-1103, June 27, 1970.

"Estrogen therapy and glucose tolerance test," by G. DiPaola, et al. AMER J OBSTET GYNEC. 107:124-132, May 1, 1970.

"Evaluation of rare adverse effects of systemic contraceptives," by R. Doll, et al. BRIT MED BULL. 26:33-38, January, 1970.

"Experience with oral contraceptives in the immediate puerperium: effect on breast engorgement and menstrual flow," by J. A. Bowman, Jr. FERTIL STERIL. 21:39-42, January, 1970.

"Experiences with IUD complications," by S. C. Green, et al. TEX MED. 66:60-63, November, 1970.

"Extra-uterine pregnancy with intra-uterine prevention," by T. Bakke. TIDSSKR NOR LAEGEFOREN. 90:1878-1879, October 15, 1970.

CONTRACEPTIVES: COMPLICATIONS & SIDE-EFFECTS

"Extra-uterine pregnancy under oral contraceptive," by G. Zographos, et al. BULL FED SOC GYNECOL OBSTET LANG FR. 22:295-296, June-August, 1970.

"Eye disorders and contraceptive agents," by G. Payeur, et al. BULL SOC OPHTALMOL FR. 70:699-703, May-June, 1970.

"FDA goes to the consumer." SCI N. 97:266, March 14, 1970.

"Failures of contraception on the lower dose ethinyl estradiol sequential therapy: a clinical trial," by J. Miyamoto. AM J OBSTET GYNECOL. 108:990-991, November 15, 1970.

"The failure of the copper IUD to inhibit fertilization in the rabbit," by J. P. Polidoro, et al. J REPROD FERTIL. 23:151-154, October, 1970.

"Fatal embolism and progestational hormones. Apropos of a case," by L. Bardonnet. LYON MED. 223:809-810, April 12, 1970.

"Fatal pulmonary embolism during oral contraception," by J. C. Glertsen, et al. TIDSSKR NOR LAEGEFOREN. 90:2252-2253, December 15, 1970.

"Fears and the pill." MANUF CHEM. 40:2+, October, 1969.

"Fibrin proteolysis in the monkey uterine cavity: variations with and without IUD," by S. T. Shaw, Jr., et al. NATURE (LOND). 228:1097-1099, December 12, 1970.

"Fibrinolytic activity and oral contraception," by I. S. Menon, et al. BR MED J. 4:621, December 5, 1970.

"Fibroadenomas in patients receiving oral contraceptives: a clinical and pathologic study," by R. E. Fechner. AM J CLIN PATHOL. 53:857-864, June, 1970.

"Fibrocystic disease in women receiving oral contraceptive hormones," by R. E. Fechner. CANCER. 25:1332-1339, June, 1970.

CONTRACEPTIVES: COMPLICATIONS & SIDE-EFFECTS

"5-hydroxytryptamine content of rat uterus with intrauterine device in one horn," by O. P. Gulati, et al. INDIAN J EXP BIOL. 8:142-143, April, 1970.

"Flocculation tests in women taking oral contraceptives," by M. J. Halpern. LANCET. 1:1065, May 16, 1970.

"Flocculation tests, oral contraceptives, and malaria," by J. F. Currin. LANCET. 1:103, July 11, 1970.

"Folate deficiency and oral contraceptives," by R. R. Streiff. JAMA. 214:105-108, October 5, 1970.

"46, XY female: anti-androgenic effect of oral contraceptive?" by L. I. Gardner, et al. LANCET. 2:667-668, September 26, 1970.

"General review of side effects of oral contraceptives," by J. Janssens. NED TIJDSCHR VERLOSKD GYNAECOL. 70:528-539, December, 1970.

"Genital candidasis and oral contraceptives," by J. J. Rohatiner, et al. J OBSTET GYNAECOL BR COMMONW. 77:1013-1015, November, 1970.

"Glucose, insulin, and growth hormone studies in long-term users of oral contraceptives," by W. N. Spellacy, et al. AMER J OBSTET GYNEC. 106:173-182, January 15, 1970.

"Glucose metabolism during the menstrual cycle. Glucose tolerance during the one cycle and under the effect of ovulatory suppressants," by J. A. Goldman, et al. OBSTET GYNEC. 35:207-210, February, 1970.

"Gravidic cholestatic icterus, icterus due to estroprogestogen substances and incomplete anicteric sarcoidosic cholestasis," by H. Merillon, et al. ANN MED INTERN. 121:711-716, August-September, 1970.

"Gravidity inspite of "coitus ante portas", by G. Ladanji. MUNCHEN MED WSCHR. 112:3, August 14, 1970.

"Gynecologic indications for oral contraceptives," by A. M. Cohen. NED TIJDSCHR VERLOSKD GYNAECOL. 70: 569-576, December, 1970.

"Haemodynamic changes in women taking oral contraceptives," by W. A. Walters, et al. J OBSTET GYNAECOL BR COMMONW. 77:1007-1012, November, 1970.

"Haemophilus endometritis in woman fitted with Lippes loop," by R. Hurley. BRIT MED J. 1:566, February 28, 1970.

"Hazards of oral contraceptive therapy," by R. K. Chandra. INDIAN J PEDIAT. 37:44-45, January, 1970.

"Hereditary haemorrhagic telangiectasia: aggravation by oral contraceptives?" by P. T. Rowley, et al. LANCET. 1:474-475, February 28, 1970.

"Hereditary haemorrhagic telangiectasia and oral contraceptives," by E. K. Blackburn. LANCET. 1:616, March 21, 1970.

"Hereditary haemorrhagic telangiectasia and oral contraceptives," by P. W. Harris. LANCET. 1:615-616, March 21, 1970.

"Hereditary haemorrhagic telangiectasia and oral contraceptives," by D. F. Harrison. LANCET. 1:721. April 4, 1970.

"Histologic study of the uterine cervix during oral contraception with ethynodiol diacetate and mestranol," by E. Carbia, et al. OBSTET GYNEC. 35: 381-388, March, 1970.

"Histological changes in the ovum following failure of intrauterine contraception," by F. Havranek, et al. CESK GYNEK. 35:377-378, July, 1970.

"Histopathological pictures of the endometrium a few years after a Lippes loop insertion," by A. Cekanski, et al. GINEK POL. 41:171-177, February, 1970.

"Hypertension in young females receiving anovulatory steroids," by A. M. Lansing. ANN SURG. 171:731-

CONTRACEPTIVES: COMPLICATIONS & SIDE-EFFECTS

734, May, 1970.

"Hysterotomy and insertion of an intrauterine device for endometrial sclerosis: importance of long term followup," by J. A. Wider, et al. FERTIL STERIL. 21:240-243, March, 1970.

"Incidence of pregnancy with the IUD in private practice in New Orleans," by L. L. Doyle, et al. J LOUISIANA MED SOC. 122:45-47, February, 1970.

"Increased antipyrine half-life in women taking oral contraceptives," by K. O'Malley, et al. SCOTT MED J. 15:454-456, December, 1970.

"Induction of hepatic delta-amino-levulinic acid synthetase by oral contraceptive steroids," by A. B. Rifkind, et al. J CLIN ENDOCR. 30:330-335, March, 1970.

"The influence of biphasic hormonal contraceptives on hair growth," by H. Zaun, et al. ARCH KLIN EXP DERMATOL. 238:197-206, 1970.

"Influence of cyclic Ovosiston therapy on plasma lipid fractions of free cholesterol, total cholesterol and phospholipid," by W. Carol, et al. ENDOKRINOLOGIE. 57:108-114, 1970.

"Influence of an IUD on the leucocytic content of the uterus and on the duration of pseudopregnancy in mice," by A. Bartke. J REPROD FERTIL. 23:243-247, November, 1970.

"The influence of a mono- and biphasic oral contraceptives on colpitis of diverse etiology," by L. Mettler, et al. Z GEBURTSHILFE GYNAEKOL. 173:168-180, 1970.

"The influence of monophasic ovulation-inhibitors on hair growth," by H. Zaun, et al. ARCH KLIN EXP DERM. 234:353-361, 1969.

"The influence of oral contraceptive and progestational drugs upon the mechanical activity of the non-pregnant human uterus in vivo," by T. K. Eskes, et al. NEDERL T VERLOSK. 70:47-56, February, 1970.

CONTRACEPTIVES: COMPLICATIONS & SIDE-EFFECTS

"The influence of an oral contraceptive on glucose-, F.F.A.-, triglyceride- and insulin levels after glucose loading," by P. Terpstra, et al. FOLIA MED NEERL. 13:44-50, 1970.

"Influence of ovulation inhibitors on body height growth," by G. K. Doering. DEUTSCH MED WSCHR. 95:241, January 30, 1970.

"The influence of several ovulation inhibiting hormone preparations on scalp hair growth," by H. Zaun. DEUTSCH MED WSCHR. 95:1433-1436, July 3, 1970.

"The influence of sex, age, synthetic oestrogens, progestogens and oral contraceptives on the excretion of urinary tryptophan metabolites," by G. E. Moursi, et al. BULL WHO. 43:651-661, 1970.

"The influence of two different doses of HMG in counteracting the inhibitory effect of an oral contraceptive observed at laparotomy," by P. Pujol-Amat, et al. J REPROD FERTIL. 22:188-189, June, 1970.

"Intracranial venous thrombosis as complication of oral contraception," by E. A. Atkinson, et al. LANCET. 1:914-918, May 2, 1970.

"Intracranial venous thrombosis complicating oral contraception," by C. Sissons, et al. LANCET. 2:419, August 22, 1970.

"The intrauterine contraceptive device and uterine perforation," by H. C. Hodes. J KANSAS MED SOC. 71:318-323, August, 1970.

"Intra-uterine contraceptive device with ectopic gestation. A case report," by A. N. Rijhwani, et al. J POSTGRAD MED. 16:42-43, January, 1970.

"Intra-uterine device and embryonic survival in the rat," by K. F. DeBoer, et al. J REPROD FERTIL. 21:343-346, March, 1970.

"Intrauterine device and pituitary follicle-stimulatine hormone and luteinizing hormone in the rat," by A. P. Labhsetwar. FERTIL STERIL. 21:177-181, February, 1970.

"Intrauterine devices and cervico-vaginal cytology," by M. Ancla, et al. PRESSE MED. 78:1541-1542, July 25, 1970.

"Intrauterine spiral and extrauterine pregnancy," by J. R. Giraud. MUNCHEN MED WSCHR. 112:2, September 25, 1970.

"Is the "pill" a cause of vaginal candidiasis? Culture study," by B. Lapan. NEW YORK J MED. 70: 949-951, April 15, 1970.

"Is the pill safe?" SR SCHOL. 96:15, March 16, 1970.

"It's an ill pill." ECONOMIST. 234:40, January 24, 1970.

"Kymographic studies of the Fallopian tubes after insertion of intrauterine contraceptive devices using the Lippes loop and the nylon ring," by A. M. Makhlouf, et al. AMER J OBSTET GYNEC. 106:759-764, March, 1970.

"Lactation and genital involution effects of a new low-dose oral contraceptive on breast-feeding mothers and their infants," by G. H. Miller, et al. OBSTET GYNEC. 35:44-50, January, 1970.

"Lactation and lactational amenorrhoea with postpartum IUCD insertions," by V. Hingorani, et al. J REPROD FERTIL. 23:513-515, December, 1970.

"Liver function in patients using depot anti-ovulation agents," by J. Rodriguez Arguelles. GINEC OBSTET MEX. 27:107-113, January, 1970.

"Lochia and menstrual patterns in women with postpartum IUCD insertions," by V. Hingorani, et al. AM J OBSTET GYNECOL. 108:989-990, November 15, 1970.

"Long-term effect of an intrauterine contraceptive device on genital organs of rhesus monkeys. A 4 and one-half year study," by A. B. Kar, et al. AMER J OBSTET GYNEC. 106:457-462, February 1, 1970.

"Long term effect of medroxyprogesterone acetate in

human ovarian morphophysiology and sperm transport," by J. Zanartu, et al. FERTIL STERIL. 21: 525-533, July, 1970.

"The long-term effects of steroid contraceptives," by R. Doll. J BIOSOC SCI. 2:367-389, October, 1970.

"Long-term toxicologic and tumorigenesis studies on an oral contraceptive agent in albino rats," by J. L. Schardein, et al. TOXIC APPL PHARMACOL. 16: 10-23, January, 1970.

"Lymphoid follicles of the endometrium in women wearing an intrauterine device," by A. Ishihama, et al. AMER J OBSTET GYNEC. 107:535-537, June 15, 1970.

"MDs blast pill's safety during Nelson hearings." AM DRUGGIST. 161:22, January 26, 1970.

"Major vascular complications during treatment with oral contraceptives and retrospective discovery of idiopathic hyperlipemia. 9 cases," by J. L. de Gennes, et al. PRESSE MED. 78:541-546, March 7, 1970.

"Malabsorption of folate polyglutamates associated with oral contraceptive therapy," by T. F. Necheles, et al. NEW ENG J MED. 282:858-859, April 9, 1970.

"Megaloblastic anemia precipitated by the use of oral contraceptive. A case report," by R. P. Holmes. N CAROLINA MED J. 31:17-18, January, 1970.

"Menstrual dysfunction following use of oral contraceptives," by H. D. Homesley, et al. OBSTET GYNEC. 35:734-739, May, 1970.

"Metabolic effects of oral contraceptives." BRIT MED J. 3:121, July 18, 1970.

"Metabolic effects of oral contraceptives," by E. C. Grant. BRIT MED J. 3:402-403, August 15, 1970.

"Microbiological study of secretion in the vagina, cervical canal and uterine cavity in women with IUD," by M. Nishijima, et al. SANFUJIN JISSAI. 19:40-43, January, 1970.

CONTRACEPTIVES: COMPLICATIONS & SIDE-EFFECTS

"Migraine and oral contraceptives," by L. Moreau, et al. THERAPEUTIQUE. 46:279-281, March, 1970.

"Modern contra conception and veneral diseases." LAKARTIDNINGEN. 67:Suppl. III:16, October 12, 1970.

"Monilial vulvovaginitis following 'the Pill'," by G. Perl. MT SINAI J MED NY. 37:699-701, November-December, 1970.

"Monitoring of adverse reactions to drugs in the United Kingdom," by W. H. Inman. PROC R SOC MED. 63:1302-1304, December, 1970.

"More about the pill; UCLA findings." NEWSWEEK. 76:78+, October 12, 1970.

"More fuel for the pill controversy; use of beagles in testing," by B. J. Culliton. SCI N. 98:402, November 21, 1970.

"Morphologic changes in the uterus associated with steroid contraceptives and intrauterine contraceptive devices," by W. B. Ober. ACTA CYTOL. 14:156, March, 1970.

"Morphological effects of intrauterine contraceptive devices," by R. M. Wynn. ILLINOIS MED J. 137:333-337, April, 1970.

"Morphological findings on the endometrium, decia and chorion following long-term use of intrauterine anticonceptive devices," by M. Stopekova, et al. BRATISL LEK LISTY. 53:146-152, February, 1970.

"Morphology of ovaries and oral contraceptives," by W. P. Plate. NEDERL T GENEESK. 114:1422-1424, August 22, 1970.

"Mortality from coronary occlusion in young women with reference to oral contraceptives as a possible etiological factor," by A. Fischer, et al. UGESKR LAEGER. 132:2480-2482, December 24, 1970.

"Mouth manifestations and oral contraceptives," by M. E. Chavallier. REV ODONTOSTOMATOL MIDI FR. 28:96-103, 1970.

"Myometrial activity and the IUCD. 3. Effect of contraceptive pills," by G. Beyer, et al. AMER J OBSTET GYNEC. 106:87-92, January 1, 1970.

"Neuro-ophthalmological complications in the wake of oral contraceptives," by J. Jablonski. POL TYG LEK. 25:1555-1557, October 12, 1970.

"Neurologic complications after oral contraceptives," by M. Orzechowska, et al. WIAD LEK. 23:2199-2201, December 15, 1970.

"Never mind the Pill---." NURS MIRROR. 131:31-32, October 2, 1970.

"New doubts about the pill." LIFE. 68:28-29, February 27, 1970.

"Notes on current drugs: oral contraceptives and thromboemboembolic disease," by C. B. Cox. MED J AUST. 2:202-203, July 25, 1970.

"Oestrogen content of oral contraceptives and thromboembolism," by E. G. McQueen. NEW ZEAL MED J. 71:317, May, 1970.

"Oestrogens and thromboembolism." BRIT MED J. 2: 189-190, April 25, 1970.

"Oestrogens in the pill." LANCET. 1:929-930, May 2, 1970.

"On a case of thrombosis of the middle cerebral artery during progestogen therapy," by G. G. Cavalca, et al. RIV SPER FRENIAT. 94:83-94, February 28, 1970.

"On some psychiatric complications of oral contraception," by M. Bourgeois, et al. BORDEAUX MED. 3:1273-1292, May, 1970.

"Once a bad'n?" by E. Williams. LANCET. 1:299-300, February 7, 1970.

"Operative laparoscopy: removal of intra-abdominal IUD with biopsy tongs," by M. B. Taylor, et al. OBSTET GYNEC. 35:981, June, 1970.

CONTRACEPTIVES: COMPLICATIONS & SIDE-EFFECTS

"Oral contraceptive steroids: effects on various nutrient balances and body composition in adult female rats," by K. Manoharan, et al. PROC SOC EXP BIOL MED. 133:774-779, March, 1970.

"Oral contraceptives and blood lipids." POSTGRAD MED. 47:256, May, 1970.

"Oral contraceptives and blood pressure," by M. P. Chidell. PRACTITIONER. 205:58-64, July, 1970.

"Oral contraceptives and copper metabolism," by M. Briggs, et al. NATURE (LONDON). 225:81, January 3, 1970.

"Oral contraceptives and depression," by J. Braham. BRIT MED J. 1:237, January 24, 1970.

"Oral contraceptives and female mortality trends," by T. W. Anderson. CANAD MED ASS J. 102:1156-1160, May 30, 1970.

"Oral contraceptives and gastrointestinal disorders," by R. L. Hurwitz, et al. ANN SURG. 172:892-896, November, 1970.

"Oral contraceptives and gestational diabetes." BRIT MED J. 1:190, January 24, 1970.

"Oral contraceptives and glucose tolerance," by P. D. Hansten. ANN INTERN MED. 73:492, September, 1970.

"Oral contraceptives and hypertension." BRIT MED J. 1:378, May 16, 1970.

"Oral contraceptives and hypertension," by D. F. Horrobin, et al. BRIT MED J. 1:285, August 1, 1970.

"Oral contraceptives and hypertension," by A. M. Macintosh. BRIT MED J. 3:346-347, August 8, 1970.

"Oral contraceptives and hypertension: the effect of guanethidine," by T. M. Clezy. MED J AUST. 1:638-640, March 28, 1970.

"Oral contraception and hypertension--once more," by O. Stenbaek. T NORSK LAEGEFOREN. 90:790-791,

CONTRACEPTIVES: COMPLICATIONS & SIDE-EFFECTS

April 15, 1970.

"Oral contraceptives and hypertensive disease: a cybernetic overview," by J. H. Laragh. CIRCULATION. 42:983-985, December, 1970.

"Oral contraceptives and the incidence of thrombosis," by A. F. Abrahamsen. T NORSK LAEGEFOREN. 90:403-408, February 15, 1970.

"Oral contraceptives and low antithrombin-3 activity," by P. Wolf. LANCET. 1:144, January 17, 1970.

"Oral contraceptives and low antithrombin-3 concentration," by M. K. Fagerhol, et al. LANCET. 1:1175, May 30, 1970.

"Oral contraceptives and low antithrombin-3 activity," by E. von Kaulla, et al. LANCET. 1:36, January 3, 1970.

"Oral contraceptives and myocardial infarction," by M. F. Oliver. BRIT MED J. 2:210-213, April 25, 1970.

"Oral contraceptives and neurologic complications," by H. H. Janzik, et al. MED WELT. 10:395-399, March 7, 1970.

"Oral contraceptives and premenstrual depression," by B. Herzberg, et al. LANCET. 1:775, April 11, 1970.

"Oral contraceptives and serum lipids," by G. M. Barton, et al. J OBSTET GYNAEC BRIT COMM. 77:551-554, June, 1970.

"Oral contraceptives and serum-proteins," by M. Elstein. LANCET. 1:367, February 14, 1970.

"Oral contraceptives and thromboembolism." NEW ZEAL MED J. 71:305, May, 1970.

"Oral contraceptives and thrombosis. Introduction," by H. Stormorken. NORD MED. 84:1472-1473, November 12, 1970.

"Oral contraceptives and thrombosis. Pathological-anatomical viewpoint," by L. Jorgensen. NORD MED. 84:1473, November 12, 1970.

"Oral contraceptives and thrombosis. Some coagulation and fibrinolysis changes," by H. Gjonnaess. NORD MED. 84:1473, November 12, 1970.

"Oral contraceptives and vascular anomalies," by L. Goldman. LANCET. 1:108-109, July 11, 1970.

"Oral contraceptives, depression, and aminoacid metabolism," by A. R. Green, et al. LANCET. 1:1288 June 13, 1970.

"Oral contraceptives, depression, and aminoacid metabolism," by D. P. Rose, et al. LANCET. 1:1117-1118, May 23, 1970.

"Oral contraceptives: depression and frigidity," by V. Huffer, et al. J NERV MENT DIS. 151:34-41, July, 1970.

"Oral contraceptives, hypertension, and toxemia," by S. M. Carmichael, et al. OBSTET GYNEC. 35:371-376, March, 1970.

"Oral contraceptives: a review of certain metabolic effects and an examination of the question of safety," by J. W. Goldzieher. FED PROC. 29:1220-1227, May-June, 1970.

"Ovarian pregnancy and the intrauterine device," by H. Lehfeldt, et al. AM J OBSTET GYNECOL. 108: 1005-1009, December 1, 1970.

"Ovarian pregnancy with in situ IUCD: report of 2 cases," by A. Pane, et al. AM J OBSTET GYNECOL. 108:672-673, October 15, 1970.

"Ovary morphology and oral contraceptives," by W. F. Plate. NED TIJDSCHR VERLOSKD GYNAECOL. 70:545-550, December, 1970.

"The oversuppression syndrome," by S. C. MacLeod, et al. AMER J OBSTET GYNEC. 106:359-364, February 1, 1970.

"The oversuppression syndrome," by W. N. Spellacy,

et al. AMER J OBSTET GYNEC. 107:1270-1271, August 15, 1970.

"Ovulation after the pill," by H. P. Dunn. BRIT MED J. 1:237, January 24, 1970.

"Ovulation inhibitor and pancreopathy," by K. Bauer-Hack. MED WELT. 40:1739-1745, October 3, 1970.

"Oxytocin levels in female rats with bilateral intrauterine devices," by K. S. Raghavan, et al. J ENDOCR. 47:255-256, June, 1970.

"Parathion, embryonic development, sterilization and estrogen effects in birds. Comparison with the effects of aldrin," by Y. Lutz-Ostertag, et al. ANNEE BIOL. 9:501-507, July-October, 1970.

"Perforation of bicornuate uterus by intrauterine contraceptive device," by S. D. Gupta. J OBSTET GYNAECOL BR COMMONW. 77:1140-1141, December, 1970.

"Perforation of the uterus by an intrauterine contraceptive device (1 case)," by M. Dumont, et al. REV FRANC GYNEC OBSTET. 65:115-117, March, 1970.

"Perils of the pill; Senate hearings." NEWSWEEK. 75:21, January 26, 1970.

"Peroral contraception (6): adverse effects," by B. Westerholm. LAKARTIDNINGEN. 67:Suppl III:63+, October 12, 1970.

"Peroral contraception (7): metabolic changes," by U. Larsson-Cohn. LAKARTIDNINGEN. 67:Suppl III: 71+, October 12, 1970.

"Peroral contraception (8): changes in laboratory test results," by S. Lindstedt, et al. LAKARTIDNINGEN. 67:Suppl III:76+, October 12, 1970.

"Physiologic responses to conception control methods in domestic animals," by H. W. Hawk. J AM VET MED ASSOC. 157:1795-1799, December 1, 1970.

"The pill, amenorrhea and ovarian cysts. Conservative surgical treatment. Pregnancy," by A. Paoli, et al. BULL FED GYNEC OBSTET FRANC. 22:90-92,

CONTRACEPTIVES: COMPLICATIONS & SIDE-EFFECTS

January-March, 1970.

"The pill and the breast," by H. P. Leis, Jr. NY STATE J MED. 70:2911-2918, December 1, 1970.

"The pill and hypertension," by R. P. Russell, et al. JOHNS HOPKINS MED J. 127:287-293, November, 1970.

"The Pill and the Pathologist." NZ MED J. 72:45-47, July, 1970. Demulen: hastily approved drug," by D. C. Goldberg. SCIENCE. 170:491, October 30, 1970.

"The pill and the public's right to know," by M. Mintz. PROGRESSIVE. 34:25-27, May, 1970.

"The pill and thrombosis," by G. J. Ottolander. NED TIJDSCHR VERLOSKD GYNAECOL. 70:556-562, December, 1970.

"Pill and your skin." VOGUE. 155:216+, May, 1970.

"Pill caution." TIME. 95:46, April 20, 1970.

"The pill controversy," by J. W. Records. SOUTHERN MED J. 63:608-610, May, 1970.

"Pill: do its benefits outweigh its hazards?" CONSUMER REP. 35:314-319, May, 1970.

"Pills and thrombosis (platelets, estrogens and magnesium)," by J. Durlach. REV FRANC ENDOCR CLIN. 11:45-54, January-February, 1970.

"Plasma-proteins and oral contraceptives." LANCET. 1:72-73, January 10, 1970.

"Platelet adhesiveness in women using oral contraceptives," by N. Oishi, et al. HAWAII MED J. 29:365-367, May-June, 1970.

"Polyethylene intrauterine contraceptive device. Endometrial changes following long-term use," by W. B. Ober, et al. JAMA. 212:765-769, May 4, 1970.

"A possible mechanism for hypertension induced by oral contraceptives. Diminished feedback suppression of renin release," by T. Saruta, et al. ARCH

INTERN MED. 126:621-626, October, 1970.

"Postoperative thromboembolism and the use of oral contraceptives," by M. P. Vessey, et al. BRIT MED J. 3:123-126, July 18, 1970.

"Pregnancy and chlormadinone acetate," by G. R. Daniel. BRIT MED J. 1:174-175, January 17, 1970.

"Pregnancy and delivery with an intrauterine contraceptive device in situ. An analysis of 44 cases," by P. Damsgaard-Sorensen, et al. UGESKR LAEG. 132:736-738, April 16, 1970.

"Problems concerning oral contraception," by A. Salvati, et al. MINERVA MED. 61:Suppl 43:10-12, May, 1970.

"Progressive inhibition of uterine sensitivity in rats fitted with intra-uterine sutures," by J. C. Wood, et al. J REPROD FERTIL. 22:339-343, July, 1970.

"Prolonged amenorrhea following oral contraception," by B. A. Hayes, Jr. N CAROLINA MED J. 31:352-354, September, 1970.

"Psychoendocrine study of oral contraceptive agents," by F. J. Kane, et al. AMER J PSYCHIAT. 127:443-450, October, 1970.

"Psychological aspects of oral contraceptives," by F. J. Huygen. NEDERL T GENEESK. 114:1436, August 22, 1970.

"Psychological aspects of oral contraceptives," by F. J. Huygens. NED TIJDSCHR VERLOSKD GYNAECOL. 70:610-617, December, 1970.

"Psychological aspects of the use of anovulatory agents," by Y. Rouleau, et al. CANAD PSYCHIAT ASS J. 15:295-300, June, 1970.

"Psychological disturbance and oral contraceptives." LANCET. 1:1378, June 27, 1970.

"Psychopathology of the pill." CANAD MED ASS J. 102:217, January 31, 1970.

CONTRACEPTIVES: COMPLICATIONS & SIDE-EFFECTS

"Psychophysiologic changes accompanying oral contraceptive use," by D. B. Marcotte, et al. BRIT J PSYCHIAT. 116:165-167, February, 1970.

"Psychosomatic effects of ovulation inhibitors," by H. J. Prill. GEBURTSH FRAUENHEILK. 30:212-224, March, 1970.

"Rabbit uterine contractile activity in the presence of an intrauterine device," by D. K. Michael, et al. AMER J OBSTET GYNEC. 107:188-193, May 15, 1970.

"Raynaud-like clinical picture during the treatment with an oral contraceptive," by H. Ebert. DTSCH GESUNDHEITSW. 25:1642-1643, August 27, 1970.

"Reactions of human endometrium to the intrauterine device. I. Correlation of the endometrial histology with the bacterial environment of the uterus following short-term insertion of the IUD," by D. L. Moyer, et al. AMER J OBSTET GYNEC. 106:799-809, March 15, 1970.

"Recalling a pill; chlormadinone." TIME. 95:39, February 9, 1970.

"Recurrent polyneuropathy with pregnancy and oral contraceptives," by R. Calderon-Gonzalez, et al. NEW ENG J MED. 282:1307-1308, June 4, 1970.

"Regression of cerebral lesions after cessation of oral contraceptives," by H. R. McFarland. SOUTHERN MED J. 63:145-151, February, 1970.

"Relation between estrogen content and the risk of thromboembolism in peroral contraception." UGESKR LAEG. 132:846, April 30, 1970.

"The relationship between endometrial mast cell count and bleeding in women following insertion of an intrauterine device," by U. Mehra, et al. AMER J OBSTET GYNEC. 107:852-856, July 15, 1970.

"A report from the Australian drug evaluation committee: oral contraceptives and thromboembolic disease." MED J AUST. 1:1267-1269, June 20, 1970.

"Review of side effects of oral contraceptives," by J. Janssens. NEDERL T GENEESK. 114:1418-1422, August 22, 1970.

"Richter's hernia resulting from displaced intrauterine contraceptive device," by G. F. Schwartz, et al. AMER SURG. 36:502-504, August, 1970.

"Role of drug-reaction monitoring in the investigation of thrombosis and 'the pill'," by W. H. Inman. BR MED BULL. 26:248-256, September, 1970.

"Safety of oral contraception," by L. Mastroianni, Jr. FERTIL STERIL. 21:281, March, 1970.

"Safety of oral contraceptives," by J. Frankenberg. BRIT MED J. 1:285, August 1, 1970.

"Safety of the pill," by J. Infield. BRIT MED J. 1:294, May 2, 1970.

"Sagittal sinus thrombosis related to oral contraceptives. Case report," by M. C. Shende, et al. J NEUROSURG. 33:714-717, December, 1970.

"Second trimester foetal death associated with an intra-uterine contraceptive device," by E. Tischler, et al. MED J AUST. 1:441-442, February 28, 1970.

"Serious sequelae of intrauterine contraceptive devices," by G. F. Schwartz, et al. JAMA. 211:959-960, February 9, 1970.

"Serum fucose levels during pregnancy and while taking oral contraceptives," by W. N. Spellacy, et al. OBSTET GYNEC. 35:39-43, January, 1970.

"The serum levels of nonesterified fatty acids and free amino acids under the effect of the oral contraceptive, Ovosiston," by H. D. Methfessel, et al. Z AERZTL FORTBILD. 64:880-882, September 1, 1970.

"Serum lipids during oral contraceptive exposure," by D. G. Corredor, et al. CLIN PHARMACOL THER. 11:188-193, March-April, 1970.

CONTRACEPTIVES: COMPLICATIONS & SIDE-EFFECTS

"Serum protein-(Xh)-changes in pregnancy and use of ovulation inhibitons in women and men," by G. Geserick, et al. ZENTRALBL GYNAEKOL. 92:1195-1200, September 12, 1970.

"Severe arterial hypertension, stenosis of the renal artery, a disorder of glycoregulation and the contraceptive pill," by H. Bour, et al. COEUR MED INTERN. 9:239-243, April, 1970.

"Side effect: pill sales slump." CHEM W. 106:26, April 1, 1970.

"Side effects of contraceptive drugs," by W. E. Schreiner. SCHWEIZ MED WOCHENSCHR. 100:778-784, May 2, 1970.

"Side effects of contraceptive steroids. I," by E. J. Plotz. GEBURTSH FRAUENHEILK. 30:193-211, March, 1970.

"Side effects of contraceptive steroids. II," by E. J. Plotz. GEBURTSH FRAUENHEILK. 30:362-379, April, 1970.

"Side effects of contraceptives," by I. V. Skorodumova. AKUSH GINEKOL. 46:41-46, March, 1970.

"Side effects of the oral contraceptive Ovosiston on the blood coagulation system," by W. Carol, et al. ZENTRALBL GYNAEKOL. 92:1641-1650, December 12, 1970.

"Side effects of synthetic progestagens," by L. A. De Luca. REV PAUL MED. 76:34-36, March, 1970.

"Some aspects of the interaction between natural and synthetic female sex hormones and the liver," by H. Adlercreutz, et al. AM J MED. 49:630-648, November, 1970.

"Some remarks on factors influencing the failure of intra-uterine devices," by A. Sadovsky, et al. HAREFUAH. 78:247-248, March 1, 1970.

"Some variations in the normal haemoglobin concentration," by J. M. Cruickshank. BRIT J HAEMAT. 18:523-529, May, 1970.

CONTRACEPTIVES: COMPLICATIONS & SIDE-EFFECTS

"Statement on the thromboembolic risk while taking oral contraceptives," by H. Rozenbaum. THERAPEUTIQUE. 46:439-441, April, 1970.

"Stimulation by ovarian hormones and intrauterine devices of vascular function in the endometrium of the ewe," by B. S. Cooper, et al. AMER J OBSTET GYNEC. 106:93-97, January 1, 1970.

"Stroke, sickle cell trait, and oral contraceptives," by J. G. Greenwald. ANN INTERN MED. 72:960, June, 1970.

"Studies on the site of action of oral contraceptive steroids. II. Plasma LH and FSH levels after administration of antifertility steroids and LH-releasing hormone (LH-RH)," by A. V. Schally, et al. ENDOCRINOLOGY. 86:530-541, March, 1970.

"A study of the endometrium in intrauterine contraceptive device users," by S. Rimdusit, et al. J MED ASSOC THAI. 53:843-848, December, 1970.

"A study of glucose tolerance in women taking oral contraceptives," by Z. Domany. ORV HETIL. 111: 1511-1513, June 28, 1970.

"Suppression of oestradiol secretion and luteinising-hormone release during oestrogen-progestagen oral contraceptive therapy," by M. Dufau, et al. LANCET. 1:271-274, February 7, 1970.

"Therapeutic considerations of side effects of hormonal contraceptives on the liver," by S. F. Gomes da Costa, et al. ARZNEIM FORSCH. 20:1246-1247, September, 1970.

"Thromboembolic complications during treatment by estro-progestational drugs. Critical study of 3 cases," by L. Croccel, et al. SEM HOP PARIS. 46: 101-108, January 8, 1970.

"Thromboembolic disease and the pill," by L. F. Nanni. BR MED J. 3:644, September 12, 1970.

"Thromboembolic disease and the steroidal content of oral contraceptives. A report to the Committee on Safety of Drugs," by W. H. Inman, et al. BRIT MED

J. 2:203-209, April 25, 1970.

"Thromboembolism and oral contraception." MED J AUST. 1:1025, May 23, 1970.

"Thromboembolism, oral contraceptives, and cigarettes," by H. Frederiksen, et al. PUBLIC HEALTH REP. 85: 197-205, March, 1970.

"Thromboembolism, oral contraceptives, and cigarettes," by A. T. Masi. ANN INTERN MED. 73:486-487, September, 1970.

"Thrombosis and the content of estrogens in oral anticonceptives," by T. J. Skobba. T NORSK LAEGEFOREN. 90:1223-1224, June 1, 1970.

"Thrombosis of a Blalock's anastomosis for Fallot's tetralogy, in the course of a contraceptive treatment," by J. C. Pony, et al. ARCH MAL COEUR. 63: 277-290, February, 1970.

"Thrombosis prophylaxis and the pill," by K. K. Meyer, et al. AMER J SURG. 119:619, June, 1970.

"Thrombotic complications in a young woman during ovocyston therapy," by Z. Babinska, et al. WIAD LEK. 23:333-336, February 15, 1970.

"Thyroid-function tests in women taking norgestrel," by A. W. Goolden, et al. LANCET. 1:624, March 21, 1970.

"Trouble with the IUD." NEWSWEEK. 75:73, May 25, 1970.

"Tubal pregnancy and oral contraceptive by continual administration," by A. Fonder, et al. BULL FED SOC GYNECOL OBSTET LANG FR. 22:329-330, June-August, 1970.

"2 cases of coralloid renal lithiasis developed in young women under prolonged treatment with the contraceptive pill," by S. Reziciner. ANN UROL. 4: 269-274, December, 1970.

"Undesirable effects of sex hormone therapy." PRESSE MED. 78:2135-2136, November 14, 1970.

CONTRACEPTIVES: COMPLICATIONS & SIDE-EFFECTS

"Ureteral dilatation and oral contraceptives," by S. Marshall. JAMA. 211:2157, March 30, 1970.

"Urinary oestrogens in pill-users may be artefacts." LANCET. 2:598, September 19, 1970.

"Urinary tract dilatation and oral contraceptives," by P. B. Guyer, et al. BR MED J. 4:588-590, December 5, 1970.

"Use of oxytocics in the control of hemorrhages after the insertion of intrauterine devices," by M. de M. Marques, et al. HOSPITAL. 78:177-189, July, 1970.

"Uterine activity and oral contraceptives," by T. K. Eskes. NED TIJDSCHR VERLOSKD GYNAECOL. 70:550-556, December, 1970.

"Uterine bleeding in rhesus monkeys after intrauterine contraceptive device insertion: effect of adrenosem salicylate and p-aminomethylbenzoic acid," by A. B. Kar, et al. INDIAN J EXP BIOL. 8:48, January, 1970.

"Uterine perforation by Lippes loop," by P. S. Alberts. OBSTET GYNEC. 36:164-166, July, 1970.

"Uterotrophic action of an intrauterine contraceptive device in Rhesus monkeys," by H. Chandra, et al. INDIAN J EXP BIOL. 8:50, January, 1970.

"Uterus activity and oral contraceptives," by T. K. Eskes. NEDERL T GENEESK. 114:1424-1426, August 22, 1970.

"Vaginal cytology in a study of cumulative effects of an oral contraceptive: acid mucopolysaccharide and keratin as indicators for cycle stages," by E. Stern, et al. ACTA CYTOL. 14:382-385, July-August, 1970.

"Vaginal smear patterns in women taking ethynodial diacetate as an oral contraceptive," by K. R. Heber. MED J AUST. 1:379-381, February 21, 1970.

"Variations in the renin-angiotensin-aldosterone system and in the antidiuretic hormone induced within

CONTRACEPTIVES: COMPLICATIONS & SIDE-EFFECTS

 5 days by a contraceptive drug. Rapid action of a contraceptive drug on the hormones controlling water and salt metabolism," by J. Menard, et al. PRESSE MED. 78:415-419, February 21, 1970.

"Vascular lesions in women taking oral contraceptives," by N. S. Irey, et al. ARCH PATH. 89:1-8, January, 1970.

"Visual loss associated with oral contraceptives," by M. S. Smith, et al. AMER J OPHTHAL. 69:874-876, May, 1970.

"Warnings," by P. Ehrlich. LISTENER. 84:215-216, August 13, 1970.

"Why there is growing concern about the safety of the pill." GOOD H. 170:129-131, January, 1970.

CONTRACEPTIVES: GENERAL
"Antifertility agents," by C. W. Emmens. ANN REV PHARMACOL. 10:237-254, 1970.

"Antifertility agents. IV. 2,3-diphenylbenzo and 5, 6-polymethylenebenzofurans, 1,2-diphenylnaphthofurans, and some related compounds," by H. P. Chawla, et al. J MED CHEM. 13:54-59, January, 1970.

"Antifertility drugs. Introductory remarks," by V. A. Drill. FED PROC. 29:1209-1210, May-June, 1970.

"Antifertility drugs. Symposium discussion," by C. R. Garcia. FED PROC. 29:1240-1241, May-June, 1970.

"The antifertility effect of Butea frondosa petals (alcoholic extract and its crystalline fraction)," by K. Kapila, et al. J INDIAN MED ASS. 55:60-61, July 16, 1970.

"Antispermatogenic agents," by H. Jackson. BRIT MED BULL. 26:79-86, January, 1970.

"Clinical and microscopic study of the inhibition of spermatic fertilizing power by 799 R. Trial of contraception in 114 cases," by A. Notter, et al. BULL FED GYNEC OBSTET FRANC. 22:58-60, January-

CONTRACEPTIVES: GENERAL

March, 1970.

"Comments on the current status of contraception," by J. Ledr. CESK GYNEK. 35:40-41, February, 1970.

"Commonsense advice on contraceptives," by L. M. Hellman. FAMILY HLTH. :37+, January, 1970.

"Conception control in doctors' families," by R. Levin, et al. PRACTITIONER. 204:694-699, May, 1970.

"Continuance of contraception post partum by patients of Cook County Hospital," by P. B. Tamblyn, et al. PUBLIC HEALTH REP. 85:220-224, March, 1970.

"Continued or discontinued use of contraceptives," by G. J. Kloosterman. NEDERL T GENEESK. 114: 1429-1432, August 22, 1970.

"Continued or intermittent use of contraceptives," by G. J. Kloosterman. NED TIJDSCHR VERLOSKD GYNAECOL. 70:576-583, December, 1970.

"Contraception," by H. Winn. CLIN OBSTET GYNECOL. 13:701-712, September, 1970.

"Contraception and abortion: american catholic responses," by D. Callhan. ANNALS OF THE AMERICAN ACADEMY OF POLITICAL & SOCIAL SCIENCE. 387:109-117, January, 1970. SA #E7669.

"Contraception before and during marriage," by V. Bartak, et al. CAS LEK CESK. 109:599-604, June 19, 1970.

"Contraception; the chemical control of fertility, by D. Lednicer. A review by V. Petrow." CHEM & IND. 1105-1106, August 22, 1970.

"Contraception: the fourth stage of labour," by P. A. Last. NURS MIRROR. 130:25-29, April 3, 1970.

"Contraception in general practice. A research project from general practice. II. Presentation of cases with special attention to the contraceptive pattern," by P. Backer, et al. UGESKR LAEG. 132: 227-231, January 29, 1970.

CONTRACEPTIVES: GENERAL

"Contraception sine comstockery," by S. H. Sturgis.
NEW ENG J MED. 283:595-596, September 10, 1970.

"Contraception hormones," by B. N. Branch. J INDIAN
MED ASSOC. 55:359-362, November 16, 1970.

"Contraceptive methods prior to hospital discharge:
the first city-wide program," by E. F. Dally.
AMER J PUBLIC HEALTH. 60:965-967, June, 1970.

"Contraceptive technology: advances needed in fundamental research," by L. J. Carter. SCIENCE.
168:805-809, May 15, 1970.

"Contraceptives," by P. A. Corfman, et al. SCIENCE.
167:1315-1316, March 6, 1970.

"Effect of infecundin in combination with ethimizol
on the reproductive capacity of white rats," by
A. N. Poskalenko, et al. AKUSH GINEKOL. 46:46-49, March, 1970.

"Effect of nonsteroidal compounds on fertility," by
G. W. Duncan, et al. FED PROC. 29:1232-1239,
May-June, 1970.

"The egg that never was," by E. Wachtel, et al. ACTA
CYTOL. 14:1-2, January, 1970.

"Ethinylated steroids," by D. Onken, et al. PHARMAZIE.
25:3-9, January 1, 1970.

"Femigen forte and mite preparations in contraception
and gynecological disorders," by Z. Sternade, et
al. GINEKOL POL. 41:1227-1236, November, 1970.

"Fertility control: health and educational factors
for the 1970's. Contraception or abortion?" by
J. H. Hughes. J BIOSOC SCI. 2:161-166, April,
1970.

"Fertility control: health and educational factors
for the 1970's. The future of oral contraception,"
by G. A. Christie. J BIOSOC SCI. 2:191-197,
April, 1970.

"Fertility control: health and educational factors
for the 1970's. Trends in contraception," by A.

CONTRACEPTIVES: GENERAL

C. Turnbull. J BIOSOC SCI. 2:157-160, April, 1970.

"Fertility control with drugs," by E. T. Tyler. POSTGRAD MED. 47:82-86, January, 1970.

"Human fertility control by transvaginal application of quinacrine on the fallopian tube," by J. A. Zipper, et al. FERTIL STERIL. 21:581-589, August, 1970.

"Ideal means of fertility control?" by A. Gillespie, et al. LANCET. 1:717, April 4, 1970.

"Ideal means of fertility control?" by J. J. Speidel, et al. LANCET. 1:565, March 14, 1970.

"Incorporation of (3H) uridine into the ribonucleic acid of rat uterus during pseudopregnancy and in the presence of I.C.I. 46474. (trans-1-(p-beta-dimethylaminoethoxyphenyl)-1,1-diphenylbut-1-ene)," by J. E. O'Grady, et al. BIOCHEM J. 119:609-613, October, 1970.

"Knowledge of and employment of contraception by young mothers," by A. Braestrup. UGESKR LAEG. 132:232-240, January 29, 1970.

"Long cycles, late ovulation, and calendar rhythm," by R. G. Potter, Jr., et al. INT J FERTIL. 12:127-140, January-March, 1970.

"Looking back upon our guidance in conception control," by Y. Ashimura. KANGO. 22:91-94, December, 1970.

"Mechanical methods of contraception," by E. Stewart. PRACTITIONER. 205:13-19, July, 1970.

"The mental and sexual aspects of contraceptives," by J. P. Hes. HAREFUAH. 78:299-300, March 15, 1970.

"Net delay of next conception by contraception: a highly simplified case," by R. G. Potter, A. K. Jain and B. McCann. POPULATION STUDIES. 24:173-192, July, 1970.

"Nurse, make it well," by E. H. Naugle. NO. 18:41, November, 1970.

CONTRACEPTIVES: GENERAL

"Ovarian suppressants in dogs: pilot study of an approach to rabies control," by C. Yasmuth, et al. LANCET. 760:1312-1315, June 20, 1970.

"Pharmacologic approach to contraception," by H. D. Johnson. J AMER PHARM ASS. 10:261-263, May, 1970.

"Prevention of pregnancy in the rabbit by subcutaneous implantation of silastic tube containing oestrogen," by M. C. Chang, et al. NATURE (LONDON). 226:1262-1263, June 27, 1970.

"Prognosis for the development of new chemical birth-control agents," by C. Djerassi. SCIENCE. 166:468-473, October 24, 1969; Discussion, P. A. Corfman. 167:1315; Reply. 1315-1316, March 6, 1970.

"Progress in contraception," by M. Vojta. CESK GYNEK. 35:129-130, March, 1970.

"Promiscuity and contraception in a sample of patients attending a clinic for venereal diseases," by A. Linken, et al. BRIT J VENER DIS. 46:243-246, June, 1970.

"Recent progress on systemic contraceptives," by S. Matsumoto. ACTA OBSTET GYNAEC JAP. 17:211-219, July, 1970.

"Schmid plans first national ads for prophylactic brands." ADV AGE. 41:6, March 16, 1970.

"Search for a preparation to prevent venereal disease and pregnancy," by R. C. Arnold, et al. PUBLIC HEALTH REP. 85:1062, December, 1970.

"Survey on induced abortion and use of contraceptives in Bogota. Method of approach," by S. Gomez, et al. REV COLOMB OBSTET GINECOL. 21:427-439, July-August, 1970.

"Temporary occlusion of ductus deferens," by K. H. Moon, et al. INVEST UROL. 8:292-298, November, 1970.

"The use of contraceptives in internal medicine," by K. Rak. ORV HETIL. 111:1913, August 9, 1970.

"Use of subcutaneous Silastic capsules for long-term

CONTRACEPTIVES: GENERAL

steroid contraception," by S. Tejuja. AMER J OBSTET GYNEC. 107:954-957, July 15, 1970.

"Users and non-users of contraception: tests of stationarity applied to members of a family planning programme," by G. E. Erbanks. POPULATION STUDIES. 24:85-91, March, 1970.

"Without sugar-coating: Jim Balog takes a searching look at drug research, the pill." BARRONS. 50:5+, February 23, 1970.

CONTRACEPTIVES: IUD

"Advantages and problems associated with the intrauterine device," by J. D. Loudon. MIDWIFE HEALTH VISIT. 6:97-99 passim, March, 1970.

"An analysis of 3 years' experience with intrauterine devices among women in the western area of the city of Santiago, July 1, 1964, to June 30, 1967," by B. Viel, et al. AMER J OBSTET GYNEC. 106:765-775, March, 1970.

"A bacteriological study in women with early postpartum intrauterine contraceptive device insertion," by G. R. Umabal, et al. INDIAN J MED RES. 58:258-267, February, 1970.

"Bacteriological study on the users of intrauterine contraceptive devices," by A. Ishihama, et al. ACTA OBSTET GYNAEC JAP. 17:77-80, April, 1970.

"Biologic mode of action of the Lippes loop in intrauterine contraception," by N. Sagiroglu, et al. AMER J OBSTET GYNEC. 106:506-515, February 15, 1970.

"Chemical composition of the deposits formed on the Lippes loop after prolonged use," by A. D. Engineer, et al. AMER J OBSTET GYNEC. 106:315-316, January 15, 1970.

"Chemical composition of I.U.C.D.s.," by P. R. Myerscough. LANCET. 2:1316-1317, December 19, 1970.

"Clinical evaluation of a plastic ring intra-uterine contraceptive device (INCON)," by E. B. Leverich, et al. J LOUISIANA MED SOC. 121:340-344, November, 1969.

CONTRACEPTIVES: IUD

"Contraception by intra-uterine device," M. Lancet, et al. HAREFUAH. 78:223-226, March 1, 1970.

"Contraception by means of a silastic vaginal ring impregnated with medroxyprogesterone acetate," by D. R. Mishell, Jr., et al. AMER J OBSTET GYNEC. 107:100-107, May 1, 1970.

"Contraception using the intrauterine device Super-DANA in combination with the rhythm method," by M. Vojta, et al. CESK GYNEK. 35:32-35, February, 1970.

"Contraceptive effect of varying dosages of progestogen in silastic vaginal rings," by D. R. Mishell, Jr., et al. FERTIL STERIL. 21:99-103, February, 1970.

"Ectopic Lippes' intrauterine devices. Hysterography," by E. Villablanca. REV CHIL OBSTET GINECOL. 35: 59-66, 1970.

"Effectiveness and adverse effects of the IUD (contraceptive loop) manufactured in Hungary," by Z. Szereday, et al. ORV HETIL. 111:2303-2305, September 27, 1970.

"An evaluation of the intrauterine contraceptive devices," by H. C. Chia. SINGAPORE MED J. 11:46-51, March, 1970.

"Evaluation of Lippes loop in planned parenthood. Present status," by S. A. Kaufman, et al. NEW YORK J MED. 70:2103-2107, August 15, 1970.

"Evaluation of the results of intrauterine contraception. 2 year analysis of the Rostock studies by means of the life table method of Tietze and Potter," by H. G. Neumann. GEBURTSHILFE FRAUENHEILKD. 30: 537-547, June, 1970.

"Evaluation of 300 cases of intrauterine devices," by G. Marty. BULL FED GYNEC OBSTET FRANC. 22:111-112, January-March, 1970.

"Experience with double-coil intrauterine contraceptive device," by B. J. Vaughn, et al. POSTGRAD MED. 47:179-183, February, 1970.

CONTRACEPTIVES: IUD

"Experience with IUD; first insertions," by J. H. Gerende, et al. PENN MED. 73:56-60, March, 1970.

"Experience with intrauterine pessaries," by M. Schulz. Z AERZT L FORTBILD. 64:1138-1141, November 15, 1970.

"Experience with DANA Super Fix contraception," by J. Sracek. CESK GYNEK. 35:277-279, 1970.

"Experience with the contraceptive effectiveness of the intrauterine DANA-Super devices," by M. Semczuk, et al. POL TYG LEK. 25:1710-1711, November 9, 1970.

"Family planning in a rural area using intrauterine devices," by C. R. Ramirez. REV CHIL OBSTET GINECOL. 35:11-13, 1970.

"Fertility after removal of the intrauterine ring," by G. Waintraub. FERTIL STERIL. 21:555-564, July, 1970.

"Frequency of expulsion of intrauterine pessaries depending upon the type and time of introduction," by S. I. Sleptsova. AKUSH GINEKOL. 46:52-55, March, 1970.

"Further experience with intrauterine contraceptive devices," by W. Mills. LANCET. 2:921-923, October 31, 1970.

"Improving mechanical birth control methods; intrauterine devices," by B. J. Cullition. SCI N. 98:121-123, August 8, 1970.

"Insertion and supervision of an intrauterine device," by J. H. Ravina. PRESSE MED. 78:31-32, January 3, 1970.

"Insertion of IUD following artificial abortion," by J. Koukal, et al. CESK GYNEKOL. 35:465-467, October, 1970.

"Interference with reproduction in water buffalo by intra-uterine devices," by K. Janakiraman, et al. J REPROD FERTIL. 22:499-507, August, 1970.

CONTRACEPTIVES: IUD

"Intrauterine administration of progesterone by a slow releasing device," by A. Scommegna, et al. FERTIL STERIL. 21:201-210, March, 1970.

"Intra-uterine contraception," by D. F. Hawkins. PRACTITIONER. 205:20-29, July, 1970.

"Intrauterine contraception and the Armed Forces," by R. Israel. MILIT MED. 135:490-494, June, 1970.

"Intrauterine contraception in Indians of the American Southwest," by C. C. Bollinger, et al. AMER J OBSTET GYNEC. 106:669-675, March, 1970.

"Is pregnancy interruption necessary following failure of the intrauterine device (IUD)," by M. Kohoutek, et al. CESK GYNEK. 35:341-342, July, 1970.

"The Lippes loop in general practice," by N. H. Fursdon, et al. NZ MED J. 72:239-243, October, 1970.

"Les loop: medicolegal aspects," by J. E. Deming. MED TRIAL TECHN QUART. 16:1-8, June, 1970.

"Majzlin intrauterine contraceptive spring. Report of a clinical study," by A. J. Sobrero, et al. OBSTET GYNECOL. 36:911-918, December, 1970.

"Mechanism of action of intrauterine contraceptives in women," by H. J. Davis, et al. OBSTET GYNEC. 36:350-358, September, 1970.

"Mechanism of the contraceptive effect of intrauterine devices," by V. I. Sakharov, et al. AKUSH GINEKOL. 46:56-57, March, 1970.

"Mechanisms of action of intra-uterine contraceptive devices in women and other mannals," by P. Eckstein. BRIT MED BULL. 26:52-59, January, 1970.

"Medical correlates of termination of use of intrauterine contraceptive devices in Taichung," by J. Y. Peng, et al. INT J FERTIL. 15:120-126, April-June, 1970.

"Microdose intrauterine progestagen associated with intrauterine contraceptive devices," by H. W. Horne, Jr., et al. INT J FERTIL. 15:210-213, October-

CONTRACEPTIVES: IUD

December, 1970.

"Mode of action of intra-uterine devices," by J. H. Ravina. PRESSE MED. 78:1063-1064, May 9, 1970.

"A new intrauterine contraceptive device. An open ring," by S. Rozin, et al. OBSTET GYNEC. 36: 304-305, August, 1970.

"Our experience with the IUD (contraceptive loop) inserted immediately after interruption of pregnancy," by Z. Szereday, et al. ORV HETIL. 111:2299-2300, September 27, 1970.

"Permanent contraception using K 18 IUD," by R. Jinno. SANFUIIN JISSAI. 19:51-53, January, 1970.

"A population policy for Britain," by M. Lancet, et al. HAREFUAH. 78:223-226, March 1, 1970.

"Rapid disruption of sperm transport mechanisms by intra-uterine devices in the ewe," by H. W. Hawk. J REPROD FERTIL. 23:139-142, October, 1970.

"Removal of Lippes loop through laparoscope," by M. O. Farooqul, et al. PRACTITIONER. 205:65-66, July, 1970.

"2nd generation IUDs are here," by H. Goldstein. AM DRUGGIST. 162:37-39, November 2, 1970.

"The shield intrauterine device. A superior modern contraceptive," by H. J. Davis. AMER J OBSTET GYNEC. 106:455-456, February 1, 1970.

"Statistical observations on IUD in the Tokyo Teishin Hospital," by I. Fuchi. SANFUJIN JISSAI. 19:44-50, January, 1970.

"3 interesting cases of insertion of the wing," by T. Fukuda, et al. SANFUJIN JISSAI. 19:763-766, July, 1970.

"Treatment of intrauterine adhesions with the use of intrauterine devices," by J. Danezis. INT J FERTIL. 15:14-23, January-March, 1970.

"Use of intrauterine devices," by H. G. Neumann. DTSCH

CONTRACEPTIVES: IUD

    GESUNDHEITSW. 25:1957-1958, October 8, 1970.

"Use of intrauterine devices for contraception," by G. V. Truevtseva, et al. AKUSH GINEKOL. 46:49-52, March, 1970.

CONTRACEPTIVES: MALE
"Blood-testis barrier--the key to male contraception in the future?" by M. Kormano. DUODECIM. 86:672-670, 1970.

"Current status of fertility restraint in males," R. Petry, et al. DEUTSCH MED WSCHR. 95:855-858, April 10, 1970.

"Male antifertility compounds: U-5897 as a rat chemosterilant," by R. J. Ericsson. J REPROD FERTIL. 22:213-222, July, 1970.

"Male contraceptive: a better pill?" by L. Witt. TODAYS HEALTH. 48:16-19+, June, 1970.

"Nature and site of action of 3-chloro-1,2-propanediol--an oral antifertility agent for the male," by B. S. Setty, et al. INDIAN J EXP BIOL. 8:49-50, January, 1970.

"Proselytizers for prophylactics; Population services, inc. promotes condoms. TIME. 96:97+, December 7, 1970.

CONTRACEPTIVES: ORAL
"AMA deslikes giving OC users info." AM DRUGGIST. 162:39, October 5, 1970.

"AMA writes OC consumer booklet." AM DRUGGIST. 162:20, August 24, 1970.

"Action mechanism of oral contraceptives," by M. Tausk. NED TIJDSCHR VERLOSKD GYNAECOL. 70:520-527, December, 1970.

"Action of trioxyethylrutin in women under estroprogestative treatment," by J. Laforet, et al. LYON MED. 223:327-329, February 1, 1970.

"The active mechanism of oral contraceptives," by M. Tausk. NEDERL T GENEESK. 114:1417-1418, August

CONTRACEPTIVES: ORAL

22, 1970.

"Alternatives for oral contraceptives," by A. A. Haspels. NED TIJDSCHR VERLOSKD GYNAECOL. 70:584-599, December, 1970.

"Antifertility effects of low dose progestin," by H. W. Rudel. FED PROC. 29:1228-1231, May-June, 1970.

"Antiuterotrophic activity of benzo-& naphthofurans: new oral antifertility agents," by B. S. Setty, et al. INDIAN J EXP BIOL. 8:139, April, 1970.

"Birth pills' marketing freedom is just about coming to an end; curbs, lower dosages in offing." OIL PAINT & DRUG REP. 197:3+, January 19, 1970.

"British experience of the pill," by C. R. Kay. J ROY COLL GEN PRACT. 19:251-257, May, 1970.

"CFM and the pill," by J. Deedy. COMMONWEAL. 91:442, January 23, 1970.

"Child plan organization endorses pill." AM DRUGGIST. 161:57, May 18, 1970.

"Chlormadinone acetate in microdosis as a contraceptive," by J. Botero, et al. REV OBSTET GINECOL VENEZ. 21:503-508, September-October, 1970.

"Chlormadinone contraceptive withdrawn," by L. Poller. BRIT MED J. 1:303-304, January 31, 1970.

"Clinical aspects of the administration of gestagen preparations (Volidan, Cyclofarlutal, Ovulen, Ciba AC-101 and Steridil)," by Z. Sternadel. GINEK POL. 41:771-776, July, 1970.

"Clinical aspects of Ovulen application as a contraceptive and in gynecological disorders," by M. Bulska, et al. GINEK POL. 41:877-882, 1970.

"Clinical evaluation of Madinon-s, an oral contraceptive," by R. Borenstein, et al. HAREFUAH. 79:8-11, July 1, 1970.

"Clinical study of a once-a-month oral contraceptive: quinestrol-quingestanol," by E. Guiloff, et al.

CONTRACEPTIVES: ORAL

"Clinical study of a once-a-month oral contraceptive: quinestrol-quingestanol," by E. Guiloff, et al. FERTIL STERIL. 21:110-118, February, 1970.

"Clinical study of an oral contraceptive, in a single monthly dose: quinestrol quingestanol," by D. Rubio, et al. GINEC OBSTET MEX. 27:123-133, February, 1970.

"A clinical study with continuous low doses of megestrol acetate for fertility control. Oil solution versus tablet formulation," by S. Avendano, et al. AMER J OBSTET GYNEC. 106:122-127, January 1, 1970.

"Clinical trial of medroxyprogesterone acetate during postpartum," by L. Beco. REV MED LIEG. 25:226-230, April 1, 1970.

"Clinical trials of a low-dose inhibitor of ovulation," by C. Poiret, et al. LILLE MED SUPPL. 4:737-739, May, 1970.

"Clinical use of steroids hormones in the control of fertility," by E. Mears. CLIN TER. 52:499-507, March 31, 1970.

"Combined oral contraceptives. A statement by the committee on safety of drugs." BRIT MED J. 2:231-232, April 25, 1970.

"Comments on the current status of our peroral contraception," by R. Sterba, et al. CESK GYNEK. 35:189-190, April, 1970.

"The Committee and the pill," by P. Diggory. LANCET. 1:86, January 10, 1970.

"Comparative clinical studies with oral contraceptives," by R. H. Richter. MED WELT. 40:1715-1726, October 3, 1970.

"Continuous microdoses of chloramadinone during lactation," by C. Gonzalez. GINECOL OBSTET MEX. 28:563-566, November, 1970.

"Contraception with a novel sequential preparation (Ovanon)," by D. Tenhaeff. MUNCHEN MED WSCHR. 112:851-857, May 1, 1970.

CONTRACEPTIVES: ORAL

"Contraceptives; once-a-month pill." CHEM & ENG N. 48:22, May 11, 1970.

"Controversy over the pill," by B. Surface. GOOD H. 170:64-65+, January, 1970.

"Cooperation of general practitioner in birth control. Legal questions about prescription of the 'pill'," by W. Becker. THER GEGENW. 109:428 passim, March, 1970.

"Current method of birth control, with special reference to oral contraceptives," by S. Suziki. JAP J MIDWIFE. 24:35-40, December, 1970.

"Current status of oral contraceptives," by R. E. Cleary, et al. MED CLIN N AMER. 54:163-171, January, 1970.

"The current status of treatment with hormonal contraceptives," by E. Robecchi. MINERVA MED. 61:2394-2404, May 30, 1970.

"Cyclic and step-up administration of ethynodiol diacetate as an oral contraceptive," by K. R. Heber. MED J AUST. 2:21-24, July 4, 1970.

"Dawn of the morning-after pill?" AM DRUGGIST. 161:35-36, February 23, 1970.

"Depo-medroxyprogesterone acetate as a contraceptive," by R. J. Seymour, et al. OBSTET GYNECOL. 36:589-596, October, 1970.

"Depot-gestagen for contraception," by A. A. Haspels. NEDERL T GENEESK. 114:61-63, January 10, 1970.

"Developments in steroidal hormonal contraception," by A. Klopper. BRIT MED BULL. 26:39-44, January, 1970.

"Develops his-or-her birth curb." AM DRUGGIST. 161:35, June 29, 1970.

"Did the pill get a fair shake from Nelson?" CHEM W. 106:21, January 28, 1970.

"D-norgestrel combined with ethinyl oestradiol as an oral contraceptive," by W. G. McBride. CURR THER

CONTRACEPTIVES: ORAL

RES. 12:177-185, April, 1970.

"Dropping of pills not serious loss to Kallir, Corbett," by N. Giges. ADV AGE. 41:16, November 2, 1970.

"The effect of age, sex, parity, haemoglobin level, and oral contraceptive preparations on the normal leucocyte count," by J. M. Cruickshank, et al. BRIT J HAEMAT. 18:541-550, May, 1970.

"The end of rapid increase in the use of oral anovulants? Some problems in the interpretation of time series of oral use among married women," by J. D. Allingham, et al. DEMOGRAPHY. 7:31-41, February, 1970.

"Evaluation of a variation in the simultaneous method of oral contraceptions," by A. Alvarado Duran, et al. GINECOL OBSTET MEX. 27:597-604, May, 1970.

"Existing stocks may be used up." AM DRUGGIST. 162:37, November 16, 1970.

"Experience with Ovosiston for contraception. II," by H. Geschke. DEUTSCH GESUNDH. 25:201-206, February 5, 1970.

"Experiences with Ovosiston in a new dosage form," by C. Zwahr. DTSCH GESUNDHEITSW. 25:635-639, April 8, 1970.

"FDA chief says Rxmen have role in educating users about the pill," by D. Wickware. AM DRUGGIST. 161:17-19, February 9, 1970.

"FDA: efficiency drive stumbles over the issue of drug efficiency; effects of Demulen," by T. P. Southwick. SCIENCE. 169:1188-1189, September 18, 1970.

"FDA is facing court action for access to pill information as a result of secrecy policy." OIL PAINT & DRUG REP. 198:7, July 6, 1970.

"FDA offers milder version OC insert." AM DRUGGIST. 161:16, April 20, 1970.

"FDA set to weigh stricter standards for the birth pills." OIL PAINT & DRUG REP. 197:5+, January 12,

CONTRACEPTIVES: ORAL

1970.

"FDA will look again into the pill's dangers." OIL PAINT & DRUG REP. 197:7+, January 26, 1970.

"FDA writes another warning." SCI N. 97:599, June 20, 1970.

"Failure of a pure progestogen contraceptive to affect serum levels of iron, transferrin, protein-bound iodine, and transaminase," by L. W. Powell, et al. BRIT MED J. 1:194-195, July 25, 1970.

"Federal Association of Physicians: 'No pills' for girls under 16 years of age." MUNCH MED WOCHENSCHR. 42:3, October 16, 1970.

"Final warning? revised pamphlet with birth-control pills." NEWSWEEK. 75:76, June 22, 1970.

"1st experiences with Ovosiston in new dosage--a comparative study of oral contraception with 'old' and 'new' Ovosiston." "Experiences with Ovosiston in contraception. II. "Viewpoint concerning works of Chr. Zwahr and H. Geschke," by D. Kuhne. DTSCH GESUNDHEITSW. 25:2245-2247, November 19, 1970.

"1st experiences with Ovosiston in a new dosage--a comparative study of oral contraception with 'old' and 'new' Ovosiston." "Experiences with Ovosiston in contraception. II. "Reply to the viewpoint of D. Kuhne," by C. Zwahr. DTSCH GESUNDHEITSW. 25: 2247-2250, November 19, 1970.

"Further doubts about oral contraceptives." BRIT MED J. 1:252, January 31, 1970.

"General view of the oral prevention of pregnancy," by D. M. Potts. KATILOLEHTI. 75:414-418, October, 1970.

"Guidelines governing the use of synthetic progestational hormones as contraceptives," by J. Okla. GINEK POL. 41:573-576, May, 1970.

"Hallelujah the pill?" by R. B. Dixon. TRANS-ACTION. 8:44-49 plus, November, 1970.

CONTRACEPTIVES: ORAL

"Hearings cause pill sales to flatten out." AM DRUGGIST. 161:18, March 23, 1970.

"Hormonal contraception," by E. Imparato. RASS INT CLIN TER. 50:86-96, January 31, 1970.

"Hormonal contraception," by R. Vokaer, et al. BULL SOC SCI MED GRAND DUCHE LUXEMB. 107:263-272, October, 1970.

"Hormonal contraception. Clinical experience, gained up to now and present-day problems," by J. Teter. POL TYG LEK. 25:1641-1643, November 2, 1970.

"How 334 gynecologists view the pill," by N. D'Amelio. MED TIMES. 98:206-212, October, 1970.

"If you want publicity, pan the pill; editorial," by D. Anderson. CHATELAINE. 43:3, April, 1970.

"Immediate postpartum oral contraception," by R. D. Gambrell, Jr. OBSTET GYNEC. 36:101-106, July, 1970.

"Immunosuppression and simultaneous contraception," by W. Creutzfeldt. DEUTSCH MED WSCHR. 95:1581, July 24, 1970.

"Industrial pressure and the population problem--the FDA and the pill," by I. C. Winter. JAMA. 212: 1067-1068, May 11, 1970.

"Inhibition of sperm capacitation in vitro by contraceptive steroids," by R. B. Gwatkin, et al. NATURE (LONDON). 227:182-183, July 11, 1970.

"Introduction of mass psychology of animals to pharmacology. I. Influence of the 3d party on the Legal questions about prescription of the 'pill'," by W. Becker. THER GEGENW. 109:428 passim, March, 1970.

"Iron and oral contraceptives." BRIT MED J. 1:320, February 7, 1970.

"Lilly, Upjohn praised: swallowed a bitter pill." OIL PAINT & DRUG REP. 198:7+, November 2, 1970.

"Long-term application of steroids enclosed in dimethylpolysiloxane (silastic): in vitro and in vivo experiments," by R. Schuhmann, et al. ACTA BIOL MED GER. 24:897-910, 1970.

"Low-oestrogen oral contraceptives," by S. M. Wood, et al. BR MED J. 4:54, October 3, 1970.

"Medical aspects of oral contraceptives," by N. J. Elgee. ANN INTERN MED. 72:409-418, March, 1970.

"Metabolism of protestogen administered in oral contraceptives," by V. Brockner, et al. MED J AUST. 1:1229-1230, June 13, 1970.

"Micro-dosage of a new progestogen (quingestanol) used as a contraceptive," by J. J. Medina del Campo, et al. GINEC OBSTET MEX. 27:471-475, April, 1970.

"Minipill in limbo." SCI N. 97:93, January 24, 1970.

"New draft of OC insert is awaited." AM DRUGGIST. 161:20, April 6, 1970.

"New oral contraceptive methods," by A. Suzuki. JAP J PUBLIC HEALTH NURSE. 26:58-59, November, 1970.

"A new oral contraceptive with a 7 plus 15 sequential formulation," by I. Brosens, et al. ARZNEIMITTEL-FORSCHUNG. 20:236-237, February, 1970.

"New report on oral contraceptives of the Advisory committee to the Food and Drug Administration. A comment on the new report," by J. W. Goldzieher. AMER J OBSTET GYNEC. 107:1106-1109, August 1, 1970.

"New report on oral contraceptives of the Advisory Committee to the Food and Drug Administration. Reply to Dr. Goldzieher's comment on the new report," by L. M. Hellman. AMER J OBSTET GYNEC. 107:1109-1110, August 1, 1970.

"A new type of oral contraceptive," by W. McBride. MED J AUST. 1:212-215, January 31, 1970.

"New use recommendations for birth control pills." GOOD H. 171:153, August, 1970.

"Nimble with the pill." NATURE (LONDON). 225:4-5, January 3, 1970.

CONTRACEPTIVES: ORAL

"O-C makers told to give MDs consumer booklets." AM DRUGGIST. 161:24, June 29, 1970.

"Off the pill?" by J. Coburn. RAMP MAG. 8:46-49, June, 1970.

"Once-a-month oral contraceptive: quinestrol and quingestanol," by B. R. Lotvin, et al. OBSTET GYNEC. 35:933-936, June, 1970.

"Oral contraception," by H. Hill. PRACTITIONER. 205: 5-12, July, 1970.

"Oral contraception. An application in family planning programme in Calcutta city," by A. S. Gupta. J INDIAN MED ASS. 54:187-194, March 1, 1970.

"Oral contraception among special clinic patients. With particular reference to the diagnosis of gonorrhoea," by A. B. Hewitt. BRIT J VENER DIS. 46: 106-107, April, 1970.

"The oral contraception controversy." CANAD MED ASS J. 102:1407 passim, June 20, 1970.

"Oral contraceptives. Current status of therapy." JAMA. 214:2316-2321, December 28, 1970.

"Oral contraceptives and acute surgery," by A. Pedersen Berget. UGESKR LAEG. 132:1628-1629, August 27, 1970.

"Oral contraceptives and amino acid utilization," by I. L. Craft, et al. AM J OBSTET GYNECOL. 108:1120-1125, December 1, 1970.

"Oral contraceptives; background, motivation, education, application," by A. Sikkel. NED TIJDSCHR VERLOSKD GYNAECOL. 70:599-604, December, 1970.

"Oral contraceptives--prescribe or proscribe?" by P. E. Sartwell. AMER J PUBLIC HEALTH. 60:1187-1189, July, 1970.

"Oral contraceptives: turmoil and aftermath," by C. A. Paulsen. JAMA. 212:873, May 4, 1970.

"Oral contraceptives warning notice is planned for

every package by FDA." OIL PAINT & DRUG REP. 197: 3+, March 9, 1970.

"Oral contraceptives: Which pill for which patient?" PT CARE. 4:135+, June 15, 1970.

"An orally active long-acting estrogen (AY-20,121)," by U. K. Banik, et al. STEROIDS. 16:289-296, September, 1970.

"Ortho 1557-O. A new oral contraceptive," by W. J. Ledger. INT J FERTIL. 15:88-92, April-June, 1970.

"Orthopedics and oral administration or contraceptives," by W. S. Kaden. JAMA. 213:301, July 13, 1970.

"Other side of the pill." NEWSWEEK. 75:45-46, March 9, 1970.

"Ovostat, a low dose oral contraceptive," by G. Linthorst, et al. BRUX MED. 50:433-437, June, 1970.

"Packaging accuracy with good tabletting speeds (Ortho pharmaceutical)," by J. Colligas. DRUG & COSMETIC IND. 106:96-97+, February, 1970.

"The 'perfect contraceptive' population," by L. Bumpass, et al. SCIENCE. 169:1177-1182, September 18, 1970.

"Peroral contraception (1): drugs," by J. Dolby, et al. LAKARTIDNINGEN. 67:Suppl III:33+, October 12, 1970.

"Peroral contraception (2): pharmacodynamics and clinical experiences," by G. Rybo. LAKARTIDNINGEN. 67:Suppl III:38+, October 12, 1970.

"Peroral contraception (3): clinical viewpoint," by M. Bygdeman, et al. LAKARTIDNINGEN. 67:Suppl III:45+, October 12, 1970.

"Peroral contraception (4): pregnancies," by M. Rutenskold. LAKARTIDNINGEN. 67:Suppl III:51+, October 12, 1970.

"Peroral contraception (5): continuing low dosage treatment," by U. Larsson-Cohn. LAKARTIDNINGEN. 67:Suppl III:56+, October 12, 1970.

CONTRACEPTIVES: ORAL

"Peroral contraception (9): use of oral contraceptives in Sweden in 1969," by U. Larsson-Cohn, et al. LAKARTIDNINGEN. 67:Suppl III:85+, October 12, 1970.

"The Pill," by G. I. Swyer. NURS MIRROR. 130:19-21 contd, June 19, 1970.

"The Pill," by G. I. Swyer. NURS MIRROR. 130:34-36, June 26, 1970.

"The 'pill'. Why not?" by M. Curwen. J R COLL GEN PRACT. 19:365-366, June, 1970.

"Pill: FDA calls it safe." CHEM & ENG N. 47:16, September 8, 1969.

"Pill: fewer takers." OIL PAINT & DRUG REP. 197:7, March 9, 1970.

"Pill for pigeons." CHEM & ENG N. 48:14-15, February 23, 1970.

"Pill goes to Washington." BSNS W. p 31-32, January 10, 1970.

"Pill: how much warning is enough?" CONSUMER REP. 35:329, June, 1970.

"Pill in court." CHEM W. 107:17, September 30, 1970.

"Pill in perspective," by E. B. Connell. READ DIGEST. 97:118-122, October, 1970.

"Pill is hard to follow." BSNS W. p 80, January 31, 1970.

"Pill: is it safe?" U S NEWS. 68:10, January 26, 1970.

"Pill is safe," ed by R. H. Berg and E. T. Tyler. LOOK. 34:65-66, June 30, 1970.

"The pill; loyalty is spite of everything," by P. Vaughan. HEALTH. 7:6-7, Autumn, 1970.

"The pill on campus," by H. E. Weinstein. WALL ST J. 175:1 plus, January 19, 1970.

"Pill on trial." TIME. 95:60+, January 26, 1970.

CONTRACEPTIVES: ORAL

"The pill parallels the placenta. A method of teaching oral contraception," by W. B. Beasley. J INDIAN MED ASS. 54:20-22, January 1, 1970.

"The pill: past, present and future," by E. J. Servy, et al. GYNECOL PRAT. 21:285-298, 1970.

"Pill--pessimism overdone?" FIN WORLD. 133:10+, February 25, 1970.

"Pill poll," by E. Damude. CHATELAINE. 43:18, March, 1970.

"The 'pill', promiscuity and venereal disease." by L. Cohen. BRIT J VENER DIS. 46:108-110, April, 1970.

"The pill--safe? Clinical evaluation of oral contraceptives," by S. T. Thierstein. J KANS MED SOC. 71:465-470, December, 1970.

"Pill scare on Washington scene is blamed for worldwide panic as Stetler reviews PMA year." OIL PAINT & DRUG REP. 197:22+, April 20, 1970.

"Pill talk at a whisper." OIL PAINT & DRUG REP. 197: 5, March 30, 1970.

"Pill trial." TIME. 95:32+, March 9, 1970.

"La pilule fait peur," by M. J. Dulac. MAG MACL. 10: 40-42, May, 1970.

"Plain talk about the pill." NEWSWEEK. 75:93, March 16, 1970.

"Poll on the pill." NEWSWEEK. 75:52-53, February 9, 1970.

"Postcoital contraception," by C. W. Emmens. BRIT MED BULL. 26:45-51, January, 1970.

"Postcoital contraception," by J. M. Morris. ANN INTERN MED. 73:656, October, 1970.

"A pox on THE PILL." JAMA. 213:1481, August 31, 1970.

"Proposed package insert for the pill," by D. Wickware. AM DRUGGIST. 161:12-14+, March 23, 1970.

CONTRACEPTIVES: ORAL

"Pros and cons of oral contraceptives," by D. Deer. J KANSAS MED SOC. 71:43-49, February, 1970.

"Pyridoxine and oral contraceptives," by A. L. Lubby, et al. LANCET. 2:1083, November 21, 1970.

"Pyridoxine and the pill," by M. J. Baumblatt, et al. LANCET. 1:832-833, April 18, 1970.

"R.C.O.G. statement on oral contraceptives," by T. N. Jeffcoate. BRIT MED J. 1:293, May 2, 1970.

"Rate of plasma protein normalization after parturition and withdrawal of oral contraceptives," by C. B. Laurell, et al. SCAND J CLIN LAB INVEST. 26: 345-348, December, 1970.

"Recent trends in pharmacologic contraception," by L. Gregoire. REV MED LIEGE. 25:224-225, April 1, 1970.

"Reduction of plasma tyrosine by oral contraceptives and oestrogens: a possible consequence of tyrosine aminotransferase induction," by D. P. Rose, et al. CLIN CHIM ACTA. 29:49-53, July, 1970.

"Rep Rogers calls for restrictions on pill advertising." ADV AGE. 41:3, April 13, 1970.

"Review of the current status of research in steroid contraception," by M. Vojta. CESK GYNEKOL. 35:431-433, September, 1970.

"Sees OC pill needing no Rx in 5 years." AM DRUGGIST. 161:39, June 1, 1970.

"Small-for-dates babies and the pill," by K. J. Dennis. LANCET. 1:195, January 24, 1970.

"Steroid contraceptives," by R. L. Vande Wiele. GYNECOL INVEST. 1:Suppl:55-68, 1970.

"Steroidal conception. Statement by the IPPF central medical committee (International Planned Parenthood Federation)." SA NURS J. 37:17-18 passim, July, 1970.

"Study of oral contraceptives and risk determination

CONTRACEPTIVES: ORAL

for life insurance," by J. G. Defares. NEDERL T GENEESK. 114:647-648, April 11, 1970.

"The survival of the chosen: three new books on the contraceptive pill," by H. Miller. LISTENER. 84: 489-490, October 8, 1970.

"Symposium: oral contraceptives. Opening address," by R. F. van Wering. NEDERL T GENEESK. 114:1416-1417, August 22, 1970.

"Syntex denies that its O-C price to OEO is unfair." AM DRUGGIST. 161:25, June 15, 1970.

"Taking the pill is just following Nature's law," by A. Jay. NOVA. p.47-48, October, 1970.

"Thin-layer chromatographic identification of estrogens and progestogens in oral contraceptives," by M. B. Simard, et al. J CHROMATOGR. 51:517-524, September 23, 1970.

"Thin layer chromatography separation of oral contraceptives and some sex steroids," by I. Szekacs, et al. Z KLIN CHEM. 8:131-133, March, 1970.

"Towards a more physiological hormonal contraception," by R. Sterba. ZENTRALBL GYNAEKOL. 92:303-312, March 7, 1970.

"A trial of a one dose a month oral contraceptive," by A. D. Claman. AMER J OBSTET GYNEC. 107:461-464, June 1, 1970.

"Use of the 'pill' on Taiwan," by F. L. Chen, et al. INDUSTRY OF FREE CHINA. 33:18-31, April, 1970.

"Useful rules in the use of estro-progestative steroids," by M. Albeaux-Fernet, et al. ANNEE ENDOCRINOL. 22:131-140, 1970.

"Various viewpoints about contraceptive pills and their use," by C. A. Ehrnrooth. KATILOLEHTI. 75:419-427, October, 1970.

"Wall Street and the pill." AM DRUGGIST. 161:23-24, March 9, 1970.

CONTRACEPTIVES: ORAL

"What you should know about the pill: text of AMA pamphlet. TODAYS HEALTH. 48:9-10, September, 1970.

"What's happened since the pill scared everyone: sales of the pill are still down, but as sales of other contraceptives rise markedly, makers of the pill tone down its potency," by G. Pluenneke. EXCHANGE. 31:1-5, August, 1970.

"Why I'll give my daughter the pill," by P. H. Wade. REDBOOK. 135:30+, June, 1970.

CONTRACEPTIVES: PARENTERAL

"A clinical evaluation of a monthly injection for conception control," by W. S. Keifer, et al. AMER J OBSTET GYNEC. 107:400-410, June 1, 1970.

"Contraception by an injectable long-acting oestrogen-progestogen agent. II. Evaluation of cycles, menstrual flows and side effects," by R. Plesner. ACTA ENDOCRINOL. 65:683-697, December, 1970.

"Evaluation of an injectable progestin-estrogen as a contraceptive," by A. Scommegna, et al. AMER J OBSTET GYNEC. 107:1147-1155, August 15, 1970.

"An injectable contraceptive with prolonged action," by P. Simon. REV FR ODONTOSTOMATOL. 46:1029-1032, December, 1970.

"Injectable long-acting progestogens for contraception," by B. Karstadt. S AFR MED J. 44:480-481, April 18, 1970.

"Ovulation inhibition with a long-acting injectable contraceptive. IV. Return of reproductive function after discontinuation," by M. A. Yussman, et al. AM J OBSTET GYNECOL. 108:901-907, November 15, 1970.

"Single monthly injection for contraception," by J. Artner, et al. GEBURTSHILFE FRAUENHEILKD. 30:554-564, June, 1970.

CONTRACEPTIVES: THERAPEUTIC USE

"A controlled trial of oral contraceptives in haemophilia," by P. Beck, et al. BR J HAEMATOL. 19:

CONTRACEPTIVES: THERAPEUTIC USE

667-673, December, 1970.

"1st clinical experiences on the use of oral contraceptive Ovosiston in diabetics," by E. Godel, et al. DTSCH GESUNDHEITSW. 25:627-631, April 8, 1970.

"Glucose tolerance in gestational diabetic women during and after treatment with a combination-type oral contraceptive," by A. J. Szabo, et al. NEW ENG J MED. 282:646-650, March 19, 1970.

"Headache and treatment with oral contraceptives," by U. Larsson-Cohn, et al. ACTA NEUROL SCAND. 46:267-278, 1970.

"Malabsorption of folate polyglutamates associated with oral contraceptive therapy," by T. F. Necheles, et al. NEW ENG J MED. 282:858-859, April 9, 1970.

"On a case of thrombosis of the middle cerebral artery during progestogen therapy," by G. G. Cavalca, et al. RIV SPER FRENIAT. 94:83-94, February 28, 1970.

"Oral ovulation inhibitors in the treatment of skin diseases," by J. Vankos. THER HUNG. 18:33-39, 1970.

"Thromboembolic complications during treatment by estro-progestational drugs. Critical study of 3 cases," by L. Croccel, et al. SEM HOP PARIS. 46:101-108, January 8, 1970.

"Treatment with an ovulation-inhibiting hormone combination with lower progestin component. Cytologic and histologic studies," by H. Breinl, et al. MED KLIN. 65:195-199, January 30, 1970.

"2 cases of coralloid renal lithiasis developed in young women under prolonged treatment with the contraceptive pill," by S. Reziciner. ANN UROL. 4:269-274, December, 1970.

"The use of continuous progestogen contraception in the treatment of migraine," by B. W. Somerville, et al. MED J AUST. 1:1043-1045, May 23, 1970.

CROWDING
SEE ALSO: ISOLATION & ALIENATION

CROWDING

"Accustoming of caged animals to the cage effect. Hypothalamo-hypophyseal repercussions," by R. Roudier, et al. C R SOC BIOL. 164:68-71, 1970.

"Anxiety arousing effects of inappropriate crowding," by J. C. Baxter, et al. J CONSULT CLIN PSYCHOL. 35:174-178, October, 1970.

"Calhoun's horrible mousery: effects of over-crowding on mice," by S. Alsop. NEWSWEEK. 76:96, August 17, 1970.

"The effects of dwelling density on mental disorders in Filipino men," by A. J. Marsella, et al. J HEALTH SOC BEHAV. 11:288-294, December, 1970.

"Effects of early experience and differential housing on susceptibility to gastric erosions in lesion-susceptible rats," by R. Ader. PSYCHOSOM MED. 32: 569-580, November-December, 1970.

"Influence of being caged together on mammary carcinogenesis due to 7, 12-dimethylbenzathracene in female rats," by J. C. Guillon, et al. C R ACAD SCI. 270: 1066-1068, February 16, 1970.

"Population crisis and extremism," by R. B. Kelman. SCIENCE. 168:777, May 15, 1970.

"Population crisis and extremism," by H. H. Suter. SCIENCE. 168:777, May 15, 1970.

"Uptake of 59Fe as a tool for study of the crowding effect in Blomphalaria glabrata," by G. Gazzinelli, et al. AM J TROP MED HYG. 19:1034-1037, November, 1970.

DEVELOPING NATIONS
SEE ALSO: SPECIFIC NATIONS & STATES

"Demographic transition: threat to developing nations," by G. A. Schnell. J GEOGRAPHY. 69:164-171, March, 1970.

"Economic value of preventing births: reply to Simon," by S. Enke. POPULATION STUDIES. 24:455-456, November, 1970.

DEVELOPING NATIONS

"Experience in education of couples about birth control in under-developed countries," by R. Traissac. BULL FED SOC GYNECOL OBSTET LANG FR. 22:187-190, April-May, 1970.

"Family planning and population control in developing countries," by H. M. Raulet. DEMOGRAPHY. 7:211-234, May, 1970.

"Family planning in the developing world," by W. G. Povey. OBSTET GYNECOL. 36:948-952, December, 1970.

"Family planning prospects in less-developed countries, and a cost-benefit analysis of various alternatives," by J. L. Simon. ECON J. 80:58-71, March, 1970.

"Intra-urban dualism in developing economics," by D. L. McKee and W. H. Leahy. LAND ECON. 46:486-489, November, 1970.

"Lessons from a 'primitive' people," by J. V. Neel. SCIENCE. 170:815-822, November 20, 1970.

"Measuring rural-urban drift in developing countries; a suggested method," by L. Roussel. INT LABOUR R. 101:229-246, March, 1970.

"Unemployment: challenge to development," by E. Thorbecke, et al. CERES. 3:24-51, November-December, 1970.

"When numbers don't mean strength," by G. Tagliacarne. SUCCESSO. 12:90-94, November, 1970.

ECONOMICS & POPULATION

"Adam Smith on population," by J. J. Spengler. POPULATION STUDIES. 24:377-388, November, 1970.

"And lest we forget: some figures to illustrate the magnitude of the problems we are facing." FREE LABOUR WORLD. p. 7-9, January, 1970.

"Architectural business: economy--ecology--and zero population growth," by J. E. Carlson. ARCH REC. 148:59-60, August, 1970.

"The assumed employment generating capacity of European immigration in Rhodesia," by D. G. Clarke. RHODESIAN

ECONOMICS & POPULATION

J ECON. 4:33-42, June, 1970.

"Characteriological deterrants to economic progress in people of Appalachia," by C. E. Goshen. SOUTHERN MED J. 63:1053-1061, September, 1970.

"Economic growth: new doubts about an old ideal." TIME. 95:72-74, March 2, 1970.

"Economic value of preventing births: reply to Simon," by S. Enke. POPULATION STUDIES. 24:455-456, November, 1970.

"Economy, ecology and zero population growth; conditions affecting construction industry," by J. E. Carlson. ARCH REC. 148:59-60, August, 1970.

"Feedbacks in economic and demographic transition," by H. Frederiksen. SCIENCE. 166:837-847, November 14, 1969.

"Magnitude of rate-of-growth effects on aggregate savings," by M. J. Farrell. ECON J. 80:873-894, December, 1970.

"Migrant labour and economic development," by M. P. Miracle, et al. OXFORD ECONOMIC PAPERS. 22:86-108, March, 1970.

"Migration and economic opportunities in West Virginia; a statistical analysis," by G. L. Rutman. RURAL SOCIOLOGY. 35,2:206-217, June, 1970.

"Migration as investment; empirical tests of the human investment approach to geographical mobility," by S. Bowles. R ECON & STAT. 52:356-362, November, 1970.

"Migration, unemployment and development; a two-sector analysis," by J. R. Harris, et al. AM ECON R. 60:126-142, March, 1970.

"The 1970 census: a statistical gold mine: the 1970 census will contain many of the facts and figures that associations need to define and achieve their goals in the 70's." ASSN MGT. 22:52-55, February, 1970.

ECONOMICS & POPULATION

"Our affluent economy will be bursting at seams by '85." ADV AGE. 41:1+, October 12, 1970.

"People and spending power, state by state," by F. Linden. CONF BD REC. 7:44-47, December, 1970.

"Population and economic change: the emergence of the rice industry in Guyana. 1895-1915," by J. R. Mandle. J ECON HIST. 30:785-801. December, 1970.

"Population change and employment policy in India," by S. V. Khandewale. ECON AFFAIRS. 15:229-236, May, 1970.

"Population growth and economic development," by D. R. Kamerschen. SCHWEIZERISCHE ZEITSCHRIFT FUR VOLKSWIRTSCHAFT UND STATISTIK. 106:79-89, March, 1970.

"Problems of economic demography," by B. Urianis. PROBLEMS ECON. 13:69-89, January, 1971.

"Putting the 1970 census of population to use," by C. R. Menke. ECON LEAFLETS. 29:1-4, January, 1970.

"The relation of migration to regional unemployment," by B. D. Phillips. AM ECONOMIST. 14:26-42, Fall, 1970.

"Relationships among population, income and retail sales in SMSAs, 1962-1966," by B. C. Liu. Q R ECON & BUS. 10:25-40. Spring, 1970.

"Some economic aspects of Norwegian population movements 1740-1940: an econometric study," by T. Moe. J ECON HIST. 30:267-270, 284-287, March, 1970.

"Survey of buying power: a preview." SALES MGT. 104:28-29, May 15, 1970.

"Survey of buying power: special issue." SALES MGT. 104:A 1-E41, June 10, 1970.

"The US labor force: projections to 1985: special labor force report sets forth BLS," by S. C. Travis. MO LABOR R. 93:3-12, May, 1970.

"Why the global income gap grows wider," by C. Ogburn, Jr. POPULATION BUL. 26:5-36, June, 1970.

EDUCATION & POPULATION

"The Asian Dropout," by S. Davies. EDUC SCI INT J. . 3, 1:93-95, May, 1969.

"College policy on abortion and sterilization. ACOG NURSES BULL. 4:2, Fall, 1970.

"Creation of new knowledge and our way of life," by D. J. Zinn. SCH SCI & MATH. 70:18-25, January, 1970.

"Curriculum should include fertility regulation," by H. E. Mizer. NURS OUTLOOK. 18:42-43, November, 1970.

"Demographic Myths: The Challenge for Education," by C. T. Lucas. EDUC. 90.2:178-181, November-December, 1969.

"Denver school dramatizes population-pollution," by B. J. Meadows. AM BIOL TEACH. 32:281-283, May, 1970.

"Educating teachers and children in law: an approach to reduce alienation in inner-city schools," by A. Elson, et al. AM J ORTHOPSYCHIATRY. 40:870-878, October, 1970.

"Education and religion as factors influencing attitudes toward population growth in the United States," by L. D. Barnett. SOCIAL BIOLOGY. 17:26-36, March, 1970.

"Family life education in a family planning clinic," by S. Okrent. BULL AM COLL NURSE MIDWIFE. 15:78-84, August, 1970.

"Fertility control: health and educational factors for the 1970s. Contraception or abortion?" by J. H. Hughes. J BIOSOC SCI. 2:161-166, April, 1970.

"Fertility control: health and educational factors for the 1970s. Family planning in the next ten years," by E. Brooks. J BIOSOC SCI. 2:171-180, April, 1970.

"Fertility control: health and educational factors for the 1970s. The future of oral contraception," by G. A. Christie. J BIOSOC SCI. 2:191-197, April, 1970.

EDUCATION & POPULATION

"Fertility control: health and educational factors for the 1970s. The role of the local authority," by D. Barnard. J BIOSOC SCI. 2:181-189, April, 1970.

"Fertility control: health and educational factors for the 1970s. The role of local authority," by D. Barnard. J BIOSOC SCI. 2:181-189, April, 1970.

"Fertility control: health and educational factors for the 1970s. Trends in contraception," by A. C. Turnbull. J BIOSOC SCI. 2:157-160, April, 1970.

"Introducing the world population crises to secondary social studies classes: an inquiry oriented instructional strategy," by R. C. Anderson. SOCIAL ED. 34:27-35, January, 1970.

"Law, policy, and behavior: educational exchange policy and student migration," by P. Ritterband. AM J SOCIOL. 76:71-82, July, 1970.

"A look at Indiana's Pupil Population in the Decade Ahead," by T. C. Hill. CONTEMP EDUC. 41,6:280-284, May, 1970.

"Mate choice and domestic life in the nineteenth-century marriage manual," by M. Gordon, et al. J MARRIAGE AND FAM. 32:665-674, November, 1970.

"Mobility among business faculty," by L. J. Shuster. ACAD MGT J. 13:325-335, September, 1970.

"1970 Census: Tool for Vocational Planning wealth," by J. C. Baker. AMERICAN VOCATIONAL JOURNAL. 45,8:83-84 passim, November, 1970.

"No Teacher Surplus," by M. Chambers. PHI DELTA KAPPAN. 52,2:118-119, October, 1970.

"Nonwage benefits of vocational training: employability and mobility," by R. L. Bowlby and W. R. Schriver. IND & LABOR REL R. 23:500-509, July, 1970.

"Population education: a challenge of the seventies." POPULATION BUL. 26:1-40, 1970.

"Population Education--A Response to a Social Problem," by I. L. Slesnick. SCIENCE TEACHER. 38,2:21-23,

EDUCATION & POPULATION

February, 1971.

"Sex education hits the British airwaves." ATLAS. 19:16, April, 1970.

"Sex education in New Orleans: the Birchers win a victory," by D. R. Mackintosh. NEW SOUTH. 25:46-56, Summer, 1970.

"Sex education: A Key to the Population Crisis," by W. G. Peter. BIOSCIENCE. 20,3:173-174, February, 1970.

"Sex education hits the British airwaves." ATLAS. 19:16, April, 1970.

"Suggestions on adding family planning to the curriculums of medical schools," by D. T. Rice. PUBLIC HEALTH REP. 85:889-895, October, 1970.

"Summary of the Social sciences and population policy: a survey," by E. D. Driver. DEMOGRAPHY. 7:379-392, August, 1970.

"The summary report of the seminar on nursing education and family planning," by M. I. Kim. KOREAN NURSE. 9:27-34, December 25, 1970.

"The teaching of fertility control and population problems in the medical schools of Brazil," by J. Yunes. REV SAUDE PUBLICA. 4:79-84, June, 1970.

"Teaching population dynamics with a simulation exercise," by E van de Walle and J. Knodel. DEMOGRAPHY. 7:433-448, November, 1970.

ENVIRONMENT, ECOLOGY & POPULATION
  SEE ALSO: HEALTH & POPULATION
          POPULATION THEORY & RESEARCH
          POPULATION FORECASTING

"Architectural business: economy--ecology--and zero population growth," by J. E. Carlson. ARCH REC. 148:59-60, August, 1970.

"The changing environment: some implications for health," by A. J. Diekema. OCCUP HEALTH NURS. 18:20-22, July, 1970.

ENVIRONMENT, ECOLOGY & POPULATION

"Congress on optimum population and environment." CHEM & ENG N. 48:34-35, June 22, 1970.

"Demography and human ecology; some apparent trends," by L. F. Schnore. ANNALS OF THE AMERICAN ACADEMY OF POLITICAL & SOCIAL SCIENCE. 390:120-128, July, 1970. SA# F0139

"Demography and thermodynamics," by E. Fein. AM J PHYS. 38:1373-1379, December, 1970.

"Ecological destruction is a condition of American life; interview, ed. by P. Collier," by P. Ehrlich. MLLE. 70:188-189+, April, 1970.

"Ecology: the new religion?" by R. L. Schueler. AMERICA. 122:293-295, March 21, 1970.

"Economy, ecology, and zero population growth; conditions affecting construction industry," by J. E. Carlson. ARCH REC. 148:59-60, August, 1970.

"The environmental crisis: through a glass darkly," by W. G. Rosen. BIOSCIENCE. 20,22:1209-1211, November, 1970.

"Environmental hucksterism." NATURE (LONDON). 227:118, July 11, 1970.

"Environmental quality: its significance in our society," by W. R. Barclay. JAMA. 213:1890-1892, September 14, 1970.

"The first National congress on optimum population and environment." POPULATION BUL. 26:2-18, November, 1970.

"Five scientists view the impacts of technology," by C. H. Waddington. IMPACT SCI SOC. 20,2:137-150, April-June, 1970.

"Healing our sick environment," by M. Michaelson. TODAY'S HEALTH. 48:21+, April, 1970.

"Health standards of a populated locality." FELDSHER AKUSH. 35:35-38, September, 1970.

"How Green is the Green Revolution?" by W. C. Paddock.

ENVIRONMENT, ECOLOGY & POPULATION

BIOSCIENCE. v20 n16 pp897-902, August, 1970.

"Implications of the changing environment to occupational health," by F. D. Yoder. OCCUP HEALTH NURS. 18:23-25, July, 1970.

"Is overpopulation really the problem? Achieving a better American way of life is not primarily a question of numbers," by H. P. Miller. CONFERENCE BD REC. 7:19-22, May, 1970.

"Life without birth," by S. Johnson. OBSERVER. colour suppt. p. 27+, June 28, 1970.

"Limits to the use of energy," by A. M. Weinberg and R. P. Hammond. AM SCIENTIST. 58:412-418, July, 1970; "Discussion,"58:618-620, November, 1970.

"Malaria control and population growth," by P. Newman. J OF DEVELOPMENT STUDIES. 6:133-158, January, 1970.

"Malaria eradication and the fall of mortality, a note," by H. Frederiksen. POPULATION STUDIES. 24:111-113, March, 1970.

"Man and His Environment," by A. J. Coale. SCIENCE. 170,3954:132-136, October, 1970.

"Man's place in the ecological pattern," by J. C. Robertson. GEOGRAPHICAL MAG. 42:254-265, January, 1970.

"Natural selection in ecologically and genetically defined populations," by C. Istock. BEHAVIORAL SCIENCE. 15:1:101-115, January, 1970.

"New tasks for the '70s," by R. N. Gardner. VISTA. 5:39+, May-June, 1970.

"On population and environment; address, June 8, 1970," by P. M. Hauser. VITAL SPEECHES. 36:696-701, September 1, 1970.

"Optimum World Population," by H. R. Hulett. BIOSCIENCE. 20,3:160-161, February, 1970.

"Palace and pollution," by A. C. Mason, et al. NATURE (LONDON). 228:693, November 14, 1970.

ENVIRONMENT, ECOLOGY & POPULATION

"People, an affluent society, and pollution," by W. R. Barclay. BULL NTRDA. 56:14+, October, 1970.

"People & pollution: the challenge to planning," by C. Hutchinson. LONG RANGE PLANNING. 2:2-7, March, 1970.

"Pollution: whence and whither," by W. H. Davis. ARCH ENVIRON HEALTH. 21:3-4, July, 1970.

"Population: EQ Index." NAT WILDLIFE. 8:38-39, October, 1970.

"Population: EQ Index." SCHOL TEACH JR/SR HIGH. pp14-15, October 5, 1970.

"Popollution--are we all guilty? The higher and higher wisdom," by J. Lederberg. CALIF MED. 113:61-62, December, 1970.

"Population and the dignity of man," by R. L. Shinn. CHR CENT. 87:442-448, April 15, 1970.

"Population and the social, political and environmental crisis," by R. B. Ragland. J FLORIDA MED ASS. 57:24-30, October, 1970.

"Population density vs per capita solid waste production," by G. P. Westerhoff and R. M. Gruninger. PUB WORKS. 101:86-87, February, 1970.

"Product pushers vs the people," by C. F. Wurster. FIELD & S. 75:60 plus, June, 1970.

"Quality of life; a proposed program for global action by the UN; address, April 21, 1970," by R. N. Gardner. VITAL SPEECHES. 36:466-470, May 15, 1970.

"Quantity or quality in dealing with human problems," by E. P. May. PERSONNEL AND GUIDANCE JOURNAL. 49, 5:376-382, January, 1971.

"The race toward misery," by D. T. Rogers, Jr. ALA BUS. 41:1-3+, October 15, 1970.

"Reducing the environmental impact of population growth," by S. F. Singer. SCIENCE. 169:1233, September 18, 1970.

ENVIRONMENT, ECOLOGY & POPULATION

"Rising population: its effect on environment," by S. J. McNaughton. CONS. 24:14-16, June, 1970.

"Safeguarding the quality of life." AMERICA. 122:548, May 23, 1970.

"Scientist looks at the human zoo," by D. Morris. U S NEWS. 68:38, March 2, 1970.

"Smoking, air pollution, bronchitis, and population mobility," by R. M. Acheson, et al. LANCET. 760:1340-1341, June 20, 1970.

"Some international implications of environmental challenges," by L. Hartley. ATLAN COM Q. 8:234-241, Summer, 1970.

"The state: an ecological phenomenon." JAMA. 214:905, November 2, 1970.

"Tomorrow's robot reports today." COMM TODAY. 1:28, December 14, 1970.

"Water pollution--an ecological perspective," by A. F. Bartsch. J WATER POLLUT CONTR FED. 42:819-823, May, 1970.

"Will the exploding human population succeed in conserving nature?" by P. A. Tschumi. EXPERIENTIA. 26:572-576, May 15, 1970.

"Will mankind survive?" by T. Philpot. HUMANIST. 85:111-112, April, 1970.

FAMILY PLANNING
"ACOG to administer hospital family planning." ACOG NURSES BULL. 4:2, Summer, 1970.

"About planned parenthood," by M. Zelenkova. ZDRAV PRAC. 20:536-540, October, 1970.

"Analysis of a family planning program in Guatemala," by D. W. MacCorquodale. PUBLIC HEALTH REPTS. 85:570-574, July, 1970.

"Assessing the demographic effect of a family planning programme," by W. Brass. PROC R SOC MED. 63:1105-1107, November, 1970.

FAMILY PLANNING

"Attitudes of married college students on overpopulation and family planning," by P. D. Darney. PUBLIC HEALTH REP. 85:412-418, May, 1970.

"Attitudes toward family planning among peri-urban Africans in Uganda," by R. E. Brown. TROP GEOGR MED. 22:87-100, March, 1970.

"Behavioral approaches to family and couple therapy," by R. Liberman. AMER J ORTHOPSYCHIAT. 40:106-118, January, 1970.

"Canadian county-sponsored family planning. 3. A second survey," by J. E. Tyson, et al. OBSTET GYNEC. 35:377-380, March, 1970.

"The challenge of family planning," by H. Hill. NURS MIRROR. 131:27-32, August 21, 1970.

"Child plan organization endorses pill." AM DRUGGIST. 161:57, May 18, 1970.

"Childlessness, intentional and unintentional," by E. Pohlman. J NERV MENT DIS. 151:2-12, July, 1970.

"Choices of parenthood." SCIENCE. 170:257-262, October 16, 1970.

"The complete family planning service at King's College Hospital," by P. Newton. NURS TIMES. 66:1399-1400, October 29, 1970.

"Continuance of family planning in a health department clinic," by J. J. Speidel, et al. AM J OBSTET GYNECOL. 108:1134-1140, December 1, 1970.

"Correlates of marital dissolution in a prospective fertility study: a research note," by L. C. Coombs and Z. Zumeta. SOC PROB. 18:92-102, Summer, 1970.

"Demographic comments on family planning," by H. Arnold. OEFF GESUNDHEITSWESEN. 32:68-70, February, 1970.

"Differential fertility and socioeconomic status of Shirazi women: a pilot study," by A. A. Paydarfar and M. Sarram. J MARRIAGE & FAM. 32:692-699, November, 1970.

FAMILY PLANNING

"Eleven myths of family planning," by A. Bose. SOUTH ASIAN R. 3:323-330, July, 1970.

"Establishing family planning services in Kenya," by N. R. Fendall, et al. PUBLIC HEALTH REP. 85:131-139, February, 1970.

"The estimation of potential fertility for family planning evaluation: a critical discussion," by D. Wolfers. PROC R SOC MED. 63:1107-1110, November, 1970.

"Evaluating the training of nurses to do family planning work in India," by J. B. Weisbuch, et al. PUBLIC HEALTH REP. 85:707-715, August, 1970.

"Experience in education of couples about birth control in under developed countries," by R. Traissac. BULL FED SOC GYNECOL OBSTET LANG FR. 22:187-190, April-May, 1970.

"Experiences in rural family planning," by J. M. Flavier. PHILIPP J NURS. 39:6+, January-March, 1970.

"Extending family planning services," by H. A. Hutcheson, et al. AMER J NURS. 70:1516-1518, July, 1970.

"Factors associated with involvement of low-income women in a public family planning program," by E. Siegel, et al. AM J PUBL HLTH. 60:1382 plus, August, 1970.

"Family life education in a family planning clinic," by S. Okrent. BULL AM COLL NURSE MIDWIFE. 15:78-84, August, 1970.

"Family planning," by A. O. Sokoya. NIGERIAN NURSE. 2:61+, January, 1970.

"Family planning," by R. L. Standard. MED ANN DC. 39:280-281, May, 1970.

"Family planning. The pace of bumbledom." NATURE (LONDON). 226:96, April 11, 1970.

"Family planning and conjugal roles in New York City poverty areas," by S. Polgar, et al. SOC SCI MED. 4:135-139, July, 1970.

FAMILY PLANNING

"Family planning and fertility in Tunisia," by R. J. Lapham. DEMOGRAPHY. 7:241-253, May, 1970.

"Family planning and the poor," by W. M. Hern. NEW REPUBLIC. 163:17-19, November 14, 1970.

"Family planning and population control in developing countries," by H. M. Raulet. DEMOGRAPHY. 7:211-234, May, 1970.

"Family planning and population problems. Concepts of 4 different eras," by M. Muramatsu. JAP J MIDWIFE. 24:27-30, December, 1970.

"Family planning: a basic human right," by J. D. Tydings. MLN BULL. 18:7-10, January, 1970.

"Family-planning bonds." CHATELAINE. 43:10, February, 1970.

"Family planning coordinator in a city hospital," by E. Smith. AMER J NURS. 70:2363-2365, November, 1970.

"Family planning counselling," by E. F. Dally. BRIT MED J. 3:345-346, August 8, 1970.

"Family planning from the viewpoint of the gynecologist," by R. Elert. OEFF GESUNDHEITSWESEN. 32:25-32, January, 1970.

"Family planning--a health priority." J MED ASSOC STATE ALA. 40:414-415, December, 1970.

"Family planning in China," by H. Suyin. JAPAN Q. 17:433-442, October-December, 1970.

"Family planning in the developing world," by W. G. Povey. OBSTET GYNECOL. 36:948-952, December, 1970.

"Family planning in England," by E. Funke. OEFF GESUNDHEITSWESEN. 32:421-429, August, 1970.

"Family planning in New York City: recommendations for action: prepared by Planned parenthood of New York City." FAMILY PLANNING PERSPECTIVES. 2:25-31, October, 1970.

FAMILY PLANNING

"Family planning in a rural area using intrauterine devices," by C. R. Ramirez. REV CHIL OBSTET GINECOL. 35:11-13, 1970.

"Family planning in rural areas: Colorado: enlisting private physicians," by S. S. Tepper. FAMILY PLANNING PERSPECTIVES. 2:30-34, June, 1970.

"Family planning in Taiwan, 1949-1970," by S. Hsu. INDUSTRY OF FREE CHINA. 34:2-20, December, 1970.

"Family planning in Taiwan, Republic of China: progress and prospects," by L. P. Chow. POPULATION STUDIES. 24:339-352, November, 1970.

"Family planning in the war on poverty," by G. D. London. FERTIL STERIL. 21:189-192, March, 1970.

"Family planning--much more than the 'pill'," by S. J. Elsea. NEBRASKA NURSE. 3:12-15, May, 1970.

"Family planning or population control?" by J. Reston. READ DIGEST. 97:163-164, December, 1970.

"Family planning problems," by J. Priddle. OCCUP HEALTH. 22:145-149. May, 1970.

"Family planning program evaluation by use of a sample survey. The Emory University Family Planning Program, Atlanta, Georgia," by C. W. Tyler, Jr., et al. AMER J PUBLIC HEALTH. 60:1264-1270, July, 1970.

"Family planning project," by J. Sigamoney. CHRIST NURSE. 232:16-17, October, 1970.

"Family planning prospects in less-developed countries, and a cost-benefit analysis of various alternatives," by J. L. Simon. ECON J. 80:57-71, March, 1970.

"Family planning: respectability at last." NATURE (LONDON). 226:992-993, June 13, 1970.

"Family planning seminars for health visitors," by D. Barnard. HEALTH VISIT. 43:81-83, March, 1970.

"A family planning services data system," by J. C. Smith and J. B. Goldsby. FAMILY PLANNING PERSPECTIVES. 2:41-46, June, 1970.

FAMILY PLANNING

"Hospital-based nurses in family planning," by A. N. K. Dan. NURS J INDIA. 61:264, August, 1970.

"Hospitals may assume role of information centres." CAN HOSP. 47:25, October, 1970.

"How to insure effective implementation of family planning activities in critical population areas," by J. P. Pasaporte. NEWSETTE. 10:4-9, January-March, 1970.

"Family-planning services within hospitals," by S. J. Steele. LANCET. 1:514-515, March 7, 1970.

"Family planning: A suggested supplementary course to health care in the home." PHILIPP J NURS. 39:12+, January-March, 1970.

"Fecundity," by B. Law. BR MED J. 1:443-445, February 20, 1971.

"Federal family planning programs: choice or coercion?" J. B. Rauch. SOCIAL WORK. 15:68-75, October, 1970.

"Fees for family planning services," by K. L. Oldershaw. BRIT MED J. 1:502, February 21, 1970.

"Fertility and family planning in Africa," by T. E. Dow, Jr. J MOD AFRIC STUD. 8:445-457, October, 1970.

"Fertility control: health and educational factors for the 1970s. Family planning in the next 10 years," by E. Brooks. J BIOSOC SCI. 2:171-180, April, 1970.

"Freedom in family planning. The abortion law and women's liberation," by H. Muramatsu. JAP J MIDWIFE. 24:10-19, December, 1970.

"Geographic distribution of need for family planning and subsidized services in the United States," by R. C. Lerner. AM J PUBLIC HEALTH. 60:1945-1955, October, 1970.

"Health aspects of family planning. Report of a WHO Scientific Group." WHO TECHN REP SER. 442:1-50, 1970.

FAMILY PLANNING

"Health visitors and family planning," by A. Cartwright. BRIT J PREV SOC MED. 24:64, February, 1970.

"Health visitors' attitudes towards family planning," by P. Woodward. HEALTH VISIT. 43:360-361, November, 1970.

"Here's where to get information and advice." CHATELAINE. 43:50, August, 1970.

"Human genetic aspects of family planning," by W. Lenz. OEFF GESUNDHEITSWESEN. 32:61-67, February, 1970.

"The impact of family planning propaganda of the younger generation," by A. Abraham. NURS J INDIA. 61:110 passim, April, 1970.

"The importance of the pediatrician in family planning," by C. C. De Silva. CLIN PEDIAT. 9:69-71, February, 1970.

"Integrated incentives for fertility control," by L. W. Kangas. SCIENCE. 169:1278-1283, September 25, 1970; "Discussion," 170:1256+, December 18, 1970.

"Integrated incentives for ertility ontrol," by L. W. Kangas. SCIENCE. 169,3952:1278-1283, September, 1970.

"International conference on family planning, Budapest, September 15-17, 1969," by M. Zelenkova. CESK GYNEK. 35:47-49, February, 1970.

"Knowledge and attitude of nursing students toward population control and family planning," by M. I. Kim, et al. KOREAN NURSE. 9:41-53, June 25, 1970.

"Lateness of contraception among recipients of subsidized family planning service," by C. F. Bennett. AM J PUBLIC HEALTH. 60:2110-2117, November, 1970.

"The literature of ethical problems in medicine," by J. R. Elkinton. ANN INTERN MED. 73:662-666, October, 1970.

"Louisiana's quiet revolution in family planning," by A. Gordon. TODAY'S HLTH. 48:38+, January, 1970.

FAMILY PLANNING

"Major federal resources for family planning programs and services: a summary." FAMILY PLANNING PERSPECTIVES. 2:40-41, March, 1970.

"Maternal nutrition and family planning," by J. G. Chopra, et al. AM J CLIN NUTR. 23:1043-1058, August, 1970.

"Mental health and family planning," by H. P. David. J NERV MENT DIS. 151:1, July, 1970.

"Morocco: family planning knowledge, attitudes, and practice in the rural areas; Morocco: family planning and an attitude survey in the urban areas." STUDIES IN FAMILY PLANNING. 58:1-10, October, 1970.

"National family-planning programs: where we stand," by B. Berelson. SCIENCE. 169:931, September 4, 1970.

"Nonmonetary commodity incentives in family planning programs: a preliminary trial," by G. W. Perkin. STUDIES IN FAMILY PLANNING. p 12-15, September, 1970.

"Nurse's role in family planning at a municipal hospital," by N. Herzig. HOSP TOP. 48:101 passim, February, 1970.

"OBG: Nurse's role in family planning at a municipal hospital," by N. Herzig. HOSP TOPICS. 48:101 plus, February, 1970.

"Observations on the instruction of family planning for outpatients of the Aiiku Hospital," by M. Horiguchi, et al. JAP J MIDWIFE. 24:50-53, March, 1970.

"On population matters and family planning programs." DEPT STATE NEWS LETTER. p 12-13, September, 1970.

"Oral contraception. An application in family planning programme in Calcutta city," by A. S. Gupta. J INDIAN MED ASS. 54:187-194, March 1, 1970.

"Physicians and methods of birth planning," by P. J. Donaldson. RI MED J. 53:419-423 passim, August, 1970.

FAMILY PLANNING

"Pilot study of patient time spent and cost analysis in a demonstration family planning and gynecology clinic. July-September, 1970, Taipei, Taiwan," by S. Fong. J NURS. 17:16-21, October, 1970.

"Planning and implementing a large-scale family planning program in Georgia," by R. W. O'Connor, et al. AMER J PUBLIC HEALTH. 60:78-86, January, 1970.

"Planning better families: education and voluntary control measures have brought Taiwan's population explosion under control even in rural areas where big families are the rule," by Y. Hsueh. FREE CHINA R. 20:20-22, March, 1970.

"Population package: Family planning services and population research act of 1970." TIME. 96:36, December 21, 1970.

"Postnatal family planning at St. Mary's Hospital and Westminster Welfare Centre, London," by A. W. Giles. MIDWIVES CHRON. 83:346-347, October, 1970.

"Prediction in family planning. Factors associated with involvement of low-income women in a public family planning program," by E. Siegal, et al. AMER J PUBLIC HEALTH. 60:1382-1394, August, 1970.

"Prediction in family planning. Prediction of the adoption and continued use of contraception," by D. Mc Calister, et al. AMER J PUBLIC HEALTH. 60:1372-1381, August, 1970.

"Problems in industry," by S. J. Vaughan. OCCUP HLTH. 22:151 plus, May, 1970.

"A program of indigent obstetric care and planned parenthood in a rural North Carolina county," by J. E. Clement. AMER J OBSTET GYNEC. 108:63-67, September 1, 1970.

"Projected effects of family-planning on the incidence of perinatal mortality in a lower-class nonwhite population," by D. V. McCalister, et al. AMER J OBSTET GYNEC. 106:573-580, February 15, 1970.

"Psychological sources of resistance to family planning," by A. B. Keller, et al. MERRILL-PALMER Q. 16:286-

FAMILY PLANNING

302, July, 1970.

"Psychosocial studies in family planning behavior in Central and Eastern Europe. A preliminary report of a developing program," by H. P. David. J PSYCHIATR NURS. 8:28-33, September-October, 1970.

"Relationship of family planning to pediatrics and child health," by H. M. Wallace, et al. CLIN PEDIATR. 9: 699-701, December, 1970.

"Removal of barriers to family planning." WIEN MED WOCHENSCHR. 120:129, May 2, 1970.

"Reserving a womb: case for the small family," by E. J. Lieberman. AMER J PUBLIC HEALTH. 60:87-92, January, 1970.

"The role of family planning in prevention of pregnancy wastage," by E. M. Gold, et al. CLIN OBSTET GYNEC. 13:145-156, March, 1970.

"The role of the pharmacist in family planning," by N. N. Wagner, et al. J AMER PHARM ASS. 10:258-260, May, 1970.

"The Singapore Family Planning Program: further evaluation data," by D. Wolfers. AM J PUBLIC HEALTH. 60:2354-2360, December, 1970.

"Social planning for the family," by R. Dore. J OF DEVELOPMENT STUDIES. 6:57-66, July, 1970.

"Socio-economic status and family planning knowledge, attitudes and practices in rural East Pakistan," by J. Stoeckel. SOCIAL & ECON STUDIES. 19:213-225, June, 1970.

"Some obstacles to family planning in India," by B. P. Singh. ECON AFFAIRS. 15:293-303, August, 1970.

"Suggestions on adding family planning to the curriculums of medical schools," by D. T. Rice. PUBLIC HEALTH REP. 85:889-895, October, 1970.

"The summary report of the seminar on nursing education and family planning," by M. I. Kim. KOREAN NURSE. 9:27-34, December 25, 1970.

FAMILY PLANNING

"Teenagers in a family planning clinic," by J. T. Cassidy. NURS OUTLOOK. 18:30-31, November, 1970.

"To teach or not to teach family planning in Kenyan primary schools," by J. B. Maathuis. EAST AFR MED J. 47:545-549, November, 1970.

"The training of nurses in family planning," by N. Loudon. NURS MIRROR. 131:28-29, July 24, 1970.

"US population growth and family planning: a review of the literature. FAMILY PLANNING PERSPECTIVES. 2: 16-page section following p. 24, October, 1970.

"United States: utilization of a family planning program in a metropolitan area," by J. D. Beasley and R. F. Frankowski. STUDIES IN FAMILY PLANNING. 59: 7-16, November, 1970.

"The use of client characteristics as predictors of utilization of family planning service," by S. M. Wishik. AMER J PUBLIC HEALTH. 60:1394-1397, August, 1970.

"Users and non-users of contraception: tests of stationarity applied to members of a family planning programme," by G. E. Ebanks. POPULATION STUDIES. 24:85-91, March, 1970.

"Vital statistics and census tract data used to evaluate family planning," by N. H. Wright. PUBLIC HEALTH REP. 85:383-389, May, 1970.

"Welfare of expectant mothers and family planning. Statistical observations on the health guidance of expectant mothers." JAP J MIDWIFE. 24:42-46, December, 1970.

"West Virginia's approach to a statewide family planning program," by L. C. Landman. FAMILY PLANNING PERSPECTIVES. 2:21-24, October, 1970.

FAMILY STRUCTURE & RELATIONS

"Changing patterns of family growth: the value of linked vital records as a source of data," by H. B. Newcombe and M. E. Smith. POPULATION STUDIES. 24: 193-203, July, 1970.

FAMILY STRUCTURE & RELATIONS

"The family. Is it basic?" by J. West. FRIENDS' Q. 16:480-484, January, 1970.

"Family breakdown and social networks," by T. Noble. BRIT J OF SOCIOLOGY. 21:135-150, June, 1970.

"Family patterns of migrant and nonmigrant retirees," by G. L. Bultena, et al. J MARRIAGE & FAM. 32: 89-93, February, 1970.

"Family planning and conjugal roles in New York City poverty areas," by S. Polgar, et al. SOC SCI MED. 4:135-139, July, 1970.

"Family size and sex-role stereotypes," by F. E. Clarkson, et al. SCIENCE. 167:390-392, January 23, 1970.

"Family therapy: an adjunct to hemodialysis and transplantation," by P. Kossoris. AMER J NURS. 70:1730-1733, August, 1970.

"On the relation between economic status and family size preferences when status differentials in contraceptive instrumentalities are eliminated," by N. K. Namboodiri. POPULATION STUDIES. 24:233-239, July, 1970.

"Parents under strain: families with a mentally handicapped child," by S. Gilderdale. NEW SOCIETY. p.777-778, May 7, 1970.

"Primary sex-ratio and size of family," by M. R. Shokeir. LANCET. 1:245, January 31, 1970.

"Size and structure of the household in England over three centuries: a comment," by J. W. Nixon. POPULATION STUDIES. 24:445-447, November, 1970.

"Smaller families: a national imperative," by G. J. Hecht. PARENTS MAG. 45:24+, July, 1970.

"The unmarried father--the forgotten man," by R. Pannor. NURS OUTLOOK. 18:36-37, November, 1970.

FERTILITY CONTROL
SEE: BIRTH CONTROL

GENETICS & POPULATION
SEE ALSO: FAMILY STRUCTURE

"Chromosomal abnormalities in the human population; estimation of rates based on New Haven newborn study," by H. A. Lubs and F. H. Ruddle. SCIENCE. 169:495-497, July 31, 1970.

"Genetic patterns," by G. E. Moore. SCIENCE. 169:328, July 24, 1970.

"Genetics of the HL-A system. A population and family study," by A. Svejgaard, et al. VOX SANG. 18:97-133, February, 1970.

"Human genetic aspects of family planning," by W. Lenz. OEFF GESUNDHEITSWESEN. 32:61-67, February, 1970.

"Natural selection in ecologically and genetically defined populations," by C. Istock. BEHAVIORAL SCIENCE. 15,1:101-115, January, 1970. SA# E9021.

HEALTH, PUBLIC HEALTH, AND MEDICINE AND POPULATION
SEE ALSO: ENVIRONMENT, ECOLOGY AND POPULATION

"Census of 1970--an important source of information on problems of social hygiene in public health," by M. S. Bednyi, et al. ZDRAVOOKHR ROSS FED. 14:8-15, January, 1970.

"The changing environment: some implications for health," by A. J. Diekema. OCCUP HEALTH NURS. 18:20-22, July, 1970.

"The detection of incidence of congenital malformations in the community," by J. A. Weatherall. PROC R SOC MED. 63:1251-1252, December, 1970.

"Dual challenge of health and hunger: a global crisis," by G. A. Borgstrom. BUL ATOM SCI. 26:42-46, October, 1970.

"Fertility control: health and educational factors for the 1970's. Contraception or abortion?" by J. H. Hughes. J BIOSOC SCI. 2:161-166, April, 1970.

"Fertility control: health and educational factors for the 1970's. Family planning in the next ten years," by E. Brooks. J BIOSOC SCI. 2:171-180, April, 1970.

HEALTH, PUBLIC HEALTH, AND MEDICINE AND POPULATION

"Fertility control: health and educational factors for the 1970's. The future of oral contraception," by G. A. Christie. J BIOSOC SCI. 2:191-197, April, 1970.

"Fertility control: health and educational factors for the 1970's. The role of the local authority," by D. Barnard. J BIOSOC SCI. 2:181-189, April, 1970.

"Fertility control: health and educational factors for the 1970's. The role of the local authority," by D. Barnard. J BIOSOC SCI. 2:181-189, April, 1970.

"Fertility control: health and educational factors for the 1970's. Trends in contraception," by A. C. Turnbull. J BIOSOC SCI. 2:157-160, April, 1970.

"Health and disease from the sociological viewpoint," by K. D. Stumpfe. THER GEGENW. 109:153-170, February, 1970.

"Health aspects of family planning. Report of a WHO Scientific Group." WHO TECHN REP SER. 442:1-50, 1970.

"Health hazards associated with urbanization and overpopulation," by B. Walker, Jr. J NAT MED ASS. 62:259-264, July, 1970.

"Health, population growth, and development in Taiwan," by Te-Hsiung Sun. INDUSTRY OF FREE CHINA. 33:17-30, June, 1970.

"Health visitors and family planning," by A. Cartwright. BRIT J PREV SOC MED. 24:64, February, 1970.

"Health visitors' attitudes towards family planning," by P. Woodward. HEALTH VISIT. 43:360-361, November, 1970.

"Implications of the 1970 census for health and medicine," by O. K. Sagen. ANN INTERN MED. 72:134-136, January, 1970.

"Isolated and migratory population groups: health problems and epidemiologic studies. I. Introduction," by D. C. Gajdusek. AMER J TROP MED. 19:127-129, January, 1970.

HEALTH, PUBLIC HEALTH, AND MEDICINE AND POPULATION

"A mass social-hygienic investigation of a very old population in various areas of the Soviet Union: program, procedure, results," by N. N. Sachuk. J GERONT. 25:256-261, July, 1970.

"Mental health and family planning," by H. P. David. J NERV MENT DIS. 151:1, July, 1970.

"Methodological issues in health statistics (symposium)" MILBANK MEMORIAL FUND Q. 48:1-87, October, 1970.

"Mumps in a general population. A sero-epidemiologic study," by L. P. Levitt, et al. AMER J DIS CHILD. 120:134-138, August, 1970.

"National surveillance network for occupational health," by V. E. Rose, et al. J OCCUP MED. 12:193-197, June, 1970.

"New biology and the prenatal child," by D. W. Brodie. J FAMILY L. 9:391, 1970.

"The obstetrician and society," by D. Baird. AMER J PUBLIC HEALTH. 60:628-640, April, 1970.

"Panel discussion on problems in population screening for cervical cancer." ACTA CYTOL. 14:161-163, March, 1970.

"Poliomyelitis surveillance in England and Wales, 1965-1968," by D. L. Miller, et al. PUBLIC HEALTH. 84: 265-285, September, 1970.

"Population increase and Public Health," by M. I. Kim. KOREAN NURSE. 9:19-24, August 25, 1970.

"Population survey for detection of frank and latent diabetes in one part of Cuttack, Orissa," by B. B. Tripathy, et al. J INDIAN MED ASS. 54:55-61, January 16, 1970.

"Prepregnancy care--a logical extension of prenatal care," by R. F. Friesen. CAN MED ASSOC J. 103: 495-497, September 12, 1970.

"Problems of health and development," by A. A. Angara. BULL INFIRM CATH CANADA. 37:133-144, May-August,

HEALTH, PUBLIC HEALTH, AND MEDICINE AND POPULATION
1970.

"Recent trends in infant and maternal health in Minnesota," by A. B. Rosenfield, et al. MINN MED. 53:807-816, July, 1970.

"Relationship of family planning to pediatrics and child health," by H. M. Wallace, et al. CLIN PEDIATR. 9:699-701, December, 1970.

"Strokes in women of childbearing age. A population study," by B. S. Schoenberg, et al. NEUROLOGY. 20: 181-189, February, 1970.

"Surveillance of poliomyelitis in Czechoslovakia in 1966-1968," by J. Vobecky, et al. J HYG EPIDEMIOL MICROBIOL IMMUNOL. 14:404-412, 1970.

ISOLATION, ALIENATION & CONFINEMENT
SEE ALSO: CROWDING

"The activity record: a measure of social isolation-involvement," by A. D. Sachson, et al. PSYCHOL REP. 26:413-414, April, 1970.

"Aggressive behavior in the rat: effects of isolation, and olfactory bulb lesions," by H. Bernstein, et al. BRAIN RES. 20:75-84, May 20, 1970.

"Alienation: another dimension of underachievement," by M. M. Propper, et al. J PSYCHOL. 75:13-18, May, 1970.

"Alienation correlates of Catholic fertility," by A. G. Neal, et al. AM J SOCIOL. 76:460-473, November, 1970.

"Alienation: an essential process of the psychology of adolescence," by S. Berman. J AM ACAD CHILD PSYCHIATRY. 9:233-250, April, 1970.

"Alienation of present-day adolescents," by L. J. Wise. J AM ACAD CHILD PSYCHIATRY. 9:264-277, April, 1970.

"Alienation of youth as reflected in the Hippie movement," by F. S. Williams. J AM ACAD CHILD PSYCHIATRY. 9:251-263, April, 1970.

"Alterations in brain sensitivity and barbiturate metabolism unrelated to aggression in socially deprived mice," by I. Baumel, et al. PSYCHOPHARMACOLOGIA. 18:320-324, 1970.

"Brain cholinesterase in grouped and singly caged adrenal-demedullated rats," by T. D. McKinney. AMER J PHYSIOL. 219:331-334, August, 1970.

"Brain weight and acetylcholinesterase activity in differentially-grouped cottontail rabbits," by T. D. Mc Kinney, et al. J MAMMAL. 51:389-391, May, 1970.

"Certain cultural and familial factors contributing to adolescent alienation," by J. D. Noshpitz. J AM ACAD CHILD PSYCHIATRY. 9:216-223, April, 1970.

"Changes in the cytology of the pars distalis of pituitary of green frog, Rana esculenta, under laboratory confinement," by R. K. Rastogi, et al. GEN COMP ENDOCRINOL. 15:488-491, December, 1970.

"Comment on 'high school yearbooks: a nonreactive measure of social isolation in graduates who later became schizophrenic'," by J. C. Schwarz. J ABNORM PSYCHOL. 75:317-318, June, 1970.

"Community homogeneity and exclusion of the mentally ill: rejection versus consensus about deviance," by A. S. Linsky. J HEALTH SOC BEHAV. 11:304-311, December, 1970.

"Companion therapy for hospitalized psychotics," by A. M. Ludwig, et al. CURR PSYCHIATR THER. 10:182-190, 1970.

"Deprivation: an essay in definition with special consideration of the Australian Aboriginal," by R. Nurcombe. MED J AUST. 2:87-92, July, 11, 1970.

"The development of tool using in wild-born and restriction-reared chimpanzees," by E. W. Menzel, Jr., et al. FOLIA PRIMAT. 12:273-283, 1970.

"Differential susceptibility to a viral agent in mice housed alone or in groups," by S. B. Friedman, et al. PSYCHOSOM MED. 32:285-299, May-June, 1970.

ISOLATION, ALIENATION & CONFINEMENT

"Disease patterns and vaccine-response studies in isolated Micronesian populations," by P. Brown, et al. AMER J TROP MED. 19:170-175, January, 1970.

"Disengagement and morale," by M. Tallmer, et al. GERONTOLOGIST. 10:317-320, Winter, 1970.

"Drug environment interactions: acute hypoxia and chronic isolation," by J. J. DeFeo, et al. FED PROC. 29:1985-1990, November-December, 1970.

"Educating teachers and children in law: an approach to reduced alienation in inner-city schools," by A. Elson, et al. AM J ORTHOPSYCHIATRY. 40:870-878, October, 1970.

"Effect of the duration of social isolation on instrumental learning acquisition in mice," by A. Ungerer. C R ACAD SCI. 271:350-352, July 20, 1970.

"Effect of two days' monotonous confinement on conditioned eyelid frequency and topography," by P. Gendreau, et al. PERCEPT MOTOR SKILLS. 31:291-293, August, 1970.

"Effectiveness of protective confinement therapy of alcoholics," by H. Skopkova. CESK PSYCHIAT. 66:165-172, June, 1970.

"Goals and some methods in psychotherapy: hypnosis and isolation," by I. Wickram. AM J CLIN HYPN. 13:95-100, October, 1970.

"Isolated and migratory population groups: health problems and epidemiologic studies. I. Introduction," by D. C. Gajdusek. AMER J TROP MED. 19:127-129, January, 1970.

"Isolation, a challenge of disability," by H. H. Hanson. J REHAB. 36:2, May-June, 1970.

"The loneliness of old age," by M. L. Conti. NURS OUTLOOK. 18:28-30, August, 1970.

"Long-term isolation in rats reduces morphine response," by D. M. Katz, et al. NATURE (LOND). 228:469-471, October 31, 1970.

ISOLATION, ALIENATION & CONFINEMENT

"Maternal effects on behavior and white blood cells of isolated female mice," by A. S. Weltman, et al. LIFE SCI. 9:291-300, March 1, 1970.

"Mothers of disabled children--the value of weekly group meetings," by R. Linder. DEVELOP MED CHILD NEUROL. 12:202-206, April, 1970.

"The problem of speech disorders and their psychosocial aspects," by L. Rubinato, et al. MINERVA PEDIATR. 22:2271-2272, November 17, 1970.

"Psychiatric care: Patients isolated from society during treatment time," by L. Gustafsson. LAKARTIDNINGEN. 67:704-708, February 11, 1970.

"Psychomotor assessment and rehabilitation of socioculturally deprived children," by H. Feldmann. ACTA PAEDOPSYCHIATR. 37:268-293, December, 1970.

"The relative importance of selected behavioral characteristics of group members in an extreme environment," by R. E. Doll, et al. J PSYCHOL. 75:231-237, July, 1970.

"Seasonal variations in the blood corticosterone level in animals kept in groups and in isolation," by E. V. Naumenko, et al. DOKL AKAD NAUK SSSR. 195:750-752, 1970.

"Sensory deprivation versus sensory variation," by M. Zuckerman, et al. J ABNORM PSYCHOL. 76:76-82, August, 1970.

"Social deprivation, housing density, and gregariousness in rats," by B. Latane, et al. J COMP PHYSIOL PSYCHOL. 70:221-227, February, 1970.

"Social isolates and urbanites in perceptual isolation," by A. As, et al. J ABNORM PSYCHOL. 76:1-9, August, 1970.

"Social isolation, activeness and leisure reading among the blind," by S. S. Guterman. SOC SCI MED. 3:349-361, January, 1970.

"Social isolation and bereavement," by F. G. Wilson. LANCET. 2:1356-1357, December 26, 1970.

ISOLATION, ALIENATION & CONFINEMENT

"Solitude and transference: a study on character neuroses," by M. Neyraut. REV FR PSYCHANAL. 34:81-100, January, 1970.

"Some relations between social isolation and communicable diseases," by F. D. Schofield. AMER J TROP MED. 19:167-169, January, 1970.

"The strange society of the physician," by N. Roth. AM J PSYCHOTHER. 24:494-498, July, 1970.

"Temporary psychosis caused by isolation," by L. Palmgren. LAKARTIDNINGEN. 67:1280-1282, March 18, 1970.

"Therapy of the alienated college student," by S. Halleck. CURR PSYCHIATR THER. 10:76-82, 1970.

"The urban setting. 3. Mental health services and the isolated citizen," by M. Mitchell-Bateman. RHODE ISLAND MED J. 53:263-266 passim, May, 1970.

"Voluntary confinement among lepers," by M. Bloombaum, et al. J HEALTH SOC BEHAV. 11:16-20, March, 1970.

LABOR & POPULATION
SEE ALSO: MIGRATIONS

"Birth rate and work load," by E. Nurge. AM ANTHROP. 72:1434-1439, December, 1970.

"The CBI industrial trends survey," by D. R. Glynn. APPLIED ECON. 1:183-203, May, 1970.

"Coping with executive mobility," by W. A. Dressel. BSNS HORIZONS. 13:53-58, August, 1970.

"The decline of the size of the domestic group in England. A comment on J. W. Nixon's note," by P. Laslett. POPULATION STUDIES. 24:449-454, November, 1970.

"Determining the labor force status of men missed in the census: special labor force report describes pilot use of a new technique for securing labor force data in urban poverty areas," by D. P. Klein. MO LABOR R. 93:26-32, March, 1970.

"Effect of out-migration of regional employment," by

LABOR & POPULATION

J. Vanderkamp. CAN J ECON. 3:541-549, November, 1970.

"Effect on unemployment rates of weekly enumeration of the current population survey," by M. D. Wann. STATIS REPORTER. p 93-98, December, 1970.

"Labor mobility and regional payment adjustments," by C. W. Hultman. LAND ECON. 46:467-473, November, 1970.

"Latin America's unemployment problem," by I. Beller. MO LABOR R. 93:8, November, 1970.

"Migrant labour and agricultural output in Ghana," by R. E. Beals and C. F. Menezes. OXFORD ECONOMIC PAPERS. 22:109-127, March, 1970.

"Migrant labour and economic development," by M. P. Miracle and S. S. Berry. OXFORD ECONOMIC PAPERS. 22:86-108, March, 1970.

"Migration, employment, and race in the deep South," by J. J. Persky, et al. SO ECON J. 36:268-276, January, 1970.

"Model for the dispersion of the migrant labor force and some results for the United State, 1880-1920," by T. J. Orsagh, et al. R ECON & STAT. 52:306-312, August, 1970.

"Negro migration and unemployment," by D. E. Kaun. J HUM RESOURCES. 5:191-207, Spring, 1970.

"Unemployment: challenge to development," by E. Thorbecke. CERES. 3:24-51, November-December, 1970.

LAWS & LEGISLATION

"Abortion and sterilization. Status of the law in mid-1970," by N. Hershey. AMER J NURS. 70:1926-1927, September, 1970.

"Birth control. Moral theological, medico-gynecologic and penal aspects," by H. D. Hiersche, et al. GEBURTSH FRAUENHEILK. 30:289-301, April, 1970.

"Brave new world: can the law bring order within traditional concepts of due process?" SUFFOLK U L REV. 4:894, Spring, 1970.

"Constitutional problems of population control," by B. S. Elkins. J LAW REFORM. 4:63-68, Fall, 1970.

"Cooperation of general practitioner in birth control. Legal questions about prescription of the pill," by W. Becker. THER GEGENW. 109:428 passim, March, 1970.

"Court-Ordered Contraception; a reasonable alternative to institutionalization for juvenile unwed mothers?" WIS L R. 1970:899, 1970.

"Critical examination of request for sterilization of mentally defective persons," by K. Grunewald. LAKARTIDNINGEN. 67:5091-5095, October 28, 1970.

"Effect of Washington hearings on contraceptive use," by E. B. Connell. DELAWARE MED J. 42:212 passim, August, 1970.

"Existing stocks may be used up." AM DRUGGIST. 162:37, November 16, 1970.

"FDA: efficiency drive stumbles over the issue of drug efficiency; effects of Demulen," by T. P. Southwick. SCIENCE. 169:1188-1189, September 18, 1970.

"FDA goes to the consumer." SCI N. 97:266, March 14, 1970.

"FDA is facing court action for access to pill information as a result of secrecy policy." OIL PAINT & DRUG REP. 198:7, July 6, 1970.

"FDA offers milder version OC insert." AM DRUGGIST. 161:16, April 20, 1970.

"FDA set to weigh stricter standards for the birth pills." OIL PAINT & DRUG REP. 197:5 plus, January 12, 1970.

"FDA will look again into the pill's dangers." OIL PAINT & DRUG REP. 197:7 plus, January 26, 1970.

"FDA writes another warning." SCI N. 97:599, June 20,

LAWS & LEGISLATION

1970.

"Federal Action for Population Policy-- What More Can We do Now?" by R. W. Lamson. BIOSCIENCE. 20,15: 854-857, August, 1970.

"Freedom in family planning. The abortion law and women's liberation," by H. Muramatsu. JAP J MIDWIFE. 24:10-19, December, 1970.

"Interference with human life; some jurisprudential reflections," by W. Friedman. COLUM L R. 70:1058, June, 1970.

"Introduction of mass psychology of animals to pharmacology. I. Influence of the 3rd party on the legal questions about prescription of the pill," by W. Becker. THER GEGENW. 109:428 passim, March, 1970.

"The law concerning voluntary sterilization as it affects doctors," by M. Mackay, et al. J UROL. 103: 483-484, April, 1970.

"Laws to limit family size," by L. Lader. PARENTS MAG. 45:58-61, October, 1970.

"Legal effects of 1970 census on Minnesota municipalities," by J. Lunde. MINN MUNIC. 55:73-75, March, 1970.

"Legal responsibility for unsuccessful sterilization," by E. Havt. HOSP MANAGE. 109:13 passim, February, 1970.

"Legality of sterilization." BRIT MED J. 1:704-705, March 21, 1970.

"National population programs and policy: social and legal implications--a symposium: Introduction," by D. A. Giannella: "Federal population policy: a decade of change," by C. S. Schultz; "National population problems and standardization of family size," by H. Y. Tien; "Population programs and policy," by S. M. Wishik; "Population policies of state governments in the United States: some preliminary observations," by E. D. Driver; "Constitutional aspects of a national population policy," by C. C. Means, Jr.; panel discussion. VILL L REV. 15:785, Summer,

LAWS & LEGISLATION

1970.

"New draft of OC insert is awaited." AM DRUGGIST. 161: 20, April 6, 1970.

"Opposition to birth control law wanes," by N. C. Miller. WALL ST J. 176:8, August 14, 1970.

"The Parliament requested overhaul in sterilization law." LAKARTIDNINGEN. 67:5732, December 2, 1970.

"Pill in court." CHEM W. 107:17, September 30, 1970.

"Population and the law: a symposium. Where does individual freedom conflict with a citizen's duty to society and the future of the environment? New role for government?" by R. O. Egeberg; "Incentives for the two-child family," by B. Packwood; "Alternative to the ant-hill society," by M. H. Stans. TRIAL. 6:10, August-September, 1970.

"Population control: the legal approach to a biological imperative." CALIF L REV. 58:1414, November, 1970.

"Population growth and international law," by A. C. Kellogg. CORNELL INTERNAT LAW J. 3:93-103, Winter, 1970.

"Population package: Family planning services and Population research act of 1970." TIME. 96:36, December 21, 1970.

"Rep. Rogers calls for restrictions on pill advertising." ADV AGE. 41:3, April 13, 1970.

"Sterilization of women in the light of Polish legislation," by W. Wieszczycki, et al. GINEKOL POL. 41: 1153-1156, October, 1970.

"US funded study hits Enovid; FDA demurs." AM DRUGGIST. 162:33, December 14, 1970.

"Voluntary sterilization and reform of the criminal law," by A. Eser. MED WELT. 40:1751-1759, October 3, 1970.

"Voluntary sterilization law recommended forms," by J. L. Moore, Jr., et al. J MED ASS GEORGIA. 59:374-

LAWS & LEGISLATION

 377, September, 1970.

LIFE INSURANCE INDUSTRY & POPULATION
 SEE ALSO: ACCIDENTS & INJURIES

 "Family history." METROPOLITAN LIFE STAT BUL. 51:4-7, May, 1970.

 "Generation life tables." METROPOLITAN LIFE STAT BUL. 51:8-11, September, 1970.

 "Profile of our children." STATIST BULL METROP LIFE INSUR CO. 51:10-11, July, 1970.

 "Profiles of American youth (ages 14-24, 1950-1969, with projections to 1980)." METROPOLITAN LIFE STATIS BUL. p 4-7, November, 1970.

 "Study of oral contraceptives and risk determination for life insurance," by J. G. Defares. NEDERL T GENEESK. 114:647-648, April 11, 1970.

MENTALLY RETARDED

 "Sexuality, contraception and the mentally retarded," by B. Fujita, et al. POSTGRAD MED. 47:193-197, May, 1970.

MIGRANT LABOR
 SEE: MIGRATIONS and specific country

MIGRATIONS
 SEE ALSO: LABOR & POPULATION
      RURAL GROWTH
      URBAN GROWTH

 "Acadian migrations," by R. G. Leblanc. CAN GEOG J. 81:10-19, July, 1970.

 "Administration of Wagina resettlement scheme," by G. Cochrane. HUMAN ORGAN. 29:123-132, Summer, 1970.

 "Age, education and occupation differentials in inter-regional migration; some evidence for Canada," by M. McInnis. DEMOGRAPHY. 8:195-204, May 1, 1970.

 "Analysis of migration to Israel," by F. S. Sherrow and P. Ritterband. JEW SOC STUD. 32:214-223, July, 1970.

MIGRATIONS

"The assumed employment generating capacity of European immigration in Rhodesia," by D. G. Clarke. RHODESIAN J ECON. 4:33-42, June, 1970.

"Bill Shaw's gate to the promised land," by A. Edmonds. MACL MAG. 83:30, January, 1970.

"The brain drain: a case study," by J. Chataparampil. ASIAN FORUM. 2:236-244, October-December, 1970.

"The brain drain: reality and paradox," by R. Du Pasquier. PANORAMA. p 2-8, July-August, 1970.

"Canadian government view on immigrant services." INTERPRETER RELEASES. 47:220-223, September 14, 1970.

"Canadian immigration," by V. Del Buono. WORLD AFFAIRS. 35:23-24, April, 1970.

"Changing pattern of immigration." METROPOLITAN LIFE STATIS BUL. p 7-9, November, 1970.

"Comparison of the migration process to an urban barrio and to a rural community: two case studies," by W. L. Flinn, et al. INTER-AM ECON AFFAIRS. 24:37-48, August, 1970.

"The convention of the Organization of African unity governing the specific aspects of refugee problems in Africa," by P. Weis. HUMAN RIGHTS J. 3:449-464, September, 1970.

"The determinants of emigration to South Africa, 1950-1967," by G. L. Chapin, et al. SOUTH AFRICAN J ECON. 38:374-381, December, 1970.

"The dispossessed: in a remarkable instance of generosity India has opened some half dozen settlements for Tibetans within her borders. VISTA. 6:16-21, November-December, 1970.

"Effect of out-migration on regional employment," by J Vanderkamp. CAN J ECON. 3:541-549, November, 1970.

"Eight assumptions concerning rural-urban migration in Colombia: a three-shanty-towns test," by W. L. Flinn, et al. LAND ECON. 46:456-466, November, 1970.

MIGRATIONS

"Emigration of Finns to Sweden: drain or benefit for Finland," by V. A. Koiranen. ECON R. 2:47-52, 1970.

"Emigrants to Canada few but independent." FIN POST. 64:J2, August 22, 1970.

"Emigration of Finns to Sweden: drain or benefit for Finland," by V. A. Koiranen. ECON R. 2:27-52, 1970.

"Ending the trek to the towns," by A. Trotter. TOWN & COUNTRY PLANNING. 38:540-543, December, 1970.

"Estimated net migration for Tennessee counties, 1960-1970," by R. A. Engels. TENN SURVEY BUS. 6:3-4 plus, September, 1970.

"European political emigrations: a lost subject," by R. C. Williams. COMP STUD SOC & HIST. 12:140-148, April, 1970.

"Fate of personal adjustment in the process of modernization," by A. Inkeles, et al. J COMP SOCIOL. 11:81-114, June, 1970.

"The fertility of migrants to and within North America," by L. H. Long. MILBANK MEMORIAL FUND Q. 48:297-315, July, 1970.

"Geography of internal migration movements in Belgium," by R. Andre. REVUE DE L'INSTITUT DE SOCIOLOGIE. 2:383-402, 1970. SA #E9001.

"Humberside; employment, unemployment and migration, the evolution of industrial structure, 1951-1966," by J. Craig, et al. YORKSHIRE BULLETIN. 22:123-142, November, 1970.

"Identification of migrants and their descendants in the United States," by W. Haenszel. J CHRONIC DIS. 23:383-387, November, 1970.

"Immigration from the U.S.A." WORLD AFFAIRS. 35:10, February, 1970.

"Immigration service statistics on immigrants with occupational preferences and other immigrants admitted by occupation." INTERPRETER RELEASES. 47:208-213, August 24, 1970.

MIGRATIONS

"Immigration statistics for 1969." INTERPRETER RELEASES. 47:131-145, June 19, 1970.

"Immigration tap still turned on with skilled young people in lead," by C. Baxter. FIN POST. 64:5, August 22, 1970.

"Immigration under review." INST PUBLIC AFFAIRS R. 24:75-79, July-September, 1970.

"Immigration yields," by G. Keeleric, et al. SCIENCE. 169:817, August 28, 1970.

"In-migration and growth of non-metropolitan urban places," by J. J. Zuiches. RURAL SOCIOL. 35:410-420, September, 1970.

"Influence of administrative reform on the immigration and naturalization service," by J. J. Green. ADMINISTRATIVE SCIENCE Q. 15:353-359, September, 1970.

"International migration of professionals," by J. A. Fortney. POPULATION STUDIES. 24:217-232, July, 1970.

"Interprovincial migration and economic adjustment," by T. J. Courchene. CAN J ECON. 3:550-576, November, 1970.

"Isolated and migratory population groups: health problems and epidemiologic studies. I. Introduction," by D. C. Gajdusek. AMER J TROP MED. 19:127-129, January, 1970.

"Italian communities abroad: migration to European and non-European nations." ITALY DOCS & NOTES. 19:7-17, January-February, 1970.

"Measuring rural--urban drift in developing countries; a suggested model," by L. Roussel. INT LABOUR R. 101:229-246, March, 1970.

"Method of analysis of a table of 'origin-destination' migrations," by Y. Tugault. POPULATION. 25,1:59-68, January-February, 1970. SA #F0140.

"Migrant labour and economic development," by M. P. Miracle, et al. OXFORD ECONOMIC PAPERS. 22:86-108,

MIGRATIONS

March, 1970.

"Migration and economic opportunities in West Virginia; a statistical analysis," by G. L. Rutman. RURAL SOCIOLOGY. 35,2:206-217, June, 1970.

"Migration and industrial development: the southern Italian experience," by A. Rodgers. ECON GEOG. 46:111-135, April, 1970.

"Migration and modernization," by F. W. Reed. INDIAN J SOCIOL. 1:104-129, September, 1970.

"Migration as investment; empirical tests of the human investment approach to geographical mobility," by S. Bowles. R ECON & STAT. 52:356-362, November, 1970.

"Migration, employment, and race in the deep South," by J. J. Persky and J. F. Kain. SO ECON J. 36:268-276, January, 1970.

"Migration flows in intraurban space: place utility considerations," by L. A. Brown and D. B. Longbrake. ASSN AM GEOG ANN. 60:368-384, June, 1970.

"Migration, functional distance, and the urban hierarchy," by L. A. Brown, et al. ECON GEOG. 46:472-485, July, 1970.

"Migration in an urban population," by A. E. Bennett. BRIT J PREV SOC MED. 24:63-64, February, 1970.

"Migration of native-born Ohioans: 1850-1960," by L. E. Gallaway, et al. BUL BUS RESEARCH. 45:4-5, June, 1970.

"Migration to and from Scotland since 1961," by H. R. Jones. INST BRITISH GEOGRAPHERS TRANSACTIONS. p 145-158, March, 1970.

"Migration, unemployment and development; a two-sector analysis," by J. R. Harris, et al. AM ECON R. 60:126-142, March, 1970.

"Migration within the US 1800-1960; some new estimates," by S. Lebergott. J ECON HIST. 30:839-847, December, 1970.

MIGRATIONS

"Negro migration and unemployment," by D. E. Kaun. J HUM RESOURCES. 5:191-207, Spring, 1970.

"The 'new' Americans--who is coming to US now." US NEWS. 69:70-71, October 5, 1970.

"A 'new town' planned for the urban and rural poor: the University of Louisville develops a controversial strategy to change the flow of migration," by S. Lawson. CITY. 4:35-38, June-July, 1970.

"On measuring geographic mobility," by L. H. Long. AM STAT ASSN J. 65:1195-1203, September, 1970.

"Patterns of migration in relation to local community structure, a study in Karasjok," by R. Mook, et al. TIDSSKRIFT FOR SAMFUNNSFORSKNING. 11,1:13-31, 1970. SA #F0134.

"Population migration and its evaluation in Lenin's works," by V. V. Pokshishevskii. SOVIET ED. 12: 86-100, January, 1970.

"Powell, the minorities, and the 1970 election," by N. Deakin, et al. POL Q. 41:399-415, October-December, 1970.

"Problems of rural-urban migration: some suggestions for investigation," by D. Warriner. INT LAB R. 101: 441-451, May, 1970.

"Radical changes in migration." REAL ESTATE ANALYST. 39:35-37, January 28, 1970.

"The reader asks to be told: on migration of the population," by V. Boldyrev. CURRENT DIG SOVIET PR. 22:18-19, September 22, 1970.

"The relation of migration to regional unemployment," by B. D. Phillips. AM ECONOMIST. 14:26-42, Fall, 1970.

"Reversing the brain drain: a case study from India," by M. F. Merriam. INTERNAT DEVELOPMENT R. 12:16-22, November 3, 1970.

"Rural slums or rural desert?" by M. Hederman. INTERPLAY. 3:23-26, June, 1970.

MIGRATIONS

"Rural-urban migration: a clue to rural-urban relations in India," by C. R. Prasada Rao. INDIAN J SOCIAL WORK. 30:335-342, January, 1970.

"Settlement patterns of Canadian emigrants to the United States, 1850-1960," by R. K. Vedder and L. E. Gallaway. CAN J ECON. 3:476-486, August, 1970.

"A short run model of inter-regional migration," by A. B. Jack. MANCHESTER SCHOOL OF ECONOMIC & SOCIAL STUDIES. 38:15, March, 1970.

"Some economic aspects of Norwegian population movements 1740-1940: an econometric study," by T. Moe. J ECON HIST. 30:267-270, 285-287, March, 1970.

"Stemming the tide of rural migration," by W. Eustis. MINN MUNIC. 55:344-345 plus, November, 1970.

"A study of disease in migrants and their siblings: development of sibling rosters," by K. Magnus, et al. J CHRONIC DIS. 23:405-410, November, 1970.

"Suburb hegira's extent startles census folk." ADV AGE. 41:1+, August 31, 1970.

"Tackling the refugee problem," by M. Louvish. JEWISH FRONTIER. 37:6-8, May, 1970.

"Three million new southerners: depopulation and migration in five southeast states, 1950 to 1968," by L. A. Eyre. FLA PLANNING & DEVELOPMENT. 21:1+, February, 1970.

"Tibetan refugees in a decade of exile," by G. Woodcock. PACIFIC AFFAIRS. 43:410-420, Fall, 1970.

"Transferred to US office? Your move may come soon," by D. Townson. FIN POST. 64:1-2, March 21, 1970.

"Trends in distances moved by interstate migrants," by J. D. Tarver, et al. RURAL SOCIOL. 35:3-33, December, 1970.

"Turkish international migrant labor," by J. Kilars. GEOG R. 60:262-264, April, 1970.

"U.S. lifts personnel transfer ban--for some," by D.

MIGRATIONS

Townson. FIN POST. 64:16, April 25, 1970.

"Victims in flight." ECONOMIST. 234:18, February 14, 1970.

"What future for the Palestine Arabs." WAR-PEACE REPT. 10:3-11, June-July, 1970.

"Why do people move?" by P. R. Ehrlich and J. P. Holdren. SAT R. 53:51, September 5, 1970.

MINORITY GROUPS & POPULATION

"Changing distribution of negroes within metropolitan areas: the emergence of black suburbs," by R. Farley. AM J SOCIOLOGY. 75:512-529, January, 1970.

"How they kept Canada almost lily white: the previous untold story of the Canadian immigration officials who stopped American blacks from coming to Canada," by T. W. Sessing. SATURDAY NIGHT. 85:30-32, September, 1970.

"Minority-group status and fertility: an extension of Goldscheider and Uhlenberg," by D. F. Sly. AM J SOCIOL. 76:443-459, November, 1970.

"Negro migration and unemployment," by D. E. Kaun. J HUMAN RESOURCES. 5:191-207, Spring, 1970.

"Obstacles to sterilization in one community," by S. C. Scrimshaw and B. Pasquariella. FAMILY PLANNING PERSPECTIVES. 2:40-42, October, 1970.

"Powell, the minorities, and the 1970 election," by N. Deakin and J. Bourne. POL Q. 41:399-415, October-December, 1970.

"Projected effects of family planning on the incidence of perinatal mortality in a lower-class nonwhite population," by D. V. McCalister, et al. AMER J OBSTET GYNEC. 106:573-580, February 15, 1970.

"Projections of the growth of the coloured immigrant population of England and Wales," by C. J. Thomas. J BIOSOC SCI. 2:265-281, July, 1970.

"Red man's plight: urban Indians, driven to cities by

MINORITY GROUPS & POPULATION

poverty, find harsh existence," by B. Isenberg. WALL ST J. 175:1 plus, March 9, 1970.

MORTALITY & MORTALITY STATISTICS

"Age-incidence of death from smoking," by S. H. Preston. AM STAT ASSN J. 65:1125-1130, September, 1970.

"Catastrophic death toll lower in first half of 1970." METROPOLITAN LIFE STAT BUL. 51:8, August, 1970.

"Crossing of mortality curves." METROPOLITAN LIFE STAT BUL. 51:10-11, November, 1970.

"Infant mortality; an urgent national problem," by F. Falkner. CHILDREN. 17:83-87, May-June, 1970.

"An international comparison of excessive adult mortality," by S. H. Preston. POPULATION STUDIES. 24:5-20, March, 1970.

"Longevity of members of Congress." METROPOLITAN LIFE STAT BUL. 51:2-5, December, 1970.

"Measures of longevity of American Indians," by C. A. Hill, Jr. PUBLIC HEALTH REPTS. 85:233-239, March, 1970.

"Mortality from diabetes mellitus at ages 45-64." METROPOLITAN LIFE STAT BUL. 51:2-4, July, 1970.

"The problem of cot deaths." ULSTER COMMENTARY. 293: 4-5, September, 1970.

"Recent mortality from cerebral vascular diseases." METROPOLITAN LIFE STAT BUL. 51:5-7, September, 1970.

"Recent mortality trends for emphysema and other chronic respiratory diseases." METROPOLITAN LIFE STAT BUL. 51:2-6, August, 1970.

"Seasonal variations in infant mortality in Belgium," by R. Andre, et al. REVUE DE L'INSTITUT DE SOCIOLOGIE. 3:587-598, 1970.

NURSING & POPULATION

"Evaluating the training of nurses to do family planning

NURSING & POPULATION

work in India," by J. B. Weisbuch, et al. PUBLIC HEALTH REP. 85:707-715, August, 1970.

"Hospital-based nurses in family planning," by A. N. K. Dan. NURS J INDIA. 61:264, August, 1970.

"Knowledge and attitude of nursing students toward population control and family planning," by M. I. Kim, et al. KOREAN NURSE. 9:41-53, June 25, 1970.

"Nurse's role in family planning at a municipal hospital," by N. Berzig. HOSP TOP. 48:101 passim, February, 1970.

"OBG: Nurse's role in family planning at a municipal hospital," by N. Herzig. HOSP TOPICS. 48:101+, February, 1970.

"Surgical nursing: abortions and sterilizations." REGAN REP NURS LAW. 11:1, June, 1970.

"The summary report of the seminar on nursing education and family planning," by M. I. Kim. KOREAN NURSE. 9:27-34, December 25, 1970.

"The training of nurses in family planning," by N. Loudon. NURS MIRROR. 131:28-29, July 24, 1970.

OVERPOPULATION: GENERAL

"Affluence and effluence: U. S.," by N. Cousins. SAT R. 53:53, May 2, 1970.

"Another approach to population control?" by N. De Nevers. BUL ATOM SCI. 27:34, March, 1971

"Are there too many of us?" by P. R. Ehrlich. MC CALLS. 97:46-47+, July, 1970.

"Crisis thinking--rhetoric vs action," by J. I. Rosoff. FAMILY PLANNING PERSPECTIVES. 2:20-28, June, 1970.

"Avalanche," by C. Merrill. INDEPEND SCH BULL. 29,2: 20-21, December, 1969.

"Beyond the exponentials; the role of geography in the great transition," by W. Zelinsky. ECON GEOG. 46: 498-535, July, 1970.

OVERPOPULATION: GENERAL

"The bigger the better." BULL NTRDA. 56:14+, July-August, 1970.

"Ecological destruction is a condition of American life," by P. Collier, et al. MLLE. 70:188-189 plus, April, 1970.

"The economy doesn't need more people," by J. G. Welles. WALL ST J. 175:22, April 22, 1970.

"The environmental crisis: through a glass darkly," by W. G. Rosen. BIOSCIENCE. 20,22:1209-1211 passim, November, 1970.

"Environmental hucksterism." NATURE (LONDON). 227:118, July 11, 1970.

"Environmental quality: its significance in our society," by W. R. Barclay. JAMA. 213:1890-1892, September 14, 1970.

"Hidden effects of overpopulation," by P. R. Ehrlich and J. P. Holdren. SAT R. 53:52, August 1, 1970.

"How to snatch survival from the jaws of pollution and overpopulation," by A. D'Amato. RIPON FORUM. 6:16-19, January, 1970.

"Human population problems," by T. C. Emmel and M. M. Sligh. SCI ED. 54:363-372, October, 1970.

"Human survival," by R. Bank. CAN MO LETTER. 51:1-4, August, 1970.

"Overpopulation and the American Catholic conscience," by P. J. Riga. WORLD JUSTICE. 12:199-215, December, 1970.

"Paul R. Ehrlich: A biologist's remarks on the 'population explosion'," by M. Sloan. ILLINOIS MED J. 138:246-247, September, 1970.

"Population overgrowth, the fertile curse," by P. R. Ehrlich. FIELD & S. 75:58+, June, 1970.

"Qualitative and quantitative problems in generation," by R. H. Williams. NORTHWEST MED. 69:92-93, February, 1970.

OVERPOPULATION: GENERAL

"Qualitative and quantitative problems in generation," by R. H. Williams. NORTHWEST MED. 69:497-501, July, 1970.

"A question of numbers," by A. Birk. TIMES. p 5, July 27, 1970.

"Third fish," by K. S. Norris. NEW REPUB. 162:16-18, May 9, 1970.

"Too many children or too many pediatricians?" by P. Banister. CANAD MED ASS J. 103:157-159, July 18, 1970.

"What is overpopulation?" by R. J. Rushdoony. FREEMAN. 20:98-105, February, 1970.

"Who's to blame?" by J. Liss. NEW SOCIETY. p 96-98, July 16, 1970.

"Who's worrying?" by M. Hold. NURS MIRROR. 131:23, October 16, 1970.

"Whose baby is the population problem?" by R. E. Miles, Jr. POPULATION BUL. 16:3-36, February, 1970.

"Why the population bomb is a Rockefeller baby," by S. Weissman. RAMP MAG. 8:42-47, May, 1970.

"Will we say 'it just happened,' when the world overpopulates itself to extinction? Louisiana family planning program," by J. Lelyveld. N Y TIMES MAG. p 24-25+, July 19, 1970.

POLITICS & POPULATION
SEE ALSO: CENSUSES; FORECASTING

"Big shifts in political power: impact of 1970 census." US NEWS. 69:26-28, September 21, 1970.

"Census and apportionment: states' gains and losses in House seats as projected from preliminary 1970 data." CONG Q W REPT. 28:2193-2196, September 4, 1970.

"European political emigrations: a lost subject," by R. C. Williams. COMP STUD SOC & HIST. 12:140-148, April, 1970.

POLITICS & POPULATION

"Generational succession as a source of foreign policy attitudes: a cohort analysis of American opinion, 1946-1966," by N. E. Cutler. J PEACE RESEARCH. p 33-47, November 1, 1970.

"Immigrants and municipal voting turnout: implications for the changing ethnic impact on urban politics," by D. N. Gordon. AM SOCIOL R. 35:665-681, August, 1970.

"The implementation of leninist national policy among the people of the USSR far north," by I. S. Gurvich. SOVETSKAYA ETNOGRAFIYA. 45,1:15-34, January-February, 1970.

"People and politics," by J. Kettle. EXEC. 12:35-36, October, 1970.

"Political affiliation and attitudes toward population limitation," by L. D. Barnett. SOCIAL BIOLOGY. 17: 124-131, June, 1970.

"Power-politics and population," by P. M. Sharma. UNITED ASIA. 22:28-34, January-February, 1970.

"Principle of population as political theory; Godwin's Of population and the Malthusian controversy," by F. Rosen. J HIST IDEAS. 31:33-48, January, 1970.

"US voting age population totals more than 124 million." COMM TODAY. 1:26, November 2, 1970.

"Who rules here? Random reflections on the national origins of those set in authority over us," by W. M. Whitehill. NEW ENGL Q. 43:434-449, September, 1970.

POPULATION: AFRICA

"Africa's population problems," by A. E. Okorafor. AFRICA R. 15:22-23, June, 1970.

"The assumed employment generating capacity of European immigration in Rhodesia," by D. G. Clarke. RHODESIAN J ECON. 4:33-42, June, 1970.

"Attitudes toward family planning among peri-urban Africans in Uganda," by R. E. Brown. TROP GEOGR MED. 22:87-100, March, 1970.

POPULATION: AFRICA

"Botswana, another developing country," by L. Buhring. SYKEPLEIEN. 57:456-457, July 1, 1970.

"Colour and colonization," by H. Tinker. ROUND TAB. 60:405-416, November, 1970.

"The convention of the Organization of African unity governing the specific aspects of refugee problems in Africa," by P. Weis. HUMAN RIGHTS J. 3:449-464, September, 1970.

"Counting heads in Africa: the experience of Zambia, 1963 and 1969," by P. O. Ohadike. J ADMIN OVERSEAS. 9:247-254, October, 1970.

"The determinants of emigration to South Africa, 1950-1967," by G. L. Chapin and others. SOUTH AFRICAN J ECON. 38:374-381, December, 1970.

"Establishing family planning services in Kenya," by N. R. Fendall, et al. PUBLIC HEALTH REP. 85:131-139, February, 1970.

"An evaluation of demographic data pertaining to the non-white population of South Africa: the population of Asian origin: the coloured population: the Bantu population," by J. L. Sadie. SOUTH AFRICAN J ECON. 38:1-34, March; 171-191, June, 1970.

"Family planning and fertility in Tunisia," by R. J. Lapham. DEMOGRAPHY. 7:241-253, May, 1970.

"Fertility and family planning in Africa," by T. E. Dow, Jr. J MOD AFRIC STUD. 8:445-457, October, 1970.

"The historical calendar as a method of estimating age: the experience of the Moroccan multi-purpose sample survey of 1961-1963," by C. Scott and G. Sabagh. POPULATION STUDIES. 24:93-109, March, 1970.

"Migrant labour and agricultural output in Ghana," by R. E. Beals, et al. OXFORD ECONOMIC PAPERS. 22:109, March, 1970.

"Morocco: family planning knowledge, attitudes, and practice in the rural areas; Morocco: family planning and an attitude survey in the urban areas." STUDIES IN FAMILY PLANNING. 58:1-10, October, 1970.

POPULATION: AFRICA

"The motivation for reproduction and the new population dimensions of Ghana," by D. A. Ampofo. E AFR MED J. 47:217-222, April, 1970.

"Nonmonetary commodity incentives in family planning programs: a preliminary trial," by G. W. Perkin. STUDIES IN FAMILY PLANNING. pp 12-15, September, 1970.

"O A U convention governing the specific aspects of refugee problems in Africa." HUMAN RIGHTS J. 3:170-181, March, 1970.

"The population of tropical Africa in the 1980's," from AFRICA IN THE SEVENTIES AND EIGHTIES, p 247-303, 1970.

"Population pressure and crop rotational changes among the Tiv of Nigeria," by D. E. Vermeer. ASSN AM GEOG ANN. 60:299-314, June, 1970.

"Problems of population pressure in tropical Africa," by R. W. Steel. INST BRITISH GEOGRAPHERS TRANSACTIONS. p 1-13, March, 1970.

"Regional aspects of the 1969 Uganda census," by S. R. Taber. EAST AFRICAN GEOG R. p 78-80, April, 1970.

"Review of the demographic levels and trends in Africa and their impact on the economic development of the region," by A. K. M. Zirky. L'EGYPTE CONTEMPORAINE. 61:351-374, October, 1970.

"The spread of anti-natal knowledge and practice in Nigeria," by J. C. Caldwell, et al. POPULATION STUDIES. 24:21-34, March, 1970.

"To teach or not to teach family planning in Kenyan primary schools," by J. B. Maathuis. EAST AFR MED J. 47:545-549, November, 1970.

"Use of the Chandrasekar-Deming technique in the Liberian fertility survey," by J. C. Rumford. PUBLIC HEALTH REP. 85:965-974, November, 1970.

"Various problems of the population in Africa," by O. P. Shchepin. SOVET ZDRAVOOKHR. 29:57-60, 1970.

POPULATION: AUSTRALIA

"Industrial decentralization policy in Victoria and its effect on the distribution of population and industry," by A. Kan. ECON ACTIVITY. 13:47-53, January, 1970.

"Note on intercensal estimates of the Australian population, classified by country of birth, 1961-1966," by P. F. Gourley. ECON REC. 46:419-423, September, 1970.

"A rejoinder to miss spencer's comments on pre-marital pregnancies and ex-nuptial births in Australia, 1911-1966," by K. G. Basavarajappa. AUSTRALIAN AND NEW ZEALAND J OF SOCIOLOGY. 6,1:79-84, 1970. SA #E9003.

"A report from the Australian drug evaluation committee: oral contraceptives and thromboembolic disease." MED J AUST. 1:1267-1269, June 20, 1970.

POPULATION: BELGIUM

"Geography of internal migration movements in Belgium," by R. Andre. REVUE DE L'INSTITUT DE SOCIOLOGIE. 2:383-402, 1970.

"Seasonal variations in infant mortality in Belgium," by R. Andre, et al. REVUE DE L'INSTITUT DE SOCIOLOGIE. 3:587-598, 1970. SA #F0121.

POPULATION: BULGARIA

"Regulation of birth rate in Bulgaria as a social experiment," by D. Sepetliev, et al. AKUSH GINEKOL. 9:115-123, 1970.

"A study of the public activity of the population in Bulgaria," by M. Radeva. FILOSOFSKIYENAUKI. 13,1:138-145, 1970. SA #E9032.

POPULATION: CAMBODIA

"The population of Cambodia 1945-1980," by G. S. Siampos. MILBANK MEMORIAL FUND Q. 48:317-360, July, 1970.

POPULATION: CANADA

"Big as it is, Canada doesn't need more people," by D. A. Chant. MACL MAG. 83:13, August, 1970.

POPULATION: CANADA

"Canadian censuses and parish registers in the 1665-1668 period; a critical examination," by H. Charbonneau, et al. POPULATION. 25,1:97-124, January-February, 1970. SA #F0127.

"Canadian county-sponsored family planning. 3. A second survey," by J. E. Tyson, et al. OBSTET GYNEC. 35:377-380, March, 1970.

"Canadian government view on immigrant services." INTERPRETER RELEASES. 47:220-223, September 14, 1970.

"Canadian immigration," by V. Del Buono. WORLD AFFAIRS. 35:23-24, April, 1970.

"Effect of out-migration on regional employment," by J. Vanderkamp. CAN J ECON. 3:541-549, November, 1970.

"Emigrants to Canada few but independent." FIN POST. 64:J2, August 22, 1970.

"Fertility patterns among religious groups in Canada," by L. H. Long. DEMOGRAPHY. 7:135-149, May, 1970.

"How they kept Canada almost lily white: the previous untold story of the Canadian immigration officials who stopped American blacks from coming to Canada," by T. W. Sessing. SATURDAY NIGHT. 85:30-32, September, 1970.

"Interprovincial migration and economic adjustment," by T. J. Courchene. CAN J ECON. 3:550-576, November, 1970.

"19 Canada dailies reject Schmid ads for prophylactics." ADV AGE. 41:68, April 6, 1970.

"Pasquia land settlement project in Manitoba," by L. Harrington. CAN GEOG J. 80:92-97, March, 1970.

"A master sampling plan for Canadian agriculture," by J. E. Graham. CAN J AGRIC ECON. 18:60-73, July, 1970.

"Plans for the 1971 census of Canada." STATIS OBSERVER. 3:3-5, July, 1970.

"Settlement patterns of Canadian emigrants to the United

POPULATION: CANADA

States, 1850-1960," by R. K. Vedder, et al. CAN J ECON. 3:476-486, August, 1970.

"Some methodological aspects of the 1971 census in Canada," by T. G. Beynon, et al. CAN J ECON. 3:95-110, February, 1970.

POPULATION: CARIBBEAN

"Cuban population estimates, 1953-1970," by L. Nelson. J INTER-AM STUD. 12:392-400, July, 1970.

"Family, fertility, and sex ratios in the British Caribbean," by A. Marino. POPULATION STUDIES. 24:159-172, July, 1970.

POPULATION: CENTRAL AMERICA

"Agricultural development in the humid tropics of Central America," by J. R. Taylor. INTER-AM ECON AFFAIRS. 24:41-49, Summer, 1970.

"Analysis of a family planning program in Guatemala," by D. W. MacCorquodale. PUBLIC HEALTH REPTS. 85:570-574, July, 1970.

"Mexico ambivalent on birth control," by F. U. Ross. CHR CENT. 87:1428-1429, November 25, 1970.

"The structure and change of mortality in a Maya community," by J. D. Early. MILBANK MEMORIAL FUND Q. 48:179-201, April, 1970.

POPULATION: CHINA

"China's birth control action programme, 1956-1964," by Pi-Chao Chen. POPULATION STUDIES. 24:141-158, July, 1970.

"Chinese provincial population data," by R. M. Field. CHINA Q. p 195-202, October-December, 1970.

"A demographic study on the relationships of nuptiality, child mortality, and attitude toward fertility to actual fertility in Hsueh-Chia township in Taiwan. I. Relationship of marriage cohort and marriage age to actual fertility," by H. Y. Wu. J FORMOSAN MED ASSOC. 69:243-255, May 28, 1970.

POPULATION: CHINA

"Family planning in China," by H. Suyin. JAPAN Q. 17:433-442, October-December, 1970.

"Family planning Taiwan, 1949-1970," by S. Hsu. INDUSTRY OF FREE CHINA. 34:2-20, December, 1970.

"Family planning in Taiwan, Republic of China: progress and prospects," by L. P. Chow. POPULATION STUDIES. 24:339-352, November, 1970.

"Health, population growth, and development in Taiwan," by Te-Hsuing Sun. INDUSTRY OF FREE CHINA. 33:17-20, June, 1970.

"Malthus versus Marx: China's population is growing more slowly than that of the US," by C. Snyder. FAR EASTERN ECON R. 69:28+, December 26, 1970.

"Marital moratorium and fertility control in China," by H. Yuan Tien. POPULATION STUDIES. 24:311-323, November, 1970.

"Planning better families," by Y. Hsueh. FREE CHINA R. 20:20-22, March, 1970.

"Taiwan: implications of fertility at replacement levels," by R. Freedman and R. Avery. STUDIES IN FAMILY PLANNING. 59:1-4, November, 1970.

"Taiwan's population characteristics and dynamics," by S. C. Hsu. J FORMOSAN MED ASSOC. 69:455-468, September 28, 1970.

"Use of the 'pill' on Taiwan," by F. L. Chen. INDUSTRY OF FREE CHINA. 33:18-31, April, 1970.

"Village campaign in China to foster birth control," by R. Harris. TIMES. p 7, January 23, 1970.

POPULATION: CZECHOSLOVAKIA

"Population development and recent population projection," by M. Kucera. DEMOSTA. 3:177-183, November 3, 1970.

POPULATION: EUROPE

"Transmission of life: certain generalizations about the

POPULATION: EUROPE

demography of Europe's nations in 1939-1941," by J. Lukacs. COMP STUD SOC & HIST. 12:442-451, October, 1970.

POPULATION: FINLAND

"Emigration of Finns to Sweden: drain or benefit for Finland," by V. A. Koiranen. ECON R. p 47-52, November 2, 1970.

POPULATION: FRANCE

"Evolution of endogenous infant mortality in France in the second half of the 19th century," by R. Nadot. POPULATION. 25,1:49-58, January-February, 1970. SA #F0135.

"Limousin: regional crisis and change," by H. D. Clout. TIJDSCHRIFT VOOR ECONOMISCHE EN SOCIALE GEOGRAFIE. 61:288-299, September-October, 1970.

POPULATION: GERMANY

"Birth rate and work load," by E. Nurge. AM ANTHROP. 72:1434-1439, December, 1970.

"Two and a half centuries of demographic history in a Bavarian village," by J. Knodel. POPULATION STUDIES. 24:353-376, November, 1970.

POPULATION: GREAT BRITAIN

"A big family isn't fun any more," by G. Tindall. GUARDIAN. p 7, April 1, 1970.

"Analyses of census data for Greater London." GREATER LONDON RESEARCH Q BULL. 11:46-61, June, 1970.

"Aspects of the intercommunity population balance in Northern Ireland," by P. A. Compton, et al. ECON & SOCIAL R. 1:455-476, July, 1970.

"Demographic factors and borough occupancy rates," by J. Peretz and H. Davies. GREATER LONDON RESEARCH Q BULL. 10:22-27, March, 1970.

"Demography in the nineteenth century," by R. Smith. LOCAL HISTORIAL. 9:27-35, February, 1970.

POPULATION: GREAT BRITAIN

"Family planning in England," by E. Funke. OEFF GES-UNDHEITSWESEN. 32:412-419, August, 1970.

"Game of human shuttlecock," by C. Adam. NEW STATESM. 79:280-281, February 27, 1970.

"The growth of population to the turn of the century," by J. Thompson. SOCIAL TRENDS. p 21-32, November, 1970.

"Humberside; employment, unemployment, and migration, the evolution of industrial structure, 1951-1966," by J. Craig, et al. YORKSHIRE BULLETIN. 22:123-142, November, 1970.

"Inhabitants of Northmavine, Shetland 18th and 19th Century," by J. C. Mowat. SCOTTISH GENEALOGIST. 17,3:91-104, 1970.

"Migration to and from Scotland since 1961," by H. R. Jones. INST BRITISH GEOGRAPHERS TRANSACTIONS. pp 145-158, March, 1970.

"National survey of U. K. births. Obstetrics in the United Kingdom," by R. Chamberlain, et al. MIDWIVES CHRON. 83:78-83, March, 1970.

"Optimizing the distribution of housing in large-scale developments," by A. W. Steiss and J. W. Dickey. TOWN PLANNING INST J. 56:95-99, March, 1970.

"People of York: 1538-1812," by U. M. Cowgill. SCI AM. 222:104-110+, January, 1970.

"Perinatal mortality in Hawkshead, Lancashire 1581-1710," by R. S. Schofield. LOCAL POPULATION STUDIES MAG. 4:11-16, Spring, 1970.

"Population change, enclosure, and the early Tudor economy," by I. Blanchard. ECON HIST R. 23:427-445, December, 1970.

"Population movement in seventeenth century England," by P. Spufford. LOCAL POPULATION STUDIES MAG. 4:41-50, Spring, 1970.

"Population of London boroughs by sex, age, and marital status," by M. Daly. GREATER LONDON RESEARCH Q BULL. 11:28-45, June, 1970.

POPULATION: GREAT BRITAIN

"Population: where have all the babies gone?" ECONOMIST. 234:22+, February 21, 1970.

"Powell, the minorities, and the 1970 election," by N. Deakin, et al. POL Q. 41:399-415, October-December, 1970.

"Projections of the growth of the coloured immigrant population of England and Wales," by C. J. Thomas. J BIOSOC SCI. 2:265-281, July, 1970.

"Sex education hits the British airwaves." ATLAS. 19: 16, April, 1970.

"A short run model of inter-regional migration," by A. B. Jack. MANCHESTER SCHOOL OF ECONOMIC & SOCIAL STUDIES. 38:15, March, 1970.

"Size and structure of the household in England over three centuries, a comment," by J. W. Nixon. POPULATION STUDIES. 24:445-447, November, 1970.

"Some aspects of immigration into the Glamorgan coal field between 1881 and 1911," by P. N. Jones. HONOURABLE SOC OF CYMMRODORION TRANS. 1969 SESSION PART I, p 82, 1970.

"Victims in flight." ECONOMIST. 234:18, February 14, 1970.

POPULATION: HONG KONG

"Hong Kong's fertility decline, 1961-1968," by R. Freedman. POPULATION INDEX. 36:3-18, January-March, 1970.

POPULATION: INDIA

"Demographic effectiveness of sterilization programme in India," by O. P. Vig. ARTHA VIJNANA. 12:398-405, September, 1970.

"Educational status and differential fertility in India," by I. Z. Husain. SOCIAL BIOLOGY. 17:132-139, June, 1970.

"Eleven myths of family planning," by A. Bose. SOUTH ASIAN R. 3:323-330, July, 1970.

POPULATION: INDIA

"India: a bleak demographic future." POPULATION BUL. 26:2-12, November, 1970.

"Migration and modernization," by F. W. Reed. INDIAN J SOCIOL. 1:104-129, September, 1970.

"Oral contraception. An application in family planning programme in Calcutta city," by A. S. Gupta. J INDIAN MED ASS. 54:187-194, March 1, 1970.

"Population change and employment policy in India," by S. V. Khandewale. ECON AFFAIRS. 15:229-236, May, 1970.

"Population control in India," by J. P. Lewis. POPULATION BUL. 26:12-31, November, 1970.

"Population survey for detection of frank and latent diabetes in one part of Cuttack, Orissa," by B. B. Tripathy, et al. J INDIAN MED ASS. 54:55-61, January 16, 1970.

"Population trends in an Indian village," by C. E. Taylor. SCI AMER. 223:106-112 passim, July, 1970.

"Presidential address: 7th National Conference of the Indian Academy of Pediatrics," by J. N. Pohowalla. INDIAN PEDIATR. 7:4-7, January, 1970.

"Reversing the brain drain: a case study from India," by M. F. Merriam. INTERNAT DEVELOPMENT R. 12:16-22, November 3, 1970.

"Rural-urban migration: a clue to rural-urban relations in India," by C. R. P. Rao. INDIAN J SOCIAL WORK. 30:335-342, January, 1970.

"Some obstacles to family planning in India," by P. Singh. ECON AFFAIRS. 15:293-303, August, 1970.

"Sterilization in India. The pill: daily bread. Cold demographic calculation should prevail over every other sentiment," by A. Fiore. MINERVA MED SUPPL. 78:20-24, September 25, 1970.

"The weight of numbers: family planning in India," by F. J. Thierry. PANORAMA. p 24-32, January-February, 1970.

POPULATION: IRAN

"Iranian censuses 1956 and 1966: a comparative analysis," by F. Firoozi. MIDDLE EAST J. 24:220-228, Spring, 1970.

POPULATION: IRELAND

"Irish fertility ratios before the famine," by G. S. L. Tucker. ECON HIST R. 23:267-284, August, 1970.

"Marriage rates and population pressure: Ireland, 1871 and 1911," by B. M. Walsh. ECONOMIC HISTORY R. 23: 148-162, April, 1970.

POPULATION: ISRAEL

"Israel's drive for manpower," by V. C. Williams. DAILY TELEGRAPH. p 11, October 29, 1970.

"Plan for a Palestinian state," by Averroes. NEW OUTLOOK. 13:19-26, May, 1970.

"Tackling the refugee problem," by M. Louvish. JEWISH FRONTIER. 37:6-8, May, 1970.

"What future for the Palestine Arabs?" WAR/PEACE REPORT. 10:3-11, June-July, 1970.

POPULATION: ITALY

"Italian communities abroad: migration to European and non-European nations." ITALY DOCS & NOTES. 19:7-17, January-February, 1970.

"Migration and industrial development: the southern Italian experience," by A. Rodgers. ECON GEOG. 46: 111-135, April, 1970.

POPULATION: JAPAN

"Changes in fertility in Japan by region: 1920-1965," by Y. Tsubouchi. DEMOGRAPHY. 7:121-134, May, 1970.

"Emigrants to Canada few but independent." FIN POST. 64:J2, August 22, 1970.

"Japan: a crowded nation wants to boost its birthrate," by P. M. Boffey. SCIENCE. 167:960-962, February 13, 1970.

POPULATION: JAVA

"Population growth in Java in the 19th century. A new interpretation," by B. Peper. POPULATION STUDIES. 24:71-84, March, 1970.

POPULATION: JORDAN

"Female fertility in the Kingdom of Jordan a statistical analysis," by W. A. Ettema. TIJDSCHRIFT VOOR ECONOMISCHE EN SOCIALE GEOGRAFIE. 61:195-206, July-August, 1970.

POPULATION: LATIN AMERICA

"Birth control wars," by J. Deedy. COMMONWEAL. 92:2, March 13, 1970.

"A reply to birth control wars," by A. C. Francia. COMMONWEAL. 92:102-103, April 3, 1970.

"Comparison of the migration process to an urban barrio and to a rural community: two case studies," by W. L. Flinn and D. G. Cartano. INTER-AM ECON AFFAIRS. 24: 37-43, Autumn, 1970.

"Comparison: population densities, land values and socioeconomic class in four Latin American cities," by P. W. Amato. LAND ECON. 46:447-455, November, 1970.

"The culture of poverty in relation to disease in Latin America," by L. S. Miranda. P RICO ENFERM. 45:14-15 concl, March, 1970.

"The decline in mortality in British Guiana, 1911-1960," by J. R. Mandle. DEMOGRAPHY. 7:301-315, August, 1970.

"Latin America's unemployment problem," by I. Beller. MO LABOR R. 93:8, November, 1970.

"The nature and effects of Latin America's non-western trend in fertility," by E. E. Arriaga. DEMOGRAPHY. 7:483-501, November, 1970.

"Population and economic change: the emergence of the rice industry in Guyana. 1895-1915," by J. R. Mandle. J ECON HIST. 30:785-801, December, 1970.

"The population question in Northeast Brazil: its eco-

POPULATION: LATIN AMERICA

nomic and ideological dimensions," by H. E. Daly. ECON DEVELOPMENT & CULTURAL CHANGE. 18:536-574, July, 1970.

"Reduced population growth as related to the urbanization process: Medellin, Colombia," by C. L. Marshall, et al. CLIN PEDIATR. 9:736-741, December, 1970.

"Survey on induced abortion and use of contraceptives in Bogota. Method of approach," by S. Gomez, et al. REV COLOMB OBSTET GINECOL. 21:427-439, July-August, 1970.

"The teaching of fertility control and population problems in the medical schools of Brazil," by J. Yunes. REV SAUDE PUBLICA. 4:79-84, June, 1970.

POPULATION: MALAYSIA

"The demographic effects of a contraceptive programme," by D. Wolfers. POPULATION STUDIES. 23:111-140, March, 1969.

POPULATION: NORWAY

"Some economic aspects of Norwegian population movements 1740-1940: an econometric study," by T. Moe. J ECON HIST. 30:267-270, 285-287, March, 1970.

POPULATION: PAKISTAN

"And the poor get babies," by R. Link. SWEDEN NOW. 4:80-85+, November, 1970.

"Trends in pregnancy and fertility in a rural area of East Pakistan," by J. Stoeckel, et al. J BIOSOC SCI. 2:329-335, October, 1970.

POPULATION: POLAND

"Aging and life space in Poland and the United States," by E. Shanas. J HEALTH SOC BEHAV. 11:183-190, September, 1970.

"Sterilization of women in the light of Polish legislation," by W. Wieszczycki, et al. GINEKOL POL. 41: 1153-1156, October, 1970.

POPULATION: SOLOMON ISLANDS

"Administration of Wagina resettlement scheme," by G. Cochrane. HUMAN ORGAN. 29:123-132, Summer, 1970.

POPULATION: SPAIN

"Structure and dynamics of the spanish human resources," by A. de Miguel. REVISTA ESPANOLA DE LA OPINION PUBLICA. 19:71-104, January-March, 1970. SA #E7671.

POPULATION: SWEDEN

"Emigration of Finns to Sweden: drain or benefit for Finland," by V. A. Koiranen. ECON R. 2:47-52, 1970.

"Sweden: a case of population policies." POPULATION BUL. 26:19-27, November, 1970.

POPULATION: THAILAND

"Sexual attitudes of Thai students: an exploratory cross-cultural study," by J. Wohl, et al. HUMAN ORGAN. 29:190-196, Fall, 1970.

POPULATION: TIBET

"The dispossessed: in a remarkable instance of generosity India has opened some half dozen settlements for Tibetans within her borders." VISTA. 6:16-21, November-December, 1970.

"Tibetan refugees in a decade of exile," by G. Woodcock. PACIFIC AFFAIRS. 43:410-420, Fall, 1970.

POPULATION: TURKEY

"Population and accessibility: an analysis of Turkish railroads," by J. Kolars and H. J. Malin. GEOG R. 60:229-246, April, 1970.

"Turkish international migrant labor," by J. Kolars. GEOG R. 60:262-264, April, 1970.

POPULATION: UNITED ARAB REPUBLIC

"Changes in the trend of crude birth rate and crude death rate of Cairo and the U. A. R. during the past ten years (1958-1968)," by S. Abdou, et al. J EGYPT MED ASSOC. 53:433-441, 1970.

POPULATION: UNITED STATES

"Aging and life space in Poland and the United States," by E. Shanas. J HEALTH SOC BEHAV. 11:183-190, September, 1970.

"American longevity in 1968." METROPOLITAN LIFE STAT BUL. 51:9-11, August, 1970.

"American population growth in 1969." METROPOLITAN LIFE STAT BUL. 51:2-4, March, 1970.

"Annals map supplement No. 13: population origin groups in rural Texas," by T. G. Jordan. ASSN AM GEOG ANN. 60:404-405, June, 1970.

"Arkansas' population growth during the 1960's: a preliminary report," by F. H. Pollard and K. D. Jones. ARK BUS & ECON R. 3:20-25, August, 1970.

"Ascertainment of men of Japanese ancestry in Hawaii through World War II Selective Service registration," by R. M. Worth, et al. J CHRONIC DIS. 23:389-397, November, 1970.

"Berkeley's demographic challenge: adjusting to population change," by G. Fox. PUBLIC AFFAIRS REPT. 11: 11-51, October, 1970.

"Big shifts in political power: impact of 1970 census." U S NEWS. 69:26-28, September 21, 1970.

"Characteriological deterrants to economic progress in people of Appalachia," by C. E. Goshen. SOUTHERN MED J. 63:1053-1061, September, 1970.

"Chromosomal abnormalities in the human population," by H. A. Lubs, et al. SCIENCE. 169:495-497, July 31, 1970.

"Colonial New England demography: a sampling approach," by R. Higgs, et al. WM & MARY Q. 27:282-294, April, 1970.

"Creation of new knowledge and our way of life," by D. J. Zinn. SCH SCI & MATH. 70:18-25, January, 1970.

"Demographic history of the West: manistee county, Michigan, 1860," by G. Blackburn and S. L. Richards, Jr. J AM HIST. 57:600-618, December, 1970.

POPULATION: UNITED STATES

"Demographic study of an Eskimo village on the north slope of Alaska; with summaries in French and Russian." by F. A. Milan. ARCTIC. 23:82-99, June, 1970.

"The ecological distribution of the elderly in the florida counties," by S. R. Ahsan. SOCIOLOGICAL SYMPOSIUM. 2:1-13, Spring, 1969.

"Estimated net migration for Tennessee counties, 1960-1970," by R. A. Engels. TENN SURVEY BUS. 6:3-4+, September, 1970.

"Family planning in New York city: recommendations for action: prepared by Planned parenthood of New York city." FAMILY PLANNING PERSPECTIVES. 2:25-31, October, 1970.

"Family planning in rural areas: Colorado: enlisting private physicians," by S. S. Tepper. FAMILY PLANNING PERSPECTIVES. 2:30-34, June, 1970.

"Fertility of American women since 1920," by W. Sanderson. J ECON HIST. 30:271-272, 285-287, March, 1970.

"Final 1970 census figures for New Mexico." N MEX BUS. 23:12, October, 1970.

"Final population figures will help US to move forward in the 70s." COMM TODAY. 1:22, November 30, 1970.

"Frustrated America: symptoms, causes, and cures," by H. K. Smith. HUMANIST. 30:14-16, January-February, 1970.

"Geographic distribution of need for family planning and subsidized services in the United States," by R. C. Lerner. AM J PUBLIC HEALTH. 60:1945-1955, October, 1970.

"Identification of migrants and their descendents in the United States," by W. Haenszel. J CHRONIC DIS. 23: 383-387, November, 1970.

"If population stops growing: impact on U. S." U S NEWS. 69:80-82, September 28, 1970.

"Immigrants and municipal voting turnout: implications for the changing ethnic impact on urban politics,"

POPULATION: UNITED STATES

by D. N. Gordon. AM SOCIOL R. 35:665-681, August, 1970.

"In-migration and growth of non-metropolitan urban places," by J. J. Zuiches. RURAL SOCIOL. 35:410-420, September, 1970.

"Indiana's metropolitan population," by M. J. Marcus. INDIANA BUS R. 45:13-26, September-October, 1970.

"L.A. county still tops in population--census." BROADCASTING. 79:38, September 21, 1970.

"Land speculation, promotion and failure: the Northern Pacific railroad, 1870-1873," by J. L. Harnsberger. J WEST. 9:33-45, January, 1970.

"Legal effects of 1970 census on Minnesota municipalities," by J. Lunde. MINN MUNIC. 55:73-75, March, 1970.

"A look at Indiana's pupil population in the decade ahead." CONTEMP EDUC. 41,6:280-284, May, 1970.

"Louisiana's quiet revolution in family planning," by A. Gordon. TODAY'S HEALTH. 48:38 plus, January, 1970.

"Major federal resources for family planning programs and services: a summary." FAMILY PLANNING PERSPECTIVES. 2:40-41, March, 1970.

"Measures of longevity of American Indians," by C. A. Hill, Jr. PUBLIC HEALTH REPTS. 85:233-239, March, 1970.

"Migration and economic opportunities in West Virginia; a statistical analysis," by G. L. Rutman. RURAL SOCIOLOGY. 35,2:206-217, June, 1970. SA #F0138.

"Migration, employment, and race in the deep South," by J. J. Persky, et al. SO ECON J. 36:268-276, January, 1970.

"Migration of native-born Ohioans: 1850-1960," by L. E. Gallaway, et al. BUL BUS RESEARCH. 45:4-5, June, 1970.

POPULATION: UNITED STATES

"Migration within the U.S. 1800-1960: some new estimates," by S. Lebergott. J ECON HIST. 30:839-847, December, 1970.

"A multivariate regression analysis of differences in fertility in United States counties," by D. M. Heer and J. W. Boynton. SOCIAL BIOLOGY. 17:180-194, September, 1970.

"Natality statistics analysis. United States, 1965-1967," by R. L. Heuser, et al. VITAL HEALTH STATIST. 19:1-38, May, 1970.

"Needed: a population policy for Arizona," by M. H. Goodwin, Jr., et al. ARIZONA MED. 27:18-22, June, 1970.

"The 'new' Americans--who is coming to U.S. now." U S NEWS. 69:70-71, October 5, 1970.

"New environment of the south," by G. Clay. ARCH FORUM. 133:42-45, December, 1970.

"New Jersey Economic Review, number 4, 1970, is a special issue entitled,'1970 preliminary census counts'." NEW JERSEY ECONOMIC REVIEW. No. 4, 1970.

"Observations on 1970 census data," by W. R. Watson. N MEX BUS. 23:17-25, November-December, 1970.

"Optimum population and environment: a Georgian microcosm," by E. P. Odum. CURRENT HIST. 58:355-359+, June, 1970.

"Overpopulated America," by W. H. Davis. NEW REPUB. 162:28-30, January 31, 1970.

"Planning and implementing a large-scale family planning program in Georgia," by R. W. O'Connor, et al. AMER J PUBLIC HEALTH. 60:78-88, January, 1970.

"Population, birth control and West Virginia," by D. T. Allen, et al. W VIRGINIA MED J. 66:167-170, May, 1970.

"Population change and mobility: a case study of an Arkansas state economic area," by D. G. Bennett. LAND ECON. 46:206-208, May, 1970.

POPULATION: UNITED STATES

"Population change in the Springfield-Chicopee-Holyoke commuter region," by L. Seig. ROCKY MOUNTAIN SOCIAL SCIENCE J. 7:77-87, April, 1970.

"Population distribution and growth patterns in Indiana," by T. E. Ryan. INDIANA BUS R. 46:15-22, January-February, 1971.

"Population estimates for Texas counties, April 1, 1969," by B. S. Bradshaw. TEX BUS R. 44:77-83, March, 1970.

"Population patterns of the sixties," by R. E. Beller. BUS & ECON DIMENSIONS. 6:18-20, January, 1970.

"Population patterns of the sixties," by R. E. Beller. FLA ECON INDICATORS. 2:1-2+, January, 1970.

"Population residing in the United States, 1790 to 1970." METROPOLITAN LIFE STAT BUL. 51:2, January, 1970.

"Portrait of a decade," by D. H. Wrong. N Y TIMES MAG. p 22-23+, August 2, 1970.

"A program of indigent obstetric care and planned parenthood in a rural North Carolina county," by J. E. Clement. AMER J OBSTET GYNEC. 108:63-67, September 1, 1970.

"Radical changes in migration." REAL ESTATE ANALYST. 39:35-37, January 28, 1970.

"Regional population geography of the northeastern United States," by M. P. Donahue. GEOG R. 60:566-568, October, 1970.

"Regionalization of population densities in Kansas," by R. T. Aangeenbrug and F. C. Caspall. TIJDSCHRIFT VOOR ECONOMISCHE EN SOCIALE GEOGRAFIE. 61:85-90, March-April, 1970.

"Small-town population change and distance from larger towns: a replication of Hassinger's study," by J. E. Butler and G. V. Fuguitt. RURAL SOCIOL. 35:396-409, September, 1970.

"Texan Appalachia," by T. G. Jordan. ASSN AM GEOG ANN. 60:409-427, September, 1970.

POPULATION: UNITED STATES

"300 million people in 30 years: where will they all live?" SAVINGS & LOAN NEWS. 91:46-49, June, 1970.

"Three million new southerners: depopulation and migration in five southeast states. 1950 to 1968," by L. A. Eyre. FLA PLANNING & DEVELOPMENT. 21:1 plus, February, 1970.

"Transferred to U.S. office? Your move may come soon," by D. Townson. FIN POST. 64:1-2, March 21, 1970.

"Trends in distance moved by interstate migrants," by J. D. Tarver and R. D. McLeod. RURAL SOCIOL. 35: 523-533, December, 1970.

"Trends in US population," by F. Pollara. AM FEDERATIONIST. 77:9-13, June, 1970.

"The US labor force: projections to 1985: special labor force report sets forth BLS," by S. C. Travis. MO LABOR R. 93:3-12, May, 1970.

"US lifts personnel transfer ban--for some," by D. Townson. FIN POST. 64:16, April 25, 1970.

"US population growth and family planning: a review of the literature." FAMILY PLANNING PERSPECTIVES. 2: 16-page section following p 24, October, 1970.

"US population growth: would slower be better?" by L. A. Mayer. FORTUNE. 81:80-83+, June, 1970.

"US voting age population totals more than 124 million." COMM TODAY. 1:26, November 2, 1970.

"United States population policy, origins and development; address, August 21, 1970," by P. P. Claxton, Jr. DEPT STATE BUL. 63:317-326, September 21, 1970.

"United States: utilization of a family planning program in a metropolitan area," by J. D. Beasley, et al. STUDIES IN FAMILY PLANNING. 59:7-16, November, 1970.

"Vital statistics publications of the registration areas of the United States," by A. S. Lunde. POPULATION INDEX. 36:125-146, April-June, 1970.

POPULATION: UNITED STATES

"West Virginia's approach to a statewide family planning program," by L. C. Landman. FAMILY PLANNING PERSPECTIVES. 2:21-24, October, 1970.

"What state governments can do," by D. Weinberg. FAMILY PLANNING PERSPECTIVES. 2:30-34, March, 1970.

"Where is 1970 US population center?" COMM TODAY. 1:25, November 16, 1970.

POPULATION: USSR

"Abortion and the birth rate in the USSR," by G. Hude. J BIOSOC SCI. 2:283-292, July, 1970.

"Baby shortage." ECONOMIST. 235:43-44, May 2, 1970.

"Call for an institute on demography: scientific council on problems of demography," by L. Degtyar. CURRENT DIG SOVIET PR. 22:15-16, July 14, 1970.

"Causes of fertility decline in eastern Europe and the Soviet Union: the influence of demographic factors," by J. Berent. POPULATION STUDIES. 24:35-58, March, 1970; 247-292, July, 1970.

"Demographic problem: female employment and the birthrate." SOVIET R. 11:76-81, Spring, 1970.

"Diffusion model for selected demographic variables: an application to Soviet data," by G. J. Demko and E. Casetti. ASSN AM GEOG ANN. 60:533-539, September, 1970.

"Have a baby for Brezhnev," by V. Zorza. GUARDIAN. p 9, January 7, 1970.

"The implementation of leninist national policy among the people of the USSR far north," by I. S. Gurvich. SOVETSKAYA ETNOGRAFIYA. 45,1:15-34, January-February, 1970. SA #F0131.

"Man in the north," by V. Ianovskii. SOVIET R. 10:24-34, Winter 1969-1970.

"A mass social-hygienic investigation of a very old population in various areas of the Soviet Union: program, procedure, results," by N. N. Sachuk. J GERONT. 25:

POPULATION: USSR

   256-261, July, 1970.

   "On the preliminary results of the 1970 all-union population census: report of the U.S.S.R. Central statistical administration." CURRENT DIG SOVIET PR. 22:22-26, May 19, 1970.

   "Problems of economic demography," by B. Urlanis. PROBLEMS ECON. 13:69-89, January, 1971.

   "The reader asks to be told: on migration of the population," by V. Boldyrev. CURRENT DIG SOVIET PR. 22:18-19, September 22, 1970.

   "Russia is growing up--but not fast enough; Baby shortage." ECONOMIST. 235:43-44, May 2, 1970.

   "Russia takes a census--what it shows." U S NEWS. 68:50-51, May 18, 1970.

   "The Soviet census." NEW TIMES. pp 13-14, January 13, 1970.

   "USSR census returns," by V. Pokshishevsky. NEW TIMES. pp 30-31, May 9, 1970.

   "Why young people leave the villages," by M. Garin and A. Druzenko. CURRENT DIG SOVIET PR. 22:4-6, September 15, 1970.

POPULATION: YUGOSLAVIA

   "One in 20 who prefers it abroad." ECONOMIST. 236:39, September 5, 1970.

POPULATION GROWTH

   "Attaining a stationary U.S. population: three views: Zero population growth: what is it?" by F. W. Notestein. FAMILY PLANNING PERSPECTIVES. 2:20-28, June, 1970.

   "COPE-ing with the environment," by A. Mull. IMPRINT. 17:7, September-October, 1970.

   "Demographic boom--doom or dud." RI MED J. 53:688-690, December, 1970.

POPULATION GROWTH

"The 'demographic explosion' or new patterns," by M. Sonin. PROBLEMS ECON. 13:58-69, March, 1971.

"Frightening talk," by J. Kettle. EXEC. 12:20-21, December, 1970.

"Growth versus the quality of life," by J. A. Wagar. SCIENCE. 168:1179-1184, June 5, 1970.

"Heading for dramatic increase of younger adults and in income," by G. H. Brown. COMM & FIN CHR. 212:1474-1475 plus, November 19, 1970.

"How many is a crowd?" NEW STATESMAN. p 429-430, March 27, 1970.

"How many people?" LANCET. 2:553-554, September 12, 1970.

"How many people is enough?" by G. Leach. OBSERVER. p 8, January 4, 1970.

"In my opinion; we must stop multiplying!" by R. Gordon. SEVENTEEN. 29:234, May, 1970.

"Magnitude of rate-of-growth effects on aggregate savings," by M. J. Farrell. ECON J. 80:873-894, December, 1970.

"Malaria control and population growth," by P. Newman. J OF DEVELOPMENT STUDIES. 6:133-158, January, 1970.

"Malaria eradication and the fall of mortality, a note," by H. Frederiksen. POPULATION STUDIES. 24:111-113, March, 1970.

"Man is the endangered species; interview," by P. R. Ehrlich. NAT WILDLIFE. 8:38-39, April, 1970.

"Man's decline as a species," by A. H. Drummond, Jr. SCI DIGEST. 68:26-31, July, 1970.

"More on pitfalls," by H. Leibenstein. POPULATION STUDIES. 24:117-119, March, 1970.

"New baby boom on the way?" METROPOLITAN LIFE STAT BUL. 51:2-3, May, 1970.

POPULATION GROWTH

"Nice baby." JAMA. 214:1108, November 9, 1970.

"Nonsense explosion," by B. Wattenberg. NEW REPUB. 162:18-23, April 4; "Discussion," 162:24-26+ May 2; 44-46, May 9; 29-31, May 16, 1970.

"Observations concerning the increase of mankind, peopling of countries, etc," by B. Franklin. PERSPECT BIOL MED. 13:469-475, Summer, 1970.

"One myth less." NATURE (LONDON). 227:874-875, August 29, 1970.

"Our affluent economy will be bursting at seams by '85." ADV AGE. 41:1 plus, October 12, 1970.

"Overpopulation: crisis today, disaster tomorrow." PARENTS MAG. 45:30, January, 1970.

"People pollution," by P. R. Ehrlich. AUDUBON. 72:4-9, May, 1970.

"People pollution: excerpt from The doomsday book," by G. R. Taylor. LADIES HOME J. 87:74+, October, 1970.

"People problem," by P. R. Ehrlich and J. P. Holdren. SAT R. 53:42-43, July 4, 1970.

"Population crisis and extremes," by R. B. Kelman. SCIENCE. 168:777, May 15, 1970.

"Population crisis and extremes," by H. H. Suter. SCIENCE. 168:777, May 15, 1970.

"Population crisis: rising concern at home," by L. J. Carter. SCIENCE. 166:722-726, November 7, 1969.

"Population explosion." US NEWS. 68:32-34, January 12, 1970.

"Population explosion," by W. P. Mauldin. AM WATER WORKS ASSN J. 62:735-739, December, 1970.

"The population explosion," by W. Veerhusen. MLN BULL. 18:3-5, July, 1970.

"Population explosion falls flat." NATURE (LONDON). 227:994-995, September 5, 1970.

POPULATION GROWTH

"Population explosion." U S NEWS. 68:32-34, January 12, 1970.

"Population explosion...a universal threat," by G. Lapointe. INFIRM CANAD. 12:25-28, October, 1970.

"Population growth," by H. C. Wallich. NEWSWEEK. 75: 70, June 29; 76:60, August 10, 1970.

"Population growth and the multi-type Galton-Watson process," by E. Seneta. NATURE (LONDON). 225:766, February 21, 1970.

"Population heads for a zero growth rate." BSNS W. p 102-104, October 24, 1970.

"Population increase and social norms," by B. M. Chung. KOREAN NURSE. 9:25-26, August 25, 1970.

"The population phenomenon: its implications and the growing crisis," by P. M. Hauser. ARIZ R. 19:1-5, June-July, 1970.

"Population policy," by J. Burkinshaw. LANCET. 2:608, September 19, 1970.

"Population policy," by P. W. Gifford. LANCET. 2:463, August 29, 1970.

"Population policy: the crucial factor," by B. Dasgupta. SOUTH ASIAN R. 3:331-346, July, 1970.

"Population pollution," by R. T. Osborne. J PSYCHOL. 76:187-192, November, 1970.

"Population problem: in search of a solution," by J. J. Spengler. SCIENCE. 167:1438-1439, March 13, 1970.

"Population problems," by J. M. Yang. KOREAN NURSE. 9:12-18, August 25, 1970.

"Population rocket," by B. Schlesinger. CHATELAINE. 43:10, September 12, 1970.

"The Population Threat," by R. S. McNamara. TODAYS EDUC. 58,9:20-23, December, 1969.

"The predicament of mankind," by A. Peccei. SUCCESSO.

POPULATION GROWTH

12:149-156, June, 1970.

"President Nixon is wrong," by J. Kettle. MON TIMES. 138:22-23, April, 1970.

"Problem of the people bomb." SR SCHOL. 97:19-20, September 28, 1970.

"Problems of expanding populations," by D. Wolfers. NATURE (LONDON). 225:593-597, February 14, 1970.

"Product pushers vs the people," by C. F. Wurster. FIELD & S. 75:60+, June, 1970.

"The prospects for zero population growth," by R. A. Engles. TENN SURVEY BUS. 5:3-6+, August, 1970.

"Reproductive revolution," by R. D. Lamm. ABA J. 56:41, January, 1970.

"We're standing on the edge of the earth," by P. Ehrlich. NAT WILDLIFE. 8:16-17, October, 1970.

"World population." NATUR HIST. 79:60-62, January, 1970.

"World population." WORLD AFFAIRS. 35:11, April, 1970.

"World population growth and related technical problems," by A. L. Austin and J. W. Brewer. IEEE SPECTRUM. 7:43-54, December, 1970.

"World population trends and controls," by D. V. Glass. PROC R SOC MED. 63:Suppl:1172-1176, November, 1970.

"World wildlife fund stresses human population; a brief review of the second international conference of the world wildlife fund," by E. Ashpole. CAN AUD. 32:127, September-December, 1970.

"ZPG: new movement challenges the U.S. to stop growing." LIFE. 68:32-37, April 17, 1970.

"Zero population growth by the year 2000?" by W. H. Draper, Jr. WAR/PEACE REPT. 10:16-17, April, 1970.

POPULATION CONTROL

"Biologists and the Crowded World," by W. Kornberg. BIOSCIENCE. 21,4:183, February, 1971.

"Containing the explosion." NATURE (LONDON). 227:110, July 11, 1970.

"Control of population; excerpt from The social contract," by R. Ardrey. LIFE. 68:48-52+, February 20, 1970; READ DIGEST. 96:116-120, June, 1970.

"Cultural determinants of population stability in the Havasupai Indians," by A. L. Alvarado. AMER J PHYS ANTHROP. 33:9-14, July, 1970.

"Cybernetic concepts in population dynamics," by H. Wilbert. ACTA BIOTHEOR. 19:54-81, 1970.

"Drive to stop population growth: Zero population growth plan." U S NEWS. 68:36-38, March 2, 1970.

"Everybody's guilty. The ecological dilemma," by G. Hardin. CALIF MED. 113:40-47, November, 1970.

"Family planning or population control?" by J. Reston. READ DIGEST. 97:163-164, December, 1970.

"Federal family planning programs: choice or coercion?" by J. B. Rauch. SOCIAL WORK. 15:68-75, October, 1970.

"Fertility control--when?" JAMA. 214:1878, December 7, 1970.

"Government seeks ways to limit population growth." CONG Q W REPT. 28:1554-1558, June 12, 1970.

"Great head count." TIME. 95:33, March 23, 1970.

"Growth in the east." NATURE (LONDON). 227:430-431, August 1, 1970.

"How many children are we entitled to have?" by A. L. Goodstadt. REDBOOK. 136:12+, March, 1971.

"Improving the quality of life," by C. E. Flowers, Jr. ALA J MED SCI. 7:297-299, July, 1970.

"Infibulation, population control, and the medical profession," by G. S. Schwarz. BULL NY ACAD MED. 46: 964-996, November, 1970.

"Licensing: for cars and babies," by B. M. Russett. BUL ATOM SCI. 26:15-19, November, 1970.

"Making plans." LANCET. 2:807-808, October 17, 1970.

"Man as an Endangered Species," by M. K. Udall. AMERICAN ASSOCIATION OF COLLEGES FOR TEACHER EDUCATION YEARBOOK. pp 69-77, 1970.

"Mendeleev; demographics in addition to chemistry." CHEM & ENG NEWS. 48:43, September 28, 1970.

"More working wives, fewer children," by H. W. Bowman. FEDERAL RESERVE CHICAGO. p 7-12, August, 1970.

"Multiple paths to population control," by G. Hardin. FAMILY PLANNING PERSPECTIVES. 2:20-28, June, 1970.

"Multiply thy kind and perish," by C. E. Gillham. FIELD & S. 75:8+, July, 1970.

"Need for a global population policy--now," by V. P. Nanda. DENVER L J. Special:17, 1970.

"Number, types and duration of human lives," by R. H. Williams. NORTHWEST MED. 69:493-496, July, 1970.

"Planning population," by T. Bendixson. TOWN AND COUNTRY PLAN. 38:124, February, 1970.

"Population alert--a case of control." BSNS MGT. 39: 24-29, December, 1970.

"Population and people," by W. H. Wisely. CIVIL ENG. 40:27, December, 1970.

"Population control in India," by J. P. Lewis. POPULATION BUL. 26:12-31, November, 1970.

"Population control: the legal approach to a biological imperative." CALIF L REV. 58:1414, November, 1970.

"Population control--a necessity for survival," by S. Pustek. COLO NURSE. 70:18-19 passim, December, 1970.

POPULATION CONTROL

"Who's worrying?" by M. Holt. NURS MIRROR. 131:23, October 16, 1970.

"Population control, sterilization, and ignorance; results of Cornell University survey," by T. Eisner. SCIENCE. 167:337, January 23; "Discussion,"168:62, April 3, 1970.

"Population strategy," by A. W. Smith. NAT PARKS. 44:2, February, 1970.

"Population: time to put the brake on," by G. Leach. OBSERVER. p 11, November 29, 1970.

"Procreation and the future of mankind. Implications of artificial insemination," by H. Muramatsu. KANGO KYOSHITSU. 14:28-31, August, 1970.

"Role of operations research in population planning," by W. A. Reinke. OP RES. 18:1099-1111, November, 1970.

"A self-regulating system of human population control," by L. Thompson. TRANS NY ACAD SCI. 32:262-270, February, 1970.

"Should public policy give incentives to welfare mothers to limit the number of their children?" by N. Dembitz; "A dissenting viewpoint," by H. F. Pilpel. FAMILY L Q. 4:130, June, 1970.

"The social ecology of hyper-fertility," by D. M. Recio. ANPHI PAP. 5:16-23, April-June, 1970.

"Stabilizing the population," by R. Haughton. MONTH. 2:150-151, November, 1970.

"Surgical control of population," by W. E. Lockhart. TEX MED. 66:24-26, November, 1970.

"Three's a crowd," by P. J. Smith. SPECTATOR. p 74-75, January 17, 1970.

"Who should take the pill? Excerpt from Two children by choice," by I. Rossman. PARENTS MAG. 45:54-57+, February, 1970.

POPULATION FORECASTING
    SEE ALSO: POPULATION THEORY & RESEARCH
               ENVIRONMENT, ECOLOGY & POPULATION
               POLITICS & POPULATION

"Charting the future; graphs," by J. Kettle. EXEC. 12:38, October, 1970.

"The climax of population growth--past and future perspective," by K. Davis. CALIF MED. 113:33-39, November, 1970.

"Critical aspects of the future of the human species," by D. Dubarie. STUD GEN. 23:998-1009, 1970.

"The determinants of fertility: a theoretical forecasting model," by M. Fish, et al. BEHAV SCI. 15:318-328, July, 1970.

"The growth of population to the end of the century," by J. Thompson. SOCIAL TRENDS. 1:21-32, 1970.

"Housing--surplus or shortage?" by J. Macey. TOWN AND COUNTRY PLAN. 38:202-206, April, 1970.

"The impact of high altitudes on human populations," by E. J. Clegg, et al. HUM BIOL. 42:486-518, September, 1970.

"Impact of a new town: application of the Garin-Lowry model," by M. Barry; "Basic model for population projection: applying the cohort survival technique," by I. Bracken. TOWN PLAN INST J. 55:428-439, December, 1969.

"Improving population estimates with the use of dummy variables," by D. E. Pursell. DEMOGRAPHY. 7:87-91, February, 1970.

"Metropolitan area projections through 1975." SALES MGT. 105:57-107, November 10, 1970.

"Necrotecture: the underground population explosion and its impact on cemetery design," by R. Slusarenko. LANDSCAPE ARCH. 60:297-300, July, 1970.

"Next decade shows promise but raises many serious urban questions." AIA J. 53:8, January, 1970.

"1984 the era of young marrieds." NATURE (LONDON).

POPULATION FORECASTING

228:206, October 17, 1970.

"1984 plus one," by G. H. Brown. CONF BD REC. 7:20-24, December, 1970.

"Our affluent economy will be bursting at seams by 1985." ADV AGE. 41:1plus, October 12, 1970.

"Population explosion," by W. G. Heim. AM BIOL TEACH. 32:244, April, 1970.

"Population projections." REAL ESTATE ANALYST. 39:417-433, October 26, 1970.

"Prediction in family planning. Factors associated with involvement of low-income women in a public family planning program," by E. Siegel, et al. AMER J PUBLIC HEALTH. 60:1382-1394, August, 1970.

"Prediction in family planning. Prediction of the adoption and continued use of contraception," by D. Mc Calister, et al. AMER J PUBLIC HEALTH. 60:1372-1381, August, 1970.

"Research techniques in structure planning, experience from the South Hampshire plan: the design and calibration of a population projection model," by M. K. Francis and P. F. Menezer. TOWN PLAN INST J. 56:216-220, June, 1970.

"The shape of things to come," by E. H. Hutten. HUMANIST. 85:182-183, June, 1970.

"Surprise for 1980's: the big city, population explosion will fizzle," by E. B. Weiss. ADV AGE. 41:65-66, May 4, 1970.

"Survival in the seventies," by M. L. Brown. OHIO NURSES REV. 45:12-20, April, 1970.

"The U.S. labor force: projections to 1985: special labor force report sets forth BLS," by S. C. Travis. MO LABOR R. 93:3-12, May, 1970.

POPULATION: HISTORY

"Colonial New England demography: a sampling approach," by R. Higgs and H. L. Stettler, 3rd. WM & MARY Q.

POPULATION: HISTORY

27:282-294, April, 1970.

"Demography of primitive populations," by N. McArthur. SCIENCE. 167:1097-1101, February 20, 1970.

"Depopulation of the central Andex in the 16th century," by C. T. Smith. CUR ANTHROP. 11:453-464, October-December, 1970.

"Edward Foote's Medical Common Sense: an early American comment on birth control," by V. J. Cirillo. J HIST MED. 25:341-345, July, 1970.

"The effect of the great blackout of 1965 on births in New York city," by J. R. Udry. DEMOGRAPHY. 7:325-327, August, 1970.

"English population in the early sixteenth century," by J. Cornwall. ECONOMIC HISTORY R. 23:32-44, April, 1970.

"Evolution of endogenous infant mortality in France in the second half of the 19th century," by R. Nadot. POPULATION. 25,1:49-58, January-February, 1970.

"Family planning and population problems. Concepts of 4 different eras," by M. Muramatsu. JAP J MIDWIFE. 24:27-30, December, 1970.

"Infibulation, population control, and the medical profession," by G. S. Schwarz. BULL NY ACAD MED. 46:964-996, November, 1970.

"Inhabitants of Northmavine, Shetland 18th and 19th Century," by J. C. Mowat. SCOTTISH GENEALOGIST. 17:91-104, November 3, 1970.

"Irish fertility ratios before the famine," by G. S. L. Tucker. ECON HIST R. 23:267-284, August, 1970.

"Land speculation, promotion and failure: the Northern Pacific railroad, 1870-1873," by J. L. Harnsberger. J WEST. 9:33-45, January, 1970.

"Marriage rates and population pressure: Ireland, 1871 and 1911," by B. M. Walsh. ECONOMIC HISTORY R. 23:148-162, April, 1970.

POPULATION: HISTORY

"Mate choice and domestic life in the nineteenth-century marriage manual," by M. Gordon and M. C. Bernstein. J MARRIAGE AND FAM. 32:665-674, November, 1970.

"Migration of native-born Ohioans: 1850-1960," by L. E. Gallaway and R. K. Vedder. BUL BUS RESEARCH. 45:4-5, June, 1970.

"Migration within the US 1800-1960: some new estimates," by S. Lebergott. J ECON HIST. 30:839-847, December, 1970.

"New look at the great landlords of eighteenth-century New York," by S. B. Kim. WM & MARY Q. 27:581-614, October, 1970.

"One hundred years of population change. Growth rate of the 100 largest metropolitan areas." REAL ESTATE ANALYST. 39:455-466, November 17, 1970.

"People of York: 1538-1812," by U. M. Cowgill. SCI AM. 222:104-110 plus, January, 1970.

"Population and economic change: the emergence of the rice industry in Guyana, 1895-1915," by J. R. Mandle. J ECON HIST. 30:785-801, December, 1970.

"Population change, enclosure, and the early Tudor economy," by I. Blanchard. ECON HIST R. 23:427-445, December, 1970.

"Population change in the Springfield-Chicopee-Holyoke commuter region," by L. Seig. ROCKY MOUNTAIN SOCIAL SCIENCE J. 7:77-87, April, 1970.

"Population growth in Java in the 19th century. A new interpretation," by B. Peper. POPULATION STUDIES. 24:71-84, March, 1970.

"Population movement in seventeenth century England," by P. Spufford. LOCAL POPULATION STUDIES MAG. 4:41-50, Spring, 1970.

"Size and structure of the household in England over three centuries: a comment," by J. W. Nixon. POPULATION STUDIES. 24:445-447, November, 1970.

"Some aspects of immigration into the Glamorgan coal-

POPULATION: HISTORY

field between 1881 and 1911," by P. N. Jones. HONOURABLE SOC OF CYMMRODORION TRANS. 1969 SESSION PART I, p 82-98. 1970.

"Some economic aspects of Norwegian population movements 1740-1940: an econometric study," by T. Moe. J ECON HIST. 30:267-270, 285-287, March, 1970.

"A source for medieval population statistics," by K. C. Newton. SOC OF ARCHIVISTS J. 3:543-546, October, 1969.

"The state: an ecological phenomenon." JAMA. 214:905, November 2, 1970.

"Two and a half centuries of demographic history in a Bavarian village," by J. Knodel. POPULATION STUDIES. 24:353-376, November, 1970.

"Victorian women and menstruation," by E. Showalter, et al. VICT STUD. 14:83-89, September, 1970.

POPULATION THEORY & RESEARCH
SEE ALSO: POPULATION FORECASTING
ENVIRONMENT, ECOLOGY, & POPULATION

"The center for population research," by J. F. O'Donnell. J AM VET MED ASSOC. 157:1786-1794, December 1, 1970.

"Current status of population research in schools of public health," by I. W. Gabrielson, et al. AMER J PUBLIC HEALTH. 60:913-918, May, 1970.

"A deterministic model for handling the birth, death, and migration processes of spatially distributed populations," by M. B. Usher, et al. BIOMETRICS. 26: 1-12, March, 1970.

"Distributional effects in demand analysis; observations and predictive tests," by D. J. Laughhunn. AM STAT ASSN J. 65:576-585, June, 1970.

"Effect of induced abortion on birth rate; a simulation model," by S. Mukherji, et al. INDIAN J PUBLIC HEALTH. 14:49-58, January, 1970.

"Estimating the effective size of human populations," by J. W. MacCluer, et al. AMER J HUM GENET. 22:176-

183, March, 1970.

"Extended family structure and fertility: some conceptual and methodological issues," by T. K. Burch and M. Gendell. J MARRIAGE & FAM. 32:227-236, May, 1970.

"Family patterns of migrant and nonmigrant retirees," by G. L. Bultena and D. G. Marshall. J MARRIAGE & FAM. 32:89-93, February, 1970.

"General theory of population by A. Sauvy; A review," by E. Hammond. TOWN & COUNTRY PLAN. 38:415, September, 1970.

"Home ownership, life cycle stage, and residential mobility," by A. Speare, Jr. DEMOGRAPHY. 7:449-458, November, 1970.

"An ideological reading of the essay on the principle of population," by A. Mattelart. L'HOMME ET LA SOCIETE. 15:183-219, January-March, 1970. SA #E7686.

"The importance of data on the age and sex structure of the population," by A. Vostrikova. PROBLEMS ECON. 12:27-39, March, 1970.

"An integrated social and demographic statistical system," by K. Bjerke. STATISTISK TIDSKRIFT. 8:173-197, November 3, 1970.

"Is there an optimum level of population?" BOSTON. 29-30, December; SCIENCE. 166:270-271, October 10, 1969.

"Learning About Population Dynamics," by L. Nilson, et al. AMERICAN BIOLOGY TEACHER. 33,1:26-28, January, 1971.

"Measuring rural-urban drift in developing countries; a suggested model," by L. Roussel. INT LABOUR R. 101:229-246, March, 1970.

"Model for the dispersion of the migrant labor force and some results for the United States, 1880-1920," by T. J. Orsagh, et al. R ECON & STAT. 52:306-312, August, 1970.

"Model for Zero Population Growth," by S. M. Dickson. BIOSCIENCE. 20,23:1245-1246, December, 1970.

POPULATION THEORY & RESEARCH

"The National Goals Research Staff report," by P. H. Abelson. SCIENCE. 169:537, August 7, 1970.

"A new deterministic model for the interaction between predator and prey," by C. Pearce. BIOMETRICS. 26: 387-392, September, 1970.

"Note on a social populations dispersing in two dimensions," by E. Bradford, et al. J THEOR BIOL. 29:27-33, October, 1970.

"Population Models in the High School," by T. M. Hunter, et al. JOURNAL OF GEOGRAPHY. 70,2:95-104, February, 1971.

"Predominance of male authors in social work publications," by A. Rosenblatt, et al. SOC CASEWORK. 51: 421-430, July, 1970.

"Primate populations and biomedical research," by C. H. Southwick, et al. SCIENCE. 170:1051-1054, December 4, 1970.

"A proposed new vital event numeration unitary system for developed countries," by F. E. Linder. MILBANK MEM FUND Q. 48:Suppl:77-87, October, 1970.

"Re-examination of some recent criticisms of transition theory," by K. C. W. Kammeyer. SOCIOL Q. 11: 500-510, Fall, 1970.

"A short-run model of inter-regional migration," by A. B. Jack. MANCHESTER SCHOOL OF ECONOMIC AND SOCIAL STUDIES. 38:15-28, March, 1970.

"Social research and privileged data," by U. L. Val. REV. 4:368, Spring, 1970.

"Stability of steady distributions of a social populations dispersing in one dimension," by E. Bradford, et al. J THEOR BIOL. 29:13-26, October, 1970.

"The value of human abortuses in the surveillance of developmental anomalies. I. General overview," by J. R. Miller, et al. CAN MED ASSOC J. 103:501-502, September 12, 1970.

"The value of human abortuses in the surveillance of

POPULATION THEORY & RESEARCH

  developmental anomalies. II. Reduction deformities of the limbs," by J. R. Miller, et al. CAN MED ASSOC J. 103:503-505, September 12, 1970.

POVERTY & POPULATION

"Characteriological deterrants to economic progress in people of Appalachia," by C. E. Goshen. SOUTHERN MED J. 63:1053-1061, September, 1970.

"Determining the labor force status of men missed in the census," by D. P. Klein. MO LABOR R. 93:26-32, March, 1970.

"Development and trends in maternal-child welfare towards the idea of family welfare," by Manciaux. REV INFIRM ASSIST SOC. 20:542-545, June, 1970.

"Factors associated with involvement of low-income women in a public family planning program," by E. Siegel. AM J PUBL HLTH. 60:1382+, August, 1970.

"Family planning and conjugal roles in New York City poverty areas," by S. Polgar, et al. SOC SCI MED. 4:135-139, July, 1970.

"Family planning and the poor," by W. M. Hern. NEW REPUB. 163:17-19, November 14, 1970.

"Family planning in the war on poverty," by G. D. London. FERTIL STERIL. 21:189-192, March, 1970.

"A 'new town' planned for the urban and rural poor: the University of Louisville develops a controversial strategy to change the flow of migration," by S. Lawson. CITY. 4:35-38, June-July, 1970.

"Participation of low-income urban women in a public health birth control program," by Z. L. Janus, et al. PUBLIC HEALTH REP. 85:859-867, October, 1970.

"A program of indigent obstetric care and planned parenthood in a rural North Carolina county," by J. E. Clement. AMER J OBSTET GYNEC. 108:63-67, September 1, 1970.

RELIGION & ETHICS & POPULATION

"Abortion: holy innocents?" CHR TODAY. 14:39, May 8, 1970.

"Alienation correlates of Catholic fertility," by A. G. Neal, et al. AM J SOCIOL. 76:460-473, November, 1970.

"Association between religio-ethnic identification and fertility among contemporary Protestants and Jews," by B. Lazerwitz. SOCIOL Q. 11:307-320, Summer, 1970.

"Baptism marriage ratios in late seventeenth century England," by E. A. Wrigley. LOCAL POPULATION STUDIES MAG. 3:15, Autumn, 1969.

"Birth control. Moral theological, medico-gynecologic and penal aspects," by H. D. Hiersche, et al. GEBURTSH FRAUENHEILK. 30:289-301, April, 1970.

"Birth control. Problem of the gynecologist from the medical, moral and religious point of view," by S. Fossati. MINERVA GINECOL. 22:664-668, July 15, 1970.

"Contraception and abortion: American catholic responses," by D. Callhan. ANNALS OF THE AMERICAN ACADEMY OF POLITICAL AND SOCIAL SCIENCE. 387:109-117, January, 1970.

"Early effect of humanae vitae?" by R. Cruz-Coke. LANCET. 2:525, September 5, 1970.

"Education and religion as factors influencing attitudes toward population growth in the United States," by L. D. Barnett. SOCIAL BIOLOGY. 17:26-36, March, 1970.

"The encyclical 'HUMANAE Vitae' and birth rate," by D. Hoogendoorn. NEDERL T GENEESK. 114:1294-1297, August 1, 1970.

"The ethics of biomedical interventions," by D. J. Ingle. PERSPECT BIOL MED. 13:364-387, Spring, 1970.

"The ethics of population control in the twentieth century," by R. Craig. CENT AFR J MED. 16:109-114, May, 1970.

"Ex-F.A.O. head charges contradiction in Pope's policies

on birth control." CHR CENT. 87:135, February 4, 1970.

"Fertility patterns among religious groups in Canada," by L. H. Long. DEMOGRAPHY. 7:135-149, May, 1970.

"How Catholics are making up their minds on birth control," by J. E. Allen. CHR CENT. 87:915-918, July 29, 1970.

"The literature of ethical problems in medicine," by J. R. Elkinton, Jr. ANN INTERN MED. 73:662-666, October, 1970.

"Marriage and malevolence: the uses of sexual opposition in a Hindu pantheon," by L. A. Babb. ETHNOLOGY. 9: 137-148, April, 1970.

"Overpopulation and the American Catholic conscience," by P. J. Riga. WORLD JUSTICE. 12:199-215, December, 1970.

"Plea for reconciliation; break between the Archbishop of Washington and his priests." AMERICA. 122:446, April 25, 1970; "Reply with rejoinder," by J. C. Ford, 122:571, May 30, 1970.

"Religious and moral aspects of population control," by H. L. Smith. RELIG IN LIFE. 39:193-204, Summer, 1970.

"Reproduction and astrology," by M. Vojta. CESK GYNEK. 35:38-40, February, 1970.

"The right to live," by J. Stallworthy. J ROY COLL GEN PRACT. 19:187-190, April, 1970.

"Science, Birth Control, and the Roman Catholic Church," by J. J. Baker. BIOSCIENCE. 20,3:143-150, February, 1970.

"Tax-supported sterilization wins in London despite Catholic drive." CHR CENT. 87:591, May 13, 1970.

"Toward a third world theology; reaction to Humanae vitae." AMERICA. 122:90, January 31, 1970.

"Vitiating Humanae vitae; Catholic renewal movements

RELIGION & ETHICS & POPULATION

  leaflet," by T. Beeson. CHR CENT. 87:1032-1033, September 2, 1970.

"Will a miracle child be born this year?" by P. S. Buck. LADIES HOME J. 87:63+, December, 1970.

RURAL POPULATION

  "Experience in rural family planning," by J. M. Flavier. PHILIPP J NURS. 39:6 plus, January-March, 1970.

  "Manpower developments," by R. J. Brown. PERSONNEL ADM. 33:2+, May, 1970.

  "Rural slums or rural desert?" by M. Hederman. INTERPLAY. 3:23-26, June, 1970.

  "Stemming the tide of rural migration," by W. Eustis. MINN MUNIC. 55:344-345 plus, November, 1970.

SANGER, MARGARET

  "Faces from the past: M. Sanger," by R. M. Ketchum. AM HERITAGE. 21:52-53, June, 1970.

SEX, SEX RESEARCH & CUSTOMS

  "Bajau sex and reproduction," by H. A. Nimmo. ETHNOLOGY. 9:251-262, July, 1970.

  "Changing sex norms in America and Scandinavia," by H. T. Christensen and C. F. Gregg. J MARRIAGE & FAM. 32:616-627, November, 1970.

  "Complexities of morality," by S. Periman. ANN INTERN MED. 72:761-762, May, 1970.

  "Context and consex: a cautionary tale," by R. M. Hauser. AM J SOCIOL. 75:645-664+, January, 1970.

  "Current morality report: standard ordinary policyholders, Metropolitan Life insurance company first half 1970." METROPOLITAN LIFE STAT BUL. 51:11, October, 1970.

  "Determinants of premarital sexual permissiveness: a secondary analysis," by C. P. Middendorp and others. J MARRIAGE & FAM. 32:369-380, August, 1970.

"Dynamics of sexual behavior of college students," by G. R. Kaats and K. E. Davis. J MARRIAGE & FAM. 32: 390-399, August, 1970.

"Extramarital sexual intercourse: a methodological note," by R. E. Johnson. J MARRIAGE & FAM. 32:279-282, May, 1970.

"Family size and sex-role stereotypes," by F. E. Clarkson and others. SCIENCE. 167:390-392, January 23, 1970.

"Flesh in the afternoon," by J. Weightman. ENCOUNTER. 34:30-32, June, 1970.

"Half-cock at the sex fair," by T. Baistow. NEW STATESM. 79:436, March 27, 1970.

"Male sex-role and response to a community problem," by F. L. Strodtbeck. SOCIOL Q. 11:291-306, Summer, 1970.

"Mate choice and domestic life in the nineteenth-century marriage manual," by M. Gordon, et al. J MARRIAGE & FAM. 32:665-674, November, 1970.

"Premarital pregnancy and status before and after marriage," by L. C. Coombs. AM J SOCIOL. 75:800-820, March, 1970.

"Premarital sex as deviant behavior: an application of current approaches to deviance," by I. L. Reiss. AM SOCIOL R. 35:78-87, February, 1970.

"Premarital sexual experience among coeds, 1958 and 1968," by R. R. Bell and J. B. Chaskes. J MARRIAGE & FAM. 32:81-84, February, 1970.

"A rejoinder to Miss Spencer's comments on pre-marital pregnancies and ex-nuptial births in Australia, 1911-1966," by K. G. Basavarajappa. AUSTRALIAN AND NEW ZEALAND JOURNAL OF SOCIOLOGY. 6,1:79-84, 1970.

"Sex-role identity and pragmatic action," by W. Bezdek and F. L. Strodtbeck. AM SOCIOL R. 35:491-502, June, 1970.

"Sexual attitudes of Thai students; an exploratory

cross-cultural study," by J. Wohl and A. Dunlop. HUMAN ORGAN. 29:190-196, Fall, 1970.

"Sexual inversion among the Azande," by E. E. Evans-Pritchard. AM ANTHROP. 72:1428-1434, December, 1970.

"Sexual responsibility in our permissive society--is it just an impossible dream?" by D. Evagorou. NURS TIMES. 66:628, May 14, 1970.

"Sexual revolution; myth or reality," by R. L. Worsnop. EDITORIAL RESEARCH REPORTS. 241-58, April 1, 1970.

"Social class and premarital sexual permissiveness: a subsequent test," by G. M. Maranell. J MARRIAGE & FAM. 32:85-88, February, 1970.

"Sociological problems of sexual morality," by S. I. Golod. SOVIET R. 11:127-147, Summer, 1970.

"Some correlates of extramarital coitus," by R. E. Johnson. J MARRIAGE & FAM. 32:449-456, August, 1970.

"What's off at the pictures?" by J. J. O'Connor. WALL ST J. 176:16, November 30, 1970.

"Why can't a woman--? 'the double standard is on the way to becoming culturally obsolete; what single standard will take its place'?" by H. M. Hacker. HUMANIST. 31:10-13, January-February, 1971.

STERILIZATION

"Abortion and sterilization. Status of the law in mid-1970," by N. Hershey. AMER J NURS. 70:1926-1927, September, 1970.

"Bacteriology of fallopian tube in relation to puerperal sterilization," by M. A. Mustafa, et al. J OBSTET GYNAEC BRIT COMM. 77:171-173, February, 1970.

"The case for voluntary sterilization," by W. C. Rattan. WIS MED J. 69:20-21, August, 1970.

"Cesarean hysterectomy," by G. T. Schneider, et al. SURG GYNEC OBSTET. 130:501-504, March, 1970.

"College policy on abortion and sterilization." ACOG

STERILIZATION

NURSES BULL. 4:2, Fall, 1970.

"Critical examination of request for sterilization of mentally defective persons," by K. Grunewald. LAKARTIDNINGEN. 67:5091-5095, October 28, 1970.

"Current trends in sexual sterilization in women," by Z. Lapinski, et al. GINEK POL. 41:219-225, February, 1970.

"Demographic effectiveness of sterilization program in India," by O. P. Vig. ARTHA VIINANA. 12:398-405, September, 1970.

"Does sterilization cause psychic faulty development?" by H. Kind, et al. NERVENARZT. 41:287-289, June, 1970.

"The effect of vasectomy upon the incidence and morbidity of post-prostatectomy epididymitis," by A. D. Beck. AUST NEW ZEAL J SURG. 39:286-289, February, 1970.

"Elective vasectomy by American urologists in 1967," by J. E. Davis, et al. FERTIL STERIL. 21:615-621, August, 1970.

"Evaluation of cesarean section hysterectomy as a sterilization procedure," by P. Brenner, et al. AM J OBSTET GYNECOL. 108:335-339, October 1, 1970.

"The expression of induced sterility in Glossina austeni," by C. F. Curtis. TRANS ROY SOC TROP MED HYG. 64:186, 1970.

"Failure of tubal sterilization accompanying cesarean section," by M. E. Husbands, Jr., et al. AMER J OBSTET GYNEC. 107:966-967, July 15, 1970.

"Female sterilization by tubal electrocoagulation under laparoscopic control," by W. A. Liston, et al. LANCET. 1:382-383, February 21, 1970.

"Fertile period after vasectomy," by J. B. Deisher. SCIENCE. 169:816-817, August 28, 1970.

"Health protection and irreversible contraception (sterilization) in women," by J. Rothe. DTSCH GESUNDHEIT-

STERILIZATION

SW. 25:555-560, March 25, 1970.

"Indications for sterilization of the mentally disturbed have to be reevaluated," by K. Grunewald. LAKARTID-NINGEN. 67:5096-5102, October 28, 1970.

"Indications for surgical sterilization," by J. R. Bopp, et al. OBSTET GYNEC. 35:760-764, May, 1970.

"Interval tubal sterilization via laparoscopy," by M. R. Cohen, et al. AM J OBSTET GYNECOL. 108:458-461, October 1, 1970.

"Is sterilization the answer?" by M. Nag, et al. SCIENCE. 168:62, April 3, 1970.

"Key points of our method of transvaginal tubal sterilization," by I. Kai. SANFUJIN JISSAL. 19:408-411, April, 1970.

"Laboratory studies on radiation-induced dominant lethality in sperms in population control of the mosquito Culex pipiens fatigans Wied," by T. Koshy, et al. INT J RADIAT BIOL. 18:521-530, 1970.

"The law concerning voluntary sterilization as it affects doctors," by M. Mackay, et al. J UROL. 103:482-484, April, 1970.

"Legal responsibility for unsuccessful sterilization," by E. Havt. HOSP MANAGE. 109:13 passim, February, 1970.

"Legality of sterilization." BRIT MED J. 1:704-705, March 21, 1970.

"Ligature of the salpinx," by H. Adachi. SHUJUTSU. 24:576-581, May, 1970.

"Male sterilization; an ultimate in family planning," by A. D. Gunn. NURS TIMES. 66:627, May 14, 1970.

"A male sterilization clinic," by P. Jackson, et al. BR MED J. 4:295-297, October 31, 1970.

"A method of tubal ligation," by S. J. Barr. AMER J OBSTET GYNEC. 107:324-325, May 15, 1970.

STERILIZATION

"Observation upon patients following vasectomy in Nepal," by B. P. Sharma. SOUTHERN MED J. 63:771-772, July, 1970.

"Obstacles to sterilization in one community," by S. C. Scrimshaw, et al. FAMILY PLANNING PERSPECTIVES. 2: 40-42, October, 1970.

"One man's answer to overpopulation; vasectomy." LIFE. 68:42-47, March 6, 1970.

"Outpatient tubal sterilization," by C. R. Wheeless. OBSTET GYNEC. 36:208-211, August, 1970.

"The Parliament requested overhaul in sterilization law." LAKARTIDNINGEN. 67:5732, December 2, 1970.

"Per-celioscopic tubal sterilization by isthmic electrocoagulation," by R. Palliez, et al. BULL FED SOC GYNECOL OBSTET LANG FR. 22:449-451, September-October, 1970.

"Pigeon control by chemosterilization; population model from laboratory results," by J. Sturtevant. SCIENCE. 170:322-324, October 16, 1970.

"Population control, sterilization, and ignorance: results of Cornell University survey," by T. Eisner, et al. SCIENCE. 167:337 plus, January 23, 1970.

"Prophylactic tubal sterilization," by C. Colmeiro-Laforet. ACTA OBSTET GINECOL HISP LUSIT. 18:263-278, November, 1970.

"Recent advances in surgical methods of control of fertility and infertility," by P. C. Steptoe. BRIT MED BULL. 26:60-64, January, 1970.

"Recent results of the sterilization of women by the Madlener's method," by J. Higier, et al. WIAD LEK. 23:637-640, April 15, 1970.

"Reversal of sterilization in the female," by G. Williams. NURS J INDIA. 61:145 plus, May, 1970.

"Semen examinations after vasectomy," by J. G. Temple, et al. LANCET. 2:1258, December 12, 1970.

STERILIZATION

"The serum level of immunoreactive LH in intact and spayed androgen-sterilized rats," by A. P. Labhsetwar. J REPROD FERTIL. 23:349-352, November, 1970.

"Sexual sterilization for non-medical reasons." CANAD MED ASS J. 102:211, January 31, 1970.

"Sexual sterilization, legal position of a doctor," by I. Maxwell. NOVA SCOTIA MED BULL. 49:18, February, 1970.

"A simple technique of re-anastomosis after vasectomy," by K. C. Mehta, et al. BRIT J UROL. 42:340-343, June, 1970.

"Statistical and sociological aspects after sterilization surgery," by H. E. Schneider. GEBURTSHILFE FRAUENHEILKD. 30:1064-1070, December, 1970.

"Sterilization," by J. S. Scott. LANCET. 2:417, August 22, 1970.

"Sterilization, an alternative to contraceptive pills," by G. Berggren. LAKARTIDNINGEN. 67:348-350, January 21, 1970.

"Sterilization and family planning," by M. Elstein. PRACTITIONER. 205:30-37, July, 1970.

"Sterilization as legitimate medical task," by R. Hellmann. MED WELT. 1:41-47, January 3, 1970.

"Sterilization by ovariotexy, a reversible technic," by C. Wood, et al. GYNECOL PRAT. 21:299-305, 1970.

"Sterilization for both sexes; vasectomy and new gynecological technique called laparoscopy." TIME. 95:33, June 1, 1970.

"Sterilization in India. The pill: daily bread. Cold demographic calculation should prevail over every other sentiment," by A. Flore. MINERVA MED SUPPL. 78:20-24, September 25, 1970.

"Sterilization of the fallopian tubes by electrocoagulation of the isthmus under celioscopy," by J. Thoyer-Rozat, et al. BULL FED GYNEC OBSTET FRANC. 22:11-13, January-March, 1970.

STERILIZATION

"Sterilization of fallopian tubes during laparoscopy," by M. Voita. CESK GYNEKOL. 35:602-603, December, 1970.

"Sterilization of women," by L. N. Jackson. LANCET. 2:463, August 29, 1970.

"Sterilization of women," by E. A. Williams. LANCET. 2:361, August 15, 1970.

"Sterilization of women," by G. F. Williams. LANCET. 2:608, September 19, 1970.

"Sterilization of women in the light of Polish legislation," by W. Wieszczycki, et al. GINEKOL POL. 41: 1153-1156, October, 1970.

"Sterilizing doses of gamma irradiation for the imported cabbageworm, Pieris rapae, and effects on longevity, mating, and fecundity," by H. M. Flint, et al. J ECON ENTOM. 63:1008-1009, June, 1970.

"Suprascrotal vasectomy," by S. M. Gupta. J INDIAN MED ASSOC. 54:561-563, June 16, 1970.

"Surgical nursing: abortions and sterilizations." REGAN REP NURS LAW. 11:1, June, 1970.

"Tax-supported sterilization wins in London despite Catholic drive." CHR CENT. 87:591, May 13, 1970.

"Trend to sterilization." NEWSWEEK. 76:90, December 21, 1970.

"Tubal electrocoagulation under laparoscopic control," by C. H. De Boer, et al. LANCET. 1:997, May 9, 1970.

"Tubal ligation and abortion in the State of Alabama," by C. E. Flowers, Jr. J MED ASS ALABAMA. 39:945-947, April, 1970.

"Tubal ligation in population control." BRIT MED J. 1:770-771, March 28, 1970.

"Tubal occlusion: a comparative study," by K. F. Omran, et al. INT J FERTIL. 15:226-241, October-December, 1970.

STERILIZATION

"Tubal sterilization. Morbidity on a charity hospital service," by C. R. Mabray, et al. OBSTET GYNEC. 36: 204-207, August, 1970.

"Tubal sterilization in an indigent population. Report of fourteen years' experience," by D. M. Haynes, et al. AMER J OBSTET GYNEC. 106:1044-1053, April 1, 1970.

"Vasectomies increase as concern over 'pill,' overpopulation grows," by E. Graham. WALL ST J. 176:1+, November 11, 1970.

"Vasectomy," by L. N. Jackson. LANCET. 1:140-141, January 17, 1970.

"Vasectomy," by D. R. Rogers. ALASKA MED. 12:60, June, 1970.

"Vasectomy and A. I.H." by B. Herzberg. LANCET. 1:90, January 10, 1970.

"Vasectomy and A.I.H." by H. Hill. LANCET. 1:191, January 24, 1970.

"Vasectomy and A.I.H." by J. K. Monro. LANCET. 1:354-355, February 14, 1970.

"Vasectomy and adverse psychological reactions," by F. J. Ziegler. ANN INTERN MED. 73:853, November, 1970.

"Vasectomy of election," by H. E. Carlson. SOUTHERN MED J. 63:766-770, July, 1970.

"Vasectomy on the N.H.S." BRIT MED J. 1:312-313, May 9, 1970.

"Vasectomy: research proposal," by A. Roe. SCIENCE. 168:1523-1525, June 26, 1970.

"Voluntary sterilization," by C. P. Blacker. BRIT MED J. 1:499, February 21, 1970.

"Voluntary sterilization," by S. T. DeLee. INT SURG. 54:304-311, October, 1970.

"Voluntary sterilization," by B. Gonzales. AM J NURS. 70:2581-2583, December, 1970.

STERILIZATION

"Voluntary sterilization and reform of the criminal law," by A. Eser. MED WELT. 40:1751-1759, October 3, 1970.

"Voluntary sterilization as a family planning measure," by P. Petersen. FORTSCHR NEUROL PSYCHIAT. 38:33-52, January, 1970.

"Voluntary sterilization in the male," by D. Urquhart-Hay. NEW ZEAL MED J. 71:230-232, April, 1970.

"Voluntary sterilization law recommended forms," by J. L. Moore, Jr., et al. J MED ASS GEORGIA. 59:374-377, September, 1970.

"Voluntary sterilization, a necessary alternative?" by P. Tierney. FAMILY LAW Q. 4:373, December, 1970.

UNDERDEVELOPED COUNTRIES
SEE: DEVELOPING NATION

URBAN GROWTH & URBANIZATION
SEE ALSO: CROWDING
ISOLATION & ALIENATION

"Abortive town expansion plan: Ipswich." TOWN PLAN INST J. 56:121, March, 1970.

"Aged people among urban population," by B. Kaufman. DEMOSTA. 3,1-2:5-26, 1970.

"Big city syndrome," by D. Behrman. UNESCO COURIER. 23:20+, August, 1970.

"Changing distribution of negroes within metropolitan areas: the emergence of black suburbs," by R. Farley. AM J SOCIOLOGY. 75:512-529, January, 1970.

"Changing urban spatial patterns; central places," by A. Getis. NAT COUNCIL SOCIAL STUDIES WRBK. 40:101-120, 1970.

"Cities shape regional growth trends," by R. M. Young. ARCH REC. 146:80, August, 1969.

"Demographic adaptations to urban conditions," by G. M. Korosteiev, et al. SOV ZDRAVOOKHR. 29:35-36, 1970.

"Determining the labor force status of men missed in the

census: special labor force report describes pilot use of a new technique for securing labor force data in urban poverty areas," by D. P. Klein. MO LABOR R. 93:26-32, March, 1970.

"Eight assumptions concerning rural-urban migration in Colombia: a three-shanty-towns test," by W. L. Flinn and J. W. Converse. LAND ECON. 46:456-466, November, 1970.

"Ending the trek to the towns," by A. Trotter. TOWN & COUNTRY PLANNING. 38:540-543, December, 1970.

"The experience of living in cities," by S. Milgram. SCIENCE. 167:1461-1468, March 13, 1970.

"Fate of personal adjustment in the process of modernization," by A. Inkeles and D. H. Smith. INT J COMP SOCIOL. 11:81-114, June, 1970.

"Function of neighborhood in ecological stratification," by G. K. Hesslink. SOCIOL & SOC RES. 54:441-459, July, 1970.

"Health hazards associated with urbanization and overpopulation," by B. Walker, Jr. J NAT MED ASS. 62:259-264, July, 1970.

"In-migration and growth of non-metropolitan urban places," by J. J. Zuiches. RURAL SOCIOL. 35:410-420, September, 1970.

"Intra-urban dualism in developing economies," by D. L. McKee, et al. LAND ECON. 46:486-489, November, 1970.

"Is dispersal the answer to urban overgrowth?" by J. P. Pickard. URBAN LAND. 29:3-10, January, 1970.

"L.A. county still tops in population--census." BROADCASTING. 79:38, September 21, 1970.

"Measuring rural-urban drift in developing countries; a suggested model," by L. Roussel. INT LABOUR R. 101:229-246, March, 1970.

"Metropolitan area projections through 1975." SALES MGT. 105:57-107, November 10, 1970.

"Migration flows in intraurban space: place utility considerations," by L. A. Brown, et al. ASSN AM GEOG ANN. 60:368-384, June, 1970.

"Migration, functional distance, and the urban hierarchy," by L. A. Brown. ECON GEOG. 46:472-485, July, 1970.

"Migration in an urban population," by A. E. Bennett. BRIT J PREV SOC MED. 24:63-64, February, 1970.

"Next decade shows promise but raises many serious urban questions." AIA J. 53:8, January, 1970.

"No greater challenge; the US urban problem," by T. L. Ashley. AIA J. 52:40-43, December, 1969; "Discussion," 53:86, February, 1970.

"Northampton--centre of megalopolis? Northampton master plan," by J. B. McLoughlin. TOWN AND COUNTRY PLAN. 38:197-199, April, 1970.

"One hundred years of population change. Growth rate of the 100 largest metropolitan areas." REAL ESTATE ANALYST. 39:455-466, November 17, 1970.

"Participation of low-income urban women in a public health birth control program," by Z. L. Janus, et al. PUBLIC HEALTH REP. 85:859-867, October, 1970.

"A policy for urban growth: Where shall they live?" by J. L. Sundquist; "Where shall the money come from?" by C. M. Haar and P. A. Lewis. PUBLIC INTEREST. p 88-112, Winter, 1970.

"Population changes in leading metropolitan areas." METROPOLITAN LIFE STAT BUL. 51:5-7, February, 1970.

"Problems of rural-urban migration: some suggestions for investigation," by D. Warriner. INT LAB R. 101:441-451, May, 1970.

"Process of cultural stripping and reintegration: the rural migrant in the city," by M. Leeds; With reply by L. E. Gary and rejoinder. J AM FOLKLORE. 83:259-270, April, 1970.

"Red man's plight: urban Indians, driven to cities by

URBAN GROWTH & URBANIZATION

poverty, find harsh existence," by B. Isenberg. WALL ST J. 175:1+, March 9, 1970.

"Reduced population growth as related to the urbanization process: Medellin, Colombia," by C. L. Marshall, et al. CLIN PEDIATR. 9:736-741, December, 1970.

"Rural slums or rural desert?" by M. Hederman. INTERPLAY. 3:23-26, June, 1970.

"Rural-urban migration: a clue to rural-urban relations in India," by C. R. P. Rao. INDIAN J SOCIAL WORK. 30:335-342, January, 1970.

"Stemming the tide of rural migration," by W. Eustis. MINN MUNIC. 55:344-345+, November, 1970.

"The stresses of urban living," by A. I. Adams. RANF REV. 1:7+, October, 1970.

"Surprise for 1980's: the big city, population explosion will fizzle," by E. B. Weiss. ADV AGE. 41:65-66, May 4, 1970.

"Towards a Rural Urban Balance," by D. L. Freeman. FUTURIST. 4,5:159-162, October, 1970.

"Urban Growth Policy," by C. W. Brubaker. ART EDUC. 23,7:16-17, October, 1970.

"Urban influence on the fertility and employment patterns of women living in homogeneous areas," by J. D. Tarver. J MARRIAGE & FAM. 32:237-241, May, 1970.

"The urban setting. 3. Mental health services and the isolated citizen," by M. Mitchell-Bateman. RHODE ISLAND MED J. 53:263-266, May, 1970.

"Urban U.S.A. - A chaotic society," by P. M. Hauser. NO. 18:48+, March, 1970.

WOMEN & POPULATION

"Birth control--the views of women," by J. A. Hurst. MED J AUST. 2:835-838, October 31, 1970.

"Freedom in family planning. The abortion law and women's liberation," by H. Muramatsu. JAP J MIDWIFE.

24:10-19, December, 1970.

"Naturalistic rationale for women's reform: Lester Frank Ward on the evolution of sexual relations," by C. H. Scott. HISTORIAN. 33:54-67, November, 1970.

"New feminism: potent force in birth-control policy," by L. J. Carter. SCIENCE. 167:1234-1236, February 27, 1970.

"Perceptual differences between married and single college women for the concepts of self, ideal woman, and man's ideal woman," by A. F. Rappaport. J MARRIAGE & FAM. 32:441-442, August, 1970.

"Predominance of male authors in social work publications," by A. Rosenblatt. SOC CASEWORK. 51:421-430, July, 1970.

"Victorian women and menstruation," by E. Showalter and E. Showalter. VICT STUD. 14:83-89, September, 1970.

"Women's magazines vs public opinion," by D. E. Schuller, et al. OHIO STATE MED J. 66:1107-1110, November, 1970.

AUTHOR INDEX

Aangeenbrug, R.T., 138
Abdel Kader, M.M., 61
Abdou, S., 41
Abello, V.B., 167
Abelson, P.H., 105
Abraham, A., 86
Abrahamsen, A.F., 114
Acheson, R.M., 146
Adachi, H., 95
Adam, C., 78
Adams, A.I., 150
Adams, J.H., 61
Adcock, L.D., 37
Ader, R., 62
Adlercreutz, H., 147
Agarwala, S.N., 1
Albeaux-Fernet, M., 161
Alberts, P.S., 161
Allen, D.T., 125
Allen, J.E., 83
Allingham, J.D., 64
Alsop, S., 37
Alvarado Duran, A., 67
Alvarado, A.L., 51
Amato, P.W., 46
Ampofo, D.A., 105
Ancla, M., 40, 91
Anderson, D., 85
Anderson, L.S., 1
Anderson, R.C., 92
Anderson, T.W., 38, 113
Andre, R., 79, 142
Angara, A.A., 132
Ansari, A.H., 64
Ardrey, R., 49
Arlen, J., 167
Armelagos, G.J., 68
Arnold, H., 53
Arnold, R.C., 142
Arriga, E.E., 1, 106

Artner, J., 146
As, A., 146
Ashimura, Y., 97
Ashley, T.L., 109
Ashpole, E., 168
Atkinson, E.A., 91
Austin, A.L., 168
Avendano, S., 44
Avery, R., 153

Babb, L.A., 99
Babinska, Z., 156
Backer, P., 48
Baird, D., 111
Baistow, T., 81
Baker, C.M., 9
Baker, J.C., 39, 109
Baker, J.J., 142
Bakke, T., 69
Banik, U.K., 116
Banister, P., 156
Bank, R., 84
Bank, S., 39
Barclay, W.R., 65, 118
Bardonnet, L., 74
Barnard, D., 73, 75
Barnett, L.D., 58, 124
Barr, S.J., 101
Barraciu, A., 131
Bartak, V., 47
Bartke, A.J., 88
Bartlett, M.S., 29
Bartok, I., 64
Barton, G.M., 114
Bartsch, A.F., 164
Basavarajappa, K.G., 138
Bauer-Hack, H., 117
Baumblatt, M.J., 135

Baumel, I., 31
Baxter, C., 86
Baxter, J.C., 32
Beals, R.E., 102
Beasley, J.D., 159
Beasley, W.B., 122
Beck, A.D., 62
Beck, P.J., 46, 48
Becker, W., 50, 92
Beco, L., 44
Bednyi, M.S., 39
Beeson, T., 163
Behrman, D., 35
Bell, R.R., 131
Beller, I., 94
Beller, R.E., 128
Belsky, R.L., 15
Bendixson, T., 123
Bennett, A.E., 102
Bennett, C.F., 94
Bennett, D.G., 125
Berelson, B., 105
Berent, J., 39
Berget, A.P., 113
Berggren, G., 149
Bergsjo, P., 145
Berkson, G., 53
Berman, S., 30
Bernstein, H., 29
Bernstein, M.C., 99
Berry, S.S., 102
Beyer, G., 105
Beynon, T.G., 148
Bezdek, W., 144
Birk, A., 136
Bjerke, K., 90
Blackburn, E.K., 82
Blackburn, G., 53
Blacker, C.P., 164
Blanchard, I., 125
Blatchley, F.R., 154
Bloombaum, M., 164
Boal, F.W., 33
Board, J.A., 65
Boerma, A.H.
Boffey, P.M., 93
Boldyrev, V., 137
Bollinger, C.C., 91
Bopp, J.R., 88
Borenstein, R., 43

Borgstrom, G.A., 57
Borkchin, M., 1
Borrie, W.D., 1
Bose, A., 64
Botero, J., 42
Bottomley, A., 1
Bour, H., 144
Bourgeois, M., 111
Bourne, J., 130
Bowlby, R.L., 109
Bowles, S., 102
Bowman, H.W., 104
Bowman, J.A., Jr., 68
Boynton, J.W., 105
Bradford, E., 110, 148
Bradshaw, B.S., 126
Braestrup, A., 93
Braham, J., 113
Brakman, P., 62
Branch, B.N., 48
Brass, W., 33
Breinl, H., 157
Brenner, P., 66
Brewer, J.W., 168
Brien, A., 98
Briggs, M.H., 49, 113
Brockner, V., 101
Broderick, C.B., 139
Brodie, D.W., 107
Brody, E.B., 2
Brooks, E., 75
Brooks, T.R., 2
Brosens, I., 108
Brown, G.H., 2, 81, 107, 109
Brown, L.A., 102
Brown, L.R., 84
Brown, M.L., 153
Brown, P., 56
Brown, R.E., 34
Brown, R.J., 99
Brubaker, C.W., 160
Buchanan, D.S., 57
Buck, P.S., 167
Buhring, L., 36
Bulsha, M., 43, 65
Bultena, G.L., 71
Bumpass, L., 119
Burch, T.K., 69
Burkinshaw, J., 128

Butler, J.E., 146
Bygdeman, M., 120

Calderon-Gonzalez, R., 137
Caldwell, J.C., 148
Callhan, D., 47
Carbia, E., 82
Cargas, H.J., 2
Carlson, H.E., 163
Carlson, J.E., 33, 58
Carmichael, S.M., 115
Carol, W., 88, 145
Carr, D.H., 42
Cartano, D.G., 46
Carter, L.J., 49, 107
Cartwright, A., 2, 82
Casetti, E., 56
Caspall, F.C., 138
Cassidy, J.T., 154
Castren, O.M., 61
Cavalca, G.G., 111
Cekanski, A., 82
Chamberlain, R., 106
Chambers, M.M., 109
Chandra, H., 161
Chandra, R.K., 81
Chang, C.C., 59
Chang, M.C., 131
Chant, D.A., 35
Chapin, G.L., 55
Charbonneau, H., 38
Chaskes, J.B., 131
Chasteen, E., 112
Chataparampil, J., 37
Chaudhury, R.R., 62
Chawla, H.P., 32
Chen, F.L., 161
Chen, Pi-Chao, 42
Chevallier, M.E., 105
Chia, H.C., 67
Chidell, M.P., 113
Chopra, J.G., 99
Chow, L.P., 73
Christensen, H.T., 41
Christie, G.A., 75
Chung, B.M., 127
Cirillo, V.J., 58
Claman, A.D., 157

Clark, C., 148
Clarke, D.G., 33
Clarkson, F.E., 74
Claxton, P.P., Jr., 159
Clay, G., 107
Cleary, R.E., 52
Clegg, E.J., 86
Clement, J.E., 133
Clezy, T.M., 114
Clout, H.D., 95
Coale, A.J., 98
Coburn, J., 111
Cochrane, G., 28
Coezy, E., 28
Cohen, A.M., 80
Cohen, L., 122
Cohen, M.R., 91
Coles, R., 2
Colligas, J., 117
Colmeiro-Laforet, C., 134
Compton, P.A., 33
Concepcion, M.B., 3
Conley, H.H., 61
Connell, E.B., 62, 122
Conti, M.L., 96
Converse, J.W., 64
Coombs, L.C., 50, 130
Cooper, B.S., 150
Corbett, N., 57
Corfman, P.A., 49
Cornwall, J., 65
Corredor, D.G., 143
Corriere, J.N., Jr., 59
Courchene, T.J., 90
Cousins, N., 29
Cowgill, U.M., 119
Cox, C.B., 110
Cox, P.R., 3
Craft, I.L., 113
Craig, J., 84
Craig, R., 66
Creutzfeldt, W., 86
Croccel, L., 155
Crow, J.F., 3
Cruickshank, J.M., 58, 148
Cruz-Coke, R., 35, 57
Culliton, B.J., 87, 104
Cumming, R., 166
Currin, J.F., 77
Curtis, C.F., 69

Curwen, M., 121
Cutler, N.E., 79

Dahlberg, B., 145
Daily, E.F., 48, 72
Daly, H.E., 129
Daly, M., 128
D'Amato, A., 84
D'Amelio, N., 84
Damsgaard-Sorensen, P., 130
Damude, E., 122
Dan, A.N.K., 83
Danezis, J., 157
Daniel, G.R., 130
Darney, P.D., 33
Dasgupta, B., 128
DaVanzo, J., 14
David, H.P., 3, 101, 135
Davies, H., 53
Davis, C.E., 32
Davis, D., 43
Davis, H.J., 100, 145
Davis, J.E., 64
Davis, K.E., 57
Davis, W.H., 104, 117, 124
Deakin, N., 130
DeBoer, C.H., 157
DeBoer, K.F., 91
Deedy, J., 36, 37
Deer, D., 134
Defares, J.G., 151
DeFeo, J.J., 57
de Gennes, J.L., 97
Degtyar, L., 37
Deisher, J.B., 75
Dejong, G.F., 4
Del Buono, V., 38
DeLee, S.T., 164
De Luca, L.A., 145
de Miguel, A., 151
Deming, J.E., 97
Demko, G.J., 3, 56
Dennis, K.J., 146
De Silva, C.C., 86
Diamond, J.M., 57
Diamond, M.T., 49
Dich, J., 30
Dickey, J.W., 112

Dickson, S.M., 103
Diekema, A.J., 41
Diggory, P., 45
Di Paola, G., 66
Dixon, R.B., 81
Djerassi, C., 35, 133
Doar, J.W., 63
Doering, G.K., 89
Dolby, J., 119
Doll, R.E., 67, 96, 139
Domany, Z., 151
Donahue, M.P., 138
Donaldson, P.J., 120
Dore, R., 147
Dougherty, C.M., 40
Douglas, B.H., 60
Dow, T.E., Jr., 75
Doyle, L.L., 87
Draper, W.H., Jr., 168
Dressel, W.A., 50
Drill, V.A., 32
Driver, E.D., 106, 152
Drummond, A.H., 99
Druzenko, A., 167
Dubarle, D., 50
Du Bois, V.D., 3
Dufau, M., 152
Dulac, M.J., 123
Dumont, M., 119
Duncan, G.W., 60
Dunlop, A., 144
Dunn, H.P., 117
Du Pasquier, R., 37
Dupree, L., 3
Durlach, J., 123

Early, J.D., 150
Ebanks, G.E., 161
Ebert, H., 136
Eckler, A.R., 133
Eckstein, P., 100
Edgell, S., 148
Edmonds, A., 35
Edwards, F., 63
Egeberg, R.O., 125
Ehrlich, A.H., 4
Ehrlich, P.R., 4, 33, 53,
    58, 82, 99, 119, 128,

164, 165, 166
Ehrunrooth, C.A., 162
Eisner, T., 126
El-Ashiry, G.M., 46
Elert, R., 72
Elgee, N.H., 100
Elkins, B.S., 47
Elkinton, J.R., Jr., 95
Elsea, S.J., 73
Elson, A., 58
Elstein, M., 114, 149
Emmel, T.C., 84
Emmens, C.W., 32, 129
Engels, R.A., 66, 134
Engineer, A.D., 42
Enke, S., 58, 95
Ericsson, R.J., 98
Eskes, T.K., 89, 161
Ettema, W.A., 75
Eustis, W., 149
Evagorou, D., 144
Evans-Pritchard, E.E., 144
Eyre, L.A., 155

Fagerhol, M.K., 32, 37, 114
Falconer, A.S., 100
Falkner, F., 88
Farley, R., 41
Farooqui, M.O., 139
Farrell, M. J., 97
Fechner, R.E., 37, 76
Fein, E., 54
Feldman, D.M., 35
Feldmann, H., 135
Fendall, N.R., 66
Fessler, L., 4
Field, A.J., 90
Field, R.M., 42
Fiore, A., 149
Firoozi, F., 92
Fisch, I.R., 51
Fischer, A., 104
Fish, M., 55
Flavier, P., 68
Fleming, A., 165
Fleming, T., 165
Flinn, W.L., 46, 64
Flint, H.M., 150

Flowers, C.E., Jr., 87, 157
Fogelholm, R., 40
Fonder, A., 158
Fong, S., 123
Ford, J.C., 124
Ford T.R., 4
Fortney, J.A., 90
Fossati, S., 35
Fox, G., 35
Foy, H., 30
Francis, M.K., 140
Frankenberg, J., 141
Franklin, B., 110
Frankowski, R.F., 159
Frederiksen, H., 98, 155
Freedman, R., 83, 153
Freeman, D.L., 156
Fregly, M.J., 60
Freire-Maia, N., 14
Friedman, S.B., 56
Friedman, W., 90
Friesen, R.F., 131
Fuchi, I., 149
Fuertes-de la Haba, A., 53
Fugita, B., 144
Fuguitt, G.V., 146
Fukuda, T., 154
Fuller, V., 4
Funke, E., 72
Fursdon, N.H., 95

Gabrielson, I.W., 52
Gaisie, S.K., 4
Gajdusek, C.D., 92. 93
Gallagher, C.F., 4
Gallaway, L.E., 102, 143
Gambrell, R.D., Jr., 85
Garcia, C.R., 32
Garcia, Ts., 4
Gardner, L.I., 77
Gardner, R.N., 108, 136
Garin, M., 167
Gary, L.E., 132
Gazzinelli, G., 159
Geary, R.C., 5
Gendell, M., 69
Gendreau, P., 61
Gerber, W., 40

Gerende, J.H., 68
Geschke, H., 68
Geserick, G., 143
Getis, A., 41
Giannella, D.A., 105
Giertsen, J.C., 74
Gifford, P.W., 128
Gilderdale, S., 118
Giles, A.W., 130
Gillespie, A., 85
Gillette, P., 5
Gillham, C.E., 105
Ginther, O.J., 61
Giraud, J.R., 92
Gjonnaess, H., 36, 115
Glass, D.V., 168
Glick, I.D., 134
Godel, E., 76
Gold, E.M., 141
Goldberg, D.C., 121
Goldberg, J.B., 45
Goldman, J.A., 36, 79
Goldman, L., 115
Goldsby, J.B., 74
Goldsmith, A., 5
Goldsmith, S., 100
Goldstein, H., 142
Goldzieher, J.W., 108, 115
Golod, S.I., 147
Gomes da Costa, S.F., 154
Gomez, S., 152
Gonzales, B., 164
Gonzalez, C., 47
Goodwin, M.H., Jr., 106
Goolden, A.W., 156
Gordis, L., 67, 100
Gordon, A., 36, 97
Gordon, D.N., 85
Gordon, M., 99
Gordon, R., 87
Goshen, C.E., 41
Gourley, P.F., 110
Graham, E., 162
Grant, E.C., 55, 101
Gray, H.P., 16
Green, A.R., 115
Green, J.J., 88
Green, S.C., 69
Greenwald, J.G., 150
Gregg, C.F., 41

Gregoire, L., 137
Grounds, D., 49
Grunewald, K., 51, 87
Gruninger, R.M., 126
Guillon, J.C., 88
Guiloff, E., 44
Gulati, O.P., 77
Gunn, A.D., 98
Gupta, A.S., 112
Gupta, S.D., 119
Gupta, S.M., 152
Gura, B., 133
Gurvich, I.S., 86
Gustafsson, L., 134
Guterman, S.S., 146
Guyer, P.B., 160
Gwatkin, R.B., 89

Haar, C.M., 124
Haenszel, W., 85
Hahn, H., 5
Halleck, S., 154
Halpern, M.J., 77
Hammond, E., 79
Hammond, R.P., 95
Han, D.W., 5
Hance, W.A., 5
Hanel, H.K., 31
Hanna, W.A., 5
Hanson, H.H., 93
Hansten, P.D., 113
Hardee, J.G., 5
Hardin, G., 5, 33, 67, 118
Hare, E.H., 36
Harman, A.J., 6
Harner, M.J., 128
Harnsberger, J.L., 94
Harrington, L., 118
Harris, J.R., 103
Harris, P.W., 82
Harris, R., 163
Harrison, D.F., 82
Hart, J.T., 55
Hartley, L., 148
Haspels, A.A., 31, 54
Haughton, R., 148
Hauser, P.M., 6, 111, 128, 160

Hauser, R.M., 47
Havens, L., 147
Havranek, F., 82
Havt, E., 95
Hawk, H.W., 120, 136
Hawkins, D.F., 91
Hayes, B.A., Jr., 133
Haynes, D.M., 158
Heber, K.R., 52, 162
Hecht, G.J., 146
Hederman, M., 141
Heer, D.M., 105
Heersema, P.H., 154
Heikel, T.A., 60
Heim, W.G., 126
Hellman, L.M., 45, 108
Hellmann, R., 149
Heltsley, M.E., 139
Henry, V.G., 29
Hern, W.M., 72
Hershey, N., 27
Hertz, R.
Hervet, E., 142
Herzberg, B.N., 41, 55, 114, 163
Herzig, N., 110
Hes, J.P., 101
Hesslink, G.K., 78
Hester, L.L., Jr., 62
Heuser, R.L., 105
Hewitt, A.B., 113
Hiersche, H.D., 35
Higgs, R., 44
Higier, J., 137
Hill, C.A., Jr., 99
Hill, H., 40, 112, 163
Hill, J.C., 96
Himes, N.E., 6
Hingorani, V., 94, 96
Hirsch, P., 168
Hobby, G.L., 131
Hodes, H.C., 91
Holdren, J.P., 53, 82, 119, 166
Holland, R., 6
Hollingsworth, T.H., 6
Holmes, R.P., 100
Holt, M., 166
Homesley, H.D., 101
Hoogendoorn, D., 64

Horiguchi, M., 110
Horne, C.H., 59, 60
Horne, H.W., Jr., 28, 101
Horrobin, D.F., 114
Howells, J.G., 69
Howie, P.W., 59
Hsu, S.C., 73, 153
Hsueh, Y., 123
Huffer, V., 115
Hughes, J.G., 5
Hughes, J.H., 75
Hulett, H.R., 112
Hultman, C.W., 94
Hurley, R., 80
Hurst, J.A., 36
Hurwitz, R.L., 113
Husain, I.Z., 58
Husbands, M.E., Jr., 71
Hutcheson, H.A., 69
Hutchinson, C., 118
Hutten, E.H., 144
Huygens, F.J., 134, 135
Huzarski, S.J., 25
Hyde, G., 27

Ianovskii, V., 99
Igun, A.I., 148
Imparato, E., 83
Ingle, D.J., 66
Infield, D., 142
Inkeles, A., 74
Inman, W.H., 103, 141, 155
Irey, N.S., 162
Isenberg, B., 137
Ishihama, A., 34, 38, 52, 97
Ishii, T., 157
Iskandar, N., 6
Israel, R., 91
Istock, C., 106

Jablonski, J., 107
Jack, A.B., 145
Jackson, H., 32
Jackson, L.N., 150, 162
Jackson, P., 98

Jacobs, J., 7, 103
Jaffe, A.J., 7
Jain, A.K., 106
Jakobovits, A., 60
James, W.H., 84
Janakiraman, K., 90
Jansen, C.J., 7
Janssens, J., 78, 140
Janus, Z.L., 118
Janzik, H.H., 114
Jay, A., 153
Jeffcoate, T.N., 136
Jelinek, J.E., 52
Jinno, R., 119
Johnson, H.D., 120
Johnson, R.E., 69, 147
Johnson, S., 7, 30, 95
Jonek, J., 28
Jones, H.R., 102
Jones, K.D., 8, 33
Jones, P.N., 147
Jones, S.B., 4
Joosse, L.A., 140
Jordon, T.G., 32, 154
Jorgensen, L., 115

Kaats, G.R., 57
Kaden, W.S., 116
Kahn, S.B., 50
Kai, I., 93
Kain, J.F., 102
Kaindl, A., 38
Kamal, I., 43
Kamerschen, D.R., 127
Kammeyer, K.C.W., 138
Kan, A., 88
Kane, F.J., 134
Kangas, L.W., 90
Kapila, K., 34
Kaplan, D.L., 123
Kar, A.B., 96, 161
Karstadt, B.S., 89
Kasindorf, M., 97
Katz, D.M., 96
Kaufman, B., 29
Kaufman, S.A., 67
Kaun, D.E., 106
Kay, C.R., 37

Keeleric, G., 86
Keeny. S.M., 8
Keifer, W.S., 44
Keller, A.B., 135
Kellogg, A.C., 127
Kelman, R.B., 126
Kelsall, R.K., 8
Kennedy, D.M., 8
Ketchum, R.M., 70
Kettle, J., 42, 78, 118, 131
Keyko, C.A., 109
Khandewale, S.V., 125
Kim, M.I., 93, 127, 152
Kim, S.B., 108
Kimurs, M., 3
Kind, H., 57
Kippley, J., 8
Kiran, O., 60
Kirk, R.S., 35
Klein, D.P., 55
Kline, T.S., 34
Klinger, G., 61
Kloosterman, G.J., 47
Klopper, A., 56
Knodel, J., 153. 158
Koehler, J.E., 8
Kohoutek, M., 92
Koiranen, V.A., 64
Kolars, J., 124, 158
Kopec, A.C., 8
Kormano, M., 36
Korostelev, G.M., 53
Koshy, T., 94
Kossoris, P., 74
Koukal, J., 90
Krigsten, W.M., 100
Kucera, M., 126
Kuhne, D., 76
Kushner, S., 43
Kznetsov, O.N., 43

Labhsetwar, A.P., 91, 143
Ladanji, G., 80
Lader, L., 94
Laforet, J., 28
Lamm, R.D., 140
Lamson, R.W., 74

Lancet, M., 48, 128
Landman, L.C., 165
Lane, M.E., 64
Lansing, A.M., 85
Lapan, B., 92
Lapham, R.J., 72
Lapinski, Z., 52
Lapointe, G., 126
Laragh, J.H., 114
Larsson-Cohn, U., 62, 81, 120
Laslett, P., 53
Last, P.A., 48
Latane, B., 146
Laughhunn, D.J., 56
Laurell, C.B., 136
Lawson, S., 108
Lazerwitz, B., 33
Leach, G., 83, 129
Leahy, W.H., 91
Lebech, P.E., 63
Lebergott, S., 103
Leblanc, R.G., 27
Lecca, U., 27
Lederberg, J., 124
Ledger, W.J., 116
Lednicer, D., 48
Ledr, J., 45
Lee, Y.L., 8
Leeds, M., 132
Lefebvre, Y., 31
Lehfeldt, H., 116
Leibenstein, H., 104
Leis, H.P., Jr., 121
Lelyveld, J., 167
Lenz, W., 84
Lerner, R.C., 79
Levin, R., 46
Levitt, L.P., 105
Lewis, J.P., 125
Lewis, P.A., 124
Liberman, R., 34
Liddle, G.G., 36
Lieberman, E.J., 140
Linden, F., 118, 159
Linder, F.E., 134
Linder, R., 104
Lindstedt, S., 120
Link, R., 32
Linken, A., 134

Linsky, A.S., 45
Linthorst, G., 117
Lipinski, A., 44
Liss, J., 166
Liston, W.A., 75
Liu, B.C., 139
Liu, F.T., 61
Liu, W.T., 16
Lockhart, W.E., 152
Lockheimer, F.R., 8
London, G.D., 73
Long, L.H., 76, 111
Longbrake, D.B., 102
Loraine, J.A., 9
Lotvin, B.R., 112
Loudon, J.D., 29
Loudon, M., 156
Louvish, M., 153
Love, G.A., 9
Love, R.M., 9
Lubs, H.A., 42
Ludwig, A.M., 45
Luhby, A.L., 135
Lukacs, J., 156
Lunde, A.S., 163
Lunde, J., 95
Lutz-Ostertag, Y., 118

McArthur, N., 54
McBride, W.G., 57, 108
McCalister, D.V., 130, 133
McCann, B., 106
McCormack, A., 9
McFarland, H.R., 138
McGaugh, M.E., 9
McGimsey, G., 109
McKay, D.A., 32
McKee, D.L., 91
McKinney, T.D., 36, 37
McLeod, R.D., 157
McLin, J., 9
McLoughlin, J.B., 109
McNaughton, S.J., 141
McQuarrie, H.G., 52
McQueen, E.G., 111

Maathuis, J.B., 156
Mabray, C.R., 158
MacCluer, J.W., 66
MacCorquodale, D.W., 31
MacDonald, A.P., Jr., 90
Macey, J., 83
Machanik, G., 27
Macintosh, A.M., 114
Mackay, M., 94
Mackintosh, D.R., 144
MacLeod, S.C., 117
Magnus, K., 151
Makhlouf, A.M., 93
Malaviya, B., 59
Malin, H.J., 124
Mandle, J.R., 53, 124
Manisoff, M.T., 9
Manoharan, K., 113
Manwell, C., 9
Maqueo, M., 65
Maranell, G.M., 146
Marcotte, D.B., 135
Marcus, M.J., 87
Marino, A., 71
Marques, M de M, 161
Marsella, A.J., 62
Marshall, C.L., 138
Marshall, D.G., 71
Marshall, J., 134
Marshall, S., 160
Martin, L., 63
Martinez-Manautou, J., 29
Marwick, C.S., 130
Marty, G., 67
Marzuki, A., 9
Masi, A.T., 40, 155
Mason, A.C., 117
Mastroianni, L., Jr., 141
Mathison, I.W., 57
Matsumoto, S., 137
Mattelart, A., 85
Mauldin, W.P., 126
Maxwell, I., 144
Mayer, L.A., 159
Meadows, B.J., 54
Means, C.C., 106
Mears, E., 44
Medina del Campo, J.J., 101
Meek, R.L., 10
Mehra, U., 139

Mehta, K.C., 145
Melandri, B.A., 120
Memon, G.N., 60
Menard, J., 162
Menczer, P.F., 140
Mendenhall, H.W., 61
Menezes, C.F., 102
Menke, C.R., 135
Menon, I.S., 46, 76
Menzel, E.W., Jr., 56
Merillon, H., 80
Merriam, M.F., 140
Methfessel, H.D., 143
Mettler, L., 89
Meyer, K.K., 155
Meyer de Schmid, J.J., 43
Michael, D.K., 136
Michaelson, M., 81
Middendorp, C.P., 55
Milan, F.A., 54
Miles, R.E., 166
Milgram, S., 68
Miller, D.L., 124
Miller, G.H., 94
Miller, H., 92, 153
Miller, J.R., 162
Miller, N.C., 112
Miller, N.N., 10
Mills, W., 78
Mintz, M., 46, 121
Miracle, M.P., 102
Miranda, L.S., 51
Mishell, D.R., Jr., 48
Mitchell-Bateman, M., 160
Miyamoto, J., 71
Mizer, H.E., 52
Moe, T.
Monro, J.K., 163
Mook, R., 118
Moon, K.H., 154
Moore, G.E., 79
Moore, J.L., Jr., 164
Moore, W.M., 67
Moreau, L., 102
Moricard, R., 42
Morris, D., 142
Morris, J.M., 129
Morrison, P.A., 10
Moses, H.A., 59
Moura, A.F., 45

Moursi, G.E., 89
Mowat, J.C., 89
Moyer, D.L., 137
Mukherji, S., 59
Mull, A., 50
Mulvihill, D.F., 10
Mulvihill, R.C., 10
Mumenthaler, M., 40
Muramatsu, H., 77, 132
Muramatsu, M., 72
Mustafa, M.A., 34
Myerscough, P.R., 42

Nag, M., 92
Namboodiri, N.K., 111
Nanda, V.P., 106
Nanni, L.F., 155
Naugle, E.H., 110
Naumenko, E.V., 142
Neal, A.G., 30
Necheles, T.F., 98
Neel, J.V., 95
Neiger, I., 44
Nelson, L., 51
Nerone, B.J., 80
Neumann, F., 63
Neumann, H.G., 67, 160
Newcombe, H.B., 41
Newman, P., 98
Newton, P., 46
Neyraut, M., 147
Nimmo, H.A., 34
Nishijima, M., 101
Nistico, G., 49
Nixon, J.W., 146
Noble, T., 71
Norris, K.S., 154
Nortman, D., 11
Noshpitz, J.D., 40
Notestein, F.W., 33
Notter, A., 43
Nurcombe, R., 55
Nurge, E., 36

Ober, W.B., 65, 104, 124
O'Connor, J.J., 166

O'Connor, R.W., 123
O'Donnell, J.F., 40
Odum, E.P., 112
O'Grady, J.E., 87
Ohadike, P.O., 50
Oishi, N., 124
Okla, J., 80
Okorafor, A.E., 29
Okrent, S., 71
Oldershaw, K.L., 74
Oliver, M.F., 114
O'Malley, K., 87
Omran, K.F., 158
Onken, D., 66
Orsagh, T.J., 103
Orzechowska, M., 107
Osborne, R.T., 128
Ottolander, G.J., 121

Packwood, B., 125
Paddock, W.C., 83
Palliez, R., 119
Palmgren, L., 154
Pane, A., 116
Pannor, R., 159
Paoli, A., 121
Pasaporte, J.P., 84
Pasquariella, B., 111
Patch, R.W., 12
Paterson, R.W., 127
Paulsen, C.A., 115
Paydarfar, A.A., 56
Payeur, G., 69
Payne, S., 30
Pearce, C., 107
Peccei, A., 130
Peel, J., 84
Pendleton, D., 12
Peng, J.Y., 9, 100
Penman, H.G., 60
Peper, B., 127
Peretz, J., 53
Perevedentsev, V., 127
Perkin, G.W., 109
Perl, G., 103
Perlman, S., 46
Persky, J.J., 102
Peter, W.G., 144

Petersen, P., 164
Peterson, M.L., 49
Peterson, R.A., 40
Petrow, V., 51
Petry, R., 51
Philipp, J., 74
Phillips, B.D., 138, 139
Philpot, T., 167
Pickard, J.P., 92
Pindyck, J., 51
Pinzello, A., 100
Pizzuto, J., 29
Plate, W.P., 104, 116
Plesner, R., 47
Plotz, E.J., 145
Pluenneke, G., 166
Pohlman, E.J., 42
Pohowalla, J.N., 131
Poiret, C., 44
Poland, B.J., 46
Polgar, S., 71
Polidoro, J.P., 70
Pollara, F., 157
Pollard, F.H., 33
Poller, L., 42
Polskin, L.J., 83
Pony, J.C., 155
Poole, P.A., 12
Poskalenko, A.N., 59
Potter, R.G., Jr., 96, 106
Potts, D.M., 62, 78
Povey, W.G., 72
Powell, L.W., 70
Prasada Rao, C.R., 141
Presser, H.B., 13
Preston, S.H., 13, 29, 90
Price, J.S., 36
Priddle, J., 73
Prill, H.J., 135
Propper, M.M., 30
Pruvot, M., 134
Pujol-Amat, P., 89
Pulay, T., 34
Pursell, D.E., 87
Pustek, S., 125

Radeva, M., 151
Raghavan, K.S., 117

Ragland, R.B., 125
Rajakumar, M.K., 38
Ramirez, R.C., 73
Rappaport, A.F., 119
Rastogi, R.K., 41
Rattan, W.C., 38
Rauch, J.B., 74
Raulet, H.M., 72
Ravenholt, A., 13
Ravina, J.H., 89, 90, 103
Recio, D.M., 146
Records, J.W., 121
Reed, F.W., 102
Reid, D.J., 37
Reinke, W.A., 141
Reiss, I.L., 131
Reitsma, W.D., 38
Reston, J., 73
Rezabek, K., 60
Reziciner, S., 158
Ricards, S.L., Jr., 53
Rice, D.T., 151
Richter, R.H., 45
Rifkind, A.B., 88
Riga, P.J., 117
Rijhwani, A.N., 91
Rimdusit, S., 151
Ritterband, P., 31, 94
Ritzmann, S.E., 51
Robecchi, E., 52
Robertson, J.C., 99
Robinson, W.C., 13
Rodgers, A., 102
Rodriguez, A.J., 95, 96
Rodwin, L., 13
Roe, A., 163
Rogers, D.R., 163
Rogers, D.T., Jr., 136
Rohatiner, J.J., 79
Rose, D.P., 115, 138
Rose, V.E., 106
Rosen, F., 131
Rosen, W.G., 65
Rosenblatt, A., 130
Rosenfield, A.B., 137
Rosoff, J.I., 33
Ross, F.U., 101
Rossman, I., 166
Roth, N., 150
Rothe, J., 81

Roudier, R., 28
Rouleau, Y., 135
Roussel, L., 100
Rowell, T.E., 34
Rowley, P.T., 82
Rozenbaum, H., 149
Rozin, S., 107
Rubinato, L., 132
Rubio, D., 44
Rubsaam, C.J., 66
Ruddle, F.H., 42
Rudel, H.W., 32
Rumford, J.C., 160
Rush, D.H., 97
Rushdoony, R.J., 165
Rusinow, D.I., 13
Russell, R.P., 121
Russett, B.M., 95
Rutenskold, M., 120
Rutman, G.L., 102
Rybo, G., 120

Sabagh, G., 83
Sabour, M.S., 38
Sachson, A.D., 28
Sachuk, N.N., 99
Sackett, G., 63
Sadie, J.L., 67
Sadovsky, A., 148
Sagen, O.K., 86
Sagiroglu, N., 35, 52
Sakharov, V.I., 100
Salvati, A., 132
Salzano, F.M., 14
Sanders, T.G., 14
Sanderson, W., 76
Sarram, M., 56
Sartwell, P.E., 115
Saruta, T., 129
Satterthwaite, A.P., 5
Saunders, F.J., 65
Sauvy, A., 79
Savel, H., 52
Schally, A.V., 151
Schardein, J.L., 96
Schlesinger, B., 129
Schmidt, A.L., 52
Schneider, G.T., 40

Schneider, H.E., 149
Schnell, G.A., 54
Schoenberg, B.S., 150
Schofield, F.D., 148
Schofield, R.S., 119
Schreiner, W.E., 145
Schriver, W.R., 109
Schueler, R.L., 58
Schuhmann, R., 96
Schuller, D.E., 167
Schultz, C.S., 105
Schultz, P.T., 14
Schulz, M., 68
Schwartz, G.F., 140, 143
Schwarz, G.S., 88
Schwarz, J.C., 45
Scommegna, A., 67, 91
Scott, C.H., 83, 106
Scott, J.S., 149
Scrimshaw, S.C., 111
Seber, G.A., 139
Sedlis, A., 65
Seidenberg, R., 109
Seig, L., 125
Semczuk, M., 69
Seneta, E., 127
Sepetliev, D., 138
Sepulveda, B., 29
Serr, D.M., 64
Servy, E.J., 122
Sessing, T.W., 84
Setty, B.S., 32, 106
Seymour, R.J., 54
Shaaban, A.H., 44
Shah, S.K., 87
Shanas, E.J., 30
Shannon, W.H., 15
Sharma, B.P., 110
Sharma, P.M., 130
Shaw, R.P., 133
Shaw, S.T., Jr., 76
Shchepin, O.P., 162
Shende, M.C., 142
Sheps, M.C., 157
Sherrow, F.S., 31
Shinn, R.L., 124
Shokeir, M.H., 131
Showalter, E., 163
Shuster, L.J., 103
Siampos, G.S., 127

Siegel, E., 70, 130
Sigamoney, J., 73
Sikkel, A., 115
Silk, M., 63
Simard, M.B., 154
Simon, J.L., 73
Simon, P., 89
Sinclair, S.G., 1
Singer, A., 60
Singer, S.F., 138
Singh, P., 148
Sissons, C., 91
Sjovall, H., 53
Skobba, T.J., 155
Skopkova, H., 62
Skorodumova, I.V., 145
Sleptsova, S.I., 77
Sligh, M.M., 84
Sloan, M., 118
Slusarenko, R., 106
Sly, D.F., 103
Smith, A.D., 8
Smith, A.W., 129
Smith, C.T., 54
Smith, D.C., 30
Smith, D.H., 74
Smith, E., 72
Smith, H.K., 78
Smith, H.L., 139
Smith, J.C., 74
Smith, M.E., 41
Smith, M.S., 163
Smith, P.J., 155
Smith, R., 54
Smith, T.L., 15
Snyder, C., 98
Sobrero, A.J., 97
Sokoya, A.O., 71
Sollins, A.D., 15
Somerville, B.W., 160
Song, J., 65
Southwick, C.H., 131
Southwick, T.P., 70
Speare, A., Jr., 83
Speidel, J.J., 47, 85
Spellacy, W.N., 51, 79, 117, 143
Spengler, J.J., 28, 128
Spufford, P., 127
Sracek, J., 68

Stacey, T., 16
Stallworthy, J., 141
Standard, R.L., 71
Stans, M.H., 125
Steel, D.J., 78
Steel, R.W., 132
Steele, S.J., 74
Stenbaek, O., 114
Stephen, D., 16
Steptoe, P.C, 137
Sterba, R., 45, 156
Stern, E., 49, 162
Sternadel, Z., 43, 75
Stettler, H.L., 44
Stewart, E., 100
Stoeckel, J., 147, 157
Stoimenov, G., 146
Stone, P.A., 16, 160
Stopekova, M., 104
Stormorken, H., 115
Streiff, R.R., 77
Strickland, P., 38
Strodtbeck, F.L., 98, 144
Stuart, M., 16
Stumpfe, K.D., 81
Sturgis, S.H., 48
Sturtevant, J., 120
Suganuma, T., 151
Sun, Te-Hsiung, 81
Surface, B., 50
Suter, H.H., 126
Suyin, H., 72
Suzuki, A., 108
Suziki, S., 51
Svejgaard, A., 79
Swyer, G.L., 121
Szabo, A.J., 79
Szekacs, I., 154
Szereday, Z., 62, 116

Taber, S.R., 138
Tada, T., 156
Tagliacarne, G., 166
Tallmer, M., 56
Tamblyn, P.B., 47
Tangri, S.S., 16
Tarver, J.D., 157, 160
Tausk, M., 28

Taylor, C.E., 129
Taylor, G.R., 119
Taylor, J.R., 30
Taylor, L.R., 16
Taylor, M.B., 112
Tejuja, S., 161
Temple, J.G., 143
Tenhaeff, D., 48
Tepper, S.S., 73
Terpstra, P., 89
Teter, J., 83
Thierry, F.J., 165, 166
Thierstein, S.T., 122
Thomas, C.J., 133
Thompson, J., 80
Thompson, L., 142
Thompson, R.P., 48
Thomson, K.W., 16
Thorbecke, E., 159
Thoyer-Rozat, J., 149
Tien, H.Y., 105, 106
Tierney, P., 164
Tindall, G., 35
Tinker, H., 45
Tischler, E., 142
Tisdall, L.H., 27
Tobin, G.A., 16
Tompkins, M.G., 141
Townson, D., 156, 159
Traissac, R., 68
Travis, S.C., 158, 159
Treas, C.E., 143
Tripathy, B.B., 129
Trlin, A.D., 16
Trobisch, W., 17
Tronnier, H., 55
Trotter, A., 65
Truevtseva, G.V., 161
Tschumi, P.A., 167
Tsubouchi, Y., 41
Tucker, G.S.L., 92
Tugault, Y., 101
Tunnadine, L.P., 17
Turnbull, A.C., 75
Tydings, J.D., 72
Tyler, E.T., 76, 122
Tyler, J.W., Jr., 73
Tyson, J.E., 38

Udall, M.K., 98
Udry, J.R., 59
Umabai, G.R., 34
Ungerer, A., 59
Urlanis, B., 132
Urquhart-Hay, D., 164
Usher, M.B., 55

Vacha, K., 33
Val, U.L., 147
Valvanne, L., 77
van de Walle, E., 128, 153
Vande Wiele, R.L., 150
Vankos, J., 116
Vaughan, P., 25, 122
Vaughan, S.J., 132
Vaughn, B.J., 68
Vedder, R.K., 102, 143
Veerhusen, W., 126
Vela, P., 40
Vermeer, D.E., 128
Vermeulen, A., 63
Vessey, M.P., 130
Viel, B., 31
Vig, O.P., 53
Villablanca, E., 58
Vobecky, J., 152
Voegeli, H., 43
Vojta, M., 28, 48, 133, 140, 149
Vokaer, R., 83
von Kaulla, E., 114
Vostrikova, A., 86

Wachtel, E., 63
Waddington, C.H., 77
Wade, P.H., 167
Wadlington, W., 33
Wagar, J.A., 80
Wagner, N.N., 141
Waintraub, G., 75
Walker, B., Jr., 81
Wallace, H.M., 139
Wallich, H.C., 127
Walsh, B.M., 25, 99
Walters, W.A., 80

Wann, M.D., 61
Warriner, D., 132
Watson, W.R., 25, 111
Wattenberg, B., 109
Waugh, A., 95
Weatherall, J.A., 55
Weightman, J., 77
Weinberg, A.M., 95
Weinberg, D., 165
Weiner, S., 25
Weinstein, H.E., 122
Weis, P., 50
Weisbuch, J.B., 66
Weiss, E.B., 152, 165
Weissman, S., 167
Welles, J.G., 58
Weltman, A.S., 99
Wering, R.F., 153
Wertheimer, R.F., 25
West, B.C., Jr., 62
West, J., 71
Westerhoff, G.P., 126
Westerholm, B., 120
Wheeless, C.R., 116
Whitehill, W.M., 166
Wickram, I., 80
Wickware, D., 70, 134
Wider, J.A., 85
Widjojo, N., 25
Wiens, H.J.H., 25
Wieszczycki, W., 150
Wigzell, F.W., 147
Wilbert, H., 52
Wilkinson, P.M., 67
Williams, E.A., 112, 150
Williams, F.S., 30
Williams, G.F., 150
Williams, R.C., 66
Williams, R.H., 110, 136
Williams, V.C., 93
Wilson, F.G., 147
Winn, H., 47
Winter, I.C., 88
Wise, L.J., 30
Wisely, W.H., 125
Wishik, S.M., 106, 160
Witt, L., 98
Wohl, J., 144
Wolf, P., 114
Wolfers, D., 66, 132, 146

Wolff, A., 103
Wood, C., 149
Wood, J.C., 60, 133
Wood, S.M., 97
Woodcock, G., 156
Woodward, P., 82
Worsnop, R.L., 144
Worth, R.M., 33
Wright, N.H., 163
Wrong, D.H., 129
Wu, H.Y., 54
Wurster, C.F., 132
Wynn, R.M., 104

Xenos, C., 26

Yang, J.M., 129
Yasmuth, C., 116
Yoder, F.D., 86
Yoder, P.S., 63
Yuan Tien, H., 99
Yunes, J., 153
Yussman, M.A., 117

Zanartu, J., 96
Zaun, H., 88, 89
Zelenkova, M., 90
Zelinsky, W., 26, 35
Ziegler, F.J., 163
Zinn, D.J., 50
Zipper, J.A., 84
Zirky, A.K.M., 140
Zographos, G., 69
Zopf, P.E., Jr., 15
Zorza, V., 81
Zuckerman, M., 143
Zuiches, J.J., 87
Zumeta, Z., 50
Zwahr, C., 69, 77

Z
7164
D3
G65
1970

APR 14 1976